Handcrafted.

BJU Press employs a team of experienced writers and artists whose best work goes into every book we produce. Because of our emphasis on quality, our textbooks are the top choice in Christian education. Each book is designed to give your student a learning experience that is enjoyable, academically excellent, and biblically sound.

bju press

BECAUSE **IT MATTERS**

To find out more, call **1.800.845.5731** or visit **www.bjupress.com**.

TABLE OF CONTENTS

CHAPTER 13

CHAPTER 14

CHAPTER 15 ──────────────────────── ◆15

CHAPTER 16

ACKNOWLEDGMENTS

A careful effort has been made to trace the ownership of selections included in this textbook in order to secure permission to reprint copyrighted material and to make full acknowledgment of their use. If any error or omission has occurred, it is unintentional and will be corrected in subsequent editions, provided written notification is made to the publisher.

CHAPTER 1
Excerpt from **Hour of Gold, Hour of Lead, Diaries of Anne Morrow Lindbergh, 1929-1932**, copyright © 1973 by Anne Morrow Lindbergh, reprinted by permission of Harcourt, Inc.

CHAPTER 2
Excerpt from pp. 25-6 from **Children of the Sun** by Adolf and Beverly Hungry Wolf. Copyright © 1987 by Adolf and Beverly Hungry Wolf. Reprinted by permission of HarperCollins Publishers, Inc.

CHAPTER 3
"Epilogue: A Word from Becky" by Rebecca Morel Vaughn from **More Precious Than Gold: The Fiery Trial of a Family's Faith** by John and Brenda Vaughn. Copyright © 1994 by John and Brenda Vaughn. Reprinted by permission.

CHAPTER 4
Baseball and the Great Depression by Bill Rabinowitz. Copyright 1945 by Penton Media, Inc. Reproduced with permission of Penton Media, Inc. via Copyright Clearance Center.

CHAPTER 6
"A Personal Account of the Fall of the Berlin Wall: The 11th and 12th of November, 1989" by Andreas Ramos. © Andreas Ramos 1989. Reprinted by permission.

CHAPTER 7
Reprinted with permission of Simon & Schuster from Charles Kuralt's American Moments by Charles Kuralt with Peter Freundlich. Copyright 1998 by Estate of Charles Kuralt. An American Moment is a trademark of Ninth Wave Productions, Inc.

CHAPTER 9
"Chameleon" by Anton Chekhov. Translation by Ivy Litvinov in **A. P. Chekhov: Short Novels and Stories** (Moscow: Foreign Languages Publishing House).

CHAPTER 10
From THE STORY OF ENGLISH by Robert McCrum and William Cran and Robert MacNeil, copyright © 1986, 1992, 2002 by Robert McCrum, William Cran, and Robert MacNeil. Used by permission of Viking Penguin, a division of Penguin Group (USA) Inc. Reprinted by permission of SLL/Sterling Lord Literistic, Inc. Copyright 1986 by Robert McCrum.

CHAPTER 11
Excerpt from **The Way of the Word** by Bryan Smith. Copyright © 2000 by BJU Press.

CHAPTER 12
Colin Powell as quoted by CNN in a speech at the Republican National Convention on July 31, 2000. Courtesy of the Republican National Committee and by permission of Colin Powell.

CHAPTER 13
Excerpt from "Looking Forward: The 12-Step Program Parents Need." Copyright © 1999 by Peggy Noonan. Reprinted by permission of William Morris Agency, LLC on behalf of the Author.

PHOTOGRAPH CREDITS

The following agencies and individuals have furnished materials to meet the photographic needs of this textbook. We wish to express our gratitude to them for their important contribution.

Abraham Lincoln Presidential Library & Museum (ALPLM)
Aeroflot Russian Airlines
Suzanne Altizer
Associated Press, AP
Bibles International/Hantz Bernard
Kim Bierman
BigStockPhoto
BJU Press Files
Bob Jones University Museum & Gallery
Anthony Bradshaw
British Airways
Jim Brooks
Collection of the House of Representatives
Corbis
COREL Corporation
Eastman Chemicals Division
Elevator World/Thyssen Aufzuege
Gene Fisher
Fotolia
Franklin Delano Roosevelt Library
German Information Center

Getty Images
Holly Gilbert
Gospel Fellowship Association
Greater Portland Convention and Visitors Association, Inc.
Brenda Hansen
Harry S. Truman Library
Carl A. Hess
The Historical Society of Pennsylvania
iStock International
Juergen Mueller-Schneck, www.dieberlinermauer.de
JupiterImages
Joyce Landis
Library of Congress
The Lindbergh Foundation
The Museum of Printing History, Houston
National Aeronautics and Space Administration (NASA)
National Archives
National Baseball Hall of Fame Library
New Jersey State Police Museum
Overseas Mission Fellowship

QA Photos Ltd.
Ronald Reagan Library
RM Photo Service
RUSSIA Illustrated Monthly Magazine
Gina Santi
Smithsonian Institution
Special Olympics, Greenville, SC
Kim Stegall
SuperStock
Carla Thomas
United States Air Force
United States Department of State
United States Navy/General Dynamics
Unusual Films
Veterans of Foreign Wars
Wake Forest University
Harry Ward
Tara Warrington
Dawn L. Watkins
The Wei Family
World Bank

Why do we study English? We learn how to understand and how to speak English while we are very young. Why, then, do we spend so much of the rest of our lives studying something we already know?

English is a living language. It changes—constantly. New words appear; obsolete words fade away as they are no longer needed. Usage patterns change; even rules occasionally change. We need to learn to speak and to write so that others can understand. Without a thorough understanding of English, we cannot communicate effectively.

English is also a flexible language. We use different levels of formality for different audiences. We speak to our friends differently than we speak to our pastor or teacher. We use one style for a letter to a friend and another style for an essay to be graded by a teacher.

WRITING AND GRAMMAR 10, Third Edition, will help you learn to communicate in English more effectively. The first step toward the goal of better speaking and writing is to acquaint yourself with the text. Take a few minutes to look through the book and become familiar with these features:

- **Combine the Skills icons** in the margin direct you to other pages in the text with more information about the topic. Each icon indicates the category of material to which that icon refers.

  A **grammar** icon refers to a concept that appears in Chapters 1-4.

  A **usage** icon sends you to material in Chapters 5-12 dealing with correct usage or mechanics.

  A **writing** icon indicates that the material is an important writing concept discussed in Chapters 13 or 14 or one of the writing activities found throughout the book.

  A **reference** icon refers to the library skills and study skills in Chapters 15 and 16 or to the special information at the end of a chapter.

- **ESL notes** explain in detail the concepts that can be difficult for students from another language background (*ESL* is an abbreviation for *English as a Second Language*). Every student can learn more about the English language from these helpful explanations.

- **Thinking Biblically** notes encourage you to step back from what you are learning and to look at it from a Christian worldview.

- **Tips** offer advice about using the grammar and usage concepts you are studying to improve your writing.

Mastering the concepts in this book will increase your appreciation for language. If you learn to use English correctly and to value the beauty of English, you will enjoy the satisfaction of becoming a more effective communicator.

Everyone enjoys receiving mail. A card from Aunt Sophie, a note from a friend you met at camp, a letter from a brother away at school—all are welcome breaks from daily routine. Getting mail is like getting a small part of the other person that you can look at over and over.

Sending mail isn't always quite so exciting. Letter writing can be difficult—especially if you forget about the target of your missive. Notice how Anne Morrow records March 27 for her fiancé, Charles Lindbergh. Her descriptions of her irritation at the press and of the street fair in Mexico City help us to learn about her and to picture her surroundings with astounding clarity. At the end of this chapter, it will be your turn to write a personal letter.

Hour of Gold, Hour of Lead *by Anne Morrow Lindbergh*

I have just gotten your letter and I feel so cheerful. You see, when you get away I feel as though you were *never* coming back again, and it was so nice to hear such very real-sounding plans.

I'm glad your letter came because I had just begun to get very hard and angry about a front-page notice of the *Times* that you and I had given it out authoritatively (or officially or whatever the word is) that we were going to be married in June—place not given out yet. It made me *boiling,* first, that they should print an absolute *lie*— that we gave it out. And in the second place, that means more letters, advertisements, etc., and people writing and asking me when and where the wedding will be—and are they coming! And sort of waiting around and expecting things in June. It was an A.P. report. My, they make me angry.

Well, that's over. Oh, today—what do you think I did today! We went down to the big Easter street fair. You walk between lines and lines of booths flaunting *everything:* dusters, dolls, toys, baskets, pink lemonade (or worse), hats and children's wagons and minute little doll's tea sets, and pots and pans and lacquer boxes, and candy, etc., etc. I bought some *more bowls.* Why is it that all the pretty pottery is . . . *bowls?* In your old age you will have to live on cornflakes alone! But these were so lovely, with a blue and green border, and deep, sloping up gracefully like some kind of flower. They were *blue.* I'll do almost anything for *blue*—hills or bowls or eyes or neckties.

By now, you have studied the parts of speech for several years. You have studied nearly everything you need to know about the traditional eight parts of speech with which all English sentences are constructed. This opening chapter will serve two purposes: to provide a diagnostic tool and to offer review.

As you work through the text and exercises for nouns, pronouns, verbs, adjectives, adverbs, prepositions, conjunctions, and interjections, take note of which parts of speech you have mastered and which you still find troublesome. Use the reviews in this worktext and the information in *The Writer's Toolbox* for further help in mastering the parts of speech.

Nouns

Spelling
Plural Nouns
pp. 430-32

Nouns comprise the largest group of words in the English language. A **noun** names a person, place, thing, or idea. **Singular nouns** name one person, place, thing, or idea; **plural nouns** name more than one.

All nouns may be classified as either common or proper. **Common nouns** name an unspecified person, place, thing, or idea: *uncle, library, dog, philosophy.* **Proper nouns** name specific persons, places, things, or ideas and are always capitalized: *Wayne, New York Public Library, Rover, Machiavellianism.*

ESL Just as all nouns are either common or proper, every common noun is either count or noncount. **Count nouns** can be singular or plural in form and are often introduced by a number word, such as *a, an,* or *one.*

Noncount nouns are always singular in form and cannot be introduced by a number word.

WRONG	We drank teas.
	We drank a tea.
	We drank one tea.
RIGHT	We drank tea.
	We drank a cup of tea.
	We drank some tea.

Count Nouns	Noncount Nouns
many animals	much wildlife
few cups (of coffee)	little cream and sugar
a chair, two chairs	furniture, some furniture
an idea	thoughtfulness

A singular count noun cannot be used without a determiner, such as an article (see pp. 14-15 for more information about determiners).

WRONG	He is teacher.
	I bought book.
RIGHT	He is **a** teacher.
	I bought **a** book.
	I bought **this** book.
	I bought **the** book.

Noncount nouns use **much** and **a little** rather than **many** and **a few,** which are only for count nouns.

NONCOUNT	"How **much** furniture did you buy?"
	"Not much."
COUNT	"How **many** chairs did you buy?"
	"Two."

A **compound noun** combines two or more words that have different meanings when used alone. Since the form of a compound noun can be one word, one hyphenated word, or two words, consult a reliable dictionary for the correct form of a questionable compound noun: *paintbrush, dining room, president-elect.*

Notice the intonation difference between compound nouns and adjectives describing nouns.

- Compound nouns in English have their main stress (their loudest syllable) in the first part of the compound: **high**chair, **black**bird.
- However, when the same two words appear as an adjective and a noun, the noun has the main stress: high **chair**, black **bird**.

Collective nouns are words that refer to groups or units: *jury, orchestra, class.* A collective noun that refers to the group as a whole takes a singular verb; a collective noun that refers to individual members of the group takes a plural verb.

SINGULAR	The *class was* excited about the trip to Williamsburg.
PLURAL	The *class were* split in their decision about where to stop for dinner.

tip

Try using concrete nouns to make your writing more vivid.

All common nouns are either concrete or abstract in meaning. The difference is one merely of meaning; it does not affect how the words are used. **Concrete nouns** refer to things that can usually be perceived with the senses: *hill, mouse, milk, teenager.* **Abstract nouns** refer to things known by the mind but usually not directly perceived with the senses: *joy, surrealism, anger, fidelity.*

Nouns function as subjects, direct objects, indirect objects, objects of prepositions, predicate nouns, nouns of direct address, appositives, and objective complements.

Sentence Patterns pp. 40-44

Prepositional Phrases, Appositive Phrases, Verbal Phrases pp. 57-75

Pronouns

A **pronoun** is a word that substitutes for a noun or for a noun and its modifiers. In the sentence *Danielle mentioned that she needs a new coat,* the pronoun *she* substitutes for the proper noun *Danielle.* In the sentence *The new red coat looks warm, and it fits well,* the pronoun *it* substitutes for the phrase *the new red coat.* A pronoun can be used in all the ways that a noun can be used—as a subject, a direct object, and so on.

Pronouns require an **antecedent,** a noun or other pronoun that the pronoun replaces. In the first sentence above, *Danielle* is the antecedent of the pronoun *she.*

Personal Pronouns

The most common type of pronoun is the personal pronoun. Each personal pronoun has four characteristics: **person, number, gender,** and **case.**

Person tells whether the personal pronoun refers to the speaker or the speaker and others (first person), the person(s) spoken to (second person), or another person(s) or thing(s) (third person).

Number tells whether the personal pronoun is singular or plural.

Gender tells whether the personal pronoun is masculine, feminine, or neuter. Gender affects only third-person singular pronouns.

Case is a change in form that reflects how a personal pronoun is used in a sentence. Subjective-case pronouns usually function as subjects or predicate nouns; objective-case pronouns usually function as objects of verbs, verbals, and prepositions; and possessive pronouns show ownership and often function as adjectives.

Pronoun
Reference
pp. 174-83

Pronoun-
Antecedent
Agreement
pp. 135-38

Pronoun Case
pp. 196-203

Singular			
	Subjective	**Objective**	**Possessive**
First person	I	me	my, mine
Second person	you	you	your, yours
Third person			
Neuter	it	it	its
Masculine	he	him	his
Feminine	she	her	her, hers
Plural			
	Subjective	**Objective**	**Possessive**
First person	we	us	our, ours
Second person	you	you	your, yours
Third person	they	them	their, theirs

We visited Monticello on vacation. (*first person plural, subjective case*)

Have *you* ever toured the house and grounds, Jim? (*second person singular, subjective case*)

Thomas Jefferson inherited the Monticello property from *his* father. (*third person singular, masculine, possessive case*)

Jefferson's many inventions include an early polygraph and a revolving music stand; visitors can view *them* at Monticello. (*third person plural, objective case*)

Demonstrative Pronouns

The **demonstrative pronouns** *this, that, these,* and *those* identify specific persons, places, things, or ideas. *This* (singular) and *these* (plural) refer to things that are near, and *that* (singular) and *those* (plural) refer to things that are far away.

Do you prefer *these* or *those?*

Determiners
pp. 14-15

Interrogative Pronouns

Interrogative pronouns are used to ask direct or indirect questions. The interrogative pronouns are *who, whom, whose, what,* and *which.* Sometimes *ever* is added to the basic interrogative pronoun for special emphasis.

The teacher inquired *who* had used the gym last.

Whatever made Lori look there in the first place?

Indefinite Pronouns

Indefinite pronouns refer to persons or things in a general way; therefore, they normally do not have antecedents. Indefinite pronouns can be classified according to whether they are singular or plural.

Agreement
pp. 129-30

ALWAYS SINGULAR	anyone, everyone, no one, someone; anybody, everybody, nobody, somebody; anything, everything, something, nothing; each, less, little, much, one
ALWAYS PLURAL	both, few, fewer, many, several
SINGULAR OR PLURAL	all, any, more, most, none, some

Considering the context of the sentence will help you decide whether one of these last pronouns is singular or plural. If one of these pronouns refers to a singular noun, it is treated as singular; if it refers to a plural noun, it is treated as plural.

SINGULAR	*Most* of the food in the refrigerator *is* okay to eat.
PLURAL	However, *most* of the bananas *are* rotten.

 ESL

Indefinite pronouns are different from nouns in several ways. Nouns, but not indefinite pronouns, can be made plural and can be preceded by determiners and adjectives. We do not say "anybodies" or "a nice anybody." However, sometimes one of these words can be used idiomatically as a noun: "She thinks he's *an absolute nobody.*" (She thinks he is not important.) "He gave *his all.*" (He gave all of his possessions or all of his effort.)

Use of Reflexive and Intensive
pp. 203-4

Reflexive and Intensive Pronouns

Reflexive and intensive pronouns are personal pronouns with *self* or *selves* added. **Reflexive pronouns** usually function as objects in sentences and refer to the same person or thing as the subject. **Intensive pronouns** intensify, or emphasize, a noun or pronoun already in the sentence. An intensive pronoun does not function as part of the sentence pattern; therefore, it can be removed without changing the basic meaning of the sentence. Grammatically, an intensive pronoun functions as an appositive: it renames the preceding noun or pronoun.

REFLEXIVE	Shakespeare's King Henry V rallies *himself* and his troops for the Battle of Agincourt.
INTENSIVE	Shakespeare *himself* could not have foreseen the popularity of the play *King Henry V.*
REFLEXIVE	We found *ourselves* on the edge of our seats during the battle scenes.
INTENSIVE	Fully engrossed in the story, we *ourselves* couldn't believe how quickly the play was over.

Relative Pronouns

Adjective Clauses
pp. 91-92
Noun Clauses
pp. 99-100

A **relative pronoun** has a noun function in a dependent clause and at the same time relates or connects that clause to the rest of the sentence. A relative pronoun has an antecedent and is part of an adjective clause. *Who, whom, whose, which,* and *that* are the relative pronouns.

Ahithophel was the man [*who* supported Absalom in a revolt against King David.]

Hushai, [*whose* advice Absalom listened to instead of Ahithophel's,] was a spy for King David.

Reciprocal Pronouns

Reciprocal pronouns express a mutual or common relationship among persons mentioned in the subject of the sentence. There are only two reciprocal pronouns: *each other* and *one another.* They are used most often as direct objects but can also be used as indirect objects or objects of prepositions.

Annie and her best friend text *each other* between every class.

I guess talking to *one another* at lunch isn't enough for them.

The reciprocal pronouns can be made into possessive adjectives and as such can modify nouns.

Of course, the girls know *each other's* cell phone number by heart.

in SUMMARY

A **noun** names a person, place, thing, or idea.

A **singular noun** names one person, place, thing, or idea; a **plural noun** names two or more persons, places, things, or ideas.

A **common noun** names a general person, place, thing, or idea; a **proper noun** names a specific person, place, thing, or idea.

Compound nouns are formed by combining two or more other words.

Collective nouns name a group. When a collective noun is singular in form, it can be either singular or plural in meaning.

Concrete nouns refer to things that can usually be perceived with the senses. **Abstract nouns** refer to concepts that are perceived with the mind.

A **pronoun** is a word that substitutes for a noun and its modifiers. The **antecedent** is the noun or other pronoun that the pronoun replaces.

Personal pronouns reflect **person, number, gender,** and **case.**

Demonstrative pronouns point out persons, places, things, or ideas.

Interrogative pronouns ask questions.

Indefinite pronouns do not refer to specific persons or things.

Reflexive pronouns are used as objects and refer to the same person or thing as the subject of the sentence; **intensive pronouns** emphasize a noun or pronoun already used in the sentence.

Relative pronouns have a noun function in a dependent clause and at the same time relate that clause to the rest of the sentence.

Reciprocal pronouns express a mutual or common relationship among persons mentioned in the subject of the sentence.

1.1 PRACTICE *the skill*

Underline the nouns once. Underline the pronouns twice.

1. Aerodynamics is the study of how moving objects interact with air.

2. The word *aerodynamics* divides into two words meaning *air* and *powerful.*

3. A person certainly hopes the air itself is powerful enough to hold him when he is in an airplane!

4. The effects of air are not always apparent to someone who is inside a plane.

5. However, the movement of air past the wings of the plane carries it higher.

6. Some of the airplanes used for passengers are quite heavy; these can be over 700,000 pounds.

7. Water in the atmosphere can significantly affect the flight of an airplane.

8. Many have studied the flight of birds as well.

9. In the United States, people have been using the air to travel in heavier-than-air objects for about a century.

10. A pilot and an engineer help each other to consider several factors; both look at viscosity, compressibility, and drag.

PRACTICE *the skill*

Identify each italicized pronoun as *personal, demonstrative, interrogative, indefinite, reflexive, intensive, relative,* or *reciprocal.*

_____ 1. Because *he* formulated the third law of motion, Sir Isaac Newton has been very important to the study of aerodynamics.

_____ 2. Nearly *everything* in a plane takes into account the laws of motion.

_____ 3. *What* could have made Aristotle think that the sun and stars travel in circles because their nature was to do so?

_____ 4. Einstein was the scientist *who* postulated the theory of relativity.

_____ 5. The theory of relativity *itself* influences the measurement of speeds approaching the speed of light.

_____ 6. Space travel concerns *itself* with entirely different forces than simple terrestrial aviation does.

_____ 7. However, the two sciences are obviously related to *one another.*

_____ 8. In order for a spacecraft to travel in space, *it* must first overcome the earth's gravitational pull.

_____ 9. *Anyone* can see the importance of the laws of gravity and motion.

_____ 10. Does Einstein refer to *that* in his writings?

USE *the skill*

Write an appropriate noun or pronoun to complete the sentence.

_____ 1. Years after Kitty Hawk, there are such _?_ as ultralights, jumbo jets, turbojet planes, and supersonic aircraft. (*noun*)

_____ 2. The Second World War greatly boosted the aviation _?_. (*noun*)

_____ 3. Demand for military aircraft, both to transport goods and to bomb enemy _?_, sharply increased during the war. (*noun*)

_____ 4. In fact, air combat was a deciding _?_ in the war. (*noun*)

_____ 5. After the war, people still wanted to fly, because _?_ were now accustomed to the convenience and speed of air travel. (*personal pronoun*)

_____ 6. They wanted to use planes more often, and many wanted to own one for _?_. (*reflexive pronoun*)

7. _?_ in weather prediction and airport efficiency also increased the use of airplanes. (*noun*)

8. In 1986, Burt Rutan designed the *Voyager,* an ultralight aircraft _?_ circumnavigated the globe without refueling. (*relative pronoun*)

9. *Voyager* was made mostly of plastic materials; _?_ allowed the aircraft to weigh just under five tons at takeoff. (*demonstrative pronoun*)

10. Most of that weight was fuel from the seventeen fuel tanks in the aircraft; _?_ began with 1,200 gallons on board. (*personal pronoun*)

Verbs

Verbs express action or state of being. They help communicate what is happening in the sentence or connect the subject with its complement.

ACTION	The politician *issued* a statement. I *considered* his words carefully.
STATE OF BEING	He *appears* unruffled. Many reporters *were* at the news conference. They *had* many questions.

Notice that some action verbs name actions we can see; others convey internal action. State-of-being verbs describe a state or condition. The verb *be* and its forms are the most common state-of-being verbs.

Verbs are perhaps the most complicated of the parts of speech because they have so many functions, forms, and types. Sentence analysis often requires that you identify a verb by its tense, person, number, voice, and mood.

TENSE	I sing; I sang; I will sing.
PERSON	He sings; you sing.
NUMBER	She sings; they sing.
VOICE	We sing the hymn; the hymn was sung by us.
MOOD	I sang; if I were singing . . .

Subject-Verb Agreement pp. 118-32

Verb Use pp. 150-64

Intransitive and Transitive Verbs

Intransitive Verbs

An **intransitive verb** is an action verb that needs nothing to complete it: the sentence can be complete with only a subject and a verb.

   S   **InV**
The opponent *counterattacked.*

   S   **InV**
Fencing contestants *engage* in attack and defense with a blunted weapon.

Sentence Pattern S-InV p. 40

Sentence
Patterns
S-TrV-DO,
S-TrV-IO-DO,
S-TrV-DO-OC
pp. 40-44

Transitive Verbs

Unlike intransitive verbs, **transitive verbs** have a word to receive the action of the verb. Transitive verbs transfer their action to receivers called **direct objects.** Some transitive verbs can also have **indirect objects.**

S   TrV   DO

One contestant *scored* a hit.

S   TrV   IO   DO

Each *gave* the other a challenging bout.

Remember that some verbs can be either intransitive or transitive, depending on the sentence pattern.

INTRANSITIVE	The taller fencer *lost* yesterday.
TRANSITIVE	He probably won't *lose* today's bout.

Linking Verbs

Sentence
Patterns S-LV-PN
and S-LV-PN
p. 41

Linking verbs connect the subject with a word in the predicate that renames or describes the subject. The most common linking verbs are forms of the verb *be.* However, other verbs may be used as linking verbs, especially these that describe the functions of the senses: *feel, look, smell, sound,* and *taste.* Verbs that express the state or position of the subject—*appear, become, grow, remain, seem, stay*—can also be linking verbs.

LINKING	The animal *looked* forlorn.
INTRANSITIVE	The animal *looked* at its prey.
LINKING	The young man *grew* tall.
TRANSITIVE	The young man *grew* a mustache.

No verb can be both transitive and linking at the same time in the same sentence. Direct objects follow transitive verbs, and predicate nouns or predicate adjectives follow linking verbs.

TRANSITIVE	The firefighter *sounded* the alarm.
LINKING	The alarm *sounded* loud.

Auxiliaries

Auxiliaries, or "helping verbs," are words that may join the main verb in making up the complete verb of a sentence. An auxiliary often joins the main verb to contribute certain minor meanings. Auxiliaries may express time, completion, progression, emphasis, possibility, and so on. (A chart of the various meanings and uses of auxiliaries is located on pages 150-51.) A complete verb may have no auxiliaries, one auxiliary, or multiple auxiliaries; but the main verb is always the last word in the verb phrase.

Be, have, and *do* can be used either as auxiliaries or alone as main verbs. When one of these is an auxiliary, it is followed by another verb.

BE AS MAIN VERB	She *is* an enjoyable person.
BE AS AUXILIARY	She *is working* on her résumé.
HAVE AS MAIN VERB	Markus *has* a job.
HAVE AS AUXILIARY	He *has* already *applied* for continuing education classes.
DO AS MAIN VERB	We *do* our own yard work.
DO AS AUXILIARY	The neighbors *do* not *mow* very often.

The **modal auxiliaries** express something about the speaker's attitude, or mood, toward the action or state he is talking about. The common modal auxiliaries are listed below.

can	could
may	might
should	would
must	ought (to)

Auxiliaries
pp. 150-51

These auxiliaries always come first in the complete verb, and in standard English only one is used at a time.

NONSTANDARD | We *might could* finish our homework before supper.

STANDARD | Perhaps we *could* finish our homework before supper.

Modal auxiliaries are different from other auxiliaries.

1. Modals never have an *s* suffix.

   WRONG | He cans go with us.

   RIGHT | He **can go** with us.

2. Except for *ought,* modals are never followed by the *to* of the infinitive.

   WRONG | You should *to* do your homework first.

   RIGHT | You **should do** your homework first.

ESL

Principal Parts of Verbs

Most verbs in English have only three basic forms. These are called the **principal parts** of the verb. Each of the different forms of a verb can be made from these three forms: the present, the past, and the past participle.

Present	Past	Past Participle
walk	walked	walked
sing	sang	sung

Note that the past participle is always used after some form of the auxiliary *have.*

in SUMMARY

Verbs express action or state of being. An **action verb** shows what the subject of the sentence does. A **state-of-being verb** describes a state or a condition.

An **intransitive verb** is an action verb that needs nothing to complete it; a **transitive verb** has an object.

A **direct object** is a noun or pronoun that receives the action of a transitive verb; an **indirect object** is a noun or pronoun that tells *to whom* or *for whom* the verb's action was done.

A **linking verb** connects the subject with a word in the predicate that re-names or describes the subject.

An **auxiliary** joins the main verb to express time or to give special meaning or emphasis.

A **modal auxiliary** is a verb that expresses something about the speaker's attitude toward the action or state he is talking about.

The **principal parts** are the three basic forms of any English verb; they are the present, the past, and the past participle.

PRACTICE *the skill*

Underline the main verb once and the auxiliary twice. Then identify the verb as action (A) or state of being (S).

A   1. In 1977, the Concorde made its first commercial takeoff from New York's Kennedy Airport.

_____ 2. It was the first supersonic aircraft in America.

_____ 3. The luxury, hundred-passenger plane could travel at twice the speed of ordinary airliners.

_____ 4. However, the British- and French-built planes were unpopular at first.

_____ 5. Even after its maiden flight, the Concorde remained a plane for the privileged few.

_____ 6. Furthermore, it produced an extremely loud sonic boom.

_____ 7. Some environmentalists wanted the Concorde to be kept on the ground.

_____ 8. After a long court battle, authorities allowed the Concorde in the United States.

_____ 9. After its initial noise test, it started regular service across the Atlantic.

_____ 10. Because of rising costs and low passenger numbers, British Airways and Air France have retired the Concorde.

USE *the skill*

Write a sentence using the type of verb indicated.

1. Tell about your last ride in a plane. If you have never ridden in a plane, tell about how you imagine a plane ride to be. (*state-of-being*)

   _____

   _____

2. Describe what a plane looks like in the sky. (*action*)

   _____

   _____

3. Write a sentence about what air travel could be like in the future. (*auxiliary*)

   _____

   _____

4. Describe an airport. (*state-of-being*)

   _____

   _____

5. Tell what you might do the next time you ride on a plane. *(auxiliary)*

_____

_____

6. Tell whether you would like to learn to fly a plane. *(present)*

_____

_____

7. Have you ever flown alone? Describe what it was like or might have been like. *(past participle)*

_____

_____

8. Write a sentence about how air travel has changed or could have changed your life. *(past)*

_____

_____

9. Describe a real or imaginary helicopter ride. *(action)*

_____

_____

10. If you could have your own plane, what kind would it be? *(state-of-being)*

_____

_____

Adjectives

Adjectives are words that modify or describe nouns or pronouns. Many adjectives will answer one of the following questions: *which one? what kind? how many? how much? whose?*

Positions of Adjectives

Most adjectives come before the nouns they modify. Sometimes adjectives will appear immediately after the nouns or pronouns they modify. A predicate adjective appears after a linking verb and describes the subject of the sentence.

BEFORE THE NOUN	Benedict Arnold was a *notorious* traitor during the Revolutionary War.
AFTER THE NOUN	Arnold, *sneaky* and *greedy*, traded secrets with the British.
PREDICATE ADJECTIVE	Vidkun Quisling, a Norwegian who allied with Hitler, was also *traitorous*.

Adjectives cannot be made plural in English.

ESL

WRONG	We saw some beautifuls sights. They live in an apartments building.
RIGHT	We saw some beautiful sights. They live in an apartment building.

One type of adjective, an **objective complement,** appears after the direct object, describing the direct object as a result of the action of the verb.

OBJECTIVE COMPLEMENT | Quisling's defection made him *infamous*.

Determiners

A **determiner** is a type of adjective that signals that a noun is coming in a sentence. Determiners point out, or limit, a following noun and come before any descriptive adjectives that may modify the same noun. There are several types of determiners.

Articles

The determiners *a, an,* and *the* are called **articles.** Articles are the most common adjectives. *A* and *an* are indefinite articles used to modify nouns not named in particular or not mentioned before. *The* is the definite article; it modifies something already known or already mentioned.

> **ESL** Use *a* before a word beginning with a **consonant sound;** use *an* before a word beginning with a **vowel sound:** *a* tent, *an* opening.

Possessives

When possessive nouns or pronouns modify nouns, they are also a type of determiner. A possessive shows ownership or other close relationship.

POSSESSIVE NOUN | The *snowshoe's* ingenious design makes it practical for walking in deep snow.

POSSESSIVE PRONOUN | *Your* leg muscles get a workout trudging through a drifted forest.

When a possessive noun is modified by at least one other adjective, the possessive and its modifiers form a **possessive phrase.** The possessive phrase modifies the following noun as a unit.

Early French trappers' snowshoes were called raquettes.

Notice that *early* and *French* modify *trappers',* not *snowshoes.* The possessive phrase *Early French trappers'* works as a unit to modify *snowshoes.*

Sometimes a possessive noun or pronoun does not function like a determiner but like a noun instead. A possessive functioning like a noun is called an **independent possessive** because it functions alone rather than as a modifier.

DETERMINER | *My* early attempts at wearing snowshoes were unsuccessful.

INDEPENDENT POSSESSIVE | What about *yours*?

Demonstratives

When a demonstrative functions alone as a subject, predicate noun, or object, it is a pronoun. However, some demonstratives modify following nouns and are then determiners. Demonstrative determiners have the same meanings and forms as the demonstrative pronouns discussed previously.

DETERMINER | *That* snowshoe is made of traditional white ash.

PRONOUN | *This* is made of aluminum.

Interrogatives

Three interrogative words can function as determiners; they are *which*, *what*, and *whose*. Used alone, interrogatives are pronouns.

DETERMINER	*Which* snowshoe do you prefer?
PRONOUN	*Which* do you prefer?

Indefinites

Just as there are indefinite pronouns, there are also indefinite determiners. The indefinites are determiners only when they modify nouns.

DETERMINER	My brother bought *some* new snowshoes.
PRONOUN	He also gave me *some* for my birthday.

Modifying Nouns

Sometimes nouns function as adjectives in a sentence. A noun that modifies another noun is called a **modifying noun.** Modifying nouns always appear directly before the nouns that they modify, after any determiners or descriptive adjectives.

NOUN	The new type of *snowshoe* grips the ice better than the old.
MODIFYING NOUN	There are approximately two dozen *snowshoe* manufacturers today.

Proper Adjectives

Adjectives that are formed from proper nouns are **proper adjectives.** Some proper nouns change form when they are adjectival; others do not change form. Proper adjectives are capitalized, just as the original proper nouns are capitalized.

Snowshoes help farmers harvest real *Vermont* maple syrup.

Some *Alaskan* trappers use extremely slender and long snowshoes.

Adverbs

Adverbs modify verbs, adjectives, and other adverbs, giving more information about the word modified. Most adverbs show manner, place, time, and negation.

MANNER (INCLUDING EXTENT AND NUMBER)	The football player ran *speedily* through a maze of defenders.
PLACE (INCLUDING DIRECTION AND ORDER)	In Australian football, there are three players who may play *anywhere* on the field.
TIME (INCLUDING FREQUENCY)	*Today,* Australian football is quite popular.
NEGATION	According to the rules, players may *not* throw the ball.

The negative word *not* can be connected to an auxiliary in the form of a contraction: *hasn't, don't, isn't, can't, weren't,* and so forth. *Not* can also be connected to the auxiliary *can* as a whole word (*cannot*).

Adverbs can appear in several different positions in the sentence. Most often, an adverb appears directly before or after the verb that it modifies. The adverb *not* appears after an auxiliary in a sentence.

In a negative sentence, the negative **not** always follows the first auxiliary, regardless of how many auxiliaries there are in the complete verb.

We could **not** have been happier.

ESL

Qualifiers

A **qualifier** is a subcategory of adverb; qualifiers modify only adjectives or other adverbs, either strengthening or weakening the idea of that word. A qualifier almost always comes directly before the word it modifies.

Adv
President Reagan recovered *somewhat* rapidly from a serious gunshot wound he received in March 1981.

Adj
It was remarkable that he was not killed, but the absence of permanent damage was *even* greater reason for amazement.

PA
God's hand of protection was *very* clear throughout the ordeal.

Conjunctive Adverbs

When a semicolon joins two independent clauses, often a conjunctive adverb helps to show the exact relationship, or meaning-link, between the clauses. **Conjunctive adverbs** modify the verb in an independent clause and join that clause to another independent clause. A conjunctive adverb can be moved within its sentence or clause and is usually set off by one or more commas, depending on where the conjunctive adverb comes in the second clause.

In earlier years people called America's vast grasslands the "great American desert"; *however,* today the area produces much of our country's food.

The grasslands support running and clustering animals such as antelope; *furthermore,* they provide homes for burrowing animals such as prairie dogs and gophers.

There is only moderate to low rainfall on the prairie; prairie grasses, *therefore,* must sink their roots deep into the soil to find moisture.

The following is a list of some common conjunctive adverbs:

also	in fact
besides	instead
for example	nevertheless
furthermore	then
however	therefore

An **adjective** modifies or describes a noun or pronoun.

A **determiner** points out a following noun and comes before any descriptive adjectives that may modify the same noun. Four common kinds of determiners are articles, possessives, demonstratives, and interrogatives.

An **article** is the most common kind of adjective. *A* and *an* are indefinite articles; *the* is the definite article.

A **possessive** is a noun or pronoun form that shows ownership or other close relationship.

An **independent possessive** replaces a noun or noun phrase.

Demonstratives and **interrogatives** (as adjectives) have the form of their pronoun counterparts but are used to describe nouns or other pronouns.

A **modifying noun** is a noun that modifies another noun. It functions as an adjective.

Proper adjectives are adjectives made from proper nouns.

An **adverb** modifies verbs, adjectives, and other adverbs.

A **qualifier** is a kind of adverb; it modifies only adjectives or other adverbs.

A **conjunctive adverb** modifies the verb in an independent clause and joins that clause to another independent clause.

1.6 PRACTICE *the skill*

Underline the adjectives once and the adverbs twice in the following excerpt from *Snow* by Catherine Farnes, published by BJU Press. Do not underline the articles unless an article is part of a possessive phrase. (There are eighteen adjectives and fourteen adverbs in the piece.)

We lined up, waited for the whistle, and, when we heard it, we started running. . . . I [hung] back . . . , waiting to see which girl [was] the most serious about getting into the lead, and then quickened my pace to catch her.

Each breath burned slightly more than it usually did at this point in the race, probably because of the higher elevation. I began to focus on the sound and rhythm of my steps on the track, ignoring the different pacing of the two girls I passed, to put myself . . . behind the leader. I [could] hear her shoelaces hitting the tops of her shoes each time she'd pick her foot up off the track . . . behind her . . . until the last 110 meters, when I stepped out to the side and began to sprint.

But she clearly did not plan to be passed.

People were shouting. . . . I could see the end of the straightaway. . . . The girl's white shoes hitting the track in pace with mine. . . .

And that's how the run ended.

Dead even.

Underline the adjectives once and the adverbs twice. Draw an arrow from each adjective or adverb to the word it modifies. Do not underline the articles unless an article is part of a possessive phrase.

1. Many scientists built unsuccessful airplanes before brothers Orville and Wilbur Wright built their airplane.

2. The brothers eagerly asked the Smithsonian Institution for a list of books on aeronautics.

3. They read several articles by Otto Lilienthal and his American counterpart, Octave Chanute.

4. The Wrights' first idea was a kite; however, they soon decided on building a glider.

5. Breezy and sandy, the beaches at Kitty Hawk, North Carolina, seemed nearly perfect for their experiments.

6. Orville and Wilbur built a rough wind tunnel out of an old starch box.

7. Their experimentation showed major flaws in the work of Lilienthal and Chanute; therefore, the brothers collected their own data.

8. The Wrights also built an engine that would fly their plane.

9. Amazingly, on December 17, 1903, the brothers made four successful flights.

10. Those flights and other future flights made the brothers quite famous.

Prepositions

A **preposition** begins a prepositional phrase and shows the relationship between its object and another word in the sentence. The **object of the preposition** is a noun or pronoun that follows the preposition. A preposition, its object, and any modifiers of the object make up a **prepositional phrase.** All prepositions appear in prepositional phrases.

Prepositional Phrases pp. 57-59

tip

Too many prepositional phrases in a row can confuse your reader.

James Forten served *in the American Navy.*

He was a wealthy sail maker *after the Revolutionary War.*

Forten was an early abolitionist who contributed *to many reform movements and causes.*

The following are the most commonly used one-word prepositions: *of, in, to, for, with, on, at, by, from.* Of course, some of these words may sometimes be adverbs. A word is not a preposition unless it appears in a prepositional phrase.

The Historical Society of Pennsylvania (HSP), *Portrait of James Forten,* Leon Gardiner Coll.

Troublesome Prepositions

Certain prepositions are commonly confused. Learn the differences between the following pairs of prepositions.

Between/Among

In most cases, use *between* when discussing two people or things and use *among* for more than two.

Ronda had to decide *between* the Advanced Math and the Physics I classes.

The soccer team voted *among* themselves to select a team captain.

In/Into

Especially in writing use *in* to show a location. Use *into* to refer to a direction.

Chemistry class meets *in* the gymnasium classroom.

The students walked *into* the gym together.

Beside/Besides

Use *beside* to indicate "next to." Use *besides* to mean "in addition to" or "except for."

Hantz kept his Bible on the table *beside* his bed.

Besides a graphing calculator, students are required to bring two sharpened pencils for the exam.

All of Mom's cakes *besides* the German chocolate fell.

Preposition or Adverb?

To determine whether a word in a sentence is a preposition or an adverb, look for an object of the preposition since prepositions must have objects.

PREPOSITION	Put the laundry *down the chute.*
ADVERB	Put the laundry *down.*

Conjunctions

A **conjunction** joins words, phrases, or clauses in a sentence. There are two main types of conjunctions: coordinating and subordinating. Correlative conjunctions are a special type of coordinating conjunction.

Coordinating Conjunctions

A **coordinating conjunction** joins sentence parts of the same type: two verbs, two direct objects, two predicates, and so on. The following are the most commonly used coordinating conjunctions: *and, or, nor, for, but, yet.*

VERBS	"Watch *and* pray, that ye enter not into temptation" (Matt. 26:41).
DIRECT OBJECTS	"Then said Jesus unto him, Except ye see signs *and* wonders, ye will not believe" (John 4:48).
PREDICATE NOUNS	"I am Alpha *and* Omega, the beginning *and* the end, the first *and* the last" (Rev. 22:13).
PREPOSITIONAL PHRASES	"Turn not to the right hand *nor* to the left: remove thy foot from evil" (Prov. 4:27).
INDEPENDENT CLAUSES	Many are called, *but* few are chosen (Matt. 22:14).

Notice that when a coordinating conjunction connects independent clauses, a comma usually precedes the conjunction.

Commas
pp. 282-83

Correlative Conjunctions

Correlative conjunctions appear in pairs and, like other coordinating conjunctions, join sentence parts having the same function. Correlative conjunctions are generally used in three ways: (1) to provide emphasis, (2) to clarify which things are being joined, (3) to alert the reader that a second thing will be added to the first. The correlative conjunctions are these:

> both—and
> either—or
> neither—nor
> not only—but also

Of course, correlative conjunctions can join any of the various types of sentence elements.

SUBJECTS	*Both* grandfather *and* granddaughter hope to catch a fish.
INFINITIVE PHRASES	Rena hopes *not only* to catch a fish *but also* to clean it herself.

When *not only—but also* joins clauses, the subject of the second clause may come between the words *but* and *also.*

Infinitive Phrases
pp. 74-76

COMPOUND SENTENCE	*Not only* did Uncle Roberto fry the fish, *but* he *also* cooked an entire meal over the campfire.

Subordinating Conjunctions

A **subordinating conjunction** joins a dependent clause to an independent clause. As part of the dependent clause, the subordinating conjunction's only function is to introduce that clause. Below is a chart of commonly used subordinating conjunctions.

after	once	when
as	since	where
because	that	wherever
before	unless	while
if	until	

Most subordinating conjunctions introduce adverb clauses. A subordinating conjunction usually expresses one of the following common types of meaning: time, place, cause, contrast, purpose, condition, and manner.

> **After** *I built my kite,* my father and I attached a long tail.

> We will fly it tomorrow **unless** *the weather is bad.*

The subordinating conjunction *that* introduces noun clauses.

> I have heard **that** *the kite was first popularized in China.*

Adverb Clauses
pp. 95-96
Noun Clauses
pp. 99-100

Interjections

Interjections can stand alone or can appear with a sentence. Grammatically, an interjection is not a necessary part of a sentence. Interjections express several different meanings.

Interjections
p. 266

STRONG FEELING	*Brrr!* Eastern Siberia often experiences temperatures of -40° F.
AGREEMENT AND DISAGREEMENT	*Yes,* over 180 days per year are subfreezing.
GREETING AND LEAVE-TAKING	*Hello!*
POLITENESS	I'll take our Florida sunshine, *thanks.*
HESITATION OR INTRODUCTION OF A SUBJECT	Part of the Yenisei River is not navigable in Eastern Siberia, *well,* except for a few months of the year.

tip

Most interjections are used in informal writing or speech.

Short phrases may also serve as interjections: *Oh, my! For sure! good evening; bless you.* Interjections can be followed by an exclamation mark or a period or can be set off by commas.

A **preposition** is a word that introduces a prepositional phrase and shows a relationship between its object and some other word in the sentence.

The **object of the preposition** is a noun or a pronoun that follows the preposition.

A **prepositional phrase** consists of the preposition and the complete object of the preposition (the object and any modifiers of the object); prepositional phrases can be used like adjectives to modify nouns or like adverbs to modify verbs.

A **conjunction** is a connecting word that joins words or groups of words in a sentence.

A **coordinating conjunction** joins sentence parts of the same type.

Correlative conjunctions are used in pairs to join sentence parts of equal rank.

A **subordinating conjunction** joins a dependent clause to an independent clause.

An **interjection** expresses strong feeling, agreement or disagreement, greeting or leave-taking, politeness, or hesitation or introduction. Interjections have no necessary part in the sentence.

1.8 PRACTICE *the skill*

Identify each underlined word as a preposition *(Prep)*, a conjunction *(Conj)*, or an interjection *(Int)*. Then identify the specific type of each conjunction: *coordinating, correlative,* or *subordinating*.

_____ 1. <u>Unless</u> you have studied the history of flight, you probably have never heard the name Otto Lilienthal.

_____ 2. A fourteen-year-old Otto strapped wooden wings to his arms <u>and</u> attempted his first flight in 1862.

_____ 3. The flight was not entirely successful, but he escaped injury and went back to his study of flight—<u>unbelievable</u>!

_____ 4. <u>Not only</u> did Lilienthal study aerodynamics, <u>but</u> he <u>also</u> studied the flights of birds.

_____ 5. <u>From</u> his study of birds, he wrote a book, *Bird Flight as a Basis for the Art of Flight,* in 1889.

_____ 6. <u>Indeed,</u> Lilienthal is believed to be the first inventor to use curved rather than flat wings.

_____ 7. In 1891 Lilienthal flew successfully <u>for</u> more than one hundred feet.

_____ 8. He held tightly to his glider, ran <u>into</u> the wind, and took off.

_____ 9. <u>Since</u> his legs were left dangling, he used them to help steer the glider.

_____ 10. Lilienthal kept detailed records <u>of</u> over two thousand glider flights.

REVIEW *the skill*

Underline the prepositions once and the conjunctions twice. Then identify the specific type of each conjunction: *coordinating*, *correlative*, or *subordinating*.

_____ 1. For centuries man wanted to fly.

_____ 2. According to Greek legend, Icarus tried to fly with wings of feathers and wax.

_____ 3. Icarus's wings fell apart because he flew too close to the sun.

_____ 4. Leonardo da Vinci recorded scientific flight principles but never designed a successful flying machine.

_____ 5. Joseph Galien hypothesized about air density.

_____ 6. The Montgolfier brothers, Joseph and Etienne, eventually engineered the first balloon flight.

_____ 7. Frightened French peasants not only attacked but also destroyed the first hydrogen balloon.

_____ 8. Jean Marie Contelle damaged enemy morale when he made military reconnaissance missions.

_____ 9. One early space flight had men flying in an open gondola-like structure featuring modified household venetian blinds.

_____ 10. Balloons have also been used widely for research purposes.

REVIEW *the skill*

Identify each italicized word as a noun (N), a pronoun (Pro), a verb (V), an adjective (Adj), an adverb (Adv), a preposition (Prep), a conjunction (Conj), or an interjection (Inter).

_____ 1. *Animal* flight consists of flapping, gliding, and soaring.

_____ 2. A gliding animal must use gravity *after* it climbs to a higher altitude.

_____ 3. Gliding is *often* used in combination with soaring or flapping.

_____ 4. Soaring flight uses energy from rising *or* horizontally moving air.

_____ 5. Large ocean birds and, *well*, some insects practice this type of flying.

_____ 6. Most animals use the flapping mode of *flight* since they must flap for takeoff and during periods of still air.

_____ 7. A diving hawk has been clocked at *nearly* five hundred miles per hour.

_____ 8. Large migratory birds can fly *between* sixty and seventy miles per hour.

_____ 9. Insects generally fly at twenty to thirty miles per hour, but *some* fly much faster.

_____ 10. Flying animals sometimes *cover* great distances during migration.

PERSONAL LETTER

As cold waters to a thirsty soul, so is good news from a far country.
Proverbs 25:25

In her letter, Anne Morrow records her thoughts about the day's experiences for her fiancé, Charles Lindbergh, who was not there to share them. Read the letter one more time and ask yourself these questions:

- How did Anne feel when she got Charles's letter?
- What was Anne's reaction to the incorrect information about her marriage in the newspaper?
- What did the bowls that she purchased at the fair look like?

The answers to these questions are clear because Anne expressed her thoughts and feelings specifically. When Charles read her letter, he could have had no doubt that she had been happy to hear from him, that she had been angered by the newspaper notice, and that the bowls she had found were a beautiful shade of blue. He could probably also tell that Anne had been thinking of *him* while she was writing. She told him news that affected both of them. She described things that she thought he would be interested in knowing. The letter you will write should have the same sense of personality and sincerity that Anne's does.

tip
A list—like Anne's about items that are blue—can be an effective tool.

Write a personal letter to someone. A letter is a little piece of you. Try to say things the way you would say them if you were talking in person. In a sense, letters are even better than conversations or e-mails, taking more deliberate thought. And as good keepsakes, letters can be read and remembered long after conversations are over and e-mails are deleted.

Planning

✔ **Choose a friend or relative to write.** A letter is a chance to share information that you might otherwise not have opportunity to share. Perhaps there is someone you should thank or offer sympathy to. A letter outlining the plan of salvation is an effective tool for sharing the gospel with someone you care about.

tip
In this day of e-writing, a handwritten letter tells the receiver that he is important to you.

✔ **Make a list of the most important things you want to communicate to your reader.** What do you really want him to know, and what do you think he would really like to know?

✔ **Think of your letter as a conversation.** Writing a letter is much like talking with someone. When you start a conversation, you bring up topics you think your listener will be interested in hearing about. You try to express your thoughts in a way that he will clearly understand and that will accurately reflect your personality.

✔ **Decide what information you would like to get from your reader and what questions would be best to ask in your letter.** People like to give information about themselves, so ask open-ended questions that invite more than a yes-or-no response from the reader.

Drafting

✔ **Be sincere.** The best letters have a conversational, sincere tone. You can tell the writer enjoys sharing his life with the letter reader. Anne's letter reads as though she is talking on the telephone to Charles, who is hundreds of miles away and whom she has not seen for a long time. Phrases like, "Well, that's over. Oh, today—what do you think I did today!" reveal the writer's personality and sincere *joie de vivre* more than the simple beginning "Today I attended a street fair" would.

ESL *Joie de vivre* is a French phrase often used by English speakers; it means "the joy of living."

✔ **Include details.** Notice the details that Anne included about her feelings and experiences. How angry was she? "Boiling." What did she see in the booths at the fair? "Dusters, dolls, toys, baskets, pink lemonade, . . . hats and children's wagons and minute little doll's tea sets, and pots and pans and lacquer boxes, and candy." Details help your reader to visualize what you are saying and to feel included in your story.

Details and
Accuracy
pp. 368-69

✔ **Make your details specific.** When you write about your thoughts or feelings, try to be as specific as possible. When you write about things you have seen or experienced, use concrete words. Include colors, sizes, and shapes of objects. Anne described the bowls that she had purchased for their future home as "lovely, with a blue and green border, and deep, sloping up gracefully like some kind of flower." Anne also informs Charles that he will "have to live on cornflakes"— not just "things that will fit in bowls"—in his old age. When you write, think of words to describe how that restaurant chili tasted or what the fabric of a shirt felt like to the touch. Make your reader feel as though he were there.

✔ **Show interest in your reader.** Include information that your reader finds especially important or interesting: news about his favorite sports team or hobby, comments on the last conversation or correspondence you had, or updates on previous topics. This lets the other person know that you listen to what he says and value his response.

Revising

✔ **Read the letter silently to yourself.** Ask yourself whether the letter will be interesting to your reader and whether the tone is conversational and sincere. Does the letter sound like you talking?

✔ **Make sure that you effectively communicated what you intended to say.** Of course, you know what you meant and what the gymnasium looked like during the banquet, but will your reader be able to tell? Does the letter contain adequate detail? Did you simply state what happened, or did you give sensory details to describe what happened?

✔ **Revise for organization.** Did you ramble about a lot of different things or did you develop each thought sufficiently? Do not be too critical of your letter writing on this point. In personal letter writing, organization can usually take a back seat to personality and sincerity.

✔ **Edit for grammar and punctuation.** Of course, since the letter is personal, you can (and should!) use fragments, contractions, and other informal conventions in this assignment. However, you should correct any agreement or reference problems since these can obscure your meaning.

✔ **Make a final copy and proofread it carefully.** An attractive, error-free copy shows that you care.

Sentence Energy pp. 368-70

---

tip

Use fragments sparingly.

Publishing

✔ **Send the letter to someone you know.** Consider adding a photograph, a drawing, or some other item to further personalize your correspondence.

 **Thinking Biblically**

Never underestimate the power of the written word. A phone call is enjoyable for the moment, but nothing takes the place of a well-written letter. Once a sentiment or belief is in print, it never goes away. The recipient may profit from (or be hurt by!) a letter for years to come. Consider the New Testament: twenty-one of its twenty-seven books are letters. God's having given us these inspired letters should emphasize to us the importance of writing about things that matter and writing about them in a way that is memorable and compelling.

Some Ideas to Consider

- Write a letter to a friend, describing a recent experience that made you happy, angry, or sad.
- Write a letter to someone you've never met, introducing yourself.
- Write a letter to a relative in another city, relating an important piece of news in your town or community.

LETTER FOR LETTER

The Fateful Letter

Whenever a person speaks or writes a letter, he is revealing something about himself. Is he being truthful, and is he acting according to truth? Ask yourself these questions whenever you are communicating or receiving communication. David thought a short note would solve all his problems. If he had known the drastic consequences this letter would have for him and his family, do you think he would have written it? Do you think David was acting according to truth?

Uriah was on his way back to the camp, a letter in his hand. He still couldn't figure out why his lord, the great king of Israel, had called him home. Had his bravery and loyalty indeed been observed, and this was how David wanted to reward him? He hoped that was it, yet deep down he wondered.

"Reporting back to camp, sir." Uriah stood before Joab. "And I have a message from the king."

"Good to have you back," the giant general responded as he hunched his bearlike frame over the map he was studying. "How was your home?"

"I presume well, my lord, but I did not go home. My orders took me to the palace."

Joab grunted. "You really are too committed, Uriah. You make the other officers look bad." He turned toward Uriah and snatched the letter from his outstretched hand. "Well, let's see what the great king wants now." He opened the letter, breaking the royal seal. His eyes darted rapidly down the page. Suddenly they stopped, widened, and then glanced up at Uriah. They ran down the page again. Then, as if

he had misread it, he held the letter up to where a ray of sunlight shone through a rip in the tent. Uriah was tempted to glance at the page since it was partially turned his way, but he refrained himself. Joab put the letter down and nervously stroked his beard. He glanced quickly at Uriah but avoided his eyes.

"Leave me," he said hoarsely without looking up.

Uriah hesitated, wondering at this response.

"Now!" Joab repeated forcefully. Uriah saluted and left, and Joab looked again at the fateful page.

It read:

> Set ye Uriah in the forefront of the hottest battle, and retire ye from him, that he may be smitten, and die.

For the full story, read II Samuel 11:1–12:25
- *Why did David send this letter?*
- *What are some of the ironies of this story?*
- *What were some of the consequences of this letter?*
- *What truths was David rejecting?*

Personal Response

"Whither shall I go from thy spirit? or whither shall I flee from thy presence? . . . If I say, Surely the darkness shall cover me; even the night shall be light about me" (Ps. 139:7, 11). David ignored the truths that God punishes sin and that God sees all things. God forgave David for the sin of murder; David did, however, suffer the consequences of sin. Write a personal response to this story and explain why God punishes sin. Be sure to support your statements with Scripture.

An injured runner describes his injury. An animal lover writes about her pet iguana. Every day you read magazines, newspapers, blogs, and letters that are full of writings on personal topics. Some writings involve in-depth research; others reflect only the author's prior knowledge. The best are perhaps a combination of both.

The authors of "Growing Up Outdoors" write about items used in child rearing. Notice the personal nature of the piece—from the details about their own hand-beaded cradleboard to the reflections of an aunt on the original use of moss bags. As you read, reflect on how the Hungry Wolfs make Native American traditions accessible to you, the reader. Later in the chapter, you will have a chance to write about a topic that interests you.

Growing Up Outdoors *by Adolf and Beverly Hungry Wolf*

An infant's first introduction to discipline came in the form of cradleboards and moss bags. An Indian baby spent very little time unbundled, lying out open, or left to crawl around in a big space. Scientists can probably make all sorts of deductions from the different practices, but we must at least recognize that children laced securely into bags start out life learning how to be still!

The cradleboard was a secure place for a baby to live during its transition from the mother's womb to walking about in the open world. For a people without cars and bassinettes, it was also a very compact and handy baby crib. We used moss bags and a cradleboard for all our children and found this to be a really safe and secure way to handle infants, even in modern times.

Our cradleboard was a very pretty one, beaded with colorful floral designs by a cousin. It was handy for going on walks, when Beverly carried it on her back with a wide leather strap, or for traveling by truck. It fit nicely between our seat and the dashboard and seemed fairly protective.

But for everyday use we found moss bags far more practical. Each of our kids had their own, decorated with different beaded designs. Along with the cradleboard, these are now heirlooms—as they often were in the past—to be used by whatever child comes next into our family.

A moss bag resembles a soft shoe, made big enough for a baby to fit in and laced up the front with strings of buckskin. In the past these bags were made of hand-tanned deer and antelope skin, but in recent years some of the nicest ones we've seen were made of velvet.

Ironically, one traditional thing we didn't put into our moss bags was the substance from which they got their name. Moss was used in place of diapers, and it seems to have worked at least as well. We learned about it from Beverly's aunt, Mary One Spot, who also made our first moss bag.

Aunt Mary said that for her own kids she and Uncle Frank would go out into the forest to pick the moss from pine trees, where it grows. They would get a big sackful of it at a time. At home they would clean it carefully by hand, picking out all the pine needles and sharp sticks. A big bunch of it was then packed around the baby before it was laced into its bag. This could soak up a lot of moisture before it needed changing, at which time the really soiled parts simply peeled away from the baby's skin, leaving it practically clean.

GRAMMAR

SENTENCES

Sentence Outlines; Paragraphing pp. 332, 334-36

Words from all the eight parts of speech can be arranged in an infinite variety of ways to capture and communicate meaning. Nouns and most verbs, adjectives, and adverbs, known as content words, usually contain most of a speaker's meaning. On the other hand, prepositions, pronouns, and conjunctions (as well as auxiliaries, determiners, and qualifiers), called function words, tie together the content words. The content words and function words combine in meaningful units called sentences. For clear communication, certain elements must appear in a sentence. Every sentence you write must contain a **subject,** an actor or something being described, and a **predicate,** the action or the description.

Recognizing Sentences

A **sentence** expresses a complete thought. These complete thoughts consist of a subject and a predicate. If you have only a noun and its modifiers, as in *the crowd,* you have just part of an idea. What is significant about that crowd? What makes the following sentence a complete thought?

Capitalizing First Words p. 249

The crowd cheered loudly.

An adjective, a noun, a verb, and an adverb combine to tell us something significant about the crowd. The crowd acted—it cheered. This particular crowd was cheering in a specific manner—loudly. Now you may be left wondering why the crowd was cheering, but the idea that there is a crowd cheering loudly has been communicated. That idea is complete with an actor and an action. A **sentence** may also be defined as a group of words that has a subject and a predicate and nothing that makes it part of another sentence.

Distinguishing Independent and Dependent Clauses p. 88

Finding the Subjects and Predicates

To find the subject of a sentence, ask yourself *who* or *what* in the sentence is acting or being described. The **simple subject** is the doer of the action, is acted upon, or is described by the predicate. The **complete subject** is the part of the sentence that includes the simple subject and all its modifiers.

> The **eye** *of the hurricane* brings an eerie calm.

> *The storm's loud* **winds** kept me awake all night.

Remember that the simple subject of a sentence never appears in a prepositional phrase.

> *Each* (of the girls) brought her camera.

Predicates say something about the subject. The **complete predicate** includes the **simple predicate,** or verb, and all the other words that tell what the subject is or what it is doing.

> The hurricane **lost** *much of its force shortly after landfall.*

> *Long after the storm,* waves *forcefully* **pounded** *the shore.*

In English, the subject of a clause almost always comes before the verb (the simple predicate).

>   **S**   **V**
> The baby traveled in a cradleboard.

>   **S**   **V**   **S**
> At home the baby would usually be in a "moss bag," which
> **V**
> was made of soft leather.

A sentence may contain two or more subjects linked with a conjunction. These **compound subjects** always share the same verb.

Subject-Verb Agreement and Compound Subjects p. 119

> *My friend* **Tanya** *and her cousin* **Eden** visited Odessa last summer.

> *A seven-mile* **hike,** *a* **cookout,** and *a marshmallow* **roast** will keep the youth group busy this Saturday.

Likewise, **compound predicates** are joined by a conjunction and share the same subject.

> Joel **played** *his guitar and* **sang** *at the cookout.*

> We **hiked** *to the top of the mountain and* **enjoyed** *the awesome view.*

Inverted Subject and Predicate

Usually, the subject comes before the predicate in a sentence. Sometimes the subject appears between two parts of the verb. **Inverted order** is often seen in sentences asking a question.

>   **V** **S**   **V**
> Will we still go hiking if it rains?

Sentences beginning with *there* or *here* usually have another kind of inverted order, in which the subject follows the verb. Rearranging the sentence may help you find the subject.

      V   **S**
Here is the weather forecast.

      S   **V**
The weather forecast is here.

Understood Subjects

Sentences giving a command usually have **understood subjects.** The subject *you* is not stated (except for special emphasis).

Wear good walking shoes.

This imperative sentence is telling the listener or reader to do something; thus the listener or reader is the subject—the understood *you.*

(You) wear good walking shoes.

in SUMMARY

A **sentence** is a group of words that has a subject and a predicate and expresses a complete thought.

The **simple subject** is the doer of the action, is acted upon, or is described by the predicate.

The **complete subject** is the part of the sentence that includes the simple subject and all its modifiers.

The **complete predicate** includes the **simple predicate,** or verb, and all the other words that tell what the subject is or what it is doing.

A **compound subject** is two or more subjects that are linked with a conjunction and share the same verb.

A **compound verb** is two or more verbs that are linked with a conjunction and share the same subject.

Inverted order occurs when the subject appears after the verb or between two parts of the verb.

Understood subjects usually occur in sentences that are commands. The subject *you* is understood but not stated.

PRACTICE *the skill*

Underline each simple subject once and each simple predicate twice. If the subject is understood, write *you* to the left of the number.

1. In the early 1600s, explorers from Europe encountered the Delaware Indians.

2. Captain Samuel Argall of the Virginia colony sailed into a bay for shelter from a storm.

3. He named the bay De La Warr Bay after the governor of Virginia.

4. The people of the Delaware River Valley spoke an Algonquian language.

5. In their language, their name for themselves is Lenni-Lenape.

6. Does that name mean "genuine people"?

7. In 1682, the Lenape signed a peace treaty with William Penn.

8. The Lenape gradually moved westward from Delaware to Indiana.

9. There are about ten thousand Lenape in the United States today.

10. Learn more about the Lenape at your library.

REVIEW *the skill*

Underline each complete subject once and each complete predicate twice. If the subject is understood, write *you* to the left of the number.

1. Tell me about Columbus's first voyage to the Western Hemisphere.

2. The European and Native American worlds met in October of 1492.

3. The Italian Christopher Columbus believed in the existence of a western trade route to Asia.

4. He landed in the Bahamas instead of Asia.

5. Columbus, thinking that he had to sail only three thousand miles to reach his destination, miscalculated the distance to Asia.

6. After sailing about two months, he finally found land on October 12, 1492.

7. Columbus's new name for the island, San Salvador, means Holy Savior.

8. Natives from the island greeted them with gifts of parrots, cotton, and spears.

9. He was certain that he had reached an island in the Indies.

10. Columbus called the natives *los indios*—the Indians.

USE *the skill*

Combine the following pairs of sentences. Some sentences may need a compound subject; others may need a compound predicate.

1. Jason visited Mesa Verde National Park.
   Tony visited Mesa Verde National Park.

   _____

   _____

   _____

2. They read about the cliff dwellers in history class.
   They researched in the library before their trip.

   _____

   _____

   _____

3. The museums at the park were interesting.
   The library at the park was interesting.

   _____

   _____

4. Jason and Tony enjoyed the information about the cliff dwellers.
   Jason and Tony did not agree with the ranger's opinions on evolution.

   _____

   _____

5. Mesa Verde National Park has dramatic scenery.
   Mesa Verde National Park includes the finest examples of cliff dwellings in the United States.

   _____

   _____

6. Canyon wall ledges held cliff dwellings.
   Flat mesa tops held cliff dwellings.

   _____

   _____

7. Richard Wetherell discovered the Mesa Verde ruins in 1888.
   Charles Mason discovered the Mesa Verde ruins in 1888.

   _____

   _____

8. They had heard of the cliff dwellings.
   They had not found them in their previous searches.

   _____

   _____

9. Can visitors hike to the cliff dwellings?
   Can visitors enter the cliff dwellings?

   _____

   _____

10. A park ranger accompanies all visitors into the cliff dwellings.
    A park ranger answers questions about the dwellings.

    _____

    _____

Identifying Four Types of Sentences

End Marks
p. 266

Sentences have four possible purposes. They express a complete thought by stating a fact, asking a question, giving an order, or expressing strong emotion.

Declarative sentences make a statement and end with a period.

> We are studying Ephesians in our Bible club.

Exclamatory sentences express strong emotion and end with an exclamation point. Some single words (interjections) are punctuated this way as well.

> That is a challenging book!

tip

Be careful not to overuse exclamatory sentences in your writing.

Imperative sentences give a command (or, with *please*, make a polite command or request). They end with a period or, sometimes, an exclamation point.

> Please join our Bible study group.

> Bring a friend!

Interrogative sentences ask a question and end with a question mark.

> Can you come this Tuesday?

ESL

In English, one of the major differences in the types of sentences is the rising and falling pitch, called *intonation.* Intonation of a sentence can be a hint about what type the sentence is.

- Declarative sentences have falling intonation at the end.
- Many interrogative sentences have rising intonation at the end.
- Imperative sentences have falling intonation at the end.
- Exclamatory sentences are stated at a higher pitch than other sentences or with a greater difference between the high and the low pitches.

in SUMMARY

Declarative sentences make a statement and end with a period.

Exclamatory sentences express strong emotion and end with an exclamation point.

Imperative sentences give a command or make a request and end with a period or, sometimes, an exclamation point.

Interrogative sentences ask a question and end with a question mark.

PRACTICE *the skill*

Identify each sentence as *declarative*, *exclamatory*, *imperative*, or *interrogative*. Place the appropriate punctuation mark at the end of the sentence.

_____ 1. The name *Basket Makers* is given to the predecessors of the Pueblo Indians

_____ 2. Remember that cliff dwellers were also members of this same culture

_____ 3. Do you know the name of this culture

_____ 4. Archaeologists refer to them as the Anasazi culture

_____ 5. Amazingly, the Anasazi made baskets that held water

_____ 6. How could a basket be waterproof

_____ 7. Read about the history of basket making

_____ 8. The Anasazi even cooked in their baskets

_____ 9. Anasazi hunters used a type of weapon called the *atlatl*

_____ 10. The *atlatl* was a throwing-stick

REVIEW *the skill*

Identify each sentence as *declarative*, *exclamatory*, *imperative*, or *interrogative*. Place the appropriate punctuation mark at the end of the sentence.

_____ 1. Did you know that a Native American clan name may be the mother's name

_____ 2. Many tribes trace family descent through the mother

_____ 3. Wow, clans of the Eastern Woodland Native Americans often had more than one hundred members

_____ 4. Count how many family members you have

_____ 5. Sometimes three or four generations lived in one house

_____ 6. Can you imagine children, parents, grandparents, and great-grandparents in one house

_____ 7. Clan members worked together, defended one another, and celebrated together

_____ 8. Boys hunted, and girls cooked and tanned hides

_____ 9. You should try that

_____ 10. Please try to work together in your own family

USE *the skill*

Write an appropriate sentence in response to the prompt. Use the type of sentence indicated in parentheses.

1. facts about the Iroquois, a confederacy of six Native American tribes *(imperative)*

   _____

   _____

2. Iroquois tribes, family tree through the women, not men *(exclamatory)*

   _____

   _____

3. Meaning of *Iroquois* = "real adders" *(declarative)*

   _____

   _____

4. beans, corn, squash = three main crops of the Iroquois *(declarative)*

   _____

   _____

5. The Iroquois lived in New York State. *(interrogative)*

   _____

   _____

6. The Iroquois tribes' living space = almost all of upper New York State = approximately 40,000 square miles *(exclamatory)*

   _____

   _____

7. The families in the tribes of the Iroquois were grouped into clans. *(interrogative)*

   _____

   _____

8. These clans combined families from different tribes. *(interrogative)*

   _____

   _____

9. the six tribes in the Iroquois confederation = Cayuga, Mohawk, Oneida, Onondaga, Seneca, and Tuscarora *(declarative)*

   _____

   _____

10. visiting today's Iroquois: New York, Wisconsin, Canada *(imperative)*

   _____

   _____

Analyzing Sentence Patterns

In English, there are a limited number of ways in which a simple sentence (or any clause) can be constructed. These ways are called the **basic sentence patterns** of English. Recognizing these patterns will help you understand how sentences work and how you can put them together yourself for variety and emphasis in your speaking and writing.

Use a variety of sentence patterns to add interest to your writing.

tip

Basic Sentence Patterns

Varying
Sentence
Patterns
p. 360

Sentences can be classified according to subject-verb-complement arrangement. After locating the subject and verb of a sentence, the next step in sentence analysis is to determine whether the sentence has any **complements.** The word *complement* means "something that completes"; a complement is a noun, a pronoun, or an adjective that completes the thought of a sentence. Ask the question *whom* or *what* of the verb, and the answer will be the complement.

NO COMPLEMENT	It didn't rain.
WHAT	Spenser and Jaimyn built the *campfire.* The flames were *bright* and *warm.*
WHOM AND WHAT	Natalie gave *Corey* a *marshmallow.*

The complement is always part of the complete predicate.

Remember to ignore any modifying words and phrases when you identify a sentence pattern, since the sentence would be complete and correct without them. Also be aware that sentences sometimes employ an understood *you* as the subject. The first five patterns below are the most common, and you have studied them before. You will add two new patterns, *S-TrV-DO-OC* and *S-Be-Advl*, this year.

Subject–Intransitive Verb (S-InV)

Intransitive Verbs
p. 9

An intransitive verb needs nothing to complete it. An intransitive verb may, however, have modifiers.

      S   **InV**
A small snake was lying across my path.

S **InV**   **InV**
I jumped and then stared blankly at the snake.

Subject–Transitive Verb–Direct Object (S-TrV-DO)

Transitive Verbs
p. 10

Reflexive
Pronouns
p. 6

This pattern has a complement called the direct object. When the verb expresses action, the direct object is the receiver of that action. The direct object, a noun or a pronoun, always refers to something other than the subject, except when the direct object is a reflexive pronoun.

    S   **TrV**   **DO**
I had been weeding the garden.

        S   **TrV**   **DO**
The snake was sunning itself.

Any verb that has a direct object is a transitive verb in that sentence.

Subject–Transitive Verb–Indirect Object–Direct Object (S-TrV-IO-DO)

This pattern adds an indirect object to the previous pattern. The indirect object, a noun or a pronoun, comes before the direct object and tells *to whom* or *for whom* the action of the verb is done.

    S   TrV IO   DO
The snake gave me a scare.

    S TrV   IO   DO
I gave the snake plenty of room.

Subject–Linking Verb–Predicate Noun (S-LV-PN)

The **predicate noun** is a noun or a pronoun in the predicate that renames or identifies the subject. In this sentence pattern the subject and the predicate noun refer to the same person or thing. The two are linked by the verb.

    S LV   PN
The snake is a copperhead.

    S   LV   PN
The copperhead is an intruder here.

Subject–Linking Verb–Predicate Adjective (S-LV-PA)

The **predicate adjective** is an adjective in the predicate that describes the subject. As in the *S-LV-PN* pattern, the subject and the word in the predicate are linked by the verb.

    S LV PA
(You) Be careful never to startle a snake.

    S   LV   PA
Copperheads are not aggressive.

    S LV   PA   PA
However, their venom is extremely poisonous and dangerous.

in SUMMARY

A **complement** is a noun, pronoun, or adjective that completes the thought of a sentence.

An **intransitive verb** is a verb that does not have (or need) a complement to complete it.

A **transitive verb** has a direct object, the receiver of action.

An **indirect object** comes before the direct object and tells *to whom* or *for whom* the action of the verb is done.

A **predicate noun** renames or identifies the subject.

A **predicate adjective** describes the subject.

PRACTICE *the skill*

Label the sentence patterns *S-InV, S-TrV-DO,* or *S-TrV-IO-DO.*

1. Roger Williams, the son of a London tailor, founded the colony of Rhode Island.

2. Williams attended Cambridge University in England.

3. After graduation in 1627, he ministered as a chaplain.

4. Williams immigrated to Boston in 1631.

5. In 1635 government officials gave Williams a sentence of banishment from the Massachusetts Bay Colony.

6. Later, he secured a charter for a new colony, Providence Plantation.

7. Williams also preached among the American Indians.

8. In 1643 he published *A Key into the Language of America.*

9. This promotional tract contains Narragansett dialogue with English translations.

10. The people of Rhode Island and Providence Plantation offered Williams the presidency over the unified colony.

PRACTICE *the skill*

Label the sentence patterns *S-LV-PN* or *S-LV-PA.*

1. Carlos Montezuma became prominent as an American Indian spokesman during the early twentieth century.

2. He was a Yavapai Apache.

3. His original name was Wassaja ("signal").

4. Wassaja became Carlos after his adoption by Carlos Gentile.

5. Montezuma seemed motivated.

6. He was a graduate from Chicago Medical College in 1889.

7. After graduation, Montezuma became a physician for the Indian Service.

8. He stayed active in Chicago as a teacher and doctor from 1896 until 1922.

9. Montezuma was also an outspoken advocate for American Indian rights.

10. Writing remained important as an outlet for his activism.

2.9 REVIEW *the skill*

Label the sentence patterns *S-InV, S-TrV-DO, S-TrV-IO-DO, S-LV-PN,* or *S-LV-PA.*

1. Many Native Americans have respect for the legends of their ancestors.

2. Most tribal peoples were conservationists.

3. They took from the land only the bare necessities.

4. In return, the land yielded them harvests of fruit and grain.

5. Sometimes the tribe needed skins or meat.

6. Then they hunted buffalo or other wild prey.

7. Early Native Americans hunted only for survival.

8. A hunt for sport was unacceptable to the Native Americans.

9. They sometimes herded buffalo over cliffs.

10. This method was strictly a last resort.

Buffalo Chase by Seth Eastman, oil on canvas, c. 1851

Additional Sentence Patterns

Subject–Transitive Verb–Direct Object–Objective Complement (S-TrV-DO-OC)

Sometimes a direct object is not enough to complete the idea in a sentence. An **objective complement**, either a noun or an adjective, renames or describes the direct object. This completer is called an *objective* complement because it completes the information about the direct object. Only a few verbs can be used in this pattern.

S   TrV   DO OC

Today wireless networks make Internet access easy.

The objective complement, *easy,* describes the direct object, *access.* Notice that the objective complement always follows the direct object, unlike the indirect object, which always precedes the direct object.

S   TrV   DO OC

Some people still find new technology difficult.

Notice the close relationship between the direct object and the objective complement. You can usually imagine that there is a form of *be* between them.

S   **TrV**   **DO OC**   **OC**
They built the wall tall and strong.

The wall *is* tall and strong because they built it that way.

S   **TrV**   **DO**   **OC**
We elected Troy class president.

Troy *is* class president because we elected him.

Adverbs
pp. 15-16

Subject–be–Adverbial (S-be-Advl)

Sentences with the verb *be* may have a prepositional phrase or an adverb acting as a complement. These completers, called **adverbials,** come only after a form of the verb *be*. They include adverbs such as *here* and *now* and prepositional phrases that express information about time, location, or condition.

S   **be**   **Advl**
My sister's cell phone is never out of her sight.

Prepositional
Phrases
pp. 57-59

Normally a prepositional phrase such as "after class" would be an optional modifier, but in the sentences below, it is the necessary complement.

S   **be**   **Advl**
The best time for texting is after class.

S   **be Advl**
Your cell phone will still be here.

in SUMMARY

An **objective complement**, either a noun or an adjective, renames or describes the direct object because of the action of the verb.

An **adverbial** is an adverb or an adverbial prepositional phrase that follows a form of the verb *be*.

2.10   PRACTICE *the skill*

Label the sentence patterns *S-TrV-DO-OC* or *S-be-Advl*. If the adverbial is a prepositional phrase, underline it.

1. The power of David Brainerd's diary made many of his readers missionaries.

2. Brainerd was often in prayer for hours before his visits to the American Indians.

3. Brainerd considered these people important.

4. Brainerd also made a young lady, Jerusha Edwards, the object of his affection.

David Brainerd, detail from *History of Evangelism* in the Bob Jones Jr. Memorial Seminary and Evangelism Center, James Brooks, artist

5. Often Brainerd was in very poor health.

6. Gentle Jerusha Edwards made Brainerd her full-time patient.

7. She was there at his death on October 9, 1747.

8. Brainerd made his wish to see her again his final message to Jerusha Edwards.

9. Only five months after his death, David Brainerd and Jerusha Edwards were in heaven together.

10. Jonathan Edwards made the biography of his friend and his daughter a legacy for David and Jerusha.

2.11 REVIEW *the skill*

Label the sentence patterns *S-InV*, *S-TrV-DO*, *S-TrV-IO-DO*, *S-LV-PN*, *S-LV-PA*, *S-TrV-DO-OC*, or *S-be-Advl*. If the adverbial is a prepositional phrase, underline it.

1. Another friend of David Brainerd was Jerusha Edwards's little brother, Jonathan Edwards Jr.

2. Like Brainerd, Jonathan Edwards Jr. had a great love for the American Indians.

3. Young Jonathan made the American Indian children his friends.

4. He was constantly among them and in their homes.

5. His knowledge of their language and their unique way of life was extensive.

6. Nine-year-old Jonathan left his family and helped an older missionary with American Indian languages and customs.

7. Later, hostility grew among the tribes, and they feared for Jonathan's life.

8. They considered their little friend valuable, and they took him back to his home.

9. At the end of the long, dangerous trip, Jonathan was safely on the shoulder of an adult American Indian.

10. By the end of his life, Edwards had given his friends years of service and a complete grammar of their own language.

2.12 USE *the skill*

Write about a Native American custom. Use as many different sentence patterns as possible.

2.13 CUMULATIVE *review*

Analyze the sentences you wrote for 2.12 Use the Skill. Label the sentence patterns for each sentence.

PERSONAL REPORT

And thou shalt teach [these commandments] diligently unto thy children, and shalt talk of them when thou sittest in thine house, and when thou walkest by the way, and when thou liest down, and when thou risest up.

Deuteronomy 6:7

Writing a research report is a little like exploration. You have a goal in mind, and you know something about where you are headed; but you don't know everything that you will find along the way. There may be pitfalls, or there may be treasures. Whatever the case, you will certainly make many discoveries. The personal report will help you discover the treasure of writing about that which interests you.

The Writing Process pp. 326-48

Adolf and Beverly Hungry Wolf wrote about what were to them two commonplace items: the cradleboard and the moss bag. Choose a topic that is of interest to you, research the topic, and write a brief personal report. In writing this report you will give both your reader and yourself new information about your topic.

Thinking Biblically

"And they brought up an evil report of the land which they had searched. . . . And the whole congregation said unto [Moses and Aaron], Would God that we had died in the land of Egypt!" (Num. 13:32; 14:2). When the ten spies returned from Canaan, they gave a kind of personal report. But it was a very bad one. The problem was not incorrect grammar, an ill-defined purpose, or a poorly worded thesis. Their report was given from the wrong perspective. Instead of reporting what they had seen from God's perspective, they reported from their own faithless viewpoint. Joshua and Caleb saw the same things, but because they loved the Lord and believed Him, they gave a very different report: "The LORD is with us: fear them [the Canaanites] not" (Num. 14:9). A person's perspective on life will affect all of his thinking and writing—even his personal reports.

Planning

✔ **Choose a topic.** The topic for this personal report should be something that you yourself are curious about, regardless of its interest to the general public. The topic should also be something that you already know a little about—a hobby, a family tradition, a current event. In "Growing Up Outdoors" Adolf and Beverly Hungry Wolf write about their continuing the family tradition of using cradleboards and moss bags.

✔ **Narrow your topic and determine your purpose.** This step can help you find the angle from which you want to write about your topic. Do you want to inform your audience about trapping? If so, you might write on the history of your topic, leaving out information on specific animals that are now illegal to trap. However, if you wanted to examine the results of trapping, its effect on certain animal populations would be relevant material to include.

✔ **Gather information.** First, list everything you already know about your topic. Since this report features a topic with which you are somewhat familiar, this step should be simple. Note any gaps in your information: missing dates and names, causes or effects, comparisons or contrasts. Next, search the library for reference works with information on your topic. Use the online encyclopedias (or bound volumes) as well as the *Readers' Guide to Periodical Literature*. Take note of any works cited within the articles you locate; you may be able to access the source for the quoted information. Your teacher or librarian will have other useful suggestions for you to try. Some topics may require personal interviews like the one with Aunt Mary One Spot in "Growing Up Outdoors." Don't neglect firsthand sources of information.

Library Skills pp. 395-401

tip

Ask your interviewee whether you can use a tape recorder while you interview. You can transcribe notes later.

✔ **Take notes and document sources.** Whether you take notes directly on your computer or make notes on paper, be sure to include all of the information you think you may need. Keep your purpose in mind as you write. As you take notes, indicate whether your information is paraphrased, quoted, or summarized from the original. Since much of the material for this report will be from your own experience, be sure to keep your own information separate from the information you glean from other sources. Document carefully each source that you use in your research. Plagiarism is the serious offense of using another's work as your own.

Drafting

Topic Sentences
pp. 334-35

✔ **Keeping your purpose in mind, write a thesis statement.** The thesis statement should name the subject of your report and tell what you intend to say about the subject. For this report, your teacher will probably want your thesis statement to be the first sentence of the report. "Growing Up Outdoors" is an excerpt from a book by the Hungry Wolfs, so the first sentence of the excerpt does not entirely meet the specifications for a thesis statement like the one you will write. However, it does name the subject (cradleboards and moss bags) and give a partial idea of what will be said (aspects of discipline—hygiene and otherwise!).

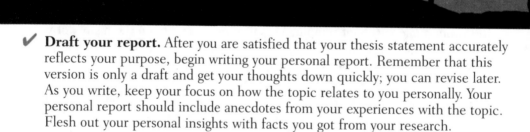

Runner's knee, or chondromalacia, is a painful overuse injury.

If you plan to run down the road of life, learn to avoid chondromalacia, a painful overuse injury.

✔ **Draft your report.** After you are satisfied that your thesis statement accurately reflects your purpose, begin writing your personal report. Remember that this version is only a draft and get your thoughts down quickly; you can revise later. As you write, keep your focus on how the topic relates to you personally. Your personal report should include anecdotes from your experiences with the topic. Flesh out your personal insights with facts you got from your research.

tip

Consider writing your draft in one sitting. This can keep ideas flowing smoothly.

Concluding
Sentence
p. 336

✔ **Draw a conclusion.** Consider ending your report with a conclusion based on what you learned about your topic from your research. Or restate your thesis statement with a slight variation or an insight relating to your report information.

So if you want to avoid being a spectator, learn to heed the warning signs of overuse.

I learned the hard way that overuse can quickly make a spectator out of a competitor.

Revising

✔ *Re-view the ideas of your report.* Look at your draft again to see whether your report clearly says what you want it to say. Does your thesis statement reflect your purpose? Is all of the information that you included relevant to your topic and purpose? Can a reader tell from your report that this topic has personal importance for you? If the answer to any of these questions is no, correct these issues in your revision.

tip

For a fresh viewpoint, allow a peer or a family member to read your report.

✔ *Re-view the style of your report.* Check for precision in your word choice. Your nouns and verbs should be especially strong. Cross out words and phrases, draw arrows, add text—mark up your first draft to indicate the changes you want to make.

First Draft

If you plan to run down the road of life, learn to avoid chondro-
malacia, ~~a painful overuse injury.~~ My ~~first hint of a problem~~ came ^introduction to this painful overuse injury^
when I started ~~running hills.~~ ~~Now~~ hills will strengthen your quadri- ^concentrating on hill work. Running consistently^
ceps, but ~~they~~ also sometimes strengthen ~~them~~ unevenly. This can ^the hill running will^ ^the muscles^
pull the kneecap out of ~~whack. Ouch!~~ (This results in a lot of pain) ^alignment^
When the kneecap is misaligned, it
~~The kneecap~~ scrapes against bone instead of tracking smoothly along ^with^
the cartilage. ^to cushion it^

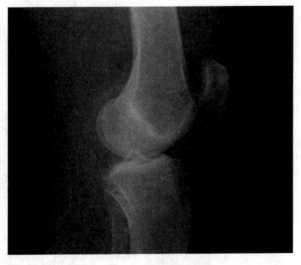

Second Draft

If you plan to run down the road of life, learn to avoid chondro-malacia. My introduction to this painful overuse injury came when I started concentrating on hill work. Running hills consistently will strengthen your quadriceps, but the hill running will also sometimes strengthen the muscles unevenly. This unevenness can pull the kneecap out of alignment. When the kneecap is misaligned, it scrapes against bone instead of tracking smoothly along with the cartilage to cushion it. This friction results in a lot of pain.

tip

Read your paper backwards to force yourself to look at each word individually.

✔ **Proofread your report.** After you have done a thorough revision and made all of the changes you noted, make a clean copy for proofreading. Check the clean copy for grammar, usage, punctuation, capitalization, and spelling errors as well as against any checklist your teacher gives you.

Publishing

✔ **Share your work.** Since this report is a personal one, consider sending it to someone who shares your interest in your topic—a grandparent, cousin, uncle, or friend. You could also post your report on your family's or school's website. If possible, read the report aloud to your family or another group.

tip

Ask the person to whom you send your piece to send one back to you. This can start an information exchange.

✔ **Submit the report.** Many magazines publish noteworthy stories written by sub-scribers. If you subscribe to a magazine dedicated to your hobby or pursuit, re-search the magazine's guidelines for submission. Newspapers also publish stories of local interest.

✔ **Save your writing.** Include this latest piece of your writing history in a writing folder or portfolio.

Some Ideas to Consider

History

- Write about an aspect of politics that inter-ests you.
- Write about your in-volvement with a local (or national) branch of government.

Family Living

- Write about your fam-ily's holiday traditions.

Bible

- Write about a lesson you are learning from your personal Bible reading.
- Write about a biblical truth that you have seen evidenced in the lives of your family members.

THINK ABOUT IT

Truth and Validity

Every person has an inborn desire to know truth. You make life decisions based on what you consider to be truth. At the same time, all kinds of people are trying to impose upon you what they believe is truth. Your parents, your teachers, and your friends tell you what they believe to be true. The books you read, the programs you watch, and even the music you listen to tends to impose on you a certain brand of truth.

The way information is presented can be misleading. Can you think of an advertisement or a popular belief that misleads many people? Or have you ever watched friends make very foolish decisions? You probably said to yourself, "What were they thinking?" Only correct thinking can lead to wise actions. Thinking comes naturally, but thinking well is a skill. Knowing how to think well produces benefits in all disciplines of life, but correct thinking is essential for a sound spiritual life. Scripture warns us against the subtle deception of the world. "Beware lest any man spoil you through philosophy and vain deceit" (Col. 2:8). The Bible highly commends those who "searched the scriptures daily, whether those things were so" (Acts 17:11).

Of course, a few critical thinking skills will not give you all knowledge and understanding. You may be a great debater and logician and still not understand the truth of Scripture. It takes a regenerated heart and a spirit that fears God to understand wisdom. With a proper attitude toward God, you can use these skills to understand the Bible and be on guard against false teaching.

Consider the following argument:

> All large gray animals can fly. Elephants are large gray animals. Therefore, elephants can fly.

Do you believe that? No, of course not. But is this argument valid? Believe it or not, the reasoning itself is valid—but the first "fact" is untrue.

The validity of an argument refers to its form. If the form of an argument is reasonable, then the argument is **valid.** The above argument says that all large gray animals can fly. If we accept this as well as the fact that elephants are large gray animals, then we must accept the conclusion that elephants can fly. A valid argument is not necessarily true, but it does have a legitimate form. An invalid argument does not have a legitimate form.

When considering an argument, first determine whether the argument is valid. Then determine whether the argument is true by considering the premises. A **premise** is a statement in an argument. The premises of an argument are the sequence of statements that are intended to establish the truth of another statement called the **conclusion.** If at least one of the premises is false, then the conclusion will also be false. Remember that some premises can be statements of evaluation or opinion that need further proof before they can be used in a valid argument. Statements can be true, false, or opinion. It is true that the sun rises every morning. It is false that there is a solar eclipse every day. The statement that exposure to the sun causes skin cancer is an evaluative statement; yet it has been proved by such a large amount of research and experience that it would be valid to call it a fact.

Identify each of the following statements as true (T), false (F), or evaluative (E).

_____ 1. The sun is the center of the solar system.

_____ 2. The earth is the center of the solar system.

_____ 3. Lemon/Lime Mist is the best-tasting soft drink.

_____ 4. Teenagers are not responsible enough to get driver's licenses until they are eighteen years old.

_____ 5. Hundreds of people are killed in car accidents each year.

Identify each argument as *valid* or *invalid*.

_____ 1. All dogs are faithful. My pet is a dog. My pet is faithful.

_____ 2. All cats are furry. My pet is furry. Therefore, my pet is a cat.

_____ 3. Eating a lot of pizza makes a person tall. I eat a lot of pizza. Therefore, I will be tall.

_____ 4. Everything that is not good for you should be outlawed. Candy bars and soft drinks are not good for you. Therefore, candy and soft drinks should be outlawed.

_____ 5. Eating candy and drinking soft drinks cause cavities. Eating candy and drinking soft drinks can cause diabetes. Therefore, candy and soft drinks should be outlawed.

Thinking It Through

Write a valid argument supporting laws that require children to attend school. Examine your essay and determine the truth and validity of your argument.

Occasionally a piece of writing is so moving that we feel compelled to respond to it. Have you ever thought for a long time afterward about something you read? discussed it with a friend? made a journal entry about it? We often respond to the literature we come into daily contact with—the newspaper, a magazine, a letter—in the same ways.

Seventeen-year-old Becky reflects on God's purposes for her life following the fire that severely disfigured her when she was two years old. As you read the piece, think about what your response might have been to this tragedy and what your responses to other problems in your life have been. In this assignment you will have an opportunity to respond to Becky's writing.

More Precious than Gold *by John and Brenda Vaughn*
Epilogue: A Word from Becky

My earliest memory is of the hospital—not the first time I was there, but later. I'm thankful I don't remember the fire. It used to scare me when I would hear Mom and Dad talk about it. It scares me now to go back to the hospital. I have had surgery fifty-seven times. I'm glad for everything the doctors have done for me, and I know that there are some things they can't do. I wish I could walk by myself. I wish I could see out of my right eye. I wish my hands were stronger. But I'm glad I made it, and I'm glad for my family and friends.

God has been very good to me. I have had 171 blood transfusions, and I don't have AIDS. I have a school across the street from my house that my Dad started. I have teachers that understand me and friends that like me for who I am. I like it best when people just treat me like a person. I know I was burned, but I don't want to be called a "victim." Several years ago I asked my Dad to write a tract that I could give to people who stared at me in public. I was saved when I was six years old, and I know that without the Lord's help I couldn't face the struggles I live with every day. I wouldn't be honest if I said I was glad for all I have been through or that I didn't want to be able to live a normal life. But really, I've never known anything else. I want to use my life for the Lord. One summer at camp I rededicated my life to Him. When I graduate from high school next year, I hope I can go to a Christian college.

This is Mom and Dad's story. I don't mind that they told some things about me, because I know they are trying to help others. But I'm glad they are going to let me tell my own story myself. I'm not sure what that story will be yet. I'm seventeen. I have a lot of decisions to make in the future. Sometimes I go to meetings

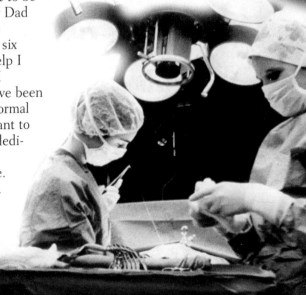

with my Mom. I'm proud of her—she saved my life—but I don't like to talk to groups. I'm too shy, I guess. I'm only telling you this because I'm writing it and you're not looking at me.

I know there are lots of other girls who feel like I do. They think they are ugly sometimes. They think no one likes them. I know that boys are sometimes interested only in how we look. But I'm learning what is really important in life. We are just here for a little while, but we will be in heaven forever. Long after I have a perfect body, others will just be starting to know the kind of suffering I have behind me—only theirs will be forever.

There have been lots of letters from people who have been saved and who have read our tract. I pray that lots of others will be helped by this book.

More people have prayed for me than I have even met. I am thankful for those prayers and those people. I know that God loves me. I know that Mom and Dad love me. We're not perfect . . . but we're working on it.

I'm glad I'm alive.

Rebecca Morel Vaughn
May 1993

GRAMMAR

PHRASES

A **phrase** is a group of related words that does not contain both a subject and a predicate. It may contain one or the other but does not contain both. In the following example there are several phrases.

> Coming around the corner, the young boy was surprised by the sound of a parade.

Coming around the corner is a participial phrase that modifies the noun *boy.* The phrase *the young boy* functions as the complete subject of the sentence. The simple predicate is the phrase *was surprised.* Both *by the sound* and *of a parade* are prepositional phrases. *By the sound* is an adverbial phrase that modifies the verb *was surprised; of a parade* is an adjectival phrase that modifies the noun *sound.* Notice that no phrase contains both a subject and a predicate.

Prepositional Phrases

A **prepositional phrase** consists of a preposition, its object, and any modifiers of the object. While the noun or pronoun object by itself is the simple object of the preposition, that word and its modifiers are the complete object of the preposition.

Prepositions
p. 19

> Snow fell lazily *on the quiet streets* and *in the nearby park.*

The sentence above contains two prepositional phrases, *on the quiet streets* and *in the nearby park.* In the first, the complete object of the preposition is *the quiet streets;* in the second, it is *the nearby park.*

A prepositional phrase may have more than one object. In the sentence below *candy* and *cookie* are compound objects of the preposition *between.*

> The toddler paused uncertainly between the *candy* and the *cookie.*

tip

Avoid using too many prepositional phrases. If you need more than two in a row, consider revising.

Functions of Prepositional Phrases

A preposition shows a relationship between its object and some other word in a sentence. The entire prepositional phrase acts as a modifier of that word, which may be either a noun or a verb. Because they perform functions similar to those of adjectives and adverbs, prepositional phrases are classified as either **adjectival prepositional phrases** or **adverbial prepositional phrases.**

Adjectival prepositional phrases modify nouns. They can answer questions that adjectives often answer: *Which one? What kind? How many?* and *Whose?*

> The antique desk *with the matching chair* will be sold today.

> Accusations *of corruption* hindered the mayor's service.

An adjectival prepositional phrase may modify the object of a preceding prepositional phrase.

> Whose is the jacket *on the desk in the hallway?*

Here the complete object of the preposition *on* is *desk* with all its modifiers: that is, *the desk in the hallway.* If we put parentheses around the prepositional phrases, the sentence would look like this:

> Whose is the jacket (on the desk (in the hallway))?

Adverbial prepositional phrases modify verbs and often show manner, place, or time.

> *In a hurried manner,* Mr. Vermicelli searched *through his pockets for his keys.*

> *On Friday afternoon* James will be *at the dentist's office for about an hour.*

in SUMMARY

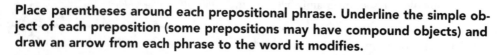

A **phrase** is a group of related words that does not contain both a subject and a predicate.

A **prepositional phrase** contains a preposition, its **object,** and any modifiers of the object. A preposition may have more than one object.

Prepositional phrases function as **adjectival prepositional phrases** (which modify nouns) and **adverbial prepositional phrases** (which modify verbs).

3.1 ◆ **PRACTICE** *the skill*

Place parentheses around each prepositional phrase. Underline the simple object of each preposition (some prepositions may have compound objects) and draw an arrow from each phrase to the word it modifies.

1. God described Job as a perfect man and an upright man.

2. Satan wished for the ruin of Job.

3. God granted Satan permission for his plan against Job's family and possessions.

4. Satan could also touch the health of Job's body but could not take his life.

5. Job's friends blamed sin for his problems.

6. Before his accusers, Job declared his innocence.

7. God taught a lesson about Himself to Job and his friends.

8. Job acknowledged his lack of comprehension of God's character and prayed for his friends.

9. God blessed Job with more children and a double portion of animals.

10. After the end of his trial, Job lived for many years.

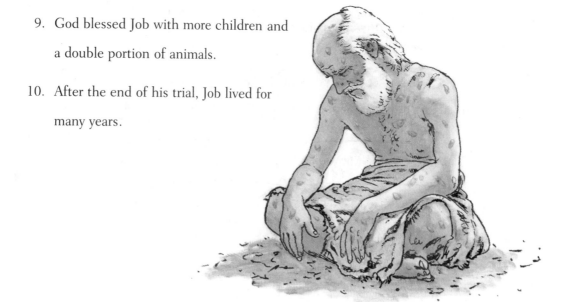

REVIEW *the skill*

Place parentheses around each prepositional phrase. Underline the complete object of each preposition (some prepositions may have compound objects) and draw an arrow from each phrase to the word it modifies.

1. The walled city of Jericho was a formidable obstacle to the Israelites.

2. The Lord solved the problem with an unusual decree.

3. He commanded a walk around the city.

4. For six days the men of war made a daily circle of the city.

5. Seven priests with rams' horns and the ark of the covenant accompanied them on their walk.

6. The men maintained silence throughout this daily routine.

7. On the seventh day, the men made seven circles of the city.

8. After the last circle and a long trumpet blast, the men shouted.

9. The walls of seemingly impenetrable strength fell down, and the men rushed in.

10. Jericho showed the Israelites their true source of victory—God.

Misplaced Prepositional Phrases

Like other modifiers, prepositional phrases can be misplaced. When the prepositional phrase is not close enough to the word it is intended to modify, the sentence may be confusing or even funny.

Misplaced Modifiers p. 226

> **UNCLEAR |** The dog barked curiously at the visitor with the wagging tail.

The solution to the problem of a misplaced prepositional phrase is to place the phrase closer to the word it should modify.

> **CLEAR |** The dog with the wagging tail barked curiously at the visitor.

in SUMMARY

A **misplaced prepositional phrase** creates confusion because it is not close enough to the word it is intended to modify.

Correct a misplaced phrase by moving it closer to the word it should modify.

PRACTICE *the skill*

Underline each misplaced prepositional phrase and insert a caret (^) at its correct location. If a sentence is already correct, write C in the blank.

_____ 1. The Midianites subdued the Israelites with their invading hordes.

_____ 2. With a strong hand, the Israelites asked the Lord to deliver them.

_____ 3. The Lord from the tribe of Manasseh chose Gideon to rescue the Israelites.

_____ 4. Although the Israelite army was much smaller than the Midianite army, the Lord told Gideon to send men home at the well of Harod.

_____ 5. With 300 men, Gideon faced an army of more than 100,000.

_____ 6. In three companies, the Midianites were surrounded by the Israelites.

_____ 7. Gideon with unusual weapons equipped the Israelites.

_____ 8. At the appointed time, men on trumpets would blow and break pitchers with lamps in them.

_____ 9. Under supernaturally induced fear, the Midianites began fighting each other.

_____ 10. God again showed the Israelites the true source of their deliverance—Himself.

REVIEW *the skill*

Correct each misplaced prepositional phrase by rewriting the sentence. If a sentence is already correct, write C in the blank.

1. Paul and Barnabas had a disagreement over the young man Mark.

_____

_____

2. Mark left Paul and Barnabas on their first missionary journey.

_____

_____

3. Out of concern for the new churches, Paul proposed that they make a second journey to Barnabas.

_____

_____

4. Barnabas sought another chance for Mark in sympathy, but Paul disagreed.

_____

_____

5. Because Paul and Barnabas could not agree, the team, over Mark, split.

_____

_____

6. Barnabas went one direction with Mark.

_____

_____

7. Paul in Silas found a new partner.

_____

_____

8. The group was able to double its efforts with two teams.

_____

_____

9. After another chance, to the church leaders Mark proved himself.

_____

_____

10. Paul requested the company of Mark as a profitable minister.

_____

_____

Appositive Phrases

An **appositive** is a noun or pronoun that follows another noun or pronoun and renames it. It can be either one word or an entire phrase.

> The entire tenth grade, *we and the other classes,* visited the museum yesterday.
> We *students* especially liked the exhibit about the space shuttle.
> Our sponsors, *the tenth grade teachers and four parents,* fixed lunch for us.
> They served us our favorite meal, *pizza and potato chips.*

As was mentioned, a pronoun may act as an appositive. (Note, however, that an appositive is more commonly a noun.) The intensive pronoun is most often used for an appositive.

> Mr. Johnson *himself* will lead the band.

A personal pronoun is also sometimes, but not often, used. (See the first example in the sentences above.)

Intensive
Pronouns
p. 6

Pronoun Case
with Appositives
p. 199

Commas to
Separate
p. 276

An appositive does not always immediately follow the noun it renames; but it could, if the sentence were restated.

Mr. Johnson will lead the band *himself*.

Miss Anderson will be discussing her favorite author next, *Charles Dickens*.

Next, Miss Anderson will be discussing her favorite author, *Charles Dickens*.

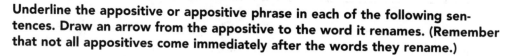

in SUMMARY

An **appositive** is a noun or pronoun that follows another noun or pronoun and renames it. It may be one word or an entire phrase.

An appositive does not always immediately follow the word it renames, but it could be moved to that position.

3.5 **PRACTICE** *the skill*

Underline the appositive or appositive phrase in each of the following sentences. Draw an arrow from the appositive to the word it renames. (Remember that not all appositives come immediately after the words they rename.)

1. Paul and Silas stopped in their travels at Philippi, a chief city of Macedonia.

2. At Philippi a young lady, a soothsayer, followed the two missionaries.

3. Paul cast out the evil spirit, the controller of the girl.

4. The girl's masters promoted hatred in the city against the "troublemakers," Paul and Silas.

5. The city leaders beat the two men and put them in a secure place, the inner prison.

6. In prison and with their feet in stocks, Paul and Silas prayed and sang praise to God, their true hope.

7. An act of God's intervention, a great earthquake, loosed all of the prisoners, but no one escaped.

8. The jail keeper wondered at the chain of events himself.

9. The jailer and his household accepted Paul and Silas's Savior, the Lord Jesus Christ, as their own.

10. The magistrates of the city personally escorted Paul and Silas, Roman citizens, out of the prison.

REVIEW *the skill*

Underline the appositive or appositive phrase in each of the following sentences. Draw an arrow from the appositive to the word it renames.

1. We Christians can expect obstacles.

2. Trials of this life, death, sorrow, crying, and pain, will not disappear until the creation of the new heaven and earth.

3. But obstacles do not have to be burdens, thieves of our joy.

4. Romans 8:28 identifies good as the outcome of all things for those who love God, those called according to His purpose.

5. According to James 1, the result of trials, patience, should cause joy.

6. I Corinthians 10:13 reminds us tempted ones of the universality of temptation.

7. It assures believers, all other Christians and us, of Christ's sufficiency for us.

8. We, the ones under temptation, will not be tempted above our capacity.

9. Philippians 4:6 advises that we avoid worry through prayer, our best defense against obstacles.

10. Peace beyond understanding, the result of reliance on prayer, is the desire of every Christian under trial.

Verbal Phrases

Verbals are special forms of verbs that function as other parts of speech in a sentence. Like true verbs, verbals show action and can have modifiers and complements. Unlike true verbs, verbals function as nouns, adjectives, or adverbs rather than as simple predicates within sentences.

Verbs
pp. 9-11

> The book still delighted young readers although its *faded* cover and *tattered* pages revealed many years of use.

Both *faded* and *tattered* are forms of verbs but function as adjectives in this sentence.

Adjectives
pp. 13-15

Participles and Participial Phrases

A **participle** is a verbal that functions as an adjective.

> The *rising* tide quickly covered the children's sand creations.

> Those *faded* curtains should be replaced.

Rising conveys the action of the verb *rise* but modifies the noun *tide*; *faded* conveys the action of the verb *fade* but modifies the noun *curtains*. Both are participles.

There are two different types of participles: present and past.

Present Participle

Principal Parts
of Verbs
pp. 151-52

The **present participle** consists of the first principal part of the verb plus *ing*. When the participle appears by itself, it generally comes right before the noun it modifies. Sometimes, though, another noun, functioning as an adjective, comes between the participle and the noun it modifies.

> A *piercing* light shone out from the lighthouse into the darkness of the night.

> The *screaming* football fans poured out of the stadium.

In the first sentence the participle *piercing* comes immediately before the noun that it modifies, *light*. In the second sentence the participle *screaming* is separated from the noun that it modifies, *fans*, by another noun, *football*.

Progressive
Tenses
p. 157

Be aware that the present participle and the progressive form of the verb look exactly alike. The two may be distinguished by their functions—the present participle is used as an adjective while the progressive verb is used as a predicate—and their forms—the participle stands alone while the progressive verb is used together with an auxiliary.

PRESENT PARTICIPLE	The *galloping* horses flew swiftly across the prairie.
PROGRESSIVE VERB	The horses *were galloping* swiftly across the prairie.

In the first example the participle *galloping* modifies the noun *horses*. In the second example the progressive verb *were galloping* conveys the action of the subject *horses*.

ESL If you have trouble distinguishing a **progressive verb** from a **participle** that follows a linking verb, try adding the qualifier **very** before the word that looks like a participle. If it is a progressive verb, the qualifier will not make sense. (If you are not sure whether it sounds right, ask a native speaker of English.)

Linking Verb Plus Participle

RIGHT	This book **is interesting.**
RIGHT	This book **is very interesting.**

Progressive Verb

RIGHT	This book **is interesting me** with its stories and pictures of mountain climbing.
WRONG	This book is very interesting me with its stories and pictures of mountain climbing.

Past Participle

The **past participle** is the same as the third principal part of the verb. (This is the form that uses *have* with the perfect tenses.) The past participle is similar to the present participle in that it expresses the action of a verb and functions as an adjective, but it is unique in that it usually has a passive meaning.

Principal Parts
of Verbs
pp. 151-52

> Pieces of the *shattered* glass flew as far as the opposite side of the room.

> Stray dogs pawed through the ruins of the *defeated* city.

The italicized participles in both sentences express passive meaning. The glass of the first sentence was shattered by someone or something. The city in the second sentence was defeated by someone.

Passive Voice
p. 160

As with the present participle, the past participle can be confused with a true verb. Remember that the past participle always functions as an adjective. Also, when the third principal part of the verb is used as part of a simple predicate, it appears together with an auxiliary.

PAST PARTICIPLE	The *opened* window allowed a breeze to enter the stuffy room.
PASSIVE VERB	The window *was opened* to allow a breeze into the stuffy room.

In the first example the participle *opened* modifies the noun *window.* In the second example the passive verb *was opened* conveys the action that happened to the subject *window.*

Participial Phrases

A participle acts as a modifier. Yet because it is made from a verb, it can itself have modifiers as well as complements. A participle and all of its modifiers and complements make up a **participial phrase.** The participial phrase may come either before or after the noun that it modifies. Depending on its position, the participial phrase is set off by one or two commas.

Sentence
Complements
pp. 40-44

PARTICIPLE WITH MODIFIER	The diver, *motivated by her coach's encouragement,* completed a flawless dive.
PARTICIPLE WITH COMPLEMENTS	*Practicing her dives repeatedly,* she had trained for the competition.
	Giving her their unanimous approval, the judges awarded the diver a perfect score.

Commas to
Separate
p. 276

In the first example, *by her coach's encouragement* modifies *motivated,* and the entire participial phrase modifies *diver.* In the next two examples, the participles have complements in addition to modifiers. *Dives* is the direct object of the participle *practicing.* *Approval* is the direct object of the participle *giving,* and *her* is the indirect object. The entire participial phrase modifies *she* in the second sentence and *judges* in the third.

tip

Starting your sentence with a participial phrase can add variety to your writing.

in SUMMARY

Verbals are special forms of verbs that function as other parts of speech in sentences.

A **participle** is a verbal that functions as an adjective. There are **present participles** (first principal part of the verb plus *ing*) and **past participles** (third principal part of the verb, usually having a passive meaning).

A **participial phrase** consists of a participle and all of its modifiers and complements.

3.7

PRACTICE *the skill*

Underline each participle or participial phrase. Then identify the word or phrase as *present participle* or *past participle*.

———————————— 1. Wanting freedom of worship, a group of English separatists sailed to the New World.

———————————— 2. Now we call these daring people Pilgrims.

———————————— 3. The Pilgrims landed at their newly discovered home of Plymouth in December of 1620.

———————————— 4. The first winter was difficult for the struggling settlers.

———————————— 5. Many Pilgrims, beaten down by the poor food, difficult work, and unfamiliar weather, became sick and died.

———————————— 6. Heading into its first spring, the colony possessed only around half of its original settlers.

———————————— 7. During the spring, a visitor entered the colony, an American Indian named Samoset.

———————————— 8. Samoset introduced the Pilgrims to his friend Squanto and to Massasoit, chief of the local ruling Wampanoag tribe.

The Landing of the Pilgrims at Plymouth, Mass., Dec. 22nd, 1620 by Currier & Ives

———————————— 9. Squanto especially was a good friend to the Pilgrims, helping them with their crops.

———————————— 10. Blessed with a good harvest, the Pilgrims invited their Wampanoag neighbors to a feast of thanksgiving.

REVIEW *the skill*

Underline the participles and place parentheses around the participial phrases. Draw an arrow from each participle to the word it modifies.

1. Born a Shoshone, Sacajawea was stolen from her tribe as a child.

2. Eventually traded to French trapper Toussaint Charbonneau, Sacajawea became the man's wife.

3. Coming into contact with Charbonneau on their travels, Lewis and Clark requested the trapper's services as a guide and an interpreter.

4. Sacajawea and her new baby boy accompanied the exploring party.

5. Sacajawea proved her value in many ways, responding courageously to difficulties and dangers of all sorts.

6. Her assistance, always appreciated, was especially prized in negotiations with her native tribe over horses for the expedition.

7. Her moving reunion with her brother, a Shoshone chief, forged a bond between the two groups.

8. Sacajawea, praised by William Clark as "a token of peace," often had a diplomatic effect just by her presence.

9. She and her husband made a qualified team of assistance for the explorers.

10. Memorials honoring Sacajawea have been erected in various spots in the West.

Rewrite each sentence below, inserting a participle or a participial phrase. In the blank before each sentence, identify your participle as *present participle* or *past participle*.

_____ 1. The construction of the Panama Canal was a large task.

_____

_____

_____ 2. The operation was made even more difficult by the presence of disease in the Canal Zone.

_____

_____

_____ 3. Yellow fever, malaria, and the bubonic plague hindered construction.

_____

_____

_____ 4. Colonel William C. Gorgas led the fight against the diseases.

_____

_____

_____ 5. This physician had learned about disease prevention in Cuba after the Spanish-American War.

_____

_____

_____ 6. Mosquitoes covered the Canal Zone, and these insects carried disease.

_____

_____

_____ 7. The major method of mosquito removal was the destruction of mosquito habitations.

_____

_____

_____ 8. These areas included brush, grassy marshes, and swamps.

_____

_____ 9. Rats, carriers of the bubonic plague, were also targets for extermination.

_____

_____

_____ 10. The triumph over diseases greatly aided the completion of the Panama Canal.

_____

_____

Misplaced and Dangling Participial Phrases

Misplaced and Dangling Modifiers pp. 226-27

If a participial phrase seems to modify the wrong word in the sentence, it is **misplaced** and may cause confusion or unintended humor. The solution to this problem is to move the misplaced phrase next to the word that it should modify.

| MISPLACED | Blinking on and off, the shopkeeper adjusted the lights in his window. |
| CORRECTED | The shopkeeper adjusted the lights blinking on and off in his window. |

Coming at the beginning of the sentence, the phrase *blinking on and off* is assumed to modify the subject *shopkeeper*. However, it should modify the direct object *lights*. The problem is corrected by moving the misplaced phrase after the word it should modify.

---
tip

Verbal phrases should appear close to the words they modify.

A participial phrase may also be intended to modify a word that is not even in the sentence. Such a phrase is said to be **dangling.**

| DANGLING | Rushing to the phone, the glass fell off the table. |
| | Opening the door, the kittens escaped from the house. |

A dangling participial phrase cannot be corrected simply by movement to another place in the sentence, since the word it should modify is not in the sentence. One way of correcting the problem is to change the phrase into a complete clause that includes the missing element.

| CORRECTED | As I was rushing to the phone, the glass fell off the table. |
| | While my little brother was opening the door, the kittens escaped from the house. |

Another way to correct a dangling participial phrase is to change the rest of the sentence so that the missing element is supplied next to the phrase.

| CORRECTED | Rushing to the phone, I knocked the glass off the table. |
| | Opening the door, my little brother allowed the kittens to escape from the house. |

---
tip

Watch for misplaced and dangling modifiers when writing sentences with introductory phrases.

---

in SUMMARY

A **misplaced participial phrase** seems to modify the wrong word in the sentence. Correct it by moving it next to the word it should modify.

A **dangling participial phrase** is intended to modify a word not in the sentence. Correct it either by changing the phrase to a clause that contains the missing element or by supplying the missing element next to the phrase.

3.10 PRACTICE *the skill*

Underline each misplaced participial phrase and insert a caret (^) at its correct location(s). If a sentence is already correct, write C in the blank.

————— 1. Rejected by other classes of society, rescue missions attempt to reach the "down-and-outs."

————— 2. Usually considered the first rescue mission in the United States, Jerry McAuley started the Water Street Mission in New York City.

————— 3. Saved in prison, McAuley had a burden for those under sin's control.

————— 4. Billy Sunday was saved at Chicago's Pacific Garden Mission, known for his great evangelistic work.

————— 5. Mel Trotter began a rescue mission in Grand Rapids, Michigan, also saved at the Pacific Garden Mission .

————— 6. Kept open day and night, the needy can find help at rescue missions.

————— 7. Rescue missions hold services consisting of music, testimonies, and simple sermons.

————— 8. Converted from the slums, testimonies of former "down-and-outs" are effective.

————— 9. Providing food and beds, rescue missions also meet physical needs.

—————10. Working for their living, some rescue missions keep their visitors busy.

3.11 REVIEW *the skill*

Underline any dangling participial phrases in the following sentences. Rewrite the incorrect sentences to supply the missing elements. If a sentence is already correct, write C in the blank.

1. Facing the Nazis alone, the Battle of Britain was important.

   _____

   _____

2. Deciding against a direct invasion of the island, air attacks were chosen.

   _____

   _____

3. Greatly outnumbered, the Nazis knew that their air force had the advantage.

_____

_____

4. Demoralized by the constant bombing, surrender would presumably come quickly.

_____

_____

5. Forgetting the character of the British people, the outcome was surprising.

_____

_____

6. Britain's pilots, making as many as five flights a day, courageously defended their homeland.

_____

_____

7. Britain's civilians remained firm, showing their unwavering determination.

_____

_____

8. Convinced of the failure of the plan, victory was sought in other directions.

_____

_____

9. Turning against the Soviet Union, a costly mistake was made.

_____

_____

10. Entering the war on the Allied side, America provided Britain with a partner across the ocean.

_____

_____

Nouns
pp. 2-3

Principal Parts
of Verbs
pp. 151-52

Gerunds and Gerund Phrases

A **gerund** is a verbal that functions as a noun.

Exercising offers many benefits.

Doctors recommend *exercising*.

Gerunds use the same form of the verb as the present participle: the first principal part plus *ing*. The two may be distinguished by their functions. Participles are adjectives, while gerunds are nouns. As nouns, gerunds can function as subjects, direct objects, predicate nouns, objects of the preposition, appositives, and occasionally indirect objects.

SUBJECT	*Stretching* builds flexibility.
DIRECT OBJECT	Endurance exercises include *bicycling* and *running*.
INDIRECT OBJECT	Some people give *walking* their attention because it is less rigorous.
PREDICATE NOUN	Another endurance exercise is *swimming*.
OBJECT OF THE PREPOSITION	Exercise should be accompanied by proper *eating*.
APPOSITIVE	Even a regular routine, *sleeping*, can make the difference between a healthy and an unhealthy body.

ESL
A gerund is the only verb form that can serve as an object of a preposition.

Tammy is afraid **of** *falling.*

Jaclyn seems interested **in** *going* along.

Do not confuse the *to* of the infinitive with the preposition *to.*

RIGHT	Paul compares the Christian life **to** *running* a race.
WRONG	Paul compares the Christian life to *run* a race.

Sentence
Complements
pp. 40-44

Gerund Phrases

Like a participle, a gerund can appear in a phrase. Because it retains some of its verb qualities, a gerund can be followed by complements and modified by adverbs. Because it functions as a noun, it can be modified by adjectives. A **gerund phrase** consists of the gerund and all of its modifiers and complements. The entire gerund phrase functions as a noun.

GERUND WITH COMPLEMENT	*Chasing a ball* is one of my dog's favorite activities.
GERUND WITH ADVERBIAL PHRASE	He can sometimes catch the ball by *jumping into the air.*
GERUND WITH ADJECTIVE	*His catching the ball* is rewarded with a biscuit.

In the first example *ball* is the direct object of the gerund *chasing,* and the entire gerund phrase is the subject of the sentence. In the second example the gerund *jumping* is modified by the adverbial prepositional phrase *into the air,* and the entire gerund phrase is the object of the preposition *by.* In the third example the gerund *catching* is modified by the adjective *his;* the entire phrase is the subject of the sentence.

Perfect Gerund

Having can be used with the third principal part of the verb to make the **perfect gerund.**

> *Having practiced parallel parking* should help her with the driving test.

The perfect gerund is used to express action that occurred before the action of the main verb, whereas the present gerund expresses action that occurs at the same time as the main verb. Notice the difference in the following sentences.

PERFECT GERUND	She is sorry for *having told the secret.*
PRESENT GERUND	*Telling the secret* ruins the fun of the surprise.

Principal Parts of Verbs
pp. 151–52

Perfect Tenses
pp. 154–55

in SUMMARY

A **gerund** is a verbal that functions as a noun. It is made up of the first principal part of the verb plus *ing.*

A **gerund phrase** consists of the gerund and all of its modifiers and complements.

The **perfect gerund** (*having* plus the third principal part of the verb) expresses action that occurred before the action of the main verb.

3.12 ## PRACTICE *the skill*

Identify each italicized gerund phrase as *present* or *perfect.*

_____ 1. *Transporting objects by elevators* is nothing new.

_____ 2. Both the ancient Greeks and Romans used elevatorlike contraptions for *heavy lifting.*

_____ 3. Until the twentieth century no one claimed *having successfully transported people.*

_____ 4. People were generally deterred from elevators by *having seen broken elevator ropes.*

_____ 5. No one wanted *a quick ending to his elevator trip.*

_____ 6. *Pondering this problem* had provided Elisha G. Otis with an idea.

_____ 7. His plan was *framing the elevator car with guide rails.*

_____ 8. *After having sensed the loss of tension,* clamps from the rails would snap around a falling car.

_____ 9. *Demonstrating his invention* required taking a potentially dangerous ride in a falling elevator.

_____ 10. *Stopping the falling car* was a triumph for Otis's invention.

Underline the gerund or gerund phrase in each of the following sentences. Then identify its function as subject (*S*), direct object (*DO*), predicate noun (*PN*), indirect object (*IO*), or object of the preposition (*OP*).

———— 1. Living to 107 is an accomplishment in itself.

———— 2. Rose Freedman could also claim the distinction of being the last survivor of the Triangle Shirtwaist Factory fire of 1911.

———— 3. The result of the fire was the killing of 146 workers at the Triangle Shirtwaist Factory in New York City.

———— 4. These deaths caused protesting from the public.

———— 5. The practice of locking the doors to stop unauthorized breaks resulted in death for many of the workers.

———— 6. Freedman escaped by following company executives to the roof.

———— 7. There firefighters pulled the surviving to a nearby roof.

———— 8. Forgetting the fire was impossible for Freedman.

———— 9. Throughout her life she gave her time and attention to campaigning for worker safety.

———— 10. Reactions to the fire included the favoring of new labor laws and stronger labor unions.

Nouns
pp. 2-3
Adjectives
pp. 13-15
Adverbs
pp. 15-17

Principal Parts
of Verbs
pp. 151-52

Prepositional
Phrases
pp. 57-59

Infinitives and Infinitive Phrases

An **infinitive** is a verbal that functions as a noun, an adjective, or an adverb.

NOUN	His primary goal in entering the competition is not *to win*.
ADJECTIVE	He wants a chance *to participate*.
ADVERB	*To improve*, he is competing against more advanced musicians.

An infinitive consists of the word *to* followed by the first principal part of the verb. Since *to* often functions as a preposition, an infinitive may look like a prepositional phrase. But *to* as part of an infinitive is followed by a verb, while *to* as a preposition is followed by a noun or pronoun.

INFINITIVE	My dog likes *to run*.
PREPOSITIONAL PHRASE	She runs *to the gate* when we come home.

ESL It is important to remember the difference between the preposition *to* and the infinitive *to*—see why on page 72.

Infinitive Phrase

Like participles and gerunds, infinitives may have modifiers and complements. An infinitive and all of its modifiers and complements make up an **infinitive phrase.** The entire phrase can function like a noun, an adjective, or an adverb.

Sentence
Complements
pp. 40-44

| INFINITIVE WITH MODIFIERS | Mrs. Chin said *to walk carefully over the rutted ice.* |
| INFINITIVE WITH COMPLEMENTS | Antonio went to the store *to buy his mother a birthday present.* |

In the first example the infinitive *to walk* is modified by the adverb *carefully* and the adverbial prepositional phrase *over the rutted ice.* The entire infinitive phrase is the direct object of the verb *said.* In the second example *present* is the direct object and *mother* the indirect object of the infinitive *to buy.* The entire infinitive phrase is adverbial, telling why Antonio went to the store.

When you can, avoid placing a modifier between the word *to* and the verb of an infinitive. This type of construction is called a **split infinitive.**

Modifiers That
Split Infinitives
p. 227

| SPLIT INFINITIVE | Kristy hopes *to better learn* Spanish this semester. |
| BETTER | Kristy hopes *to learn* Spanish *better* this semester. |

tip

In most cases, good writers avoid splitting infinitives. However, it is better to split an infinitive with a one-word modifier than to create an awkward sentence by placing the adverb too far from the infinitive.

You will sometimes see an infinitive without a *to.* If the infinitive sounds natural either way, more formal English will include the *to.* If, however, the *to* would sound odd, it can be omitted at any level of English.

CORRECT	All she did was *raise* a question.
MORE FORMAL	All she did was *to raise* a question.
CORRECT AT ANY LEVEL	With the very little that he studied, he will likely do nothing except *fail.*

ESL

Some verbs are more likely to be followed by a gerund (*enjoy, avoid, admit, finish, risk, consider, appreciate, understand,* and so forth). These verbs often refer to something that has already happened.

I enjoy **going** to camp each summer.

Some verbs are more likely to be followed by an infinitive (*want, wish, offer, hope, decide, ask, plan, wait,* and so forth). These verbs often refer to something only wished for or planned, but not yet fulfilled.

I want **to go** to camp next summer.

Some verbs can be used with either meaning.

I like **going** to that restaurant; it has good food.
I would like **to go** there tomorrow.
I tried **opening** the window (but it's still hot in here).
I tried **to open** the window (but it was painted shut).

in SUMMARY

An **infinitive** is a verbal that functions as a noun, an adjective, or an adverb. It is made up of *to* followed by the first principal part of the verb.

An **infinitive phrase** consists of the infinitive and all of its modifiers and complements.

An infinitive that has a modifier between the *to* and the verb is referred to as a **split infinitive**. Avoid this type of construction when you can do so without awkwardness.

3.14 **PRACTICE** *the skill*

Identify the function of each italicized infinitive or infinitive phrase as noun (*Noun*), adjective (*Adj*), or adverb (*Adv*).

———— 1. Automobile accidents are the source *to blame for many fatalities in the United States annually.*

———— 2. *To discover the cause of an accident* requires an examination of the driver, the vehicle, and the road.

———— 3. The driver is often the one *to cause the accident.*

———— 4. He may not take precautions *to drive safely.*

———— 5. Alcohol consumed stays in his system *to impair his driving.*

———— 6. Voluntary changes in driver behavior are the way *to prevent many accidents.*

———— 7. Automobile manufacturers have made adjustments in vehicles *to improve their safety.*

———— 8. *To protect the people inside the car,* carmakers add safety features.

———— 9. Roadmakers attempt *to insure quality road construction.*

———— 10. *To consider the flow of traffic* is also part of their attention to safety.

3.15 **REVIEW** *the skill*

Underline each infinitive and place parentheses around each infinitive phrase. Then identify its function as noun (*Noun*), adjective (*Adj*), or adverb (*Adv*).

———— 1. Signaling is a good way to communicate over a distance.

———— 2. Different signal methods are used around the world to transmit critical information.

———— 3. To send a signal may require the use of an electrical impulse or a visual or sound indicator.

———— 4. One purpose of electrical signals is to communicate, as through the telephone.

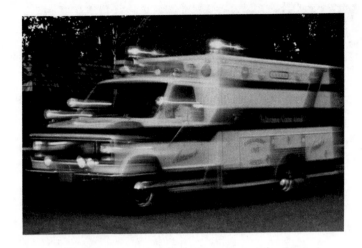

_____ 5. Electrical signals are used to send messages all over the world through communications satellites.

_____ 6. A traffic light is a visual signal to direct people on the roads.

_____ 7. A sound signal is often installed on an emergency vehicle to warn people of the vehicle's approach.

_____ 8. To navigate safely through the air, airplanes use certain kinds of signals.

_____ 9. For ships, signals are warnings to steer clear of danger.

_____ 10. One of the greatest uses for signals may be to call for help.

Passive Infinitive

The simple infinitive (_to_ + verb) has an active meaning. But an infinitive can be made passive if it is taken from a transitive verb.

Passive Voice
p. 160

| ACTIVE | I want _to wash_ the windows Saturday. |
| PASSIVE | The car needs _to be washed_. |

In the first example the subject of the sentence, _I,_ will be washing. In the second example the subject of the sentence, _car,_ will be washed; someone or something will wash it.

The **passive infinitive** consists of the word _to,_ the passive auxiliary _be,_ and the third principal part of the verb. It, like the simple infinitive, can be used as a noun, an adjective, or an adverb.

NOUN	My laptop needs _to be fixed_.
ADJECTIVE	Some enthusiasts view blogs as the least biased news sources _to be found_ currently.
ADVERB	Many new computer products are designed _to be accessible_ to all kinds of users.

_in_ SUMMARY

A **passive infinitive** combines _to_ with _be_ and the third principal part of the verb. It expresses action that occurs _to_ something.

Underline the infinitive or infinitive phrase in each of the following sentences. In the blank, identify it as *active* or *passive*.

_____ 1. Special education was created to help students with distinct learning needs.

_____ 2. Many of these needs present challenges to be overcome by the students.

_____ 3. The challenge may be to work with either a physical or a mental disability.

_____ 4. In either case, the goal is to be taught as much as possible in a regular classroom.

_____ 5. This mainstreaming, as it is called, often requires certain equipment to be purchased for the student's classroom.

_____ 6. For example, a child with limited mobility may need a desk to accommodate his wheelchair.

_____ 7. Resource rooms provide additional help to supplement the student's learning in the regular classroom.

_____ 8. Teachers often take classes to be trained specifically for work with disabled children.

_____ 9. Teaching in a resource room focuses on the skills to be mastered by each student.

_____ 10. With the help of special education, disabled students can learn to overcome their particular challenges.

Underline the infinitive or infinitive phrase in each of the following sentences. Then identify its function as noun *(Noun)*, adjective *(Adj)*, or adverb *(Adv)*.

_____ 1. Special Olympics was created in 1968 to be used for the physical development of mentally disabled individuals.

_____ 2. It gives participants opportunities to be trained in various sports.

_____ 3. Its competitions help to challenge participants in their training.

_____ 4. Special Olympics events are designed to be held annually on a regional basis in the United States.

_____ 5. Other countries choose to be organized on a national level for their annual or biannual competitions.

_____ 6. All athletes want to be prepared for the International Special Olympics Games.

_____ 7. Like the Olympics, the International Special Olympics Games are arranged to be rotated between summer and winter every two years.

_____ 8. There is a wide variety of sports to be mastered, ranging from gymnastics to powerlifting.

_____ 9. Besides improvement in physical fitness, Special Olympics helps to encourage athletes in their self-confidence.

_____ 10. Another benefit of Special Olympics is the relationships to be built among the athletes.

Label the sentence patterns in each of the following sentences. Identify the italicized word or phrase as a prepositional phrase (Prep), an appositive phrase (App), a participial phrase (Part), a gerund phrase (Ger), or an infinitive phrase (Inf). Then identify the function of the word or phrase as noun (Noun), adjective (Adj), or adverb (Adv).

_____ _____ 1. Hudson Taylor was a missionary pioneer to the almost *closed* land of China.

_____ _____ 2. From his early experiences in the country, Taylor decided *to start his own mission board* and to adopt Chinese dress.

_____ _____ 3. Together with twenty-four other missionaries, Taylor, *the founder of the China Inland Mission,* and his wife, Maria, left for China in 1866.

_____ _____ 4. *Starting a new work* was not easy.

_____ _____ 5. Four years after *arriving in China,* Taylor endured the death of his wife.

_____ _____ 6. Opposition came *from other missionaries, Chinese officials, and even members of the China Inland Mission.*

_____ _____ 7. *Rioting* Chinese citizens were a concern to the missionaries.

_____ _____ 8. Yet God made the ministry *of Taylor* successful.

_____ _____ 9. The China Inland Mission permeated China and laid the groundwork for *the founding of other missions.*

_____ _____ 10. Taylor died in 1905 in the capital of the last province *to be opened to the gospel.*

WRITING

God is my strength and power: and he maketh my way perfect.
II Samuel 22:33

Think of your favorite book, short story, or piece of writing. Why is it your favorite? Does it address some issue that is important to you? Does it have characters you like? Does it comfort you, make you laugh, make you think?

When people read literature, they have many kinds of responses. Sometimes people look at how the piece is written. They enjoy the sounds of the words and the rhythm of the sentences. They think about the figures of speech and the images.

tip

To record your responses to reading, keep a journal with you while you read, or if you own the book, take notes directly in the margins of the book.

For example, Stephen Crane's short story "The Open Boat" begins this way:

None of them knew the color of the sky. Their eyes glanced level, and were fastened upon the waves that swept toward them. These waves were of the hue of slate, save for the tops, which were of foaming white, and all of the men knew the colors of the sea. The horizon narrowed and widened, and dipped and rose, and at all times its edge was jagged with waves that seemed thrust up in points like rocks.

Someone reading this might respond to the rhythm of the sentences, especially the third and fourth sentences. Because they are somewhat long and contain phrases set off with commas, they seem to mimic the rise and fall of waves.

Another person may focus mainly on the meaning. He sees how the piece agrees or disagrees with how he sees the world. He silently makes applications to his own life from lessons the characters learn. How would someone reading for meaning respond to the passage from "The Open Boat"? Perhaps he would watch to see how the men in the open boat would deal with a rough sea and their own apprehension and take from that a lesson about being "seaworthy" in life.

At other times, a reader has a much more personal response to a piece of literature. He may think of times he has been in a boat or ship; he may identify with a character for some reason; he may be drawn by the drama of the situation, whether or not he has experienced any such event. Your response to Becky Vaughn's writing will probably be highly personal.

And in some cases, a reader responds to a piece in all these ways at once. Someone reading the beginning of Crane's short story might be drawn by the sailors' precarious position, be reminded of some experience of his own, and be aware of how the writing is supporting these effects on him. In such a moment, he might well begin to feel a bit seasick.

We respond to literature because literature is based on life experiences. A good writer can take a special event or even a very ordinary one and describe it in a way that attaches significant meaning to it. A good writer uses the setting, the language, the characters, and other elements of the work to create a certain impression on the reader and to reinforce the theme of the work. Reading a broad selection of literature will increase your understanding of people and enable you to view situations from someone else's point of view.

How did you respond to the piece by Becky? Could you identify with her in any way? Did you think of a trauma your family has faced? Did you think the writer seemed courageous? Does she speak like other seventeen-year-olds you know?

How you respond to something you read says as much about you as it does about the piece. And for this writing assignment, there is no one correct approach. You should simply write in a clear and direct way about how "A Word from Becky" struck you as you read it.

Perhaps you can write about something in your own experience, or perhaps you can say how Becky's style shaped your impression of her. Just remember—this is *your* response.

Planning

Thinking Biblically

The Christian should know how to recognize and respond to good literature: he should be able to say why a book is worthwhile and enjoyable. But he should also know how to recognize and respond to literature that violates biblical principles and the Christian worldview. He should know how to identify problems in what he sees or hears and further be able to suggest how those problems could be corrected. Job listened to the speeches of his three friends, and he was able to evaluate them. Paul knew what false teachers were saying, and he knew how to respond (1 Tim. 1:2-11; 2 Tim. 2:16-19). And Peter states that Christians should be able to defend their beliefs to unbelievers (1 Pet. 3:15-16).

✔ **Begin by reading through the piece two or three times.** Jot down your initial reactions to the story. How do you feel about Becky's attitude toward her circumstances? What do you think other people's responses to Becky might be? Why? Were you surprised, encouraged, saddened? What is your response to the last line, "I'm glad I'm alive"?

A short final sentence can make an effective ending. **tip**

✔ **Consider Scriptures that might influence your response.** What verses have comforted you in times of trouble? What verses might you give to someone like Becky?

✔ **Decide which response you would like to describe.** You may want to focus on one particular response, or you may want to explore two or three different responses.

✔ **Select a form for your response.** You may want to write an essay describing your response to "A Word from Becky"; however, you may want to draft a letter to her or to her parents. Another possibility might be a letter describing Becky's piece to someone who is experiencing difficulty. Your teacher will help you decide on an appropriate form for your response.

Drafting

✔ **Begin with a brief synopsis.** You do not need a detailed summary of the work, but you do need one or two sentences so that the reader will be able to understand your response.

✔ **Write your response, giving concrete details.** As you describe your response, you need to give specific details. Tell exactly what event, setting, dialogue, or description evoked the response. A reader's response to the story "The Open Boat," which ends with all aboard getting ashore except the character who is the strongest swimmer and the most likely to survive, might begin like this:

> When I read this short story, I kept thinking of the time my father and I were camping in Wyoming. I think I made that connection because my father broke his arm, just as the captain in the open boat did, and like the captain, my father was still in charge and capable even though he was injured. We had to walk a long way, just as the people in the boat had to row a long way. And when we got to the road and someone stopped to help us, I felt how the one sailor felt when he finally made the shore—"grateful."

Your response to Becky's story may include details about Becky's attitude, her injuries, her feelings, or her goals—whatever made you respond in some way to her story.

✔ **If appropriate, end your essay by summarizing your response.** Becky's summary statement was "I'm glad I'm alive." You may choose to write something brief and to the point, or you may decide to elaborate on your theme. Whatever the case, leave your reader knowing the emphasis of your piece.

Student Model

In Stephen Crane's short story "The Open Boat," a group of men are stranded on the ocean and face a hostile environment in their quest to get to shore safely. While reading this story, I felt saddened, but I could not relate to these men. I think Stephen Crane accurately portrayed the harshness of the sea, but he did not factor in the presence of a loving God. I could not help thinking of the story of Jesus and the disciples in the storm on the sea. The disciples were scared, like the men in the story, but Jesus calmed the seas. Overall, I felt sadness for those who do not know and trust in God.

Revising

✔ **Review your initial responses to the piece.** Have you included the most important ones in your response? Did you tie your response to what other people might think?

✔ **Make sure that you have summarized enough about the story to be clear.** Saying that Becky "responded well to what happened to her" and that she "handled the consequences better than most people" does not communicate the tragic nature of her circumstances or the horrific difficulties she faced following the fire. This step includes checking to be sure that your writing is detailed and specific.

✔ **Revise for spelling, grammar, and punctuation.** The personal nature of this response will probably lend itself to a less formal style of writing. The use of contractions and the first person is expected for this assignment.

✔ **Invite a peer to edit your response.** You will benefit from hearing how your classmates responded to Becky's piece and from analyzing how their responses differ from yours. Read as many other responses as you can to consider as many viewpoints as possible.

Publishing

✔ **Share your response with your classmates, your teacher, and/or your family.** Listen closely for attitudes and insights that you had not considered before.

✔ **Put this essay into your writing portfolio or enter it in a devotional journal.** This piece of writing could be one that you return to often for encouragement.

✔ **Consider reworking your response.** Perhaps your essay could be revised for submission to a Christian publication or for recording as a radio spot on a local Christian radio station.

Some Ideas to Consider

• Read Psalm 139 and write a personal response to the psalm. How would you compare this poem to Becky's testimony?

• Write about something you have read recently that you think relates to Becky's story.

LETTER FOR LETTER

Tall Order

The letter being discussed was written by someone who believed what a servant girl had said. Was the writer of this letter acting according to truth? This letter was at first misunderstood by its readers. What were some of the presuppositions that the readers had that caused them to "read between the lines" and thus misinterpret the letter?

In the courtyard of the palace, two of the king's closest advisors whisper together under the shadows of a large date palm.

"Have you seen the king?"

"Yes, I saw him. What do you think of all this?"

"I'm afraid I don't know. Twice already the king has called me into his presence and asked for my advice. I'm afraid I didn't have much hope to give him."

"I was there when he first received the letter from Aram. You should have seen his reaction. He must have torn his robe from the neck to the waist."

"That bad. Just what exactly did the letter say?"

"It's precisely as you have heard, I'm sure. I read it myself. It said that the cursed King Aram had sent his chief commander, Naaman, the one who has led so many victories against us, to King Joram to be healed of his leprosy—"

"Yes, well, I wonder what Aram would say if we sent all our lepers to them—"

"Obviously it's just a poor attempt at an excuse to start a war. This time they want to take Samaria itself, no doubt. I wouldn't be surprised if Naaman's army is just beyond Mount Ebal, waiting for the order to sack Samaria because we couldn't heal him of his wretched leprosy."

"Quietly, my friend. We should be careful that the king doesn't see our pessimism. He has enough on his hands. Besides, I'm not so sure we can't find some way out of this."

"Why, what do you want to do?"

Hammelech, the elder advisor, did not answer immediately. He stroked his thin beard thoughtfully.

"Come on, Hammelech," the other asked, probing him, "I know you've got an idea; now what is it?"

Hammelech looked up. "I want to talk to the prophet of Jehovah."

"Who? Elisha? What can that old sage do? You don't really believe in those miracles they say he performs!"

"What I believe about Elisha is immaterial. What I believe about Jehovah is what's important."

Hammelech turned from his colleague to his servant nearby.

"I want you to take a message to the prophet Elisha. Tell him . . ."

For the full story, read II Kings 5:1-14.

- *To whom was this letter written?*
- *How did Naaman know about Elisha?*
- *Why was the receiver of this letter afraid?*
- *What were the ultimate results of this letter?*

Personal Perspective

You have probably never received healing from leprosy, but God may have done something miraculous in your life. God is a healer of both body and soul. Write a personal response to this story or write about something significant that God has done in your life or in the life of someone you know.

Everyday occurrences often become more interesting when we go beyond the actual event and investigate its causes and effects. Examining the past or the future of a subject can help you find reasons for and consequences of a particular occurrence. Bill Rabinowitz looks at the evolution of baseball—from the addition of radio broadcasting and the All-Star game to fixing ticket prices and the first night game—and the causes and effects of the changes in America's pastime. The excerpt below, which comes in the middle of Rabinowitz's piece, examines one effect of the Great Depression on baseball. At the end of this chapter, you will learn how to write a cause-and-effect essay about something that interests you.

Baseball and the Great Depression *by Bill Rabinowitz*

Several innovations instituted during the Depression, for example, changed the sport of baseball forever. One was the advent of public address systems. Because many teams, especially those in the National League, were inexplicably reluctant to follow the Yankees' example of numbering players, and the megaphones used to relay information to fans were often not loud enough for many fans to hear, many spectators had a difficult time knowing who was playing or exactly what was going on. For example, in a late-season game in 1933 when the New York Giants, just after the Cardinals had taken a four-run lead, broke into a wild celebration, fans at Sportsman's Park in St. Louis probably thought the visiting team had gone berserk. Unbeknown to most fans, the Giants were celebrating having clinched the National League pennant after receiving word that the second-place Pittsburgh Pirates had been eliminated after a loss.

Though it is difficult, if not impossible, to determine whether the Depression's impact on attendance led to the installation of loudspeakers or whether it was simply a natural development that would have happened anyway, the fact is that by the end of the 1930s, almost every owner had installed public address systems and the change was advertised as a means of attracting fans.

Distinguishing Independent and Dependent Clauses

Subjects and Predicates
pp. 33-34

Four Types of Sentences
p. 37

Subordination
pp. 365-66

A **clause** is a group of words that contains both a subject and a predicate. There are two major categories of clauses: independent clauses (sometimes called main clauses) and dependent clauses (also called subordinate clauses).

An **independent clause** can stand alone as a sentence. The sentence may be a statement, a question, or a command.

> The earliest "books" were sets of clay tablets with carved inscriptions.
>
> Have you ever seen clay tablets in a museum?
>
> Please tell me more about the exhibits in the museum.

A **dependent clause** cannot stand alone as a sentence; it is subordinate to an independent clause. A dependent clause may be an important part of the sentence, but it contains a word that makes it incomplete. It depends on the independent clause grammatically and for its complete meaning.

> Historians have discovered sets of clay tablets that are numbered like the pages of a book.
>
> They have also found clay cylinders in a case on which the title of the "book" was written.
>
> This book says that these clay tablets exist in many shapes and sizes.

Modern plaster impression from an Akkadian Cylinder Seal,
From the Bowen Collection of Antiquities
Bob Jones University Museum & Gallery

ESL When identifying dependent clauses, look for subject and predicate pairs introduced with words such as relative pronouns (*who*, *which*, *that*) and subordinating conjunctions (*if, since, because*).

in SUMMARY

A **clause** is a group of words that contains both a subject and a predicate.

An **independent clause** can stand alone as a sentence.

A **dependent clause** cannot stand alone; it must be attached to an independent clause.

PRACTICE *the skill*

Place parentheses around each dependent clause. Some sentences may not contain a dependent clause.

1. (Although there is much speculation about the cause of the Great Depression,) most people agree (that the stock market crash of 1929 played a major role.)

2. Many people invested in the New York Stock Exchange throughout the 1920s (because the market was experiencing a period of continual growth and soaring dividends.)

3. However, large swings in the market were ignored in 1928 and 1929, and during these latter years of the '20s, many middle class investors lost their entire savings (when they purchased large amounts of stock on credit.)

4. Thus, (when stock prices dropped at the beginning of the crash,) people panicked.

5. In September of 1929, many investors believed (that the market had reached its peak) and began selling or trading their stocks; (as the number of stocks for sale went up,) their value went down.

6. The stock market crash began on October 24, (which has been nicknamed "Black Thursday.")

7. Anxious investors wanted to sell their stocks before prices could drop any lower.

8. On "Black Tuesday" (Oct. 29) alone, more than 16,000,000 shares of stock were traded.

9. (After the crash occurred,) people made "runs" on the banks and on the stock market. (When United States banks could not repay their loans,) thousands of them went out of business.

10. By 1932 stocks were worth twenty percent of their original value, and over a million people had lost their savings, jobs, and even homes.

Place parentheses around each dependent clause. Some sentences may not contain a dependent clause.

1. Because many people lost their jobs at the outset of the Depression, "hoboing" became common.

2. A hobo is typically a poor, homeless person who travels from town to town looking for work.

3. Hoboes had their own culture and even a code of honor; they did not consider themselves bums because they asked for work and not a handout.

4. Many hoboes were teenagers who left their homes in search of adventure or freedom, but many ran away or were forced out when their families could no longer support them.

5. As many as 250,000 teenagers lived as hoboes during the peak of the Great Depression.

6. Many hoboes traveled across the country by jumping freight trains. This illegal and dangerous activity was called "riding the rails."

7. Hoboes would jump on the train after it started and jump off before it stopped; there was less chance that they would be caught this way.

8. In 1933, as a deterrent to teenage freight hopping, Warner Brothers Studio made a film, *Wild Boys of the Road*, about a boy who lost his leg in a train accident.

9. Some teenagers who became hoboes said that the film did not scare them but actually made them more interested in the activity.

10. Thousands of hoboes were injured or killed while they were riding the rails.

Identifying Kinds of Dependent Clauses

A dependent clause can function like an adjective, an adverb, or a noun. Adjective clauses and adverb clauses act as modifiers in a sentence. Noun clauses perform the same functions that nouns perform; they act as subjects, objects, predicate nouns, or appositives in sentences.

Adjective Clauses

An **adjective clause** is a dependent clause that functions like an adjective in a sentence. It modifies a noun or a pronoun in another clause.

Relative Pronouns

Most adjective clauses begin with **relative pronouns.** A relative pronoun is *relative* because it relates an adjective clause to the noun or pronoun that the clause modifies. It is a *pronoun* because it appears in the dependent clause as a replacement for a noun or another pronoun in the independent clause (its antecedent). A relative pronoun also functions as a subject, an object, or an adjective within the adjective clause.

Adjectives
pp. 13-15

Commas to
Separate
pp. 276-77

| who | whom | whose | which | that |

(S) **(InV)**
The papyrus plant is a reed *that* grows in the marshes along the Nile River.

(DO) **(S)** **(TrV)**
Papyrus, *which* Egyptian scribes used for historical and legal records,

was a significant improvement over clay tablets.

Papyrus documents include the works of the Greek poet Homer, *whose*
(S) **(TrV)** **(DO)**
famous epics each filled at least twenty-four rolls of papyrus.

Although relative pronouns look like interrogative pronouns, there is no subject and verb inversion in clauses introduced by relative pronouns. The relative pronoun comes at the beginning of the clause and functions as the subject or is followed by the subject and verb in normal order. **ESL**

Sometimes the relative pronoun *that* is omitted (simply "understood") when it is the direct object or the object of a preposition in the adjective clause.

(DO) (S)
During the fourth century, flat-folded sheets replaced the scrolls *[that]* we
(TrV)
associate with papyrus documents.

Relative
Pronouns
p. 6

Just as an adjectival prepositional phrase can modify the object of another prepositional phrase, an adjective clause may modify a noun or pronoun in another dependent clause.

                         (S)   (TrV)   (DO) [DO] [S] [TrV]
The sheets [that replaced the scrolls [that we associate with papyrus]] were

much easier to store.

Relative Adverbs

Adverbs
pp. 15-16

Some adjective clauses begin with **relative adverbs.** Like a relative pronoun, a relative adverb relates the adjective clause to a word in the independent clause. Unlike a relative pronoun, which has a noun or adjective function in the adjective clause, a relative adverb modifies the verb in the adjective clause.

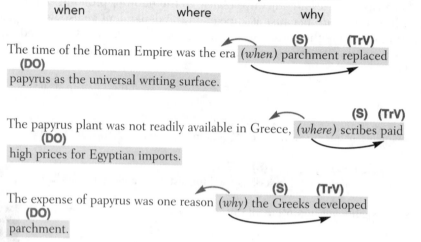

when   where   why

                                           (S)   (TrV)
The time of the Roman Empire was the era *(when)* parchment replaced
        (DO)
papyrus as the universal writing surface.

                                                   (S)   (TrV)
The papyrus plant was not readily available in Greece, *(where)* scribes paid
        (DO)
high prices for Egyptian imports.

                                        (S)   (TrV)
The expense of papyrus was one reason *(why)* the Greeks developed
        (DO)
parchment.

ESL An adjective clause beginning with **when** modifies a "time" noun, such as *year* or *era*. An adjective clause beginning with **where** modifies a "place" noun, such as *Greece* or *city*. An adjective clause beginning with **why** modifies a "cause" noun, usually *reason* or *cause*.

Remember that an adjective clause may consist of several elements: it always has a subject and a predicate, and it may include modifiers and complements. Although an adjective clause (also called a "relative clause") may begin with either a relative pronoun or a relative adverb, the adjective clause always functions like an adjective. The clause modifies the word that the relative pronoun or relative adverb relates to.

in SUMMARY

An **adjective clause** is a dependent clause that functions like an adjective in a sentence. It modifies a noun or a pronoun in another clause.

A **relative pronoun** relates an adjective clause to the noun or pronoun that the clause modifies. It functions as a subject, an object, or an adjective within the adjective clause.

A **relative adverb** relates an adjective clause to the noun or pronoun that the clause modifies. It modifies the verb in the adjective clause.

PRACTICE *the skill*

Place parentheses around each adjective clause. Draw an arrow from each adjective clause to the word it modifies.

1. In the 1930s, a time when most people had few possessions, people treasured their radios.

2. Families sometimes sold things that they considered less important, such as their beds. Many simply refused to sell their radio.

3. In the 1920s and early '30s, the radio had served primarily as a tool, but during the Depression it turned into a medium that focused more on entertainment.

4. Radio programs, which were broadcast during each day and in the evening, helped pass the time for people who could not find work.

5. They could listen to the exploits of Dick Tracy, Amos and Andy, the Lone Ranger, Fibber McGee and Molly, or even Superman, whose first appearance came in 1938.

6. Radio shows like *Little Orphan Annie* addressed issues that were prevalent in the '30s, such as economic policy, labor problems, and unemployment.

7. There were also regional variety shows that featured singers and comedians. These performers, who were hired and promoted by individual studios, became local celebrities.

8. President Franklin D. Roosevelt spoke to the American people through the radio in broadcasts that became nicknamed "fireside chats."

9. The 1930s was also the time when national broadcasting networks, like NBC and CBS, began to appear.

10. In 1938, a broadcast that dramatized H. G. Wells's novel *The War of the Worlds,* frightened many people who believed the report of Martian invasion.

Place parentheses around each adjective clause. Draw an arrow from each adjective clause to the word it modifies. Underline each relative pronoun once; underline each relative adverb twice.

1. Charles Lindbergh, whom many considered the most famous man in the world after his flight across the Atlantic, became the recipient of some unwanted attention because of his celebrity status.

2. On March 1, 1932, between 8:00 and 10:00 P.M., Charles and Anne Lindbergh's twenty-month-old boy, Charles Jr., was kidnapped from a newly built house, which they had located in a secluded area.

3. The kidnapper used a homemade ladder to reach the second-story nursery, where the child was at the time of his abduction.

4. A ransom note, which demanded $50,000, was found on the nursery windowsill.

5. Negotiations lasted until April 2, the day when Dr. John Condon, a go-between, delivered the ransom to a German man in a cemetery.

6. The Lindberghs, who had been given false information by the man from the cemetery, searched for their son until May 12. On that day, a truck driver found a child's corpse, which the baby's nurse and father identified as Charles Jr., a few miles from the Lindbergh home.

7. Bruno Hauptmann, an illegal German immigrant with a criminal record, was arrested, convicted, and executed after his trial, which took place three years after the kidnapping.

WANTED

INFORMATION AS TO THE WHEREABOUTS OF

CHAS. A. LINDBERGH, Jr.
OF HOPEWELL, N. J.
SON OF COL. CHAS. A. LINDBERGH
World-Famous Aviator
This child was kidnaped from his home in Hopewell, N. J., between 8 and 10 p. m. on Tuesday, March 1, 1932.

DESCRIPTION:
Age, 20 months	Hair, blond, curly
Weight, 27 to 30 lbs.	Eyes, dark blue
Height, 29 inches	Complexion, light

Deep dimple in center of chin
Dressed in one-piece coverall night suit

ADDRESS ALL COMMUNICATIONS TO
COL. H. N. SCHWARZKOPF, TRENTON, N. J., or
COL. CHAS. A. LINDBERGH, HOPEWELL, N. J.

ALL COMMUNICATIONS WILL BE TREATED IN CONFIDENCE

March 11, 1932   COL. H. NORMAN SCHWARZKOPF
Supt. New Jersey State Police, Trenton, N. J.

8. Because of Lindbergh's fame, the trial drew international media attention, and nearly seven hundred journalists flocked to Flemington, New Jersey, where the trial was held.

9. Hauptmann never confessed, and people who believe in his innocence have offered several other theories on the events surrounding the baby's disappearance.

10. According to some people, the body that the truck driver found was not really the Lindbergh baby, and several individuals have publicly claimed to be "the missing baby."

Adverb Clauses

An **adverb clause** is a dependent clause that functions like an adverb in a sentence. Usually, an adverb clause modifies the simple predicate in the independent clause. Occasionally, an adverb clause modifies the entire independent clause. Most adverb clauses appear before or after the independent clause.

Adverbs
pp. 15-16

Subordinating Conjunctions

Adverb clauses begin with subordinating conjunctions. A **subordinating conjunction** is a conjunction that joins a dependent clause to an independent clause; in other words, it joins unequal elements, subordinating one statement to another. Subordinating conjunctions show the logical relationship of an adverb clause to an independent clause.

Conjunctions
p. 21

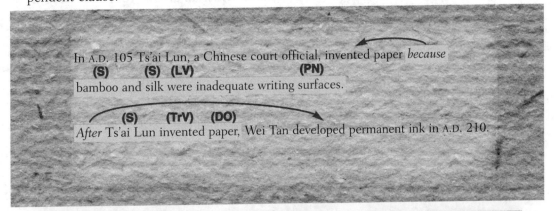

In A.D. 105 Ts'ai Lun, a Chinese court official, invented paper *because*
(S)   (S) (LV)   (PN)
bamboo and silk were inadequate writing surfaces.

After Ts'ai Lun invented paper, Wei Tan developed permanent ink in A.D. 210.
(S)   (TrV)   (DO)

Some Common Subordinating Conjunctions

after	because	now that	so	when
although	before	once	so that	whenever
as	if	on condition that	till	whereas
as if	inasmuch as	provided that	unless	wherever
as though	in order that	since	until	while

Commas to
Separate
p. 277

Some adverb clauses are elliptical. An **elliptical adverb clause** is a clause that keeps the subordinating conjunction but drops one or more other words—words that will be clearly understood from the context.

While living in Spain, Arabs introduced the Chinese inventions to Europe.

The subordinating conjunction identifies the group of words as an elliptical adverb clause. The reader can supply the missing words from the context. The rest of the sentence makes it clear that *While living in Spain* is short for *While they were living in Spain.*

in SUMMARY

Dangling
Modifiers
p. 227

An **adverb clause** is a dependent clause that functions like an adverb in a sentence.

A **subordinating conjunction** joins a dependent clause to an independent clause. It can show the relationship of an adverb clause to an independent clause.

An **elliptical adverb clause** is a clause that keeps the subordinating conjunction but drops one or more other words that will be clearly understood from the context.

4.5 PRACTICE *the skill*

Place parentheses around each adverb clause. Draw an arrow from each adverb clause to the word or words it modifies.

1. Until it exploded on May 6, 1937, the *Hindenburg* was the largest airship in existence.

2. Once completed, the massive flight machine measured 804 feet long and just over 135 feet in diameter.

3. The Zeppelin Company designed the ship so that it was capable of carrying 112.1 tons in addition to its own weight.

4. Although helium had been Zeppelin's first choice, hydrogen, a more accessible but highly flammable gas, was used to give the ship lift.

5. With a maximum speed of eighty-four miles per hour, the *Hindenburg* could travel from Europe to America easily in two days, whereas other aircraft needed to stop and refuel frequently.

6. After it was launched in the spring of 1936, the zeppelin made ten round trips between Germany and the United States.

7. On its first 1937 trip, the *Hindenburg* caught fire during its landing attempt, and the ship crashed just outside the naval base at Lakehurst, New Jersey, after less than a minute had passed since the appearance of the first flames.

8. Herbert Morrison, a radio announcer, delivered his famous broadcast as he and his sound engineer, Charley Nehlson, witnessed the crash.

9. Before the tragedy ended, thirty-six of the ninety-seven people on board had died.

10. Because the *Hindenburg* belonged to Nazi Germany, the explosion on board may have been an act of anti-Nazi sabotage.

Place parentheses around each adverb clause. Draw an arrow from each adverb clause to the word it modifies. Underline each subordinating conjunction that introduces an adverb clause.

1. When just twenty-six years old, Eliot Ness began working for the United States Department of Justice as a special agent in charge of the Prohibition Bureau in Chicago.

2. As soon as Ness took over the Bureau, he began disrupting the criminal activities of Al "Scarface" Capone, Chicago's most famous gangster.

3. Capone had been involved with numerous gangs and a variety of crimes since he was very young.

4. Capone quickly rose to the top of the organized crime scene, but once Eliot Ness had enlisted his crime-fighting force, things became difficult for Capone.

5. Whereas many government agents would accept bribes, the young agents recruited by Ness would not accept bribes.

6. Because they would not be bribed, one journalist nicknamed Ness and his men "the Untouchables."

7. The Untouchables crashed Capone's bootlegging operations wherever the breweries and speakeasies were found.

8. According to biographer Paul Heimel, the fictional detective Dick Tracy was patterned after Ness, while Capone was the model for Tracy's archrival, "Big Boy."

9. Whenever people think of Eliot Ness, they usually think of Al Capone's arrest, but three IRS agents actually deserve most of the credit for the charges that sent Capone to prison.

10. Eliot Ness was never well known during his lifetime. He became famous after the television show *The Untouchables* began airing in 1959, two years after his death.

Noun Clauses

A **noun clause** is a dependent clause that functions in the sentence as if it were a noun. In other words, noun clauses function as subjects, predicate nouns, objects, and appositives.

Nouns
pp. 2-3

Subordinating Conjunctions

Many noun clauses begin with certain subordinating conjunctions. The most common kind of noun clause begins with the subordinating conjunction *that*. Another subordinating conjunction that can introduce noun clauses is *whether*.

Commas to
Separate
pp. 276-77

tip The subordinating conjunction *if* sometimes substitutes for *whether* in informal speech and writing.

| | **S** | | **LV** | **PN** | **(S)** | **(TrV)** | **(DO)** |

A common misconception is *that* Johann Gutenberg invented movable type

(DO)

and the printing press.

| | **S** | | **TrV** | **DO** | **(S)** | **(TrV)** |

Most people do not realize *that* printers in Asia had developed movable

(DO)

type centuries earlier.

| | **S** | | **App.** | **(S)** | **(TrV)** |

The answer to one question, *whether* the Asian inventions influenced Euro-

(DO) **LV** **PN**

pean printers, is probably no.

In each of these examples, the entire noun clause works together as a unit to perform the function of a single noun.

Sometimes the subordinating conjunction *that* is not expressed but simply understood when the noun clause acts as the direct object of the sentence.

| | **S** | **TrV** | **DO** | **(S)** | **(LV)** |

Some historians say *[that]* an appropriate title for Johann Gutenberg is the

(PN)

Father of Printing.

Indefinite Relative Pronouns

Some noun clauses begin with **indefinite relative pronouns.** Like all relative pronouns, an indefinite relative pronoun functions as a subject, an object, or an adjective in the noun clause. Unlike a relative pronoun that begins an adjective clause, an indefinite relative pronoun does not have an antecedent in the independent clause. An indefinite relative pronoun substitutes for something indefinite (identity unknown) in the noun clause itself.

| | **S** | **InV** | | **OP** | **(DO)** | **(S)** |

Various Europeans had experimented unsuccessfully with *whatever* they

(TrV)

could devise.

| | **S** | **(S)** | **(TrV)** | **(DO)** | | **TrV** |

Whoever developed a usable kind of movable metal type would have a new

DO

tool for meeting medieval society's increasing demand for books.

| | **S** | | | | **S** |

The perfection of movable metal type and the development of the modern

LV **PN** **(S)** **(TrV)** **(DO)**

printing press are *what* we remember Gutenberg for today.

(OP)

Gutenberg Press, The Museum of Printing History, Houston

Indefinite Relative Pronouns

what	whatever
which	whichever
who	whoever
whom	whomever
whose	whosever

in SUMMARY

A **noun clause** is a dependent clause that functions in the sentence as a noun. Most noun clauses begin with the subordinating conjunction *that;* some begin with an indefinite relative pronoun; and a few noun clauses begin with the subordinating conjunction *whether.*

An **indefinite relative pronoun** functions as a subject, an object, or an adjective in the noun clause. An indefinite relative pronoun does not have an antecedent in the independent clause.

4.7 PRACTICE *the skill*

Place parentheses around each noun clause. Identify the function of each noun clause as subject (S), predicate noun (PN), direct object (DO), indirect object (IO), object of the preposition (OP), or appositive (App).

_____ 1. That the Great Depression lasted so long is partially attributable to the Dust Bowl, which lasted eight years.

_____ 2. Poor farming techniques and several years of successive drought were what caused the Dust Bowl.

_____ 3. Although the entire United States felt the effects of the disaster, the fact is that the Dust Bowl actually took place in the southern part of the Great Plains.

_____ 4. Dust Bowlers continually experienced what they called "dust storms" or "black blizzards."

_____ 5. High winds would pick up dried-out soil and fill the sky with dust clouds. Whatever stood in the way of the clouds would be permeated with dust.

_____ 6. After a storm had been through, people would find that dirt had sifted into everything—drawers, cabinets, and even clothes.

_____ 7. The dust storms gave whoever was not strong a sickness called dust pneumonia. The disease most affected the old, the young, and animals.

_____ 8. Most people know that a lot of Dust Bowlers migrated to California, but few people realize it was only twenty-five percent of Plains dwellers who left.

9. During the Depression employers would often hire whoever would work for the least amount of pay. Because migrators would work for less, many Californians saw "Okies," a derogatory name used for migrant workers, as job stealers.

10. In 1939 the literary world witnessed the publication of what became the most famous portrayal of Dust Bowl migrators, Steinbeck's *The Grapes of Wrath*.

REVIEW *the skill*

Place parentheses around each noun clause. Identify the function of each noun clause as subject (S), predicate noun (PN), direct object (DO), indirect object (IO), object of the preposition (OP), or appositive (App). Underline each subordinating conjunction once; underline each indefinite relative pronoun twice.

1. Many people know who J.R.R. [John Ronald Reuel] Tolkien was. He was a professional scholar who became famous for his fiction writings.

2. What began as stories that he told his boys during their "Winter Reads" eventually were put together to form his most famous written work, *The Hobbit*.

3. While grading exams one day, Tolkien jotted something on a blank page he found amidst the papers. The seed of his first book, what he wrote on that page, was this line: "In a hole in the ground there lived a hobbit."

4. In the early 1930s Tolkien began writing what became a literary classic.

5. The story's basic plot is that hobbit Bilbo Baggins and a group of dwarfs attempt to rescue the dwarfs' treasure from a dragon.

6. Tolkien wrote out most of *The Hobbit* and gave whichever friends were interested copies of the partially completed story.

7. C. S. Lewis, a close friend who had read the story, told Tolkien he should have it published, but Tolkien had no such intention.

8. In 1936 a publisher from George Allen & Unwin obtained a manuscript from a friend of Tolkien's. Her opinion was that Tolkien should publish the story—even though it was still unfinished.

9. The question of whether the book would be a success was settled when the first printing, released in the fall of 1937, sold out by Christmas.

10. That *The Hobbit* was so popular created a demand for more "hobbit books." The result was Tolkien's series, *The Lord of the Rings*.

USE *the skill*

Combine the following pairs of sentences by making one of them a dependent clause. Then identify the kind of dependent clause you used as adjective (*Adj*), adverb (*Adv*), or noun (*Noun*). Try to use all three kinds of dependent clauses.

————— 1. Richard Drew was an engineer at 3M Corporation. He invented self-adhesive cellophane tape in 1930.

————— 2. Drew was already a successful engineer. Drew had invented masking tape five years earlier.

————— 3. Food distributors needed a moisture-proof method for sealing cellophane packaging material. Drew's research was inspired by this fact.

————— 4. Could anyone provide a solution to the problem? This question was common.

————— 5. He spent a year experimenting with different formulas. Drew developed a workable new adhesive.

————— 6. The new tape was waterproof and transparent. The new tape allowed food distributors to seal cellophane wrap easily.

————— 7. Drew and his employers named the new invention Scotch Cellulose Tape. The name was inspired by a customer's comment.

————— 8. A new method of using heat to seal cellophane packages was introduced. The usefulness of the new tape seemed limited.

_____ 9. Many people could not afford to replace broken items during the Depression. People used cellophane tape to mend household items.

_____

_____

_____ 10. The original tape was difficult to use. The difficulty led to John Borden's design in 1932 of a tape dispenser with a cutting blade.

_____

_____

Using Independent and Dependent Clauses

Every sentence includes at least one independent clause, and many sentences consist of a combination of two or more clauses. All sentences can be categorized by the number and kinds of clauses they contain.

A **simple sentence** consists of only one independent clause. There are no dependent clauses in a simple sentence.

> Many European printers tried to improve Gutenberg's famous inventions.
>
> Early improvements affected illustration and type design.

A **compound sentence** contains two or more independent clauses, usually joined by a semicolon or by a comma and a coordinating conjunction. There are no dependent clauses in a compound sentence.

> Peter Schoeffer introduced colored ink, and Albrecht Pfister combined movable type with woodcut illustrations.
>
> Gutenberg's type resembled a monk's handwriting, but printers in Italy designed a plainer type.

A **complex sentence** contains one independent clause and one or more dependent clauses. The dependent clause may appear before, within, or after the independent clause.

> The new roman type *that* printers [*who* lived in Italy] designed was small and compact.
>
> *Whereas* Gutenberg's type was ornate, roman type was plain and easy to read.

A **compound-complex sentence** includes two or more independent clauses and one or more dependent clauses.

> Aldus Manutius was a printer *who* lived in Italy; he commissioned the first italic type.
>
> Italic type is slanted, but roman type, *upon which* italic type was based, is vertical.

Sentence
Expansion
and Reduction
pp. 372-76

Conjunctions
pp. 20-21

Commas;
Semicolons
pp. 270, 286

Commas
pp. 273, 277

Coordination
and Subordination
pp. 365-66

in SUMMARY

A **simple sentence** consists of only one independent clause.

A **compound sentence** contains two or more independent clauses.

A **complex sentence** contains one independent clause and one or more dependent clauses.

A **compound-complex sentence** includes two or more independent clauses and one or more dependent clauses.

4.10 PRACTICE *the skill*

Identify each sentence as simple (S), compound (Cd), complex (Cx), or compound-complex (Cd-Cx).

_____ 1. After SPAM luncheon meat was introduced in 1933, the popularity of processed food grew quickly in America.

_____ 2. Processed food is somehow altered from its original form; it is often precooked, frozen, or dehydrated.

_____ 3. This process can alter the food's nutritional value or taste.

_____ 4. Processed food often has color and flavor additives so that the appearance and taste of the food will be pleasant; other additives are added for preservation and nutrition.

_____ 5. Marketers know people buy food for its taste, appearance, and smell.

_____ 6. If you could see or taste your favorite processed food without its color and taste additives, you might be surprised at the difference.

_____ 7. Don't be deceived by an ingredient label that says "natural flavors"; both artificial and natural flavors are produced in a laboratory.

_____ 8. A few drops of chemicals can smell and taste like a grilled hamburger.

_____ 9. Approximately 90% of the food that Americans eat is processed food.

_____ 10. Before you eat your next processed food snack, look for "natural flavors" or "artificial flavors" on the list of ingredients.

4.11 USE *the skill*

Using each set of sentences, create the type of sentence indicated in parentheses.

1. In the 1930s a phenomenon known as the Dust Bowl occurred. This changed the way of life for many people living in the Great Plains. (*simple*)

_____

_____

2. Before the Dust Bowl, farmers had not been using good soil conservation practices. These farmers had been harvesting wheat for years. (*complex*)

_____

_____

3. By 1931 improper farming and overgrazing had destroyed the ground cover. Ground cover had held the topsoil. A severe drought had also begun. (compound-complex)

_____

_____

4. Fierce winds carried the dry, unprotected topsoil away. Fierce winds caused terrible dust storms. (simple)

_____

_____

5. Millions of acres of land lost topsoil. The country experienced the worst drought ever. (compound)

_____

_____

6. The Dust Bowl intensified the Great Depression. There was little food or work to be found. Thousands of people evacuated the plains. (compound-complex)

_____

_____

7. In order to save the land, the government initiated new programs. The programs included teaching soil conservation methods and planting trees. (complex)

_____

_____

_____

_____

_____

8. Farmers began using better planting methods. The condition of the land improved. (complex)

_____

_____

9. Thousands of trees were planted across the plains. The trees protected the land from wind erosion. (compound)

_____

_____

10. The rains returned at the end of the decade. Afterwards, the plains once again held bountiful fields of wheat. (complex)

_____

_____

Avoiding Errors

Fragments

A **fragment** is a group of words wrongly punctuated as if it were a complete sentence. A fragment could be either a phrase or a dependent clause. Although we often use incomplete sentences in our speech, fragments are usually considered errors in writing.

> William Caxton, who was also a translator and an editor.

> The most important printer in British history.

> Because he introduced printing to England and helped to shape the English language.

Correct a fragment either by adding the missing element (a subject or a predicate if the fragment is only a phrase) or by joining the dependent clause to an independent clause.

> William Caxton, who was also a translator and an editor, was the most important printer in British history.

> We remember him because he introduced printing to England and helped to shape the English language.

Comma Splices and Fused Sentences

A **comma splice** is two sentences incorrectly joined by only a comma. A **fused sentence** is two sentences incorrectly joined without any punctuation. Because these errors can confuse your reader, it is important to avoid them.

COMMA SPLICE	William Caxton learned the art of printing in Germany, he opened his first printing press in the Netherlands.
	Caxton printed some books in French or Latin, he also translated books into English.
FUSED SENTENCE	Caxton established the first printing press in England in 1476 he also published the first book printed in the English language.
	Caxton's books were famous for their literary content he was the first to publish a printed version of Chaucer's writings.

To correct these errors, use one of the following methods:

- Separate the two sentences with a period or a semicolon.

  > William Caxton learned the art of printing in Germany. He opened his first printing press in the Netherlands.

  > Caxton printed some books in French or Latin; he also translated books into English.

- Combine the two sentences correctly with a comma and a coordinating conjunction.

  > Caxton established the first printing press in England in 1476, and he published the first book printed in the English language.

- Change one of the sentences into a dependent clause.

  > Caxton, whose books were famous for their literary content, was the first to publish a printed version of Chaucer's writings.

Periods
p. 266
Commas
p. 270
Semicolons
p. 286

Conjunctions
pp. 20-21

Subordination
pp. 365-66

Be careful not to correct a fused sentence by inserting only a comma—the resulting comma splice would be no improvement.

in SUMMARY

A **fragment** is a group of words wrongly punctuated as if it were a complete sentence.

A **comma splice** is two sentences incorrectly joined by only a comma.

A **fused sentence** is two sentences incorrectly joined without any punctuation.

4.12

PRACTICE *the skill*

Thinking Biblically

Have you ever thought about the fact that God is the "First Cause," the cause for everything? Even baseball. You might wonder what caused baseball to become such a well-loved sport. Most people would identify the combination of competition, suspense, and athletic prowess as their reasons for enjoying the game. But for a Christian with a Christian worldview, the reason must ultimately be God. After all, it is God who created us to be delighted by these things. Since God made humans in His own image (Gen. 1:26-27), God Himself must delight in competition (the Bible is filled with stories about conflicts and resolutions), suspense (the Bible regularly uses suspense as a story-telling device—consider Abraham, Joseph, and Samson), and athletic prowess (God made humans with athletic ability). So, since a person's love for baseball comes ultimately from God, a Christian can freely enjoy baseball for God's glory. Write a cause-and-effect essay that shows God as the cause of our delight in some aspect of life.

Identify each group of words as a sentence (S), a fragment (F), a comma splice (CS), or a fused sentence (FS).

_____ 1. Joe DiMaggio was born in California in 1914 his parents were immigrants from Sicily.

_____ 2. In 1930, he dropped out of high school and began working various jobs; in his spare time he played baseball.

_____ 3. Joe DiMaggio's older brother Vince DiMaggio played for the minor league San Francisco Seals, he recommended his little brother for the open position of shortstop in 1932.

_____ 4. After Joe DiMaggio played an outstanding season in 1933, the Seals sold DiMaggio to the New York Yankees.

_____ 5. In 1936 DiMaggio played for the Yankees, and the rookie helped his team defeat the Giants that year in the World Series.

_____ 6. DiMaggio played in spite of his injuries he had a bad back, a weak right shoulder, and bone spurs in both of his feet.

_____ 7. Always known for being consistent and for rarely making mistakes.

_____ 8. He performed well during important games, however, he also played his best when the game was unimportant.

_____ 9. DiMaggio, winning ten pennants and nine World Series titles in thirteen years.

_____ 10. His fans voted him "Greatest Living Player."

REVIEW *the skill*

Identify each group of words as a sentence *(S)*, a fragment *(F)*, a comma splice *(CS)*, or a fused sentence *(FS)*. If the sentence contains a sentence error, rewrite the sentence correctly.

———— 1. Alcatraz, an island in the middle of the San Francisco Bay, is famous for the prison that it once housed.

_____

_____

_____

———— 2. In the 1850s the government used the island as a citadel and a military prison, the island had one hundred cannons and the first operational lighthouse.

_____

_____

_____

———— 3. In 1909 the Citadel was torn down the basement became the foundation for the new prison called "The Rock."

_____

_____

_____

———— 4. The Army continued to use the prison until 1933, when ownership of the island was transferred to the United States Department of Justice.

_____

_____

_____

———— 5. The government decided to use the island for a maximum-security prison for the toughest criminals, in fact, Al Capone was one of the prisoners who landed himself in Alcatraz.

_____

_____

_____

———— 6. The prison, open for three decades while fourteen escape attempts were made.

_____

_____

_____

_____ 7. In all but one of the escape attempts, the men either were captured on the island or drowned in the cold waters of the San Francisco Bay.

_____

_____

_____

_____ 8. In the most famous escape attempt, Frank Morris and brothers John and Clarence Anglin left the island and made it to the water the men were never found.

_____

_____

_____

_____ 9. In 1963 the prison closed because shipping supplies to the island was too expensive.

_____

_____

_____

_____ 10. Alcatraz is now part of the Golden Gate National Recreational Area the park attracts over one million visitors each year.

_____

_____

_____

Read the following paragraph. Write the letter of the best description for each italicized word or group of words. Identify the word or group of words according to the context of the sentence.

In 1930, the members of Moody Church in Chicago made Harry Allen Ironside their new ¹*pastor.* One may be surprised to know ²*that the new pastor's formal education had ended in the eighth grade.* Harry Ironside was born in 1876 in Toronto, Canada, but moved to Los Angeles, California, when he was only ten years old. Two years later, a famous evangelist, D. L. Moody, came to the city. Harry was ³*excited.* After hearing Moody preach, Harry prayed that the Lord would allow him someday ⁴*to preach* to great crowds. Moody had no idea that someone ⁵*who* was listening to his sermon would be one of his successors someday. Even in his early teens, Harry preached on the streets and witnessed to thousands of people. When he was twenty-one, he assisted an evangelist in his campaign, and he fell in love with the pianist. He and Helen Schofield were married soon afterwards. Once while traveling home from a speaking engagement in Minnesota, the couple was ⁶*in need of funds,* and they had to stop in Utah. Together they prayed for forty cents for food. ⁷*That* evening after his ⁸*preaching* on the streets, two men put forty cents into Harry Ironside's hand. In 1900, the first of many books written by Ironside appeared. ⁹*Although* he had only a limited education, Ironside had studied and taught the Scriptures many years. When he died in 1950, he had preached ¹⁰*to millions* of people. He left a legacy of books and Bible commentaries.

———— 1. pastor

———— 2. that the new pastor's . . .

———— 3. excited

———— 4. to preach

———— 5. who

———— 6. in need of funds

———— 7. That

———— 8. preaching

———— 9. Although

———— 10. to millions

A. complement in S-*be*-Advl

B. adverbial prepositional phrase

C. demonstrative adjective

D. gerund

E. infinitive

F. noun clause

G. objective complement

H. predicate adjective

I. relative pronoun

J. subordinating conjunction

And the work of righteousness shall be peace; and the effect of righteousness quietness and assurance for ever.

Isaiah 32:17

How much do you know about the Declaration of Independence? You may know that Thomas Jefferson wrote it in 1776. But do you know why the document was written? Did you know that it was written partly as a persuasive document to justify the colonies' actions and to persuade Americans to support the war? Have you considered the effects of this single document on the Revolutionary War, on the United States of America, and on the world? Bill Rabinowitz's essay on the effects of the Depression could hardly be termed revolutionary, but it does document a cause and its effect on an ordinary occurrence: a baseball game.

A cause-and-effect essay analyzes a phenomenon in relation to its cause or its effect. The essay can inform or persuade, but it primarily shows the link between cause and effect. Choose a topic that interests or puzzles you, go backward or forward in time to look for causes and/or effects, then write an essay about your findings.

Planning

✔ **Begin brainstorming for topics that are interesting or puzzling to you.** What historical event would you like to examine? What caused the event? What were the effects? Does the event affect us today? How did a specific person change the course of history? Consider scientific achievements. What were the effects of landing a man on the moon? How has the Internet and wireless communication changed our society? Does a current problem in society concern you? Do you think your country's educational system is substandard? Why? You may find the topic of baseball interesting. Were you surprised to learn that a historical and economic event such as the Great Depression had long-term influence on the methods and marketing of modern baseball? The following is a brainstorming list of possible topics.

> highways/roads/travel
> cars—big, little, economy, speed
> paper production
> pollution
> electricity
> pets—leash laws
> television/radio/mass communication

✔ **Choose a few topics and write down as many causes and effects related to your topics as you can.** Group these ideas together and decide which topic works best for your paper. Look at the list below for ideas that one group of students came up with after their brainstorming session.

> highway system—effect on travel in America; effect on auto industry, hotel chains, fast food, gas stations; tourism
> cars—different models' effects on other models; Volkswagen in Germany; Saturn company

pollution—effect on environment (pollution laws?); water, air, soil pollution; conservation; overemphasis on creation over the Creator

television—effect on radio, moving pictures, newspapers, other forms of print communication

✔ **Narrow your topic.** After you decide on a topic, determine what part or parts of the topic you will analyze. The cause-and-effect relationship should be clear in your paper. If you have a long list of causes or effects, choose the most important ones to discuss. Be careful not to waste time on facts that your audience already knows. For example, the fact that Napoleon's ambition caused conflict in Europe is common knowledge. One student chose to write about the effect of the automobile's invention on the American road system.

✔ **Determine your audience and purpose.** Are you writing to your classmates about a school-related issue? Are you writing to a young audience? An educated audience? Is your essay something that would appear in a newspaper column, a history book, or an academic journal? The purpose of your paper may be to inform, as in the piece on baseball. If you are writing a humorous paper, your purpose is to entertain. If your topic is controversial, you may be writing to persuade. Before you write, ask yourself these questions:

- Who is my audience?
- What is my purpose?
- What does my audience already know about my topic?
- What specific parts of my topic will my audience find interesting?
- Based on the expected knowledge of my audience, what details will best achieve my purpose?

✔ **Gather information for your paper.** The topic you choose will determine the amount of research necessary for your paper. However, the more support you have, the more informative and convincing your paper may be. As you research, ask yourself the same questions about the information you find that you asked while narrowing your topic and considering your audience and purpose.

✔ **Clarify the relationships between the causes and effects.** Sometimes a single cause has a single effect (e.g., running over a nail in the road caused a flat bike tire), but more often a single cause has multiple effects (e.g., running over the nail caused the flat tire, which caused a crash into a tree, which caused a broken thumb). When a single cause creates an effect that in turn becomes the cause of another event, we call it the chain effect. In the baseball example, the Depression caused ticket sales to go down, which caused the industry to consider methods to attract fans, which caused the installation of loud speakers, which may have caused ticket sales to go back up. Look for chain effects in your topic and make a chart or an outline to help clarify the steps in the process.

Truth and Validity pp. 51-53

Fallacious Argumentation pp. 322-23

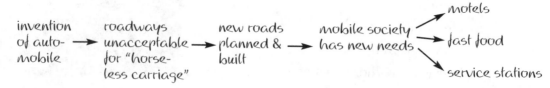

invention of automobile → roadways unacceptable for "horse-less carriage" → new roads planned & built → mobile society has new needs → motels / fast food / service stations

Drafting

✔ **Write an opening that captures the audience's attention.** As you are well aware, your first sentence will set the tone for your piece. Tell your reader what you will discuss and how it is important to him or to what is happening around him. Rabinowitz's claim that "several innovations . . . changed the sport of baseball forever" shows the significance of the piece and encourages the reader to continue reading. The writer of the automobile essay decided to focus only on the effect of the highway system. Two possible opening sentences appear below:

> In 1912 the newly invented automobile had the run of the road—that is, if there was a road.

> Few inventions have caused a greater stir than the automobile, and its effect on the American road system changed forever how—and where—we drive.

✔ **Define the cause-and-effect relationship clearly.** Give background information that will set up the situation for your reader. Use the chain effect diagram or the outline you made in the planning stage to be sure you have left nothing out of the picture. Three methods of organization will help you include your examples and details:

Chronological Order

Use the order in which the details of your effect occurred. Most of the time, this method works best and helps the writer to include all necessary information. In the essay about the highway system, the writer might briefly mention the invention of the automobile, then describe road conditions at the beginning of the 1900s, and then move on to who first began planning a national system of roads, what the first highway was, and so on.

Order of Importance

Begin with the most important information and proceed to the least important. Or do the reverse of that. Discussing who planned the roads, how much they cost, and whom the roads were named for is an example of least-important-to-most-important order.

Familiar-to-Unfamiliar Order

Start with the details that most people have heard of and continue to the more obscure details. This type of organization works well when there are details that are important but not well known. Starting with road location, proceeding to cost, and ending with local contests to name the roads and the shenanigans that went on to pay for them would take the reader from relatively familiar to unfamiliar territory.

✔ **Use at least one good example.** Notice the example in the baseball story that gives us a good picture of what baseball was like before loudspeakers: losing players celebrate wildly as those in the grandstands gape in bewilderment. Your essay will likely contain more than one, but be sure to include at least one fascinating illustration.

✔ **Come to a good conclusion.** Tell your audience the significance of all that you have stated. Your conclusion may be a summary, a persuasive plea, or a prediction based on the facts you have presented. If you have presented several effects, consider restating the most important one and contrasting it with the cause to end the piece.

> The effect of the interstate highway system on the national and individual states' economies is immeasurable. Today billions of dollars in toll and tax revenue and in hotel and food expenditures pour in from those who travel the country by "horseless carriage." In the years since Carl Fischer and his Coast-to-Coast Rock Highway burst onto the scene, thousands of highways have come and gone. Lincoln Highway is only a 150-mile stretch of lonely Pennsylvania road. Romantic Route 66 has been replaced by more modern Is (I-40, I-55 . . .). But America's roadway adventurers roll on—with miles of paved and well-lighted highway to go before they sleep.

Revising

✔ **Question yourself about your draft.** Or ask a classmate to read your draft and to tell you his answers to these questions. Peer input will help you spot potential problems—and successes—of your essay.

- Is my "cause" a legitimate cause? Or is it merely an event that preceded another event?
- Is my topic interesting?
- Did my opening paragraph arrest the audience's attention?
- Are my points stated in an order that is logical and clear?
- Am I assuming that my audience knows more (or less) than they actually do?
- What is the significance of my statements?
- Are my transitions and transition words (*as a result of, because, if . . . then, therefore*) clear?
- Have I used correct grammar, usage, and mechanics?

✔ **Revise your draft.** After you have worked through the questions above, make those revisions that you and your peers have decided on. Take as many suggestions from as many people as you can, but make the final decision yourself.

Publishing

✔ **Include this piece in your writing portfolio.** An expository cause-and-effect essay is a good contrast to some of the personal and creative writing you have done.

✔ **Read your paper aloud for the class.** Especially if your paper is a persuasive one, an oral presentation is a good publication choice. See whether you can sway any of your audience to your point of view.

✔ **Develop your outline or chart.** Rework your final paper into a detailed outline or chart to be posted in your classroom. Include illustrations or photographs if appropriate.

✔ **Submit the essay to a website or other publication.** Many websites welcome information from outside sources on their particular topic. Check the site's homepage for links that encourage submission.

Some Ideas to Consider

History

- Write about the effects of the American Revolution on the French Revolution.

 Consider writing about cause and effect related to some event or situation in the history of your family's homeland. Talk with your family for some ideas and see what information you can find (in either language).

Church History

- Write about how Luther affected church history when he nailed the Ninety-five Theses on the church door.

Literature

- Research a book such as *Uncle Tom's Cabin* and write about its effects on society and politics.

THINK ABOUT IT

Conjunctions and Disjunctions

You have already studied true and false statements as well as valid and invalid conclusions as part of an argument. Now we are going to consider more complex statements. Some statements have at least two parts that are joined by a connective. The two most common connectives are *and* and *or*. If you say, "I will finish my homework and play basketball," then you must do both activities in order for the statement to be true. A two-part claim joined by the word *and* is called a **conjunction.** Several words mean the same as *and*, including *yet, both,* and *also.* If you say, "I will finish my homework or play basketball," then you will have to do only one activity for the statement to be true. For a statement with two parts joined by the word *or* to be true, one or both of the statements may be true. Such a statement is called a **disjunction.**

Basing your answer on the example sentences, identify the following statements as true or false.

Sandra says, "I have volleyball games on Tuesday and on Thursday."

1. Sandra does not have a game on Thursday. Then her claim is

   _____ .

2. Sandra does have a game on Thursday. If she also has a game on Tuesday, then her statement is _____ .

3. Sandra does not have a game on either Tuesday or Thursday. Then her statement is _____ .

Sandra says, "I have a volleyball game on Tuesday or Thursday."

4. Sandra has a game on Tuesday. Her statement is _____ .

5. Sandra does not have a game on Tuesday, but she has a game on Thursday. Her statement is _____ .

6. Sandra does not have a game on Tuesday or Thursday, but she does have a game on Wednesday. Her statement is _____ .

Thinking It Through

Consider the following statements:

- You can go to college, or you can be a failure in life.
- You can wear a certain brand of clothing, or you can be out of style.
- Every country will disarm its nuclear weapons, or the whole world will destroy itself.

Are these statements true? Examine the validity of using these kinds of statements in an argument. Write statements similar to these that might be used in an argument. Determine whether the statements are true or false.

Poetry is an important vehicle for getting a message across. Several books of the Bible use the language of poetry: the book of Psalms contains some of the world's best-known Hebrew poems; Proverbs makes use of many poetic devices. In Ecclesiastes, Solomon employs poetry to warn of the vanity, or emptiness, of life lived without God. Note how effectively Ecclesiastes 12 describes growing old using poetic metaphor. In this chapter's writing assignment you will practice using both poetry and metaphor.

Ecclesiastes 12

[1]Remember now thy Creator in the days of thy youth, while the evil days come not, nor the years draw nigh, when thou shalt say, I have no pleasure in them;

[2]While the sun, or the light, or the moon, or the stars, be not darkened, nor the clouds return after the rain:

[3]In the day when the keepers of the house shall tremble, and the strong men shall bow themselves, and the grinders cease because they are few, and those that look out of the windows be darkened,

[4]And the doors shall be shut in the streets, when the sound of the grinding is low, and he shall rise up at the voice of the bird, and all the daughters of musick shall be brought low;

[5]Also when they shall be afraid of that which is high, and fears shall be in the way, and the almond tree shall flourish, and the grasshopper shall be a burden, and desire shall fail: because man goeth to his long home, and the mourners go about the streets:

[6]Or ever the silver cord be loosed, or the golden bowl be broken, or the pitcher be broken at the fountain, or the wheel broken at the cistern.

[7]Then shall the dust return to the earth as it was: and the spirit shall return unto God who gave it.

[8]Vanity of vanities, saith the preacher; all is vanity.

[9]And moreover, because the preacher was wise, he still taught the people knowledge; yea, he gave good heed, and sought out, and set in order many proverbs.

[10]The preacher sought to find out acceptable words: and that which was written was upright, even words of truth.

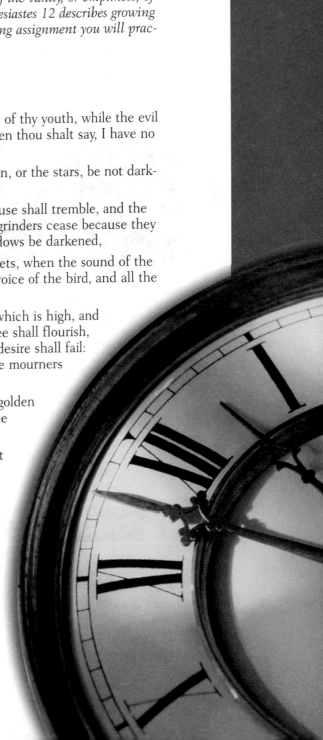

[11]The words of the wise are as goads, and as nails fastened by the masters of assemblies, which are given from one shepherd.

[12]And further, by these, my son, be admonished: of making many books there is no end; and much study is a weariness of the flesh.

[13]Let us hear the conclusion of the whole matter: Fear God, and keep his commandments: for this is the whole duty of man.

[14]For God shall bring every work into judgment, with every secret thing, whether it be good, or whether it be evil.

AGREEMENT

Subject-Verb Agreement

Subjects and Predicates

Clear communication requires agreement in number between subjects and verbs. In other words, a singular subject takes a singular verb, and a plural subject takes a plural verb.

Plural Nouns p. 2

Most singular nouns become plural by the addition of the suffix *s* or *es.* Verbs, however, are plural in just the opposite way. Singular verbs usually end in *s* or *es,* while plural verbs do not. A good rule to remember is that if your subject ends in the suffix *s,* your verb usually should not.

SINGULAR	The *chef prepares* chicken for the banquet.
PLURAL	The *chefs prepare* chicken for the banquet.

Present Tense p. 154

This form change in verbs occurs only in the present tense with subjects in the third person. With the exception of the verb *be,* verbs in the past and future tenses stay the same, whether singular or plural.

Spelling pp. 430-31

Forms of *Be*

	Present		Past	
	Singular	**Plural**	**Singular**	**Plural**
First Person	I am	we are	I was	we were
Second Person	you are	you are	you were	you were
Third Person	he is	they are	he was	they were

Compound Subjects

Sentences often have compound subjects. If the compound subject is joined by *and* or *both—and,* the verb should be plural. If it is joined by *or, nor, either—or,* or *neither—nor,* the verb must agree with the subject that is closer to it.

Compound Subjects p. 33

Conjunctions pp. 20-21

PLURAL	**S** **S** **TrV** **DO** Lakes *and* streams cover this part of the country.
	S **S** **TrV** **DO** *Both* Tom *and* his father like to fish.

In the first example the two parts of the compound subject are joined by *and.* In the second example they are joined by *both—and.* Both instances require plural verbs.

SINGULAR	**S** **S** **TrV** **DO** *Either* cookies *or* cake makes a good birthday treat.
PLURAL	**S** **S** **TrV** **DO** *Either* cake *or* cookies make a good birthday treat.

In both examples the compound subject is joined by *either—or.* The verb in the first example is singular because it is closer to the singular subject *cake.* The verb in the second example is plural because it is closer to the plural subject *cookies.*

ESL

If a complete verb contains one or more auxiliaries, then the first auxiliary agrees with the subject. Only the first auxiliary shows agreement; auxiliaries that appear later in the complete verb do not change form. However, the only auxiliaries that change form to agree with a singular or plural subject are **be, have,** and **do.** Other auxiliaries do not have different singular and plural forms.

	Singular	Plural
be	I **am starting** a blog on my website.	We **are going** to start it this week.
have	He **has been reading** a psalm every night.	They **have been studying** Psalms in their Sunday school class.
do	**Does** she **speak** French?	They **do** not **speak** French.
may (and other auxiliaries)	She **may find** a laptop easier than a desktop computer.	They **may provide** wireless access by this fall.

in SUMMARY

Subjects and verbs must agree with each other in number.

If a compound subject is joined by *and* or *both—and,* the verb should be plural. If it is joined by *or, nor, either—or,* or *neither—nor,* the verb should agree with the subject that is closer to it.

PRACTICE *the skill*

Underline the simple subject(s) in each sentence. Then underline the correct verb from the choices in parentheses.

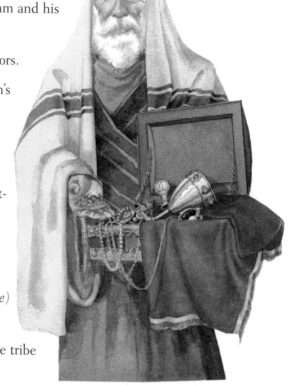

1. Melchizedek's offices (*was, were*) King of Salem and priest of the most high God.

2. In Genesis 14 Melchizedek (*meets, meet*) Abraham and his men as they return from battle.

3. Refreshments (*is, are*) offered to the weary warriors.

4. The bread and the wine (*renews, renew*) the men's energy.

5. Abraham (*receives, receive*) a blessing from Melchizedek.

6. Then Abraham (*gives, give*) him a tithe of the battle spoils.

7. Psalm 110:4 and Hebrews 5:6 (*compares, compare*) Melchizedek with Christ.

8. Both Melchizedek and Christ (*combines, combine*) the offices of king and priest in one person.

9. Yet neither Melchizedek nor Christ (*is, are*) of the tribe of Levi.

10. Their priesthood (*supersedes, supersede*) Aaron's because it is everlasting.

REVIEW *the skill*

Underline the simple subject(s) in each sentence. In the blank, write the correct present tense form of the verb given in parentheses.

_____ 1. Jubilee (*occur*) every fiftieth year.

_____ 2. Seven Sabbatic years (*pass*) before the arrival of the year of Jubilee.

_____ 3. Rest and redemption (*come*) in that special year.

_____ 4. Three general laws (*regulate*) the activities of the Jubilee.

_____ 5. First, neither the people nor the land (*be*) to be active that year.

_____ 6. A much-needed rest (*benefit*) both men and fields.

_____ 7. Second, a man or his heirs (*receive*) back any family property that had to be sold.

_____ 8. Third, Israelite slaves (*gain*) their freedom.

_____ 9. Oppression and want (*be*) to cease in the year of Jubilee.

_____ 10. God (*provide*) refreshment for His people.

"Be to" *(is/am/are/was/were + to)* has the same meaning as *must*, expressing necessity imposed by another. Notice its use in sentences 5 and 9 above.

Problems with Subject Identification

The verb in a sentence must agree with its subject, but sometimes the subject may be difficult to identify. Intervening phrases between subjects and verbs, predicate nouns that are the opposite of their subjects in number, and inverted word order in sentences may all be confusing.

Intervening Phrases

Often words come between the subject and the verb in a sentence. These **intervening phrases** can be distracting. Remember that the verb must agree with the true subject, not with a word in an intervening phrase.

Two common intervening phrases are the **negative phrase** and the **prepositional phrase.** When you are faced with a sentence that contains one of these types of phrases, be sure to make your verb agree with the true subject of the sentence, not with a word or words in the phrase.

NEGATIVE PHRASES	*Self-discipline and financial restraint,* not more money, *are* the answers to their problems with debt.
	My *brothers,* but not my sister, *want* to ski on Saturday.
PREPOSITIONAL PHRASES	*Divisions* into chapter and verse in the Bible *help* the reader locate specific text.
	Her favorite *verse* in the Gospels *is* John 3:16.

In the two examples of negative phrases, the subjects are plural (although the negative phrases are singular) and require plural verbs. In the first prepositional phrase example, the subject *divisions* is plural and takes the plural verb *help* even though *Bible,* the object of the preposition *in,* is singular. The second example is just the opposite. The singular subject *verse* takes the singular verb *is* although the plural *Gospels,* object of the preposition *in,* comes immediately before the verb.

Another phrase that sometimes comes between a subject and its verb is the **appositive phrase.** Remember that an appositive is a noun or pronoun that follows another noun or pronoun and renames it. The presence of an appositive does not affect the number of the verb. The verb should still agree with the true subject.

Appositive Phrases pp. 61-62

His *punishment,* kitchen duties, *was* fitting for the offense of throwing food.

These *tickets,* the gift of a congressman, *allow* the bearers to take an extensive tour of the White House.

The *bridge,* two rotted logs connected by flimsy boards, *poses* danger for hikers.

Notice that in each example the verb agrees with the subject of the sentence, not the appositive. In the first sentence the singular verb *was* matches the singular subject *punishment,* not the plural appositive *duties.* In the second sentence the plural verb *allow* matches the plural subject *tickets,* not the singular appositive *gift.* And in the third sentence the singular verb *poses* agrees with the singular subject *bridge,* not the plural appositive *logs.*

Predicate Nouns of a Different Number

Sometimes a subject and a predicate noun are not of the same number. In such a case the verb must agree with the subject, not the predicate noun.

    S   **LV**   **PN**

The *subject* of the picture *is* two friends at play, a child and a small dog.

    S **L**   **PN**

The *trip is* two weeks in the Italian countryside.

       S **LV**   **PN**

Two small *candles are* the only source of light in the powerless house.

Inverted Order

In most sentences the verb follows the subject. But occasionally that order is reversed, or **inverted.** The word *there* or *here* at the beginning of a sentence followed by the verb is often a clue that such inversion has taken place. Since *there* or *here* is almost never the subject of a sentence, the presence of one or the other indicates that you should look after the verb for the true subject. The verb must agree with the delayed subject.

SINGULAR |
Advl *be*   **S**
There *is* a *controversy* over the answer to the question.

Advl *be*   **S**
Here *is* my *opinion.*

PLURAL |
Advl *be*   **S**
There *are* many *questions* to be answered still.

Advl *be*   **S**
Here *are* the most important *ones.*

The verb also comes before the subject in certain other declarative sentences and in some interrogative sentences. In many interrogative sentences the subject comes after the first auxiliary. Always make sure that you have identified the true subject before you decide which verb to use.

SINGULAR |
Advl   *be*   **S**
Behind the doors *is* a full-length *mirror.*

PLURAL |
(Aux)   **S**   **TrV**   **DO**
Have your *cousins* ever *spent* the night before?

When compound subjects appear in a sentence with inverted order, follow the general rules for compound subjects. Notice the following examples in which the verb agrees with the closer of the two subjects joined by *or.*

SINGULAR |
LV **S**   **S**   **PN**
Is Cole Porter or *the Gershwins* your favorite songwriter?

PLURAL |
be **S**   **S**   **Advl**
Are pears or *pineapple* in that salad?

Ignore any intervening phrases when determining agreement between a subject and its verb.

In a sentence with a predicate noun, the verb should always agree with the subject of the sentence.

In some sentences the subject comes after the verb. Be sure to find the true subject and make the verb agree with it.

5.3 **PRACTICE** *the skill*

Underline the simple subject(s) in each sentence. Then underline the correct verb from the choices in parentheses.

1. In Daniel 2 there *(is, are)* a crisis in the kingdom of Babylon.

2. The king, not his subjects, *(causes, cause)* the crisis.

3. The wise men *(is, are)* the target.

4. On them *(is, are)* laid the responsibility of telling the details and meaning of the king's dream.

5. Daniel, not the other wise men, *(performs, perform)* the task.

6. A human image of many metals *(dominates, dominate)* Nebuchadnezzar's dream.

7. The metals that make up the image *(decreases, decrease)* in worth from the head downward.

8. Among the dream's interesting points *(is, are)* the conclusion, the destruction of the image by a great stone.

9. The image's metals *(is, are)* the representation of major Gentile kingdoms of the earth.

10. The actions of the stone *(symbolizes, symbolize)* the end of Gentile world domination at the second coming of Christ.

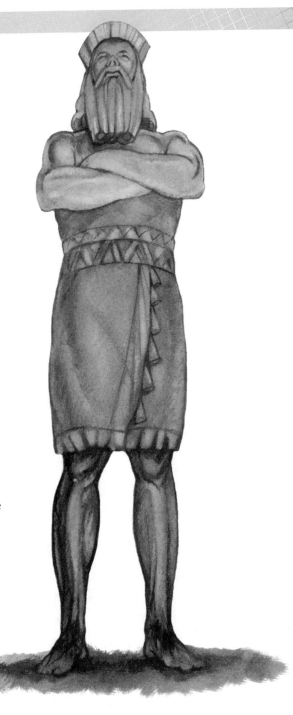

Underline the simple subject(s) in each sentence. In the blank, write the correct present tense form of the verb given in parentheses.

_____ 1. Out of the Old Testament *(come)* many types, symbols of other things or ideas.

_____ 2. The tabernacle, the structure and furnishings, *(be)* full of typology.

_____ 3. The tabernacle in its several parts *(signify)* the presence of the Lord with His people.

_____ 4. There *(be)* many types of Jesus Christ within the tabernacle furnishings.

_____ 5. The sacrifices on the brazen altar *(represent)* Christ's final atonement for sin on the cross.

_____ 6. The laver *(picture)* the washings from sin that the believer receives from Christ.

_____ 7. The Light of the World, Jesus Christ, *(be)* typified by the golden candlestick.

_____ 8. The table of shewbread *(represent)* Jesus Christ as the Bread of Life.

_____ 9. Through the altar of incense *(emerge)* the dual images of Christ as Intercessor and the Christian as believer-priest.

_____ 10. The supernatural rending of the veil, not its construction and presence, *(reveal)* the true significance of the veil, Christ's body rent on the cross to grant us access to God.

Problem Nouns and Pronouns

Often the hardest part of achieving subject-verb agreement is identifying the subject. However, some subjects cause problems even after they have been identified. These types of subjects merit special mention.

Nouns of Plural Form

Certain nouns have only one form, a form that appears to be plural. Many of these words are used in only one way, either as singular or as plural nouns.

SINGULAR | The *United States is* my country of origin.

PLURAL | My best *scissors are* in my sewing box.

Below is a list of common plural-form nouns, divided according to whether they need singular verbs or plural verbs.

Need Singular Verbs	Need Plural Verbs
billiards	clothes
checkers	eyeglasses
measles	goggles
molasses	pants
news	riches
Niagara Falls	scissors
the United States	tweezers

Some of the nouns that always require a plural verb can also be used with *a pair of* to make clear how many items are meant. In such a case the subject would be *pair* instead of the plural noun.

A *pair* of glasses *was* left on the platform.

Two pairs of pants *are* ready to be picked up at the cleaners.

Plural-sounding names of teams and organizations usually require a plural verb.

The *Tigers are* playing an important game tonight.

The *Brownies are* a branch of the Girl Scout program.

Many words ending in *ics* may be used as either singular or plural, depending on the meaning intended. When referring to such a word as a field of study, use a singular verb; when referring to it as an activity, product, or characteristic, use a plural verb.

SINGULAR | *Economics is* a valuable course for any student.

PLURAL | *Economics affect* our daily lives, from managing our money to making purchases.

A good dictionary will help you distinguish between the singular and plural meanings of *ics* words.

Collective Nouns

Collective nouns are nouns such as *club* and *audience* that refer to groups. Like other count nouns, collective nouns can be made plural (*clubs*). Even when singular, however, a collective noun can take a plural verb if the sentence focuses specifically on the individual members of the group.

SINGULAR USE	The *club meets* at a new time this week.
	The *audience waits* expectantly for the start of the program.
PLURAL USE	The *club turn* their chairs around for a group discussion.
	The *audience raise* their voices in cries for an encore.

In both of the singular sentences, the group is performing one action as one unit. But in the plural-use sentences, the members of the group are acting individually. Each person in the club turns around his own chair, and individual members of the audience call out for an encore.

ESL

Americans often reword a sentence to avoid using a collective noun such as **club** with a plural verb.

The club **members turn** their chairs around for a group discussion.

The British, on the other hand, treat many more words as collective nouns (including singular-sounding names of teams and corporations); and they freely treat these nouns as plural.

The **government are** considering new regulations to solve this problem.
Hampton are ahead, 6-0.

Americans would use **is** in both of these sentences.

in SUMMARY

Certain nouns have only one form, which appears to be plural. Some of these nouns are always used with singular verbs, and others are always used with plural verbs.

A **collective noun** refers to a group. It usually takes a singular verb but may take a plural verb if the sentence focuses on the individual members.

5.5 PRACTICE *the skill*

Underline the simple subject in each sentence. Then underline the correct verb from the choices in parentheses. You may use a dictionary.

1. Our thanks *(is, are)* due to those who pursue the field of archaeology.

2. A team of archaeologists *(provides, provide)* much information about how people lived in the past.

3. The United States *(classifies, classify)* archaeology under anthropology, the study of humanity and human culture.

4. News of ancient cultures *(comes, come)* through various sources.

5. For example, clothes (*is, are*) considered artifacts, objects that are man-made and movable.

6. Ceramics (*composes, compose*) another significant set of artifacts.

7. The riches of an earlier civilization often (*manifests, manifest*) themselves in large structures such as houses that are not easily moved.

8. A whole army of workers (*was, were*) required to complete a magnificent structure like the Great Pyramid at Giza.

9. An agricultural club (*discusses, discuss*) a common interest in ecofacts, natural objects like seeds, among themselves.

10. A collection of natural objects from an area (*reveals, reveal*) how people interacted with their environment.

5.6 REVIEW *the skill*

Underline the simple subject in each sentence. Then underline the correct verb from the choices in parentheses. You may use a dictionary.

1. The class (*imagines, imagine*) together a future archaeologist unearthing the remains of the twentieth century.

2. His crew (*puzzles, puzzle*) over the evidence of daily life in America.

3. The clothes (*presents, present*) a special curiosity.

4. A pair of pants (*is, are*) made of a sturdy blue material.

5. The New York Yankees, a group of some sort, (*receives, receive*) tribute on a hat found near the pants.

6. Eyeglasses (*was, were*) apparently needed to correct vision.

7. Economics (*seems, seem*) to have occupied the minds of many Americans.

8. Checkers (*shows, show*) that Americans also engaged in mind games.

9. The team (*concludes, conclude*) from their individual explorations that Americans had many possessions.

10. The United States (*is, are*) judged to have been an affluent society.

For each of the following sentences, write a new sentence that uses the same subject but requires a verb of a different number (plural instead of singular or singular instead of plural).

1. The family plans a vacation to an archaeological dig.

2. The jury deliberates the case of the accused archaeologist.

3. The team of archaeologists take their places around the site under excavation.

4. The committee decides to continue financing the underwater recovery project.

5. The antiquities club show their treasures to each other.

6. The organization of adjoining nations plans a joint search for the missing manuscripts.

7. The archaeology class receive their assignments for their personal projects.

8. The touring choir learns some of the history of the country.

9. The army discovers traces of a long-deserted camp while on maneuvers in the jungle.

10. The legislature debate among themselves the value of the Mackenzie Project of artifact recovery.

Indefinite Pronouns

Indefinite
Pronouns
p. 5

When an indefinite pronoun is used as a subject, the verb must agree with it in number. Most indefinite pronouns are singular. But some are plural, and some can be either singular or plural depending on the meaning of the sentence.

Always Singular				
another	each	everything	neither	one
anybody	either	less	nobody	somebody
anyone	everybody	little	no one	someone
anything	everyone	much	nothing	something

Always Plural				
both	few	fewer	many	several

Singular or Plural		
all	more	none
any	most	some

ALWAYS SINGULAR	*Everybody wants* to take a picnic lunch today.
ALWAYS PLURAL	*Many prefer* to eat at the falls.
SINGULAR OR PLURAL	*Some* of the hikers *bring* water to drink.
	Some of the water *is* warm.

To determine whether to use a singular or a plural verb with an indefinite pronoun that can be either way, check the prepositional phrase that typically follows the pronoun. An *of* phrase with a singular object requires a singular verb; an *of* phrase with a plural object requires a plural verb. (Note that the nouns *half, part,* and *percent* also take singular or plural verbs according to these same guidelines.)

SINGULAR	*Some* of the *picture was* blurry.
	Most of the *painting is* finished.
	I need clean paper, but *all is* used.
PLURAL	*Some* of the *pictures were* dark.
	Most of the *paintings are* nature scenes.
	I wanted to read the papers, but *all were* sold.

Notice from the last example in each category that the *of* phrase can be understood. (All *of the paper* is used. All *of the papers* were sold.)

Additional explanation is required for the word *none. None* is always singular when followed by an *of* phrase with a singular object but may be singular or plural when followed by an *of* phrase with a plural object, depending on the meaning intended.

SINGULAR OBJECT	*None* of the *milk is* spoiled.
PLURAL OBJECT	*None* of the *students are* at school today.
	None of the *students* in this class *is* the lead in the play.

When the object of the preposition is plural, you should decide whether to use a plural or singular verb based on whether the group is being looked at as a whole or individually. In the first of the two examples of plural objects, the students are absent from school as a whole group. But in the second example, there is not one of the individuals in the class who is the lead in the play.

The word *number* follows special rules of agreement. **The number of** (like *the number*) is always singular, but **a number of** (meaning "several") is always plural.

SINGULAR	**The number of people** in the room **has** increased. **The number is** now twenty.
PLURAL	**A number of people have** joined the celebration.

in SUMMARY

When an indefinite pronoun is used as a subject, the verb must agree with it. Some indefinite pronouns are always singular; some are always plural; and some can be either.

An indefinite pronoun that can be either singular or plural will often be followed by a prepositional phrase. The number of the object of the preposition is a clue for determining whether to use a singular or plural verb.

5.8   PRACTICE *the skill*

Underline the simple subject in each sentence. Then underline the correct verb from the choices in parentheses.

1. Everyone (*loves, love*) the book of Psalms.

2. Some of the Bible's best-known passages (*is, are*) found within its pages.

3. Each of the psalms (*is, are*) a Hebrew poem.

4. Anyone with a church background (*knows, know*) Psalm 23.

5. Many also (*quotes, quote*) from familiar passages such as Psalm 1.

6. Several of our Scripture songs (*comes, come*) from Psalms.

7. All of Psalm 1 (*has, have*) been made into a song.

8. Many of these songs, though, (*uses, use*) only a portion of a psalm.

9. Few (*learns, learn*) that *psalm* is a Greek word meaning a song accompanied by stringed instruments.

10. Most of the identified psalms (*was, were*) written by David.

REVIEW *the skill*

Write a correct form of the verb *be* to complete each sentence.

_____ 1. No one except Jesus Christ ? wiser than Solomon.

_____ 2. Many of Solomon's wise sayings ? contained in the book of Proverbs.

_____ 3. A number of these sayings ? direct teaching on the subject of wisdom.

_____ 4. Several ? also focused on specific aspects of wise living.

_____ 5. Anybody with spiritual understanding ? interested in wise living and eternal rewards.

_____ 6. Not one of the world's self-help books ? able to give adequate direction in either area.

_____ 7. Both ? addressed by the book of Proverbs.

_____ 8. Nobody ? left out in the discussions of right human relationships.

_____ 9. All of the book's teaching ? applicable to a wide audience.

_____ 10. Some of the book's final proverbs ? written by men other than Solomon.

Titles, Quotations, and Amounts

Certain subjects are viewed as singular although they may contain or consist of plural words. **Titles** are an example of this type of subject. Although words in the title may be plural, the entire title refers to one work.

Great Expectations is the play we will be performing this spring.

"Showers of Blessing" *is* the song she played.

A **quoted word or phrase** is also viewed as a single item although it may contain plural words.

"Free soil, free men, free speech, Frémont" *was* the rallying cry of the Republican party in 1856.

Alumni is the plural form of the word *alumnus.*

Finally, an **amount** is viewed as a single item although the items that make up the amount may be plural. This principle applies to measured amounts, amounts of money, and periods of time.

Six cups of flour *makes* a large batch of cookies.

Five dollars is all that I have in my wallet.

Nine months is the length of a typical school year.

Relative
Pronouns
p. 6

Antecedents
p. 4

Relative Pronouns

When a relative pronoun (e.g., *who, which, that*) is a subject, it is treated as if it has the same number as its antecedent. Therefore, in effect, the verb agrees with the antecedent.

S TrV DO
This is the *house that faces* the lake.

S TrV DO
These are the *houses that face* the woods.

In the first sentence the antecedent of the relative pronoun *that* is the singular noun *house*; therefore, the singular verb *faces* is used. The antecedent of *that* in the second sentence is the plural noun *houses*; therefore, the plural verb *face* is used.

Be aware that the antecedent can be tricky to find. Make sure that you have correctly identified the antecedent before you decide which verb to use.

S TrV DO
Hand me the *box* of crayons *that has* a sharpener built into it.

S LV PN
Hand me the box of *crayons that are* sixty-four different colors.

The meaning of the dependent clause in each sentence above helps to reveal the intended antecedent of the relative pronoun. For instance, in the first sentence it is obviously the box and not the crayons that has a sharpener built into it, so the singular noun *box* is the antecedent. But in the next sentence, it is not the box that is sixty-four different colors, but the crayons. Therefore, the plural noun *crayons* is the antecedent.

Sentences with "the only one of the" or "one of the" before a noun and a relative pronoun are sometimes a problem. Usually, "the only one of the" is used before a singular verb while "one of the" is used before a plural verb. Notice the difference in the emphasis of the following two sentences.

S TrV DO
Mrs. Pearson is *the only one of the secretaries* who *answers* the phone.

S TrV DO
Mrs. Pearson is *one of the secretaries* who *answer* the phone.

There is only one person who performs the action of the dependent clause (answering the phone) in the first sentence, but several people perform it in the second sentence.

in SUMMARY

Titles, quoted words and phrases, and amounts are considered singular, although they may contain or consist of plural words.

When a relative pronoun is a subject, it is treated as having the same number as its antecedent.

PRACTICE *the skill*

Underline the correct verb from the choices in parentheses.

1. Three years (*was, were*) the length of Jesus' public ministry.

2. Though not a long period, it was enough time to incur the resentment of the Pharisees, who (*was, were*) a powerful contemporary religious group.

3. *Separatists* (*is, are*) the name sometimes given to the Pharisees.

4. It is a title that (*identifies, identify*) the Pharisees' desire to separate from uncleanness both inside and outside of Israel.

5. The ceremonial law was the concern that (*was, were*) of great significance to the Pharisees.

6. In fact, to the law they added the tradition of the scribes, which (*was, were*) elevated to the level of Scripture.

7. For example, two thousand cubits (about two-thirds of a mile) (*was, were*) the distance that a person could travel without breaking the Sabbath.

8. The Pharisees hated Jesus, who (*was, were*) teaching against reliance on tradition.

9. "Whited sepulchres" (*was, were*) Jesus' description of these men with outward but not inward piety.

10. Written by R. Travers Herford, *The Pharisees* (*is, are*) a potential resource for further information on this religious party.

Underline the subject of the dependent clause and draw an arrow to its antecedent. Then underline the correct verb from the choices in parentheses.

1. The Sadducees were also one of the religious parties that (*was, were*) active in Jesus' day.

2. Generally, a Sadducee was a person who (*was, were*) aristocratic in background.

3. The high-priestly families of the New Testament era, who (*was, were*) of the highest class of Jewish society, belonged to the Sadducees.

4. The politically minded Sadducees differed from the Pharisees, who (*was, were*) most concerned with religious matters.

5. The Pharisees had more power among the common people, who often (*responds, respond*) to the influence of religion.

6. In fact, religion may be the force that (*rallies, rally*) the people in an oppressed country toward nationalism.

7. In beliefs, the Sadducees did not feel obliged to follow the scribal traditions that (*was, were*) so important to the Pharisees.

8. They were the only one of the religious parties that (*was, were*) in disagreement with the concept of resurrection and the reality of spiritual beings (other than God).

9. The doctrine of free will, which (*emphasizes, emphasize*) man's choice in decisions, was important to the Sadducees.

10. The Sadducees disappeared when the Jewish political power, which (*was, were*) their source of strength, was overturned by the Romans.

Pronoun-Antecedent Agreement

Just as a verb must agree with its subject, so a pronoun must agree with its antecedent, the word or phrase to which the pronoun relates.

Antecedents
p. 4

Nouns as Antecedents

The antecedent of a pronoun is often a noun or a noun phrase. The agreement of the pronoun with its antecedent is similar to that of a verb with its subject in that it reflects number. If the antecedent is singular, the pronoun must be singular. If the antecedent is plural, the pronoun must be plural.

SINGULAR	The *car* has been fixed, and *it* needs to be picked up.
PLURAL	The *cars* are lined up, and *they* are ready for the parade.

In addition, unlike verbs, pronouns often show gender as well as number. Therefore, the pronoun must also agree with the gender of its antecedent—masculine, feminine, or neuter.

MASCULINE	*James K. Polk* was a dark horse candidate for president. *He* was little known before *his* nomination.
FEMININE	*Mary Todd Lincoln* was born in Kentucky. *She* met *her* future husband in Illinois.
NEUTER	The *book* about the presidents is on the shelf. *It* is well worn.

If a singular antecedent refers to a person but does not specify gender, use a singular masculine pronoun.

The *student* is responsible for *his* conduct.

If the antecedent refers to an animal, use a neuter pronoun unless the context of the sentence indicates that the animal is a male or female.

NEUTER	The *dog* chased *its* mother down the length of the fence.
FEMININE	The *mother dog* allowed *her* excited offspring to jump up on *her* back.

Compound Antecedents

The rule for compound antecedents is the same as the rule for compound subjects. If the antecedents are joined by *and* or *both—and,* the pronoun should be plural. If they are joined by *or, nor, either—or,* or *neither—nor,* the pronoun should agree with the antecedent that is closer to it.

Conjunctions
pp. 20-21

PLURAL	*Jon and Shawn* passed *their* test.
SINGULAR	*Neither the girls in the chorus nor Mrs. Peters* remembered to bring *her* music.
PLURAL	*Beth or her sisters* will bring *their* mother.

- Although **either—or** indicates a choice, **neither—nor** is different. The meaning of **neither—nor** is the same as **both—and** plus **not.**

   Neither the girls **nor** Mrs. Peters is here.

This sentence means that the girls are not here **and** Mrs. Peters is not here. In the sentence above about bringing music, no one brought music.

- **Or** works the same way when **not** is present: it makes **not** apply to all the items named.

   Sarah has**n't** met Julie **or** Michael.

   Sarah likes strong colors—not gray, pink, or orchid.

In these sentences Sarah has met no one (neither person), and she dislikes all three colors named.

Sometimes agreement with the nearer antecedent can create an awkward sentence.

> *Either Julie or Michael* dropped *his* ticket.

You may want to reword such a sentence.

> *Either Julie* dropped *her* ticket, or *Michael* dropped *his.*

Either of the above sentences is a better choice, however, than incorrectly using a plural pronoun with a singular antecedent.

> **WRONG** | *Either Julie or Michael* dropped *their* ticket.

in SUMMARY

A pronoun must agree with its antecedent in number and gender.

If a compound antecedent is joined by *and* or *both—and*, the pronoun should be plural. If the antecedent is joined by *or, nor, either—or,* or *neither—nor*, the pronoun should agree with the antecedent that is closer to it.

5.12 PRACTICE *the skill*

Underline the correct pronoun from the choices in parentheses.

1. The New Testament character of Luke is known for (*his, their*) medical and literary abilities.

2. Paul and Luke were sometimes travel companions, and (*his, their*) acquaintance may have aided Luke in his writing of the book of Acts.

3. Luke, a physician, wrote the third Gospel, and (*its, their*) style reflects Luke's distinctive abilities.

4. Most likely, Luke's writings are the only ones in the New Testament that owe (*its, their*) authorship to a Gentile.

5. Not surprisingly, a Gentile writer took Gentiles as (*his, her*) primary audience.

6. Neither Matthew nor the other Gospels have Luke's emphasis, Christ the Son of Man, as (*its, their*) theme.

7. The events that Luke includes are often notable for (*its, their*) demonstration of Christ's humanity.

8. For example, both Christ's birth and childhood are described in more of (*its, their*) details by Luke than by any of the other Gospel writers.

9. The inclusion of the detail of Mary and (*his, her*) Magnificat shows the interest in individuals and the place of prominence given to women in the book of Luke.

10. Neither Jew nor Gentile finds (*himself, herself, themselves*) excluded from the promise of salvation for the whole world.

REVIEW *the skill*

Write an appropriate personal pronoun to complete each sentence.

_____ 1. Luke wrote the Gospel that bears his name, but _?_ was not the only book that he authored.

_____ 2. The book of Acts, an early history of the church and _?_ activities, is also attributed to Luke.

_____ 3. In _?_ first chapters, both Luke and Acts are addressed to Theophilus.

_____ 4. Bible scholars suggest in _?_ notes that Theophilus was a recent convert and possibly a Roman official.

_____ 5. The title "most excellent" (Luke 1:3) would be used for a high official in honor of _?_ rank.

_____ 6. Luke could describe some of _?_ personal experiences in Acts, having traveled with Paul.

_____ 7. The first section of the book discusses Jerusalem and the surrounding areas, focusing on _?_ reception of Christianity.

_____ 8. In the rest of the book, Paul becomes the prominent figure as _?_ ministers to the Gentiles.

_____ 9. Both missionary work and church life have _?_ beginnings in Acts.

_____ 10. Neither men nor science needs to give _?_ stamp of approval to the book of Acts, yet archaeological evidence does support the book's historicity.

Indefinite Pronouns as Antecedents

An indefinite pronoun may also be the antecedent for a personal pronoun. As with a noun antecedent, the pronoun must agree in number with the indefinite pronoun.

SINGULAR	*Either* of the options has *its* merits.
PLURAL	*Several* of the plans have *their* supporters.

Indefinite Pronouns p. 5

As you saw earlier (p. 129), some indefinite pronouns can be either singular or plural, depending on the meaning of the sentence. Often a prepositional phrase gives a clue to the number of the indefinite pronoun.

SINGULAR	*All* of the *field* has stones in *it*.
PLURAL	*All* of the *lakes* have fish in *them*.

In the first sentence *all* is considered singular because the object of the preposition that follows is the singular *field*. In the second sentence *all* is considered plural because the object of the preposition that follows is the plural *lakes*.

An indefinite pronoun does not show gender, but sometimes the context of the sentence may indicate a specific gender. If so, the pronoun should agree in gender with the meaning of the indefinite pronoun.

MASCULINE	*Either of the men would do his best if chosen.*
FEMININE	*Each of the sisters has her own interests.*
NEUTER	*One of the chairs has lost its back left leg.*

If the indefinite pronoun is singular and clearly refers to a person without indicating a specific gender, use a singular masculine pronoun. Do not use a plural personal pronoun to refer to a singular indefinite pronoun.

WRONG	*Nobody wanted their picture in the newspaper.*
RIGHT	*Nobody wanted his picture in the newspaper.*

in SUMMARY

A pronoun should agree in number and, where applicable, in gender with an indefinite pronoun that acts as its antecedent.

If an indefinite pronoun is singular and refers to a person without indicating a gender, use a singular masculine pronoun to refer to it.

5.14 PRACTICE *the skill*

Write an appropriate pronoun to complete each sentence.

_____ 1. Everybody wants to have peace in ? life.

_____ 2. But few of the world's people know how ? can have peace.

_____ 3. Christ promised His disciples that He would give them peace so that ? hearts would have no reason to be troubled (John 14:27).

_____ 4. John 11 demonstrates that neither of Lazarus's sisters felt peace in ? heart before Jesus arrived.

_____ 5. A major difference between biblical and worldly peace is that the one finds ? source in God and the other in circumstances.

_____ 6. Because circumstances change, nobody should try to base ? contentment on them.

7. The unchanging God is the only source of true peace, but all of man's sin has done _?_ part to separate man from God.

8. Many try to achieve _?_ own peace with God, but the Bible says that peace comes through the blood of Jesus Christ shed on the cross (Col. 1:20).

9. Anybody who by faith accepts that payment for _?_ sin will be at peace with God.

10. One day the world and its inhabitants will be ruled by Christ, and then both will have _?_ peace guaranteed (Is. 9:6-7).

5.15 REVIEW *the skill*

Decide whether each italicized pronoun agrees with its antecedent. If it does not, write the correct pronoun in the blank. If it does, write C in the blank.

1. Some people may not think of humility as something *they* want to have.

2. But few of the Christian virtues have *its* praises sung as highly as humility.

3. One does not have to be constantly criticizing *himself* to be humble.

4. What everyone needs is a proper opinion of *themselves*.

5. People must admit that none of their good deeds can in *itself* earn them favor with God.

6. Each must base *his* salvation solely on the merit of Jesus Christ.

7. Many accept Christ as *their* Savior but forget that Christian humility does not stop with salvation.

8. Continued dependence on God and honor for others are manifestations of humility, and both should have *its* part in the Christian's life.

9. Any of the proud ones will find *himself* resisted by God (James 4:6).

10. God knows the person who is humble, and He will bless *them* with riches, honor, and life (Prov. 22:4).

Rewrite the following paragraph, correcting the ten errors from these categories: misplaced prepositional phrases, misplaced or dangling participial phrases, fragments, comma splices, fused sentences, or disagreement.

Angels are spiritual beings that acts as the messengers of God. According to Christ's teaching, they is personal, sinless, and immortal. Created by God with a higher level of intelligence, men profit from their example of willing and complete obedience to God. Angels play an active role in the Christian's life. They rejoice over him at conversion they minister to him throughout his Christian walk. There is a great number of angels there are fewer ministering to saints today than at the beginning. A portion of the original angels rebelled against God and fell away from his position in heaven. These fallen angels can apparently be divided into two categories. The first category are fallen angels that are currently free and under the leadership of Satan. These angels are called demons and will fight with Satan against the forces in the end times of God. The other category is currently imprisoned and awaiting judgment. God punished the fallen angels in this class. For violating the order that He established in Creation.

_____

_____

_____

_____

_____

_____

_____

_____

_____

_____

_____

_____

_____

_____

_____

_____

_____

_____

POETRY AND METAPHOR

I will praise thee; for I am fearfully and wonderfully made: marvelous are thy works; and that my soul knoweth right well.

Psalm 139:14

Thinking Biblically

It is apparent that God loves poetry since one quarter of the Bible is poetry. Psalms, one of the longest books in the Bible, extols God's greatness and goodness through poetry. Because God created man in His image, man also loves poetry and has for centuries used poetry to express his deepest feelings. Toward the end of Adam's first day, the first man spontaneously wrote a poem about the first woman (Gen. 2:23). Even after Adam's sin God used poetry to express His promise of salvation (Gen. 3:15). And years later Jacob used poetry to predict Messiah's coming (Gen. 49:8–12). But sinful man used poetry to express evil thoughts and desires: Lamech, a descendant of Cain, boasted in a poem that he had murdered another man (Gen. 4:23–24). Poetry is a powerful tool—for evil as well as for good. Today, how can Christians use poetry for redemptive purposes?

What makes a poem a poem? How do you distinguish true poetry from prose broken up into lines on a page? The major characteristic of poetry that sets it apart from prose is *density*, or *compression*. A poem packs as much meaning as possible into few words.

Look again at the passage from Ecclesiastes in the chapter opener. As you read verses 1-7, all sorts of pictures come to mind—and each one is a comparison. Solomon, the writer of Ecclesiastes, here uses metaphoric language to describe the process of aging by describing the body as a house. When we read Ecclesiastes 12, not only do we discover a number of lovely word pictures, but we also get a vivid impression of a person's body slowly failing, moving toward death, which is described for us in verses 6 and 7. Can you guess what is being compared to each of the following? (See page 146 for some possible answers.)

1. the "keepers of the house" trembling
2. the "strong men" bowing themselves
3. the "grinders" ceasing because they are few
4. "those that look out of the windows" being darkened
5. the "doors" being shut when the sound of the grinding is low
6. rising up "at the voice of the bird"
7. the "daughters of music" being "brought low"
8. the "almond tree" flourishing

What is the point that Solomon is making in this poem? Verse 1 tells us. "Remember now thy Creator in the days of thy youth, while the evil days come not, nor the years draw nigh, when thou shalt say, I have no pleasure in them." Solomon is speaking to a young person—someone like you. He is warning this person that life will not always be the way it is now. Youth does not last forever; everyone grows old and loses his strength, and his body eventually fails. We need to focus on knowing and serving the Lord *now*—not wait until we are old and feeble, unable to seek and serve Him with our full strength.

Write a poem that describes a person, place, thing, or idea using metaphor. If you would like an extra challenge, write your poem as an *extended metaphor*.

Planning

✔ **Look for examples of metaphor.** Below is an example of a poem using a metaphor.

Remedy

O God, the Comfort of the mind,
The Balm of battered soul,
Quiet tumult,
Soothe desire,
Make true and plain the way
That leads to last repose.

The author uses the metaphor of ointment to develop the picture of what the Holy Spirit can do for the human soul. Read poems like "A Bird Came Down the Walk" by Emily Dickinson or "A Noiseless Patient Spider" by Walt Whitman to look for other examples of metaphor in poetry. Make notes about your favorite poems, especially noticing the images that occur to you as you read the poems.

tip

Try to write in different locales—the park, the gym, your attic, a garden. This will help to give you fresh insights.

✔ **Be observant.** Look carefully at the plants and people and things around you. What do you notice about the person sitting beside you that you've never really seen before? Make it your goal to observe five things a day while you are planning this assignment. Write your impressions down in a writing journal.

girl on bus—young, 12 (?); carrying violin in worn, black case; tennis shoes w/no laces; backpack crammed full; hair falling out of clip in back; eating red apple; key on green yarn around neck; "p. 117" written in blue ink on right hand; front row of bus

daffodils covered in snow—it's late for snow this year; it was 70 degrees last week—and now snow! the snow might hurt the flowers; the daffodils are even more bent; they look sad but very clean; I wonder if they'll survive??? look like they're sleeping

✔ **Enlist the help of your memory.** Think about moments from your childhood: the Christmas that you got the bike you asked for, the first fireflies you caught, fishing with your grandpa. The moments could be happy, funny, or sad. Write the details you remember and fill in any thoughts you have about the memories that might make your poem interesting.

ESL If you write about a memory from another country—or a different area of this country—try to include some details that will let your readers see it as a place different from where you live now.

Brainstorming
p. 327

- ✔ **Practice writing metaphors.** After you observe and write, try to describe what you see in terms of something else; for example, the tree in your front yard could be an old woman, withered and bent; your three-year-old brother could be a windstorm. What about the girl in the description above? You could draw conclusions about where she is going and where she has been.

- ✔ **Brainstorm with your classmates.** Collaborate with your peers and your teacher about the metaphors, images, and memories you have collected. Read portions of your observations aloud and collect the impressions of others about what you have described. Enlist the help of your classmates in settling on a metaphor that you want to use for your description.

tip

Your best writing will come when you write about something you care deeply about.

- ✔ **Choose a topic that you want to write about.** After your brainstorming session, choose one or two phrases or images that you want to expand upon. Have the comments from the brainstorming handy when you begin to write.

Drafting

- ✔ **Set a time limit and begin freewriting.** Allow yourself the liberty to write without worrying about making mistakes or finding the perfect word. Write without stopping for five or ten minutes. Remember that much of poetry reflects only the main points of a story. Your poem will be a very condensed version of the entire impression or image that you have. But do not worry about editing yourself for now.

- ✔ **Use the figurative language of the metaphor.** If you were writing a poem, how would you describe the moon? In "The Highwayman," Alfred Noyes calls it "a ghostly galleon tossed upon cloudy seas." In a few words, he gives a vivid picture of how the moon looks. This type of figurative language is called *metaphor.* Metaphor makes a comparison between two objects or ideas without using any comparison words such as *like* or *as.* How does metaphor make a poem more dense? The words used in a metaphor have a meaning in themselves, but they also have an unstated meaning beyond themselves. Using metaphor can double the amount of meaning the reader draws from a poem.

You can use several metaphors to make several comparisons, or you can use an extended metaphor, in which one comparison is drawn out through the entire poem. Ecclesiastes 12 is an extended metaphor; parts of the body are being compared to parts of a household throughout the entire poem. "The Highwayman," on the other hand, compares the moon to a ship, but the entire poem is not about the moon or a ship.

✔ **Adhere to certain conventions of poetry.** Contemporary poetry does not have to adhere to any line length, meter, or rhyme scheme; however, that does not mean that your poem will be entirely without structure. The following tips should make your work conform to the genre of poetry.

Your poem should be written in lines instead of sentences. Divide thoughts or sentences by breaking the lines to make the most of the text's natural rhythm and to emphasize its most important ideas. Sometimes the way the lines look on the page is actually part of the message of the poem. Look at the example below.

First Draft
An army of ants
   tramped by in fine array
Their feelers finely tuned antennae
   searched high and low for food, for enemies, for fair weather or foul.

The mighty warrior in boots, with arm held high
   came glumping to investigate their mountain retreat
only to step and step and step
   Right on their installations and
Crush
Every
One.

Farewell, Warriors Brave.
New comrades will soon be by to bear you bravely home.

Your poem should be very condensed or compressed. Only the images that are the most important ones are included in a poem. Extraneous thoughts will be cut either now or during revision. This will involve using exact vocabulary—strong verbs and nouns especially.

Your poem may include words or word order that at first seems stiff. This is a natural outcome of compressed speech. You may need to change the word order to achieve a certain effect, to eliminate unnecessary phrases, or to end on a given word (for rhyming purposes).

✔ **Consider using other sound devices.** Techniques such as **alliteration** (repeating beginning sounds) and **onomatopoeia** (using words that themselves imitate the sound they represent) are effective tools for communicating condensed thought.

And there they heard the **b**ooming of the **b**ig, **b**road drum.
The pebble hit the water with a **splish.**

Read the poem "All Day I Hear" by James Joyce for good examples of alliteration and onomatopoeia.

Revising

✔ **Read your poem aloud.** Which parts do you like? Which parts would you like to change? Are there any words or phrases that you could do without and still retain the meaning? Remember that a poem is "word music"; therefore, the language may sound a bit more lofty than your normal speech. As long as the vocabulary and syntax are appropriate for your audience, this heightened language is acceptable (and perhaps preferred).

✔ **Make sure that your poem focuses on one main topic.** Have you tried to cover too many things at one time? The topic that you chose in the prewriting stage should be obvious to you and to any others who read your draft.

✔ **Look for ways to condense your poem further.** Delete all unnecessary words and phrases. Decide which phrases you can change to make the meaning more compact. Are there any phrases that can be changed into metaphors? If so, change them. Get rid of overdone sound devices.

Sentence
Reduction
pp. 374-76

Revision

An army ~~of ants~~

    tramped ~~by in fine array~~

~~Their feelers~~ finely tuned ~~antennae~~

    ~~searched high and low~~ for food, for en^{foe}~~emies~~, for fair weather ~~or~~, foul.

The ~~mighty warrior~~^{foe} in boots, with arm^{club} held high

    ~~came~~ glump^{ed}~~ing~~ to investigate the^{hill}~~ir mountain~~ retreat

But
~~only to~~ step^{ped} and step^{ped} and step^{ped}

    ~~Right~~ on ~~their~~^{tiny} installations and

Crush^{ed}

Every

One.

_{new line} ← Farewell, (Warriors Brave.)

    New comrades will soon be by⌐ to bear you bravely home.   _{new line}

Final Draft

An army
Tramped,
finely tuned
for food, for foe, for fair weather, foul.

The foe in boots, with club held high,
    glumped to investigate the hill retreat.
But stepped and stepped and stepped
    on tiny installations and
Crushed
Every
One.

Farewell,
Warriors Brave.
New comrades will soon be by
    to bear you bravely home.

✔ **Ask a friend to read your poem.** Does he understand the comparison being made in your metaphor? Can he find the topic that you chose to focus on? Ask him to comment on what he found confusing or distracting in the poem. Are the sound devices clear to him? Does your reader have any suggestions for a title? Remember that you are not bound by others' comments, but they are a good tool to help you see your work through someone else's eyes.

Poetry and Metaphor | Chapter 5 **145**

✔ **Put your poem away for a while and then reread it.** Is the image still clear? Does your description seem fresh and vivid? Avoid clichés and trite phrases.

If you've seen a phrase in print before, it's probably trite. **tip**

Publishing

✔ **Title your piece.** Pique audience interest by adding a title that makes the reader want to find out more about your poem. A good title suggests the subject of the poem and at least hints at your approach to the topic.

✔ **Read your completed poem aloud in class or to your family.** Organize a poetry reading—perhaps including students from other language arts classes.

✔ **Make a class collection of poems.** Display a collection of poems from your class, with a picture illustrating the topic of each poem if possible.

✔ **Print your poem . . . literally.** Make a greeting card, poster, T-shirt, mug, or gift bag with your poem on it. Use calligraphy or computer-generated writing to publish your written art form. Send your poem to someone who would enjoy both the sentiment and the presentation.

Your local copy center can help you put your poem on just about anything. **tip**

✔ **Include your poem in a writing portfolio.** Any attempt at poetry is a candidate for inclusion in your permanent collection. Look at the poem again in a week or a month to see whether your feelings on the topic have changed.

Some Ideas to Consider

Physical Education
• Compare your quest for physical fitness to firefighting.

Bible
• Note the comparisons between your spiritual development and some other process.

Business
• Look at the similarities between your finances and a soufflé.

Here are some possible answers to the questions on page 141.
1. arms and hands
2. legs
3. teeth
4. eyes
5. lips
6. waking early in the morning
7. loss of hearing
8. hair turning gray or white

(The images in verse 6 probably refer to the final shutting down of the body's various systems before death.)

LETTER FOR LETTER

Frightening News

The instigator of this letter intended to pacify his hurt pride by committing geno-cide. Was he acting according to truth? What were the consequences of his sin?

Elam held tightly to his mother's hand. He felt her tighten her grip as she swept him through the city streets. She was following his father, whose strong, dark figure led the struggle to get through the crowds. The boy caught glimpses of the usual orange carts on either side of the street. In the background, he could smell and sometimes hear the Choapses River over the din of the city. Little Elam quickened his steps to keep up with his mother. Finally they stopped at the outskirts of a crowd near the heart of the great city.

Elam noticed some of his friends among the crowd. Their parents were present also. Some men near the front of the crowd were shouting, and everyone seemed to be talking at once. Presently, Elam noticed a court official approaching the crowd. Guards surrounded the official on every side and pushed people out of the way.

"Make way there!" A burly soldier threw Elam's father to the side.

Identified by his clothing as a king's courier, the man held a scroll at his side and, having approached the door of the satrap's mansion, handed the scroll to a guard. The guard took it and was about to tack it to the heavy wooden door—

"Read it!" a man from the crowd yelled.

Several others took up the call. "Read the command!" "What does it say?"

The official took the notice back and with his hand quieted the crowd.

"By royal decree of King Xerxes, sovereign of all Persia. There is an order 'to destroy, to kill, and to cause to perish, all Jews, both young and old, little children and women, in one day, even upon the thirteenth day of the twelfth month, which is the month Adar, and to take the spoil of them for a prey.' This is the command of the king. Let every man hasten to obey his will."

The courier repeated the decree in three other dialects, but no one really heard him. The cries, moans, and angry threats that followed drowned out his voice.

For the full story, read the book of Esther.
- *Who instigated this decree?*
- *What truths was the instigator of this decree ignoring?*
- *If God had not intervened, what would have been the results of this decree?*
- *A second letter was sent throughout the kingdom. What did this decree say?*
- *What do you think was the response of the Jews to the second letter?*

Personal Response

Mordecai told Esther that God would certainly deliver the Jewish people with or without her help. However, he reminded Esther that God might have brought her into such a high position "for such a time as this." God brought you into the world at the perfect time to accomplish His will for you. Esther lost her parents and lived in a strange country. Maybe, like Esther, you have gone through some changes that you would not have chosen. Perhaps there is something about the way you look or about your personality that you wish you could change. God has made you the way you are for a purpose, and He will use everything about you for His glory. Write about some things that you have wished you could change and then thank God for those things.

You are an eyewitness to the events that happen around you. Every day you see people and places and things that may never be the same. Today's bus ride could be tomorrow's headlines.

In 1989 Andreas Ramos witnessed the fall of an empire. He was at the Berlin Wall in then-communist East Germany when thousands of people literally pulled the concrete barrier down with hammers and drills and their bare hands. Note how Ramos captures the tense thrill of driving his VW through throngs of people heady with the taste of new liberty. In this chapter you will write about an event to which you have been an eyewitness.

A Personal Account of the Fall of the Berlin Wall

by Andreas Ramos

On Thursday, the 9th of November, 1989, and Friday the 10th, the TV and radio in Denmark was filled with news about the events in Berlin. The Wall was about to fall. On Saturday morning, the 11th of November, I heard on the radio that East Germany was collapsing. At the spur of the moment, I suggested to Karen, my Danish wife, and two Danish friends, Rolf Reitan and Nana Kleist, that we should go to Berlin. We talked about what one should take to a revolution: it was a very cold, dry November day. We settled on a dozen boiled eggs, a thermos pot of coffee, extra warm clothes, sleeping bags, and a battery-powered radio. The four of us packed into my 25 year old Volkswagen bug and we drove off.

Along with everyone else headed towards Berlin were thousands of East Germans; they had been in West Europe for a blitz tour with the kids and grandmother in the back, to look around and drive back again. Without passports, they had simply driven through the borders. Amused West European border guards let them pass. They smiled and waved to everyone.

At the checkpoint, which is a 25 lane place, people milled around. It was nearly 3 a.m. by now. It had taken us three hours to go through the traffic jam of cheering and applause. West Germans are environmentally conscious and if they're stuck in traffic, they turn off the engine and push their cars. East Germans, on the other hand, sat in their Trabis, putting out clouds of exhaust. Everyone had their radios on and everywhere was music. People had climbed up into trees, signs, buildings, everything, to wave and shout. Television teams stood around filming everything. People set up folding tables and were handing out cups of coffee. A Polish engineer and his wife had run out of gas; someone gave us some rope, so we tied the rope to his car and pulled them along.

We walked through the border. On both sides the guard towers were empty and the barbed wire was shoved aside in great piles. Large signs told us that we needed sets of car documents. The East German guard asked if we had documents. I handed him my Danish cat's vaccination documents, in Danish. He waved us through.

We walked to Potsdammer Platz. This used to be the center of Berlin. All traffic once passed through the Potsdammer Platz. Now it was a large empty field, bisected by the wall. Nearby was the mound that was the remains of Hitler's bunker, from which he commanded Germany into total defeat. We talked to Germans and many said that the next break in the wall would be here. It was still very dark and cold at 5 a.m. Perhaps 7,000 people were pressed together, shouting, cheering, clapping. We pushed through the crowd. From the East German side we could hear the sound of heavy machines. With a giant drill, they were punching holes in the wall. Every time a drill poked through, everyone cheered. The banks of klieg lights would come on. People shot off fireworks and emergency flares and rescue rockets. Many were using hammers to chip away at the wall. There were countless holes. At one place, a crowd of East German soldiers looked through a narrow hole. We reached through and shook hands. They couldn't see the crowd so they asked us what was going on and we described the scene for them. Someone lent me a hammer and I knocked chunks of rubble from the wall, dropping several handfuls into my pocket. The wall was made of cheap brittle concrete: the Russians had used too much sand and water.

VERB USE

Verbs have many functions, forms, and types; in fact, they may be the most complicated of the parts of speech. This chapter examines verbs in detail so that you can understand how verbs work and how to use them effectively in the sentences that you write.

Auxiliaries

An auxiliary, or "helping verb," never appears alone. It joins the main verb to make up the complete verb, or simple predicate, of a clause. (Of course, some clauses may contain only a main verb without any auxiliary.) Auxiliaries act as grammatical signals and contribute certain minor meanings to the complete verb.

Auxiliaries
pp. 10-11

Auxiliary	Meaning	Use	Example
will, shall	future	with the basic present form of the verb	Each of us *will speak* for five minutes. *Shall* I *speak* a word for you?

Auxiliary	Meaning	Use	Example
have (has, had)	perfect	with the past participle	Ivonne *has spoken* with the chairman already. When I got there, she *had* just *spoken* with him. In two minutes he *will have spoken* for an hour.
be (am, is, are, was, were, being, been)	progressive	with the present participle	Tram Nguyen *was speaking* just then.
	passive	with the past participle	That word *was spoken* just in time.
can, could, may, might, should, would, must, ought (to)	modal expressions of ability, possibility, obligation, necessity, etc.	with the basic present form of the verb (use only one at a time)	Anyone *can speak* who wants to. We *should speak* up for the Lord.
do (does, did)	emphasis, question inversion, negative—all in present or past tense only	with the basic present form of the verb	That parrot *does speak* too much. *Do* you often *speak* in public? Ed *did* not *speak* at our meeting.

Principal Parts

Almost all verbs have three basic forms called their **principal parts:** present, past, and past participle. Because we use these principal parts (or "main" parts) to make all the different forms of verbs, an effective writer must understand the principal parts to use verbs correctly.

Principal Parts
p. 11

---

tip

Always use the past participle after any form of the auxiliary *have*.

Regular Verbs

Regular verbs form their past and past participle forms by adding *d* or *ed* to the first principal part (or present form) of the verb. Most verbs fall into this category.

Adding Suffixes
p. 433

brush	brushed	brushed
serve	served	served

Irregular Verbs

Irregular verbs form the past and past participle some way other than by adding *d* or *ed* to the first principal part. Many common verbs fall into this category. A dictionary lists the principal parts of any verb, usually right after the pronunciation of the verb.

All three principal parts of the verb are the same.

| hit | hit | hit |
| shut | shut | shut |

Two principal parts of the verb are the same.

| dig | dug | dug |
| mean | meant | meant |

All three principal parts of the verb are different.

| bite | bit | bitten |
| fly | flew | flown |

in SUMMARY

The three **principal parts** of the verb are the **present, past,** and **past participle.**

Regular verbs form the second and third principal parts by adding *ed* to the first principal part.

Irregular verbs form the second and third principal parts by some method other than by adding *ed* to the first principal part.

6.1 PRACTICE *the skill*

Underline each complete verb. Write *Aux* above each auxiliary. Be prepared to identify the principal part of the verb and to tell whether the verb is regular or irregular.

1. The name of Notre Dame de Paris, probably the most famous cathedral in the world, means "Our Lady of Paris" in English.

2. Maurice de Sully, a bishop of Paris, initiated the construction of the cathedral in 1163.

3. At the time of his death in 1196, he had served as overseer of the construction for thirty-six years.

4. After the completion of the main part of the building in 1250, additions continued for the next hundred years.

5. Centuries after its construction, Notre Dame remains famous for its Gothic architecture, flying buttresses, gargoyles, statues, and rosette windows.

6. The rosette windows in Notre Dame still retain the stained glass from the thirteenth century.

7. During the centuries (and revolutions) following construction, Notre Dame sustained a large amount of architectural damage.

8. Victor Hugo chose Notre Dame as the setting for his 1831 novel, *The Hunchback of Notre Dame*.

9. Eugène Viollet-le-Duc, like many others, had read Hugo's novel and had become interested in Notre Dame and its architecture.

10. Viollet-le-Duc became the overseer of Notre Dame's restoration (1845-1868) to its original beauty.

6.2 REVIEW *the skill*

Write the correct past or past participle form of the verb in parentheses.

_____ 1. Construction of the Arc de Triomphe, or Arch of Triumph, was (*begin*) by Napoleon in 1806.

_____ 2. Napoleon had just (*win*) the Battle of Austerlitz the year before.

_____ 3. He (*want*) to honor his victorious army with a triumphal arch similar to those that the Romans had (*build*).

_____ 4. However the arch was not (*finish*) until 1836, fifteen years after Napoleon's death.

_____ 5. Construction had (*halt*) in 1814 at the time of Napoleon's abdication and had not (*resume*) until 1826.

_____ 6. Today this triumphal arch, the largest in the world, commemorates all the soldiers who (*die*) in World War I.

_____ 7. On November 11, 1920, the French (*honor*) these soldiers by burying an unknown soldier in a tomb located beneath the Arc.

_____ 8. Jean-François-Thérèse Chalgrin, the Arc's designer, (*incorporate*) large relief sculptures on each side of the Arc's legs.

_____ 9. Starting in 1923, a flame called the Flame of Remembrance, also dedicated to the heroes of World War I, has (*burn*) beneath the Arc.

_____ 10. The Arc de Triomphe has (*rest*) on a hilltop at one end of the Champs Elysées, one of the world's most famous streets, for almost two hundred years.

Tense

A verb's tense tells the reader the time frame of the action or state of being expressed by the verb.

Simple Tenses

Verbs have three simple tenses: present, past, and future.

Present tense verbs express either a state that is true now or an action that occurs habitually. The present tense is formed from the first principal part of the verb.

> Pierce *likes* to go places with his older brother Perry.

> They *walk* to basketball practice together every day.

> **ESL** The first principal part of nearly every verb is used almost unchanged throughout the present tense, simply adding *s* or *es* to agree with third-person singular subjects (see p. 118). However, three verbs are irregular. As you know, **be** uses **is, am,** and **are** instead of a principal part (p. 118). Two other verbs have an irregular form for third-person singular in the present: **have** ("he **has**") and *do* ("he **does,**" which is irregular only in pronunciation).

Past tense verbs show a state or an action that occurred in the past. The past tense of the verb is the same as the second principal part.

> Perry *was* taller than Pierce until last year, when Pierce *grew* several inches.

Future tense verbs show a state or an action that will occur in the future. The future tense of the verb is formed by adding the auxiliary *will* (or *shall*) to the first principal part.

> Pierce *will be* taller than Perry soon.

> *Shall* we *watch* them in tonight's basketball game?

tip

Today *shall* is used primarily with the first-person pronouns *I* and *we* in questions of preference or in formal statements.

Perfect Tenses

The perfect tenses express completion of a state or an action. Perfect tenses are formed from the third principal part and a form of the auxiliary *have*. The name of each perfect tense matches the form of *have* used with the past participle.

The **present perfect tense** describes a state or an action that is completed during the present time period or one that began in the past and has continued up to the present moment. Use the auxiliary *have* or *has* to form the present perfect tense.

> The weather *has been* rainy all week.

> We *have waited* in vain for sunny skies.

The **past perfect tense** describes an action that was completed (or a state that existed) before a certain time in the past. Use the auxiliary *had* to form the past perfect tense.

> The weather *had been* clear before this storm front developed.

> When the rain began, the groundskeeper *had* just *prepared* the soccer field.

Perfect Gerund
p. 73

The **future perfect tense** describes an action that will be completed (or a state that will exist) by or before a certain time in the future. Use the auxiliaries *will have* (or *shall have*) to form the future perfect tense.

By tomorrow, the soccer field *will have been* wet for several days.

The soccer team *will have practiced* indoors several times before the rain stops.

One unusual thing about English is the expression of future time in dependent clauses that begin either with **if** or with a time-word such as **when, while, as, before** and **after**. Instead of future tense, these dependent clauses use the simple present to express future time.

When you **get** home, please feed the dog.

If you **do**n't **find** dog food on the shelf, you will need to get some from the pantry.

When the verb in the independent clause is in the future perfect tense, the *if* clause or time clause can use either present tense or present perfect to express future time.

When I **have done** (or: When **I finish**) these two exercises, I will have completed my homework.

in SUMMARY

A **present tense verb** expresses either a state that is true now or an action that occurs habitually.

A **past tense verb** shows action that occurred or a state that existed in the past.

A **future tense verb** shows action that will occur or a state that will exist in the future.

A **present perfect tense verb** describes an action completed or a state that existed during the present time period or one that began in the past and has continued up until the present moment.

A **past perfect tense verb** describes an action that occurred or a state that existed before a certain time in the past.

A **future perfect tense verb** describes an action that will occur or a state that will exist by or before a certain time in the future.

PRACTICE *the skill*

Underline each complete verb. Then identify its tense as *present*, *present perfect*, *past*, *past perfect*, *future*, or *future perfect*.

————————————— 1. On Salisbury Plain in southern England stand gigantic hand-hewn stones.

————————————— 2. Where have they come from?

————————————— 3. Perhaps scientists will never know the answer to that question.

————————————— 4. Early scientists and historians imagined the stones as a temple of sorts.

————————————— 5. By the end of the 1950s, archeologist R. J. C. Arkinson had excavated several areas around Stonehenge.

————————————— 6. According to some historians, Stonehenge monument took about one thousand years to construct.

————————————— 7. In the first phase of construction, builders dug a ring of fifty-six shallow pits.

————————————— 8. Mathematicians have calculated the weight of the stones at approximately forty-five tons.

————————————— 9. By the time they finished, the builders had transported at least eighty-two stones from Wales to form the original double circle of Stonehenge.

————————————— 10. After this trip, my friend Fayez will have visited Stonehenge four times.

REVIEW *the skill*

Write a correct form of the verb in parentheses.

————————————— 1. The construction of any large structure (*involve*) both technical skill and danger.

————————————— 2. The builders of Stonehenge (*lift*) seven-ton lintels to the tops of upright stones.

————————————— 3. Most modern cranes (*hoist*) between one and 250 tons at a time.

————————————— 4. Builders (*secure*) the lintels with peg-and-socket joints.

————————————— 5. Before Stonehenge was built, carpenters (*use*) the peg-and-socket joint for centuries.

————————————— 6. The purpose of Stonehenge (*be*) mysterious since its discovery.

_____ 7. Originally, historians (*think*) that Stonehenge was solely a religious site.

_____ 8. Recent studies of Stonehenge (*focus*) on its remarkable correspondences with solar and lunar cycles.

_____ 9. Historians no doubt (*continue*) their study of Stonehenge.

_____ 10. Probably many more people (*write*) on the subject by the end of the twenty-first century.

Progressive Tenses

Each of the simple tenses and perfect tenses also has a progressive form. The **progressive tense** of the verb shows continuous action. Use a form of *be* as an auxiliary and the *ing* form of the verb to form the progressive tense. The form of *be* reflects the simple or perfect tense of the verb.

Present Participles
p. 64

Tense	Meaning	Form of *Be*	Example
Present Progressive	present continuing action	present tense of *be: am, is, are*	I *am learning* Spanish after school. Señora Suarez *is teaching* me. We *are studying* the uses of subjuntivo.
Past Progressive	past continuing action	past tense of *be: was, were*	We *were reviewing* my homework when the power went out. The lightning *was flashing* at the time.
Future Progressive	continuing action in the future	future tense of *be: will be*	My family *will be leaving* for Mexico in July.
Present Perfect Progressive	continuing action performed during the present time period	present perfect tense of *be: has been, have been*	My father *has been planning* this trip for several months. All of us *have been looking* forward to it since then.
Past Perfect Progressive	continuing action completed before a certain time in the past	past perfect tense of *be: had been*	I *had been hoping* for a chance to visit Mexico or Central America.
Future Perfect Progressive	continuing action that will be completed before a certain time in the future	future perfect tense of *be: will have been, shall have been*	By the time we leave, Señora Suarez *will have been helping* me for two years.

PRACTICE *the skill*

Underline each verb. Then identify its tense.

_____ 1. Our class has been studying the Sears Tower in Chicago.

_____ 2. We are planning a trip to visit the Windy City.

_____ 3. On Monday our class will have been trying to get tickets to the Tower for two months.

_____ 4. Our teacher is hoping for the tickets in the mail soon.

_____ 5. By the time of its completion in 1974, the builders had been working on the Sears Tower for four years.

_____ 6. Until 1996 the Sears Tower had the title of tallest building.

_____ 7. In the 1990s the builders of the twin Petronas Towers in Malaysia succeeded with a taller structure—by about thirty feet.

_____ 8. In the future many other builders will probably seek the title for their structures.

_____ 9. The 1454-foot Sears Tower has been impressing visitors for many years.

_____ 10. The Sears Tower will be rising above the rest of the Chicago skyline for years to come.

REVIEW *the skill*

Write the progressive form of each italicized verb. Do not change the tense of the verb.

_____ 1. Premier John Joseph Cahill *will hear* Goossens's recommendations for a new opera house in Sydney, New South Wales, Australia.

_____ 2. Architect Jørn Utzon *had submitted* a unique design for the new opera house.

_____ 3. The committee *awarded* his design first prize in 1957.

_____ 4. An American team of architects *will have submitted* the second-place design.

_____ 5. Some *describe* the roof of the Sydney Opera House as sails of boats.

_____ 6. Utzon himself *had taken* inspiration from palm leaves.

_____ 7. The platforms in Mexican architecture *have inspired* Utzon as well.

_____ 8. Construction of the beautiful roof shells *proved* extremely difficult.

_____ 9. Glazed and matte tiles *cover* the concrete shells.

_____ 10. From design to dedication, the Sydney Opera House *took* over sixteen years to complete.

6.7 USE *the skill*

Complete each sentence by writing a verb in an appropriate tense. Use a variety of verbs and tenses.

_____ 1. From 1948 until 1989 Germany _?_ two separate countries: East Germany and West Germany.

_____ 2. The Allied Powers _?_ the capital city of Berlin as well.

_____ 3. In the 1950s thousands of persons suffering under communism _?_ through East Berlin into West Berlin.

_____ 4. By 1961 approximately one thousand East Germans _?_ to West Germany every day.

_____ 5. By August of 1961, East German police _?_ a wall separating East and West Berlin.

_____ 6. More than one hundred seventy people _?_ during escape attempts at the Berlin Wall.

_____ 7. Border guards _?_ most of those who died.

_____ 8. However, no one else _?_ at the Berlin Wall.

_____ 9. During the late 1980s, partly as a result of negotiations by United States President Ronald Reagan, the East German government _?_.

_____ 10. In November, 1989, the Western world watched their television sets in amazement: West German guards and onlookers _?_ the Berlin Wall!

Voice

Like tense, voice is another characteristic of verbs. Voice signals the role of the subject in relation to the verb. Sentences with intransitive verbs and linking verbs are in active voice. A sentence with a transitive verb can be in either active or passive voice. In **active voice,** the subject of the clause is the doer of the action. In **passive voice,** the subject of the clause is the receiver of the action.

Passive Infinitive
p. 77

Active or Passive
p. 363

ACTIVE VOICE	The frog jumped from the pond to the shore. The frog was green. The frog caught an insect.
PASSIVE VOICE	The insect was caught by the frog.

You can identify a passive sentence by looking at the verb. A passive sentence contains a form of the auxiliary verb *be* followed by the past participle form of the transitive verb.

As with perfect and progressive tenses, the tense of the passive voice verb matches the tense of the auxiliary.

Tense	Active Voice	Passive Voice
Present	The chef *prepares* the meal.	The meal *is prepared* by the chef.
Past	The chef *prepared* the meal.	The meal *was prepared* by the chef.
Future	The chef *will prepare* the meal.	The meal *will be prepared* by the chef.
Present Perfect	The chef *has prepared* the meal.	The meal *has been prepared* by the chef.
Past Perfect	The chef *had prepared* the meal.	The meal *had been prepared* by the chef.
Future Perfect	The chef *will have prepared* the meal.	The meal *will have been prepared* by the chef.

Active voice usually makes sentences more direct and interesting. To change a sentence from passive voice to active voice, make the doer of the action the subject of the sentence.

PASSIVE VOICE	The fire alarm was heard throughout the building.
ACTIVE VOICE	Everyone in the building heard the fire alarm.

ESL

Most English textbooks for native speakers present only the usual passive forms with *be,* as seen above. However, in spoken English you may also notice a special passive using *get* instead of *be* as the auxiliary.

ACTIVE	The falling tree limb **hit** him.
NORMAL PASSIVE	He *was hit* by the falling tree limb.
GET-PASSIVE	He *got hit* by the falling tree limb.

As in this example, *get*-passives usually express unfavorable occurrences. Because they tend to be informal, you should usually use the normal *be*-passive in your writing for school or business.

In **active voice,** the subject of the clause is described or is the doer of the action.

In **passive voice,** the subject of the clause receives the action. A passive sentence contains a form of the auxiliary *be* followed by the past participle form of the transitive verb.

6.8

PRACTICE *the skill*

Underline the verb in each independent clause. Then identify its voice as *active* or *passive.*

_____ 1. After receiving the law on Mount Sinai, Moses told the Israelites that God had commanded the construction of the tabernacle.

_____ 2. The tabernacle, a place of worship and sacrifice, was a huge portable tent.

_____ 3. The people were asked to bring offerings of valuable metals, expensive cloths, oil for light, spices for incense, wood, and precious stones for the construction of the tabernacle.

_____ 4. The people were bringing so much that Moses finally told them to stop.

_____ 5. God filled the head workmen, Bezaleel and Aholiab, with His Spirit. Therefore, the tabernacle was completed according to God's plan.

_____ 6. The tabernacle's construction included weaving, dyeing, and embroidering, as well as carpentry and metalworking.

_____ 7. The tabernacle comprised the outer court, the holy place, and the holy of holies.

_____ 8. The laver, the altar of burnt offering, and the holy place were housed in the outer court.

_____ 9. Only the priests were allowed to enter the holy place.

_____ 10. Separated from the rest of the holy place by a thick veil, the holy of holies was actually an inner room accessible only to the high priest.

Rewrite each sentence, changing the voice of each passive verb to active. Do not change the tense of the verb.

1. David was told by God that his son, and not he, would build the temple.

   _____

   _____

2. All the plans for the temple were made by David, but it was built by Solomon.

   _____

   _____

3. The collection of materials for the temple was begun by David during Solomon's childhood.

   _____

   _____

4. The basic layout of the tabernacle was followed by workers in the temple's construction.

   _____

   _____

   _____

5. Hiram, the Phoenician king, was requested by Solomon to send skilled laborers for the temple's construction.

   _____

   _____

6. That the Phoenician and Israelite workmen work together was decreed by Solomon.

   _____

   _____

7. Cedar, cypress, and juniper wood was imported from Lebanon.

   _____

   _____

8. Purple dye from Tyre was probably used for coloring the embroidered curtains in the temple.

   _____

   _____

9. Masons were commanded to mine and prepare large stones from quarries at Tyre and Byblos.

_____

_____

10. Hiram was asked by Solomon to send a man skilled in engraving to help with the furnishing of the temple, so Huram, a master craftsman, was sent.

_____

_____

Mood

English verbs can also express different moods. The mood of a verb reflects the attitude of the speaker or writer. The three moods of verbs in English are indicative, imperative, and subjunctive.

Indicative

The most common mood is the **indicative mood.** Sentences in the indicative mood consist mostly of factual sentences—sentences that indicate something. Most English sentences are in the indicative mood.

> The Needhams recently bought a new beagle.

> Greta and Carl take turns walking their dog around the neighborhood.

Four Types of Sentences
p. 37

Imperative

Sentences in the **imperative mood** give direct commands. Use the simple present form of the verb, with no auxiliary. Often the subject is understood *you,* although the *you* can be stated for clarity or emphasis.

> Carl, catch the dog!

> Look at that dog run.

Understood Subjects
p. 34

Subjunctive

The **subjunctive mood** is used less frequently today than it was in the past. Sentences in the subjunctive mood often express the idea that something is untrue though perhaps desired. Use the subjunctive mood to express a wish or a condition contrary to fact. These are clauses that begin with *if* (condition clauses) and that speak of something known to be untrue (contrary to fact). However, if you do not know whether a condition is true or not, use an indicative verb.

UNKNOWN	If Greta *is watching,* she must be amused.
UNTRUE	If Greta *were watching,* she would be amused.

The indicative mood in the first sentence tells us that Greta's actions are unknown. We do not know whether she is watching her brother chase the dog or not. The subjunctive mood in the second sentence tells us that Greta is definitely not watching the chase. Do not use the indicative mood for a condition contrary to fact: only the subjunctive mood is acceptable in standard English usage. Remember, "I say 'if I *were* you' because I am *not* you."

The forms of verbs in the subjunctive mood are familiar forms used differently. To make a statement about something in the present or future, use the simple past form of the verb. If the verb is *be,* use *were* (not *was*). To make a statement about something in the past, use the past perfect form of the verb.

PRESENT	If their dog *had* more obedience training, Carl could control it more easily.
PRESENT	I wish that Greta *were* here now.
PAST	When she heard the story, Greta wished that Carl *had paid* closer attention to the dog.
PAST	Perhaps Carl would have caught the dog more quickly if Greta *had been* here to help.

ESL In conversation you will sometimes hear English speakers use *was* instead of *were* as the present subjunctive of *be*. In written or formal use, however, *was* is considered nonstandard for conditions contrary to fact.

in SUMMARY

Use the **indicative mood** for factual sentences.

Use the **imperative mood** for commands.

Use the **subjunctive mood** for a wish or a condition contrary to fact.

6.10 PRACTICE *the skill*

Identify the mood of each italicized verb as indicative, imperative, or subjunctive.

_____ 1. Jill's cousin Martin *lives* in Newbury, England.

_____ 2. Martin recently received a message from his employer in Ireland saying, "Martin, please *take* the Wickens file to our Paris office tomorrow."

_____ 3. If he *had received* the message earlier, his travel arrangements wouldn't have been so rushed.

_____ 4. His parents suggested, "*Try* the Chunnel. It's the fastest way to get there."

_____ 5. The Channel Tunnel, also called the Chunnel, *connects* Great Britain and France by an underground railway system running beneath the English Channel.

_____ 6. Martin went to his friend Karl's house to reserve some Eurostar tickets online. If Martin's computer *had been* operational, he could have done it at home.

_____ 7. The Eurostar, the high-speed passenger train running through the Chunnel, *transported* Martin across the Channel in just twenty minutes.

_____ 8. If Martin *had failed* to make the trip in time, his job could have been in jeopardy.

_____ 9. When Martin returned home the next day, he found an e-mail message from Jill marked "*Reply* ASAP."

_____ 10. Jill told him later, "If you *had told* me you were going to Paris, I would have told you to visit some missionary friends of mine, the Eaveses."

Write a sentence in the mood indicated in parentheses.

1. Tell someone how he can help in the garden. (*imperative*)

   _____

   _____

2. What would you do if you were caught inside a glass box? (*subjunctive*)

   _____

   _____

3. Write a sentence about a garden in a glass box. (*indicative*)

   _____

   _____

4. Tell your friend she needs to see the snowfall. (*imperative*)

   _____

   _____

5. Describe the sound of leaves in the wind. (*indicative*)

   _____

   _____

6. If it snowed leaves, what effect would it have on your yard? (*subjunctive*)

   _____

   _____

7. If you were to adapt a novel for a stage performance, which novel would you pick? (*subjunctive*)

   _____

   _____

8. Warn someone standing in the road that a car is coming. (*imperative*)

   _____

   _____

9. Write a sentence about gorillas that have been trained to "talk" with their hands. (*indicative*)

   _____

   _____

10. If your friends were in a play about car-driving gorillas, what would you bring them for an opening night gift? (*subjunctive*)

    _____

    _____

Rewrite the paragraph, correcting the ten errors from these categories: misplaced prepositional phrases, fragments, comma splices, fused sentences, subject-verb disagreement, pronoun-antecedent disagreement, and incorrect verb use (principal parts, tense, or mood).

The idea of building an underwater tunnel beneath the English Channel date back to 1802. In 1994, when a transport company called Eurotunnel completed the Channel Tunnel, a fixed link from Britain to mainland Europe. The company is using satellite technology to find the best path for the Channel Tunnel. The Chunnel, as it were commonly called, were actually the result of a collaborative effort of the British and the French, the Chunnel consists of three separate tunnels; one is for repairs, and two have one-way tracks for freight and passenger trains. If anyone want to ride the passenger train, they can bought tickets over the Internet to London, Paris, or Brussels.

_____

_____

_____

_____

_____

_____

_____

_____

_____

_____

_____

_____

_____

_____

_____

_____

_____

_____

_____

For the nation and kingdom that will not serve thee shall perish; yea, those nations shall be utterly wasted.

Isaiah 60:12

Imagine being on the scene when Lewis and Clark first saw the Pacific Ocean. Or when Leonardo da Vinci was holding art lessons. Or when Mount Vesuvius erupted. Or when commanders signed surrender papers at the end of World War II. Or when a man stepped onto the moon. Dramatic historical events like these can be obviously significant to everyone. To millions of people watching their TVs when Neil Armstrong took that little hop into the lunar dust, the importance of the action was apparent. And many people recorded what they saw and how they felt in diaries and essays and books.

Other events may seem rather commonplace to the observers at the time. Probably the man who wrote about da Vinci's daily work was not completely aware his words would be studied and reprinted for centuries. But in all cases, much of what we know about large and small dramatic events comes from what eyewitnesses record for us. Until the invention of still and motion picture cameras, such records were preserved only in words and art.

Choose a dramatic event that you have witnessed. It can be something from your own family—someone getting married, finding a lost dog, attending a family reunion. It can be from school history—winning a championship, having a famous visitor, meeting the new principal.

Or perhaps you can draw on local or national history for some event to recount. Whatever you choose, your writing should

1. Use specific, concrete details, such as names and dates, actions and speech.

2. Engage as many senses as possible.

3. Reveal your response to the scene.

Planning

—————————————————————————————**tip**

Keep a journal with you so that you record events as they happen.

✔ **Train yourself to be observant.** What in Ramos's piece about the Berlin Wall gives you the sense of being there? The author engages your senses of sight, hearing, touch, taste, and smell. There is no substitute for such description in getting a reader to feel a part of the action. Can't you hear the commotion—violins and accordions playing, horns honking, people talking and cheering, drills and hammers tearing at the wall? Can you smell the exhaust from the cars? Can you taste the coffee? Can you see that huge, mysterious light from the tens of thousands of headlights shining through a cloud of Trabi fumes? Can you imagine the rough rope in your hands and the crush of passing through such a crowd of people? Look around you right now—at the people, the place, the circumstances. Note what your five senses tell you: what do you see? smell? taste? feel? hear?

✔ **Decide on an event to report about.** Start looking for an event going on currently. The event may seem mundane to you now, but some time in the future your eyewitness account may become famous! Not every personal report records world news like Ramos's. You might tell about a basketball game or about working backstage at the school play. Report on the bus ride to school or a trip to the grocery store.

Drafting

✔ **Use specific details.** Ramos names places—Potsdammer Platz—and people—his wife, Karen, and his friends Rolf and Nana. It is 3:00 A.M. on November 12. The cars are not just cars—they are Trabis or a twenty-five-year-old Volkswagen. Being specific makes the scene real for the reader. Write about the specifics of your event—the clothing, the weather, the street noises.

Try changing some of the common nouns in your piece to proper nouns. **tip**

Proper Nouns
p. 2

✔ **Connect personally with what you describe.** Ramos says that the traffic jam was spectacular. How does that compare with the information that over 20,000 Germans were gathered near the border? The word *spectacular* interjects the writer's emotion into what might have been a strictly objective report. We suddenly feel the scene with the writer. Most of the time, traffic jams are not considered happy events. Ramos inserts himself through humor and irony as well. He reports that he and his wife and friends talk about "what one should take to a revolution." His comment is understatement, with humorous effect. He hands a guard his cat's vaccination papers, and they are accepted. The lightness of the moment—against so hard a history—is comical. And then there is irony: the wall that had divided a people for so long and cost so many lives was made only of "cheap, brittle concrete."

Paragraph
Organization
p. 338

✔ **Write your account in chronological order.** Most personal reports are organized from what happens first to what happens last. The Berlin Wall piece starts with the four friends jumping into the car and heading for Germany and ends with the author's participating in breaking down the wall. Chronological order uses words like *by, during,* and *later* as well as actual dates to show time progression. Although most of your eyewitness report will use chronological order, parts of your piece may include spatial or order-of-importance writing. For example, Ramos uses spatial order in describing the traffic jam: he records the cars, the radios, the noise, and the folding tables at the checkpoint.

Revising

✔ **Read your draft over.** Is your report an accurate account of what you witnessed? Have you used specific and sensory details? Can your reader sense the significance of the event? Is the order understandable?

✔ **Allow someone else to read your account.** A peer's comments will help you know what you need to work on. Ask your peer reader to tell you what is unclear or missing from your report. Think about the peer responses but do not feel bound by them. Your teacher will also probably want to read your report.

✔ **Make corrections based on peer feedback and your own reading.** Retype your report to reflect the input of your peers and/or teacher. Double-check to make sure that this version is free of errors. Do not allow new errors to creep in as you make corrections.

tip

If you are going to submit your piece to a magazine, check the publication guidelines of the magazine before reprinting.

✔ **Make a clean copy.** Once you have corrected the errors in your piece, print out a fresh copy of your report.

✔ **Proofread your clean copy.** Use multiple read-throughs to check further for spelling, punctuation, grammar, and usage problems. Look at previous papers you have written to note the kinds of errors you are likely to make and then read your paper looking especially for those.

Proofreading p. 346

Thinking Biblically

An eyewitness report from a credible person can challenge people's beliefs about God as almost nothing else can. It is one thing to have heard about God's marvelous works; it is quite another to have—with proof—experienced God at work. John 9 records Jesus's healing of the blind man. This man's healing caused quite a stir, and the Pharisees, not wanting people to believe in Jesus, desired to prove that Jesus was not the Christ. They summoned the man who had been blind in order to discredit his story. His simple testimony thoroughly frustrated them. "One thing I know," he said, "whereas I was blind, now I see" (John 9:25). His testimony did not convince the Pharisees to accept Jesus's claims. It did, however, show them that those claims could not be ignored. Are you an eyewitness of the power of God? Perhaps you could testify to being healed, to having a financial need met, to seeing a great change in a friend's life, or to experiencing a great change in your own life.

Publishing

tip

Include photographs from the event you report on to make your piece more publishable.

✔ **Submit your report to a magazine or newspaper.** If your eyewitness report has local significance, your city's newspaper may be interested in publishing it. Use caution in naming names in a published report. Some people will not want their names mentioned in print; others will not mind if you check with them first.

✔ **Put the eyewitness report in your portfolio.** This report is a personal one that you will want to keep and share with others in the future. Make it a part of your permanent writing collection.

✔ **Read your report aloud to your family or friends.** Your family and friends will be interested in your eyewitness report—especially if some of them witnessed the same event with you. Ask them their impressions of what you wrote compared with what they experienced.

Some Ideas to Consider

Mathematics
- Describe watching the construction of a building, mentioning the angles of the I-beams, walls, joists, etc.

History
- Write about an event you witnessed that may (or may not) have lasting significance.

Literature
- Tell about hearing an author lecture or about visiting an author's home.

If-Then Statements

We have already studied two kinds of complex statements: conjunctions and disjunctions. Now we will look at conditional statements. These appear in business arrangements, in legal documents, in computer programming, and on standardized tests. More important, the Bible contains conditionals. Understanding the logic behind a conditional statement will increase your ability to make wise decisions as well as give you a better understanding of Scripture.

Conditional statements are in the form "If *P*, then *Q*."

P **Q**

If Buttons is a cat, then Buttons has four legs.

The sentence above is a conditional statement. The first part of the statement, *P*, is the **condition.** The second part of the statement, *Q*, is the **conclusion.**

There are three cases of a conditional statement that make the entire statement true and one case that renders the statement false. Let's consider the possibilities. First, suppose Alex has a cat named Buttons and Buttons has four legs. The condition has been met, and the conclusion is obviously true, so the entire conditional statement is true.

Second, let's suppose that Alex has a dog named Buttons. In this instance, the condition (the "if" clause) would be false, but the conclusion would still be true because dogs have four legs. If Alex, referring to Buttons the dog, made the statement "If Buttons is a cat, then Buttons has four legs," he is not telling a lie. The condition has not been met, so his hypothetical claim is still valid.

Third, what if both parts of the conditional statement are false? Buttons may be a fish. The fish is not a cat, nor does it have four legs. These facts, however, have still not proved the conditional statement false because the conditional statement claims only that Buttons has four legs if Buttons is a cat. Therefore, when *P* and *Q* are false, the conditional statement is still true.

There may be a cat, however, that has only three legs. If Buttons is a cat and has only three legs, then the conditional statement is false. The only false conditional statement is one in the form of "*P* is true and *Q* is false." In order to prove a conditional statement false, an example must be given where *P* is true and *Q* is false. This is called a **counterexample.**

If Buttons is a cat, then Buttons has four legs.

(Buttons is a cat, but Buttons has only three legs.)

The truth table demonstrates the four cases of conditional statements. The shaded column at the end represents the truth of each case.

P	*Q*	*P*→*Q*
T	T	T
T	F	F
F	T	T
F	F	T

Identify each conditional statement as *true* or *false*.

_____ 1. If Nate is a good soccer player, then he will be the captain of the team. *(Nate is a good soccer player, but he is not the captain.)*

_____ 2. If the team practices hard, it will reach the playoffs. *(The team practiced hard, and the team reached the playoffs.)*

_____ 3. If Nate is not injured, then he will play the entire game. *(Nate was not injured, but he did not play the entire game.)*

_____ 4. If the opposing team plays poorly, then Nate's team will win the game. *(The opposing team played well, and Nate's team lost the game.)*

_____ 5. The coach promised to take the team out for burgers and fries if they won the game. *(They lost the game, and the coach took them out for burgers and fries.)*

For each conditional statement, give a counterexample that would prove the conditional statement false.

1. If our pet has large ears, then our pet is a dog.

   _____

2. If a person is a teenager, then he is irresponsible.

   _____

3. If Shane is not Emily's brother, then he is not her cousin.

   _____

4. If Ron is not the most popular boy in school, then everyone dislikes him.

   _____

5. If Damon does not like coffee, then he likes to drink tea.

   _____

Thinking It Through

Write an argument making your thesis a conditional statement. Be sure to provide adequate support for your argument. Examine your argument to see whether you can find a counterexample.

As you read "Proof Through the Night," think about the style of the essay. Do you feel as though you are listening to someone speak rather than actually reading an essay? Do you get some idea of the kind of person the writer is?

An oral anecdote relates experiences and information in a style that sounds informal and personal—like someone talking to a friend. Notice how reporter Charles Kuralt incorporates facts into his piece on Annin & Company while rousing feelings of patriotism. Later, when you write your oral anecdote, try to make your story meaningful to your listener or reader and at the same time keep the personal flavor of an oral story.

Proof Through the Night *by Charles Kuralt with Peter Freundlich*

There may not be a more American place anywhere than the one you're looking at. Not because Annin & Company in New Jersey has been the source of a river of red, white, and blue since its founding in 1849. Annin *is* the oldest and largest flag maker in America.

Its flags have flown at every inauguration since Zachary Taylor's, and at the North Pole, and the South Pole, and on the moon.

But look around. A woman of China sews flags here. And a man of Haiti rivets them. A worker from Burma folds the flags, and another from Ecuador sees to the stars. They are from everywhere.

You know how fabric is made, of threads laced together so that the whole is stronger than any of its parts. Who are these workers but the threads of our fabric?

This is not the dawn's early light nor twilight's last gleaming, but there is something to hail here nonetheless among these flagmakers who are a living flag themselves.

Does the star-spangled banner yet wave o'er the land of the free and the home of the brave? Ask the workers at Annin & Company. They'll tell you.

PRONOUN REFERENCE

Pronoun-
Antecedent
Agreement
pp. 135-38

Antecedents
p. 4

A pronoun takes the place of a noun, and the word that a pronoun replaces is called the **antecedent.** If the antecedent is ambiguous or unclear, then the entire sentence will be ambiguous or unclear. Not all pronouns have antecedents, but we do usually expect them for the third-person personal pronouns (*it, he, she, they*), the relative pronouns in adjective clauses (*who, which, that*), and the demonstrative pronouns (*this, that, these, those*). These pronouns must have clear antecedents.

Ambiguous Reference

For clear reference, a pronoun should have a single noun nearby that is clearly the antecedent of the pronoun.

When two nearby nouns are possible antecedents, the sentence is confusing.

AMBIGUOUS	When Keaton sees Thomas at the library, he will probably be surprised.
CLEAR	When Keaton sees Thomas at the library, Keaton will probably be surprised. *or* Keaton will probably be surprised when he sees Thomas at the library.

Sometimes the antecedent can be made clearer by using a more specific pronoun in a direct quotation.

AMBIGUOUS	Keaton told Thomas that his sister was coming with them.
CLEAR	Keaton said, "My sister is coming with us." *or* Keaton said, "Your sister is coming with us."

Remote Reference

A reference can be unclear when the antecedent is simply too far away from the pronoun.

REMOTE	Health experts say that swimming is an excellent way to exercise. The cardiovascular workout strengthens the heart, and the leg and arm motion builds upper body and lower body muscle. It is also fun and relaxing.
CLEAR	. . . lower body muscle. *Swimming* is also fun and relaxing.

If the antecedent is too far away from the pronoun, replace the pronoun with a noun.

in SUMMARY

To prevent **ambiguous reference,** a pronoun should have a single noun nearby that is clearly the antecedent of the pronoun.

To prevent **remote reference,** the antecedent should not be too far away from the pronoun.

PRACTICE *the skill*

Rewrite each sentence to correct any unclear pronoun reference. If the reference is already clear, write C.

1. Technology has changed the way people receive news. It has made information accessible to most people.

   _____

   _____

   _____

2. People got their news mainly from newspapers before the radio, the television, and the Internet were invented. They were the most common news medium.

   _____

   _____

   _____

3. Before newspapers, news was spread mostly by word of mouth or letters. A town might send out a rider to deliver its important news to another location.

   _____

   _____

   _____

4. If a man were waiting for an important message from a rider, a long time could elapse before he received the news.

   _____

   _____

   _____

5. Often the news the rider and his horse carried would be outdated even before it had reached its destination.

   _____

   _____

   _____

6. In the War of 1812, Andrew Jackson led the Americans to victory against the British in the Battle of New Orleans before they heard that it was already over.

   _____

   _____

   _____

7. The slow communication kept the people of the world separated because they could not find out what was happening in other parts of the globe. It also caused people to be less aware of the politics and culture of other people.

_____

_____

_____

8. Today, efficient communications have unified the globe. Now if Jenny in America wants to talk to Sharon in Japan, she can hear from her friend in seconds.

_____

_____

_____

9. Now the television and the Internet have reduced the dependency on newspapers. They easily relate the news to Americans every day.

_____

_____

_____

10. Satellites now orbit the earth continuously, conveying world news to newspapers, radio stations, and television networks. Along with news script, they send photo images all around the world.

_____

_____

_____

7.2 REVIEW *the skill*

Rewrite each sentence to correct any unclear pronoun reference.

1. Sarah Josepha Hale was the mother of five children and a spokeswoman for women in America. Through her popular ladies' magazine, she shaped much of their style and tastes.

_____

_____

_____

2. Born in 1788 in New Hampshire, Sarah had an unquenchable thirst for knowledge. Sarah's mother assisted her in her self-education, but she never attended college.

_____

_____

_____

3. Sarah married a young lawyer, David Hale, and they had five children. Each night they would set aside a couple of hours for study and discussion.

_____

_____

_____

_____

4. David's unexpected death was a shock to Sarah, and the responsibility of running the household discouraged her. It left her with no source of income and five children to provide for.

_____

_____

_____

_____

5. Sarah and her sister-in-law Hannah started a business, but she also desired to be a writer.

_____

_____

_____

6. Hannah and Sarah worked together until she had made enough money to quit the business and become a writer.

_____

_____

_____

7. Sarah published a novel, _Northwood,_ and in 1834 she became editor of _American Ladies Magazine._ It was very popular among American women.

_____

_____

_____

8. Advocating the advancement of women, Sarah supported one woman who wanted to be an overseas missionary. She believed that women should be allowed to be missionary doctors.

_____

_____

_____

9. Although she supported women's rights, she emphasized a woman's role as a wife and mother. To her, it was the most influential position a woman could have.

_____

_____

_____

10. "Mary Had a Little Lamb" is Sarah Josepha Hale's most famous poem, although most people do not recognize her as the author. It is certainly one of the best known in America.

_____

_____

_____

Reference to an Implied Noun

A pronoun needs to refer to a stated noun, not an implied noun.

IMPLIED NOUN	When I checked out these books, she said that I need to return them in seven days.
CORRECT	When I checked out these books, the librarian said that I need to return them in seven days.

In the first example, *she* probably refers to the librarian, but the antecedent does not appear in the sentence or passage. Correct this kind of error by replacing the pronoun with the needed noun.

Reference to a Noun That Is a Modifier

When we read a pronoun, we usually expect the antecedent to be in a noun position. Nouns functioning as adjectives are less noticeable and make poor antecedents.

MODIFYING NOUN AS ANTECEDENT	We're going to build a new tool shed since we have so many of them.
BETTER	We're going to build a new shed for our tools since we have so many of them.
A POSSESSIVE AS ANTECEDENT	Isaac volunteered to take care of John's dog, who was going to camp for a week.
BETTER	Isaac volunteered to take care of John's dog because John was going to camp for a week.

Either use the intended antecedent instead of the pronoun or revise the sentence so that the antecedent is no longer a modifier.

Possessives;
Modifying
Nouns
pp. 14-15

in SUMMARY

An antecedent must be a stated noun, not an **implied noun.**

An antecedent must be in a noun position. An antecedent cannot be a **modifier.**

PRACTICE *the skill*

Rewrite each sentence to correct any unclear pronoun reference.

1. Many students aspire to be journalists, and it is a respectable profession.

   _____

   _____

   _____

2. Constantly expanding technology increases a journalist's career options, who can choose print, radio, or television journalism.

   _____

   _____

   _____

3. They can strongly influence a country's opinions and actions.

   _____

   _____

   _____

4. Because citizens learn about their government and important issues from watching television, checking Internet sites, and reading the newspaper, it influences the people's views and opinions.

   _____

   _____

   _____

5. A story can be reported from two different journalists' perspectives, who can give two completely different views of the situation.

   _____

   _____

   _____

6. Journalism must always be accurate, and they have a responsibility to be fair in their presentation.

   _____

   _____

   _____

7. Many people feel that the news is biased and that they do not report the news impartially.

   _____

   _____

   _____

8. Many journalists enjoy excitement and adventure, and it can provide opportunities for writing and speaking.

_____

_____

_____

9. Relatively few dedicated Christians perceive a need to participate in the media, but it is a much-needed profession.

_____

_____

_____

10. Journalism is an exciting profession, and often they are some of the best-known voices in America.

_____

_____

_____

7.4 REVIEW *the skill*

Rewrite each sentence to correct any unclear pronoun reference.

1. In John Milton's *Areopagitica,* he strongly advocates freedom of the press.

_____

_____

_____

2. Freedom of the press forbids the government's restriction of news or opinions that may not be favorable toward them.

_____

_____

_____

3. Religious groups' beliefs are protected by freedom of the press, for the lack of restriction allows them to voice their opinions publicly in print.

_____

_____

_____

4. Even before the printing press, written materials were restricted by the government and by religious leaders' control, who destroyed anything that disagreed with their teachings.

   _____

   _____

   _____

5. After the invention of the printing press, the government or a religious group would issue a printer's license, and he had to publish within strict guidelines.

   _____

   _____

   _____

6. The government or religious authority could take away the printer's license, who would no longer be allowed to publish.

   _____

   _____

   _____

7. After Milton's work in the 1600s, the license system began to fade, and they were not used at all in many countries by the 1800s.

   _____

   _____

   _____

8. The First Amendment protects freedom of the press, and they can print almost anything without intervention from the government or private groups.

   _____

   _____

   _____

9. Most democratic countries do practice national security censorship, which could be endangered if certain things were printed.

   _____

   _____

   _____

10. Most democratic countries also have obscenity laws to prevent it from being published.

    _____

    _____

    _____

Indefinite Reference of Personal Pronouns

Personal
Pronouns
pp. 4-5

Indefinite pronouns such as *someone, one,* and *everybody* do not require antecedents. Personal pronouns, however, are different from indefinite pronouns: they need an antecedent. Three personal pronouns that are misused as if they were indefinite pronouns are *they, it,* and *you.*

Do not use *they* without an antecedent.

INDEFINITE *THEY*	In Hawaii they ride mopeds.
CORRECTED	In Hawaii people ride mopeds.
MORE EXACT	Many Hawaiians ride mopeds.

Avoid using *it* as an indefinite pronoun in the phrase "it says." Replace *it* with the name of the source of information.

INDEFINITE *IT*	In the introduction to the book it says that the author has done extensive research on this topic.
CORRECTED	The introduction to the book says that the author has done extensive research on this topic.

The pronoun *you* generally refers to the person being addressed, but it is sometimes used as an indefinite pronoun when it refers to people in general. While the indefinite *you* is acceptable in informal writing and speaking, it should not be used in formal writing and speaking. Replace the *you* in formal contexts.

INFORMAL	If you want to save money, you have to develop a good budget.
FORMAL	If a person wants to save money, he has to develop a good budget.
VERY FORMAL	If one wants to save money, he must develop a good budget.

In very formal writing, including most academic writing, the use of *you* should be avoided altogether.

Reference to a Broad Idea

Another mistake is using a pronoun to refer to a general idea rather than a noun. Be sure to clarify the sentence.

REFERENCE TO GENERAL IDEA	Sam was asked to be on the all-star basketball team, and it surprised him.
CLEAR	Sam was asked to be on the all-star basketball team, and the invitation surprised him.
UNCLEAR	Jessie had to get up early every morning and run several miles, but this was not difficult for her.
CLEAR	Jessie had to get up early every morning and run several miles, but getting up early was not difficult for her. Jessie had to get up early every morning and run several miles, but running for long periods of time was not difficult for her.

Exception: **It** does not refer to a specific noun in certain common English expressions referring to time, distance, weather, and environment.

TIME	**It's** 1:00, time for lunch.
DISTANCE	**It's** only seven blocks to the library from my house.
WEATHER	The forecast says that **it** is going to rain later today.
ENVIRONMENT	**It** is very quiet here today.

in SUMMARY

Always have an antecedent for the word *they.*

Do not use *it* as an indefinite pronoun in the expression "it says." Replace *it* with the name of the source of information.

Do not use the indefinite *you* in formal writing and speaking.

A pronoun must refer to a noun, not a general idea.

PRACTICE *the skill*

Identify the following sentences as *clear* or *unclear.*

_____ 1. Muckraking became a common journalistic practice at the beginning of the twentieth century. They would write exposés on corruption in big businesses and politics.

_____ 2. Theodore Roosevelt knew of a character in *Pilgrim's Progress* who busily raked up filth, which caused him to nickname these writers "muckrakers."

_____ 3. Many journalists resented the name, but some were proud of it.

_____ 4. Roosevelt's appreciation of the muckrakers' work was genuine, but the president feared that the journalists could be unnecessarily stirring up unrest, and this bothered him.

_____ 5. Ida Tarbell's work was very popular in the early 1900s. In *McClure's Magazine,* it featured a series of her exposés on the Standard Oil Company.

_____ 6. Other magazines began to copy *McClure's* example, and soon there were many magazines, such as *Cosmopolitan, Pearson's,* and *Collier's,* that focused on muckraking.

_____ 7. Ida Tarbell, the first reform journalist, had her articles on Standard Oil compiled, and it was published as a book.

_____ 8. Muckraking is the ancestor of investigative reporting, which is a more respectable profession than muckraking.

_____ 9. Not everyone approved of muckraking, but this did not keep the profession from instigating several important reforms in America.

_____ 10. Muckraking eventually disappeared, mainly because in America they lost interest in it.

7.6 REVIEW *the skill*

Rewrite each sentence to correct any unclear pronoun reference. Avoid informal English.

1. Each week our church presents a broadcast on the radio. This is an exciting and valuable ministry.

2. Our pastor prepares a fifteen-minute message, and it is done weekly.

3. He then records a public presentation that will make them consider things that are eternal.

4. After recording the message, he delivers the tape to the radio station. This gives him the opportunity to speak to thousands of people.

5. As people hear the broadcast, it gives a refreshing word of truth in the midst of their busy day.

6. They give a phone number with the presentation, and often people will respond to the message.

7. If a person responds to the broadcast, we record it, and we usually send him some useful literature.

8. Sometimes our follow-up leads us to a person searching for truth, which gives us the opportunity for further ministry.

_____

_____

_____

9. In order to have an active ministry, you first have to establish a point of contact with people.

_____

_____

_____

10. In the Bible it says to tell the gospel to all people, and radio broadcasting offers many opportunities to obey this command.

_____

_____

_____

CUMULATIVE *review*

Rewrite the following paragraph, correcting the ten errors from these categories: subject-verb agreement, pronoun-antecedent agreement, verb use (principal parts, tense, or mood), and pronoun reference.

A war correspondent reports news directly from the battle scene. Assignments to the battlefield, not without risk, never lacks excitement. One of the first efficient war correspondence efforts was George Kendall's work. He will cover the Mexican War. During the American Civil War, both the North and the South sent its reporters to the battlefield, and both World Wars were covered by United States correspondents. Marguerite Higgins covered the Korean War and had became the first woman to receive the Pulitzer Prize for war correspondence. During the Vietnam War, you could receive eyewitness reports from television and from the newspapers. David Halberstam wrote controversial reports during this time, and this raised questions about a reporter's right to criticize national policy during a war. In the 1980s the United States set up a press pool system, which limited the number of correspondents at the battle scene and required him to reveal all information to other reporters. During the Persian Gulf War of the 1990s, the United States continues the press pool system. War correspondence, although it includes dangerous activities, are certainly one of the most exciting branches of journalism.

_____

_____

_____

_____

_____

_____

_____

_____

_____

_____

_____

_____

_____

_____

_____

_____

_____

_____

ORAL ANECDOTE

Some trust in chariots, and some in horses: but we will remember the name of the Lord our God.

Psalm 20:7

Oral stories are among the oldest of language traditions. Throughout much of history, only a few people in a culture knew how to read and write. The rest would relay information and report events orally. Perhaps they sat around a fire or beside a stream telling tales. For some storytellers even today, in a world full of high-speed technology, a story just isn't told right unless it is told aloud.

Accounts such as "Proof Through the Night" read like conversations and reveal the opinions and character of the author. They are in the tradition of oral history, a form of literature that lets people tell stories in their own words. Because oral accounts are usually personal, their styles are as varied as their authors.

Choose some event, experience, thought, or person to write about. Look for something that will strike other people as familiar. Then present the subject in your own voice.

Planning

✔ **Decide what event you want to feature or what personal account you want to give.** What story do you have a unique angle on? Think about people or items around you that might be of interest to someone else and choose one to highlight in your oral anecdote. Or perhaps you have a skill or hobby that is unusual.

✔ **Brainstorm your ideas about your chosen topic.** Write down everything you know about your topic. Ask yourself questions about what people might want to learn about your topic. If you are writing about an item, you might ask how and where it is made, who makes it, how the item has changed through the years, and whether there are any unusual uses for the item. An anecdote focusing on a person might ask when and where the person was born, what he does for a living, and how he came to choose that job.

Brainstorming
p. 327

> water-skiing
> jumps
> slalom courses
> ski ropes
> boats—motors, hulls
> skis—how they're made, materials, new technology in,
>   trick skis
> ski competitions—famous ones, ones I've competed in
> trick skiing
> famous skiers

tip

Don't reject any idea in a brainstorming session as long as the idea is biblically appropriate.

Considering Your
Audience
p. 329

✔ **Consider your audience and your genre.** Remember that this assignment features an oral presentation of a written work. Your audience will expect your anecdote to sound like natural speech. "Proof Through the Night" sounds like a person speaking because it uses sentence fragments, imperatives mingled among informative sentences, and second person. Suppose the first sentence of the fourth paragraph read like this: "Fabric is made of threads laced together so that the whole is stronger than any of its parts." The basic information is unchanged, but the tone has changed dramatically because the reader is not pulled in with "You know how," including him and acknowledging his experience. And the more formal sentence structure seems less friendly somehow. Using contractions will also make your piece seem more appropriate for oral presentation.

Drafting

Introductory
Paragraphs
p. 340

✔ **Write an introduction.** Introduce the facts of your anecdote in your introduction. "Proof Through the Night" effectively presents the topic (Annin & Company); the theme ("There may not be a more American place . . . than . . ."); and several facts about the piece (New Jersey, 1849, oldest and largest flagmaker). You should avoid making your opening paragraph merely a listing of facts; inject interest by using a question, quotation, or story. Kuralt uses the metaphor of a river running red, white, and blue and makes you ask yourself what kind of river he is speaking of. The next sentence delivers the unusual but apt answer: a river of flags. Sometimes keeping your audience in suspense for a sentence or so will generate interest in your topic. Try several options to see which works best for this piece.

✔ **Use a conversational style, but don't sacrifice correctness.** Just because anecdotal accounts are casual does not mean that they can be careless. While Charles Kuralt's voice in this work is warm and neighborly, it is never ungrammatical or uncrafted. Never confuse conversational style with unskilled expression.

Style should never interfere with understandability. **tip**

✔ **Aim for a universal theme.** Oral essays such as this aim for one effect by commenting on a theme that all of the hearers would agree with. Kuralt wants his reader or hearer to finish reading and realize that, yes, unity of purpose is American, and Kuralt wants him to feel pride in that unity. Try to stir in your hearers a sense of pride or indignation or appreciation—whatever emotion is appropriate for your topic. A theme that is universal strikes the reader as though he is reading his own thoughts. "Proof Through the Night" makes a point that large numbers of Americans already believe in. They read the essay and say, "That's true, isn't it? We are a wonderful mixture, with people from everywhere." Perhaps the reader has never stopped to verbalize this idea, but he recognizes it and responds warmly.

✔ **Use recognizable allusions.** Kuralt strengthens his theme with good allusions. His title is the best example. You know where it comes from right away—a line from "The Star-Spangled Banner": "Gave proof through the night that our flag was still there." Kuralt also uses a long-standing image: weaving. Even though many modern readers may not know how to weave, they will understand the analogy.

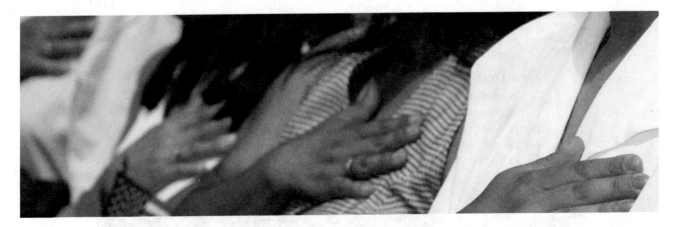

✔ **Include common experiences.** Common experience is another universal writers use. Although visiting a flag factory is not all that common an experience, singing the national anthem is. So Kuralt quotes from the well-known song in his closing paragraphs: "This is not the dawn's early light nor twilight's last gleaming." Your audience will recognize a baseball game, a hamburger, a flat tire, or a host of other experiences that you could include in your anecdote.

✔ **Provide detail and support throughout your piece.** As with all good writing, your oral anecdote should include specific details: Zachary Taylor's inauguration, 1849, Annin & Company in New Jersey. Good support anchors your writing and lends credence to what you are saying. When drafting the body of your piece, keep the interest level high by further developing the theme, allusions, and experiences you began at the beginning. Kuralt keeps interest high in the middle of his piece by addressing the listener in the second person and by asking a question: "Who are these workers but the threads of our fabric?"

✔ **Strive for a dramatic ending.** Suppose the last sentence of Kuralt's piece were "The workers at Annin & Company will tell you." What is the same? The basic idea—that the workers know the answer to the question preceding. What has changed? The drama of the presentation. The pause between the last two sentences in the essay creates a boost of emotion for the last sentence. And it adds to the impression that someone is talking to you.

Revising

✔ **Check your purpose.** Make sure that you have fulfilled your purpose in writing your anecdote. Will your readers respond to your piece in the way that you planned? Is the theme clear? If not, your piece probably needs reworking for either organization or unity.

✔ **Read your piece aloud.** Since this assignment is an oral one, read your piece to yourself or to a friend. You could also try recording the piece to play back to yourself. Listen to how you sound; check for a conversational style.

Thinking Biblically

Paul's epistles in the New Testament read like oral anecdotes. These letters are written communication, but they have a personal and informal style. Some interpreters have suggested that this style is the natural result of Paul's employing an amanuensis—a person who writes from dictation (cf. Rom. 16:22). We seem to hear Paul speaking as we read Galatians because he composed Galatians by speaking. Not all of the New Testament epistles were authored through an amanuensis. Hebrews seems to have been put in writing by its author. Read Galatians 1 and Hebrews 1. Note the differences between these two styles. What are the strengths of each style? What does the style that Paul uses in Galatians suggest about oral anecdotes?

✔ **Look for proper emphasis.** Do the important ideas in your anecdote stand out? Sentence rhythm—the ebb and flow of long and short, parallel and contrasting sentences—is an excellent tool for attaining proper emphasis in your piece. Check to see whether altering sentence types, especially at the beginning of your piece, would improve the rhythm.

tip

Count the words of each of your first six sentences. If the numbers are not significantly different from one another, revise by lengthening or shortening sentences to create variety.

First Draft

Sometimes I dream about water-skiing. In my dreams I ski for exhibitions. My driver starts, and we hurtle toward the jump. Sometimes it seems like we're going a hundred miles an hour. The whipping wind rushes through my hair and ears. I almost signal to turn back, but I'm there.

Second Draft

In my water-ski dreams, I compete at Cypress Gardens. One signal and the high-speed hurtle toward the jump begins. Whoosh, whoosh—the wind whips through my hair and whistles in my ears. Buoys and boats and water rush by. For a split second, I almost wish myself back at the safety of the dock. Too late—I'm at the jump.

✔ **Avoid clichés . . . like the plague.** Phrases like the previous one and many others have been used so often that they have lost their effectiveness. This is especially true of comparisons; for example, *hard as a rock* and *light as a feather* are overused comparisons. Also, if you have overused a word or phrase in your piece (unless the repetition is purposeful), check a thesaurus for alternatives. However, never use a word that you do not fully understand: sometimes a word can have shades of meaning that contradict what you intend.

tip

Read your paper through, looking for one error that is common for you.

✔ **Proofread for correctness.** Reread your paper for grammar, usage, spelling, and other conventions. Do not expect to find every error in one reading. You will need to read your piece through several times, looking for different types of errors.

Publishing

✔ **Read your oral anecdote aloud to your family.** Your family will probably have a personal interest in what you have written. Read the anecdote at dinner or family devotions or any time that your family is gathered together.

✔ **Record your anecdote.** Make a final recording of your piece and play it for family or friends. Consider sending the recording to someone as a personal and unique gift.

✔ **Read or play your oral anecdote for the class.** Your teacher may set aside part of a period in which to hear or play several anecdotes at a time.

✔ **Compile your class's oral anecdotes.** For display purposes, prepare neatly written copies and put them in a three-ring binder. Encourage other classes to read your anecdotes or display them for parents during parent-teacher conferences.

✔ **Post your anecdotes.** If your class has a website with audio capabilities, record your class anecdotes for a webpage. If not, post the anecdotes as written pieces.

Webpage Design pp. 207-12

Some Ideas to Consider

Science
∞ Write about the Curies' discovery of radium.
∞ Describe current research in cancer treatments.

History
∞ Relate a story in the life of Robert Wadlow, the tallest human being in modern history.
∞ Tell about a scene from a battle you have studied.

Home Economics
∞ Write an anecdote about a local bakery or candy store.

ESL

Most people can relate to the idea of going to a new place and needing to make many adjustments. (Many of your classmates have probably gone away to summer camp, or they may have left home to visit someone for a few days.) Consider writing an oral anecdote about your first day in the United States or your first day in a new school.

∞ What surprised you? What puzzled you? Or what was your main impression, and why? Mention a few specific details.

∞ You can simply tell how it was on that day. Or you can add a sentence at the end to give the idea that things are different now.

Now I _____, but that's how it was on Day One.

Feel free to complete that sentence and use it at the end of your anecdote.

LETTER FOR LETTER

A Desperate Prayer

A powerful king wrote a threatening letter, but the threats were based on falsehood. What truths did Hezekiah depend on to keep him from despair?

The few candles in the sanctuary flickered. They cast a dim shadow against the heavily curtained wall. The king's form, on which the candles glowed, bent in fervent prayer. Beyond his head a royal parchment lay, spread as an offering before the Lord.

The king's voice was tense and quiet. Finally he rose, smoothed out his royal garments and turned with the parchment in hand to leave. His weary face, so overloaded with emotions, made him seem older than he was. Only his eyes revealed the strength the prayer had given him.

The parchment was a letter from Sennacherib, the great king of Assyria. In it, he had threatened Hezekiah and his country with total destruction. He had even brought colonists with whom to inhabit Jerusalem after he had wiped out the defiant Jews. Soon after taking the matter to Jehovah, King Hezekiah was greeted by a messenger.

"A message from the prophet Isaiah to King Hezekiah," he began and held up a parchment from which to read. His trained voice echoed the powerful message across the chamber.

"This is the word of the Lord concerning Sennacherib, king of Assyria:

> The virgin, the daughter of Zion,
> hath despised thee, and laughed thee to scorn;
>
> The daughter of Jerusalem hath shaken her head at thee.
>
> Whom hast thou reproached and blasphemed?
>
> And against whom hast thou exalted thy voice, and lifted up thine eyes on high?
>
> Even against the Holy One of Israel."

The king's eyes widened, allowing two trapped tears to fall.

> "Because thy rage against me, and thy tumult, is come into mine ears,
>
> Therefore will I put my hook in thy nose, and my bridle in thy lips,
>
> And I will turn thee back by the way by which thou camest."

That night, as the king slept, an angel of Jehovah stepped into the enemy's camp. His soundless tread woke no one, and his fiery blade made little sound, but when he left the Assyrian host that night, 185,000 soldiers had died.

The remaining Assyrians did not stay around to ask questions; they packed up camp and headed home.

For the full story, read Isaiah 37.
* *Whom did the Assyrian king offend by sending the letter?*
* *Why does Hezekiah pray that God will save the nation from the Assyrians?*
* *How does the Lord send His message to Hezekiah?*

Personal Response

Until Christ returns, Satan and the world will oppose Christians. Christians can be sure, however, that God will supernaturally protect His children. Write about a time when God provided protection for you.

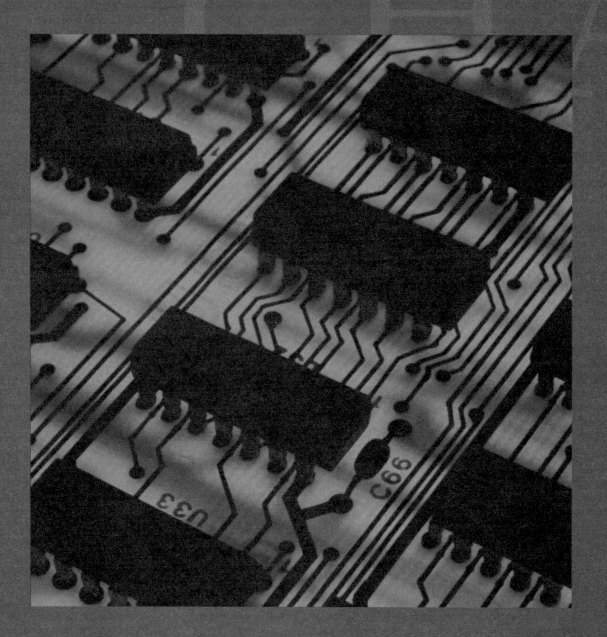

The last century boasted a multitude of technological advances. Someone born in the early 1900s saw everything from the beginning of flight to the advent of radio and television. Toward the end of the twentieth century, scientists and mathematicians tackled a project that to some seemed infeasible: the linking of every computer in the world with every other computer in the world. Despite skepticism, the experiment worked, and the Internet was born. The Internet's impact on daily life has been likened to that of Gutenberg's printing press, and today's Internet users log on to obtain information on everything from weather to airline fares to e-texts of books and plays. This webpage writing project requires that you use the Web, not for consuming content, but rather for creating content on the Web.

Alumni | Opinion Poll | Poetry | School News | Weekly Information

BAKER CHRISTIAN SCHOOL

Soccer: Rain, Mud, and Gold

At 6:00 A.M. on Thursday morning, the soccer team packed the Gator Bus and headed north. After ten hours the team arrived ready to play. The Patriots gave them an easy victory, 6-1. On Friday the Gators met the Eagles—the defending champions. After an intense game the reign of the Gators prevailed 3-2.

That afternoon the Gators defeated the Tigers in the semifinal. Then the team waited anxiously for Saturday.

The game and the rain began simultaneously. By halftime the players' uniforms were so muddy that it was hard to distinguish the teams. The determined Gators splashed through the puddles on the field and scored two goals. Goalkeeper Josh made several amazing saves, and the Lions never made it past him. Covered in mud, the Gators carried the shining trophy off the field. The scoreboard shone through the fog: 2-0.

Choir Tour

After weeks of practicing, the choir is in the final stages of preparation for its annual tour. On Tuesday at 7:00 P.M. the choir will be performing its program in the auditorium. The ten-day trip will include singing at several churches, performing in a few parks, and some sightseeing. While in the parks, half the team will conduct a children's Bible club, and the others will pass out tracts.

Remember to pray for the choir's safety. Also pray for those who will hear the gospel through the choir's witness.

It's a Boy!

Coach Mallary is the proud father of a baby boy! At 3:30 A.M. October 26, Mrs. Mallary gave birth to Jaimin Bradley Junior, who weighed 7 pounds and 7 ounces.

Calendar

November

1 Final basketball cuts
6 Choir recital 7:00 P.M.
8 Choir leaves
18 Choir returns
20 Elementary Thanksgiving program/ Thanksgiving break begins
22 Thanksgiving
26 Back to School
29 Pep rally/ Spirit Day
30 Home game

USAGE

PRONOUN USE

Correct Use of Pronoun Case

Personal
Pronouns
p. 4

The case of a personal pronoun is the form of the pronoun that reflects the way the word is used in a sentence. Pronouns have three cases: subjective, objective, and possessive.

The **subjective case** is used most often for subjects but is also the correct case for predicate nouns. The subjective case pronouns are *I, we, you, it/he/she,* and *they.*

> *We* have enrolled in Introduction to Physics.

The **objective case** is used primarily for objects: direct objects, indirect objects, and objects of the preposition. The objective case pronouns are *me, us, you, it/him/her,* and *them.*

> Jorge told *me* that the subject interests *him.*

The **possessive case** is used to show ownership and other close relationships. It may appear in one of two forms. The more common form modifies nouns. The possessive pronouns that are used as modifiers are *my, our, your, its/his/her,* and *their.*

> It was *my* choice to take an advanced class.

> The teacher will do *her* best to challenge us.

ESL The form that shows ownership (possessive) can show a number of other relationships as well. Here are some of the relationships expressed by possessives.

OWNERSHIP	This is **my book.** (I just bought it.)
DOER OF ACTION	It was **my choice** to take the class. (I chose.)
PRODUCER	**Your poem** is beautiful. (You wrote it.)
OBJECT OF ACTION	**His punishment** was severe. (Someone punished him.)
FAMILY RELATIONSHIP	I'll ask **my father.**
REPRESENTATION	Thank you for giving me **your picture;** you look good in it.
OTHERS	He loves **his country.**
	I'll do **my best.**
	I skinned **my elbow** when I fell.

The other possessive pronoun form stands alone as a subject, predicate noun, or object. It is called an **independent possessive.** The pronouns that are used in this way are *mine, ours, yours, its/his/hers,* and *theirs.*

SUBJECT	*Mine* is the first jacket on the right.
PREDICATE NOUN	That last piece of pizza is *yours.*
DIRECT OBJECT	I can wait for my coat, but they need *theirs* before they can leave.

Most possessive modifiers make the noun definite in meaning—that is, the noun refers to a specific person or thing. My pen is a specific pen, and Jack's wife is a specific woman. However, a special construction with independent possessives enables us to express possession and yet keep the noun indefinite.

He borrowed *a pen of mine* (some pen that I own).

I met *a friend of Jack's* (an unspecified one of Jack's friends).

As you see in the examples, this is the construction for possession of indefinite nouns: *a/an*   (Noun)   *of*   (Independent Possessive)

in SUMMARY

Use **subjective case pronouns** for subjects and predicate nouns.

Use **objective case pronouns** for direct objects, indirect objects, and objects of prepositions.

Use **possessive case pronouns** to show ownership.

The **independent possessive** form of a pronoun shows ownership and functions as a subject, a predicate noun, or an object.

8.1   PRACTICE *the skill*

Underline each personal pronoun and identify it as subjective (S), objective (O), possessive (P), or independent possessive (IP).

_____ 1. Cuneiform is an ancient west Asian writing system; travelers discovered it in the seventeenth century.

_____ 2. The Egyptians developed their own writing system, hieroglyphics.

_____ 3. Theirs is not the oldest, though; Akkadian writing predated Egyptian writing by several centuries.

_____ 4. Choosing whether to use cuneiform or hieroglyphics may have been difficult; each writer would have wanted to use the writing system that was his.

_____ 5. To appeal to his audience, the writer would probably have used the reader's writing system.

_____ 6. The ancient writing systems had their strengths and weaknesses.

_____ 7. They developed in somewhat different ways.

_____ 8. The Egyptians used a logographic and phonographic system; in other words, they used symbols that represented both words and sounds.

_____ 9. Cuneiform, on the other hand, was a logographic system; that is, each symbol in it represented a word.

_____ 10. Neither of them was an alphabet; the Phoenicians later developed one.

Egyptian Pottery Tablet, 20th century reproduction, from the Bowen Collection of Antiquities, Bob Jones University Museum & Gallery

REVIEW *the skill*

Provide an appropriate pronoun. Then identify the pronoun as subjective (S), objective (O), possessive (P), or independent possessive (IP).

_____ _____ 1. The Phoenicians were predominantly coastal people, and ? used the Mediterranean Sea to become a prospering commercial civilization.

_____ _____ 2. ? was one of the first alphabets.

_____ _____ 3. Actually, some scholars believe that ? developed from a precursor alphabet, North Semitic.

_____ _____ 4. These first alphabets used only consonants; there were no vowels in ? .

_____ _____ 5. The Hebrew alphabet developed from these systems, and ? still have many examples of ancient literature from the Jews.

_____ _____ 6. Nearly all of this ancient literature is part of the Old Testament, an example of God's preservation of ? Word.

_____ _____ 7. Isaiah wrote in Hebrew, producing the book that bears ? name.

_____ _____ 8. Hebrew is still written today; ? was revived when Israel declared itself an independent state.

_____ _____ 9. Hebrew speakers can even find Dr. Seuss books translated into ? language.

_____ _____10. Hebrew uses an alphabet different from the one English uses; ? does not use the Latin alphabet.

Torah Scroll, from the Bowen Collection of Antiquities, Bob Jones University Museum & Gallery

Compound Constructions

Choosing the right pronoun case in a compound construction can sometimes be difficult. When faced with such a construction, remember that the rules are the same as those for simple constructions. The case you use depends on the function of the word in the sentence.

SIMPLE	*They* will finish the project after lunch.
COMPOUND	*They* and their mother will finish the project after lunch.

In both sentences the word *they* functions as the subject (or part of the subject) of the sentence. Therefore, the subjective pronoun *they* is used.

If you are having trouble deciding which case to use, try dropping the rest of the compound construction. Without it, you should have an easier time determining the function of the word in question. In the following sentence, drop the words "Mom and" to isolate the questioned pronoun. You will see that it is acting as part of the subject of the sentence; therefore, the subjective case pronoun *I* is required.

COMPOUND	Mom and *(I, me)* picked up Susan at the airport.
SUBJECTIVE	*I* picked up Susan at the airport.
OBJECTIVE	*Me* picked up Susan at the airport.
CORRECT	Mom and *I* picked up Susan at the airport.

Appositives

There are two general rules regarding pronoun case in sentences with appositives. First, ignore an appositive when determining the case of a pronoun it renames.

Appositive
Phrases
pp. 61-62

    S (App) TrV   DO

We campers chose a new tent site for this year. (*we* chose)

    S   LV PA OP (App)

The location of the lake is ideal for *us* fishermen. (for *us*)

Second, the case of a pronoun within an appositive should match the case of the word that is renamed.

    S   (App)   InV

Our whole family, Mom, Dad, and *I,* went to the play.

    S TrV   IO   (App)   DO

My friend's parents gave their children, her sisters and *her,* a car to use for

school transportation.

In the first sentence the appositive renames the subject, *family;* therefore, the subjective pronoun *I* is used. In the second sentence the appositive renames the indirect object, *children;* therefore, the objective pronoun *her* is used.

Comparisons Using *Than* or *As*

Sometimes in a comparison using *than* or *as,* the second part of the comparison is "understood" (in other words, it is left out of the sentence). Decide which pronoun case to use after the comparative word (*than* or *as*) according to how the pronoun would function in the full understood clause.

Her sister is taller than *she.* (than *she* is tall)

My best friend is as old as *I.* (as *I* am old)

John owes Jason as much as *me.* (as much as he owes *me*)

John owes Jason as much as *I.* (as much as *I* owe Jason)

Notice from the last two examples that in some sentences you will have a choice of pronouns, depending on the meaning you intend.

in SUMMARY

Compound constructions follow the same rules for pronoun case as do simple constructions.

The presence of an **appositive** does not affect the case of the pronoun it renames.

The case of a pronoun in an appositive is determined by the case of the noun it renames.

Determine the case of a pronoun after *than* or *as* by determining how the pronoun would function in the full understood clause.

PRACTICE *the skill*

Underline the correct pronoun from the choices in parentheses.

1. Diana and (*I, me*) wrote Poppa Stein a letter.

2. (*We, Us*) sisters frequently correspond with him by using e-mail.

3. She checks her e-mail more often than (*I, me*).

4. However, Poppa Stein writes to me as much as (*she, her*).

5. We all—Diana, Marie, and (*I, me*)—sent him a birthday card.

6. Our parents do not use e-mail; Philip and (*they, them*) will mail their cards tomorrow.

7. The granddaughters—Diana, Marie, and (*I, me*)—will send a gift too.

8. The invitation to dinner was addressed to (*we, us*) grandchildren.

9. The authors of the invitation were Nana Stein and (*he, him*).

10. Was the postcard from (*they, them*) too?

REVIEW *the skill*

Underline the correct pronoun from the choices in parentheses.

1. My family—Mom, Dad, Carlos and Samuel (the twins), and (*I, me*)—is studying the inspiration of the Bible.

2. Although Carlos studied this topic in Sunday School, Samuel has memorized more verses than (*he, him*).

3. "How did God give us the Bible?" Dad asked Samuel and (*I, me*).

4. Samuel remembered that II Timothy 3:16 says, "All scripture is given by inspiration of God," and so we know He gave the Bible to (*we, us*) believers by inspiration.

5. Dad directed the next question to the twins, Carlos and (*he, him*): "What does *inspiration* mean?"

6. Samuel told Carlos and (*I, me*) that God prompted men to write down His Word.

7. Mom informed Samuel and (*we, us*) that the Greek word for inspiration means "God-breathed."

8. Dad added that inspiration is essentially divine control: the Holy Spirit completely directed the men as (*they, them*), the human authors, penned the Bible.

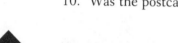

9. "A perfect God inspired every word of the Bible, so we can trust it to be completely accurate," Dad assured the family, Mom, the twins, and (*I, me*).

10 I think that this study has taught Dad as much as (*we, us*).

Using *Who* and *Whom*

The pronouns *who* and *whom* are often confused. Remember that *who* is a subjective case pronoun and that *whom* is an objective case pronoun.

Interrogative Pronouns p. 5

Who	**S LV PN** *Who* is your group leader?
	S LV PN (S) (TrV) (DO) She is the one *who is blowing the whistle.*
Whom	**DO (Aux) S TrV** *Whom* did you see at the meeting?
	S TrV DO (DO) (S) (TrV) I saw the speaker *whom we heard last spring.*

Relative Pronouns p. 6

If *who/whom* is used in a dependent clause (see second and fourth examples above), determine its case by its function within its clause, not by the function of the entire clause within the sentence.

If you cannot decide on the correct case, try substituting a personal pronoun for *who/whom* and rearranging the sentence if necessary. Notice how the following examples use this technique.

Original	*Who/Whom* is your group leader?
Substitute	*She/Her* is your group leader.
Original	He is the guard *who/whom* we saw at the gate.
Substitute and Rearrange	We saw *he/him* at the gate.

In the first example the substituted sentence should help you see that the word in question is functioning as the subject of the sentence. The subjective *she* would be the correct choice in the substituted sentence, so you should use the subjective *who* for the question. In the second example, words are rearranged as well as substituted. You can see from the rearranged section that the pronoun is functioning as the direct object of the dependent clause and should be the objective case *him*. Therefore, use the objective case *whom* in the original sentence.

ESL

In deciding the right case for **who/whom** in a question, ignore "do you think" if it comes in the middle of the question. (Consider it parenthetical.)

Who do you think will lead our group? (**Who** will lead?)

Whom do you think I saw? (I saw **whom?**)

As you may notice, in colloquial English (informal conversation) there is a strong tendency to use *who* at the beginning of all questions, regardless of its function. In written and formal use, however, you should follow the rules stated here in the text.

in SUMMARY

Use **who** for subjects and predicate nouns.

Use **whom** for direct objects, indirect objects, and objects of prepositions.

Determine whether to use *who* or *whom* in a dependent clause by determining the function of the pronoun in the dependent clause itself.

8.5 PRACTICE *the skill*

Underline the correct pronoun from the choices in parentheses.

1. The Newbery Medal goes to the novelist (*who, whom*) writes the best junior novel of the year.

2. The book that won the first Newbery Medal was written by (*who, whom*)?

3. (*Who, Whom*) picks the winner of the Newbery Medal?

4. The American Library Association is the group (*who, whom*) is responsible for selecting the Medal winner for the year.

5. (*Who, Whom*) did this year's Medal winner use as his main character?

6. (*Who, Whom*) do you think wrote that story?

7. This is the writer (*who, whom*) they picked.

8. This year's winner is not the author (*who, whom*) I would have picked.

9. Yesterday, they announced the authors (*who, whom*) won the Honor Book distinction.

10. (*Who, Whom*) is the Newbery Medal named after?

8.6 REVIEW *the skill*

Write the appropriate pronoun (*who* or *whom*) for each sentence.

_____ 1. _?_ was John Newbery?

_____ 2. By _?_ was the Newbery Medal designed?

_____ 3. Whoever designed the Medal must have been someone _?_ had both artistic ability and a love for children.

_____ 4. For _?_ is adolescent literature written?

_____ 5. _?_ won the Newbery this year?

_____ 6. He is the writer _?_ won the award last year.

_____ 7. To _?_ was that Honor Book dedicated?

_____ 8. She was one of the librarians ? were chosen for the committee that selects the Newbery Medal winner.

_____ 9. ? did she replace on the selection committee?

_____ 10. The Medal is given only to someone ? is a resident or citizen of the United States.

Courtesy Order

Observe two general rules of courtesy when joining a personal pronoun with another personal pronoun or a noun in a compound construction.

Always mention yourself last.

> **SAY** | Kris saved a seat for Haley and *me*.
>
> **NOT** | Kris saved a seat for *me* and Haley.

In most circumstances mention your hearer before anyone else.

> **SAY** | We will wait for *you* and Craig.
>
> **NOT** | We will wait for Craig and *you*.

Correct Use of Reflexive and Intensive

Reflexive and intensive pronouns are personal pronouns that have a *self* or *selves* suffix. A **reflexive pronoun** usually functions as an object: direct object, indirect object, or object of the preposition. The reflexive pronoun is unique in this function in that it refers to the same person or thing as the subject of the clause, whereas an object typically refers to someone or something different. Notice the objects in the following sentences.

Reflexive and Intensive Pronouns p. 6

> Dave surprised *himself* when he volunteered to clean the garage.
>
> In fact, Dave surprised *me* too.

You can see that in the first example, the doer of the action (*Dave*—the subject) and the receiver of the action (*himself*—the direct object) are the same person. In the second example, however, the doer (*Dave*) and the receiver (*me*) are two different people.

Reflexive and other personal pronouns should not be used interchangeably. If an object refers to the same person or thing as the subject, use a reflexive pronoun. If it does not, choose another personal pronoun.

> **INCORRECT** | *Grandmother* took pictures of Kendra and *myself*.
>
> **CORRECT** | *Grandmother* took pictures of Kendra and *me*.

An **intensive pronoun** intensifies, or emphasizes, a noun or pronoun already in the sentence. Grammatically it functions as an appositive, renaming the preceding noun or pronoun. Unlike the reflexive pronoun, it could be removed without changing the basic meaning of the sentence.

> The supervisor *himself* read my report.
>
> I hope that they *themselves* will move the furniture.

Although an intensive pronoun often comes immediately after the word it renames, it may also come later in the sentence.

> The supervisor read my report *himself*.
>
> I hope that they will move the furniture *themselves*.

In a compound construction, mention your hearer first and yourself last.

Use a **reflexive pronoun** as a direct object, indirect object, or object of a preposition only when the object refers to the same person or thing as the subject of the clause.

Use an **intensive pronoun** as an appositive to emphasize a noun or another pronoun already in the sentence.

8.7 **PRACTICE** *the skill*

Underline the correct pronoun or pronouns from the choices in parentheses.

1. The man whose name became synonymous with fountain pens, Lewis Waterman *(he, himself)*, invented the first internationally successful fountain pen in 1884.

2. Though it is probably not a favorite with *(me or you, you or me)*, the fountain pen was the favorite in the West until the invention of the ballpoint pen after World War II.

3. In 1938 brothers Georg and Ladislao Biro, a chemist and an editor, perfected the ballpoint pen by *(they, themselves)*.

4. The Japanese helped *(them, themselves)* by developing the felt-tip pen.

5. It is ideally suited to the Japanese writing style, with which *(you and he, he and you)* are familiar.

6. Just between *(you and me, me and you)*, I would rather not have to use a felt-tip pen.

7. Though it may seem that school children have used pencils forever, William Monroe gave *(them, themselves)* the sharpenable lead pencil in 1812.

8. The developers of the mechanical drafting pencil, which came much later, initially marketed *(it, itself)* for drafters, engineers, and artists.

9. Extravagant materials are sometimes used for writing; even diamonds *(they, themselves)* are used to inscribe very hard materials like glass, plastic, or metal.

10. The computer *(it, itself)* can be considered a writing tool; it writes with the erasability of a pencil but prints with the permanency of a pen.

REVIEW *the skill*

Underline the part of the sentence that contains an error in courtesy order or the use of reflexive and intensive pronouns. Write the correction in the blank. If the sentence is already correct, write C in the blank.

1. My friend and I recently read *The Elements of Style* by William Strunk and E. B. White.

   _____

2. The authors themselves were already quite familiar to Kerri and myself.

   _____

3. In fact, themselves are so well known that the book is sometimes referred to as "Strunk and White."

   _____

4. Itself was first published as the text for a college class taught by Strunk.

   _____

5. E. B. White was a student of himself.

   _____

6. I and my friends know White best as the author of *Charlotte's Web*.

   _____

7. I hope the book was helpful to Brenna and yourself.

   _____

8. *The Elements of Style* has been re-released several times and is itself a classic book on writing.

   _____

9. Lee and you should read the book yourselves.

   _____

10. Strunk and White's work made myself and my class rethink our writing strategies.

   _____

CUMULATIVE *review*

Rewrite the following paragraphs, correcting the ten errors from these categories: subject-verb agreement, pronoun-antecedent agreement, verb use, pronoun reference, pronoun case, pronoun courtesy order, and use of reflexive and intensive pronouns.

In some cultures, the act of writing is an art in itself. Us students have been studying about calligraphy. China, Korea, and Japan has valued beautiful calligraphy for centuries. In the Middle Ages, Japanese poetry is often written in a particularly graceful style called *hiragana*. Japanese artists combined calligraphy with illustration. His skill is evident in the paintings of the *Yamato-e* style. One famous example is the *Genji* scrolls, containing an eleventh-century tale of Japanese court life.

Everyone in class must present a report on their favorite aspect of Japanese culture. Me and Toby have began the research for his report about the Japanese poet Buson. He was a famous painter and poet of the eighteenth century whom wrote many haiku in the traditional style of his teacher, Basho.

WRITING

Ponder the path of thy feet, and let all thy ways be established.
Proverbs 4:26

Christians and the Internet

You may well have a question about whether Christians have any business trafficking on the Internet. There are many legitimate and beneficial reasons to use the World Wide Web. E-mail is inexpensive and speedy. Missionaries report that e-mail has aided their ministries and their family relations immensely. Persons in underprivileged parts of the world have access to important and potentially life-saving medical information. And that information is available twenty-four hours a day, can be kept extremely current, and is usually free. You can bank, shop, read the Bible, order tickets, get groceries and medicine, send a greeting card, and do much, much more. But there is a negative side. Besides the many good things, pornography, gambling, Satanism, and suggestive e-mail, not to mention fraudulent information, are readily available on the Web. One pastor said that he has counseled more people about inappropriate Internet use than he has about any other issue in his several decades of ministry.

So how should Christians handle the question of what to do with the Internet? For some families, the best approach to the Internet may be to avoid it entirely. After all, Christians must be "strangers and pilgrims" (Heb. 11:13) whose affections are on "things above" (Col. 3:2). They are enjoined to "stand against the wiles of the devil" (Eph. 6:11). Therefore, the argument that "everyone else is online" is not, by itself, sufficient to persuade the committed Christian to use the Internet. On the other hand, Christians are also not to be hidden but are to be out in the open for others to see (Matt. 5:14-15). Christ also prayed "not that thou shouldest take them out of the world, but that thou shouldest keep them from the evil" (John 17:15). The matter is one to be discussed thoroughly and considered carefully.

If you and your family should decide to use the Internet, one way to avoid problems is to remove the element of secrecy that ensnares many users. Make sure that your computer is located in a high-traffic area of your house—that way other family members can help with accountability. Don't use the Internet when you are home alone or when everyone else is asleep. Many people avoid secrecy by sharing a password with someone else in their family (each one knows half); that way, both people must be present in order to log on. Of course, nothing done by computer is truly secret, but the Internet can lull you into thinking that only you know what you view. Anyone can check your browser; every site you visit has a record of your being there; and your Internet service provider (ISP) knows what you view. Above all, before Christ "all things are naked and opened unto the eyes of him with whom we have to do" (Heb. 4:13).

Danger on the Internet is often only a click away. A reliable filter is one of the best ways to avoid the immediacy of viewing wrong material, perhaps by accident. The best suggestion is a filtered ISP that is difficult to bypass. However, there are several other options for those who want to protect themselves. Remember that no filter can keep all harmful material from appearing on your screen. Filters are, after all, only as reliable as their programmers; and with the vast amount of information being added to the Internet daily, no filtering system can be expected to work perfectly.

This is why all Christians who choose to use the Internet must accept personal responsibility to heed biblical warnings. No one is above temptation, for the very one who thinks he is strong must "take heed lest he fall" (I Cor. 10:12). The devil, a "roaring lion," seeks people to "devour" (I Pet. 5:8), and the Internet is one of his favorite stomping grounds. The book of Proverbs is replete with warnings against sins done in secret, persons lying in wait, and the deceit of the wicked. As with books read, television viewed, and music listened to, the biblical injunction governing the use of the Internet calls for vigilance, discernment, and personal holiness. Like David, a Christian must decide before going online that he "will set no wicked thing before [his] eyes" (Psalm 101:3).

Many, if not most, Internet users are consumers of Web content rather than creators of it. They access dictionaries and encyclopedias for research, browse various sites for news, and use search engines to discover bits of information. They stay in touch with relatives through e-mail and locate bargains on auction sites. However, *creating* Web content becomes an increasingly important skill for students of the twenty-first century. In this assignment, you will learn a little of how to create good Web content.

Working with your teacher and your classmates, design a webpage for your class or school. Make your webpage as informal or as formal as you decide is appropriate for your purposes. This assignment will give you a chance to enhance your visual and verbal communication skills.

Planning

✔ **Preview successful websites.** To get a feel for what works well, look at some proven websites. Your teacher may give you a list of suggested sites to access. Look at what makes those sites attractive, readable, and usable. What about the site makes you want to return to it? What about the site makes you frustrated? Or what would you like to change?

✔ **Brainstorm about the purpose of your webpage.** Decide whether your page will be a place for school notices and news articles of school events or whether it will be a place for your class to post examples of your writing. Will your purpose be to inform or to amuse? to analyze or to persuade? Most school-wide webpages inform readers of events on the school calendar and then post photographs after the event is over. Some include a homework schedule or sports roster. You may decide instead to make your page class specific, e.g., your writing and grammar class or the sophomore class. If so, what you post on your page can be more targeted. Keep your purpose in mind throughout the planning and drafting stages.

✔ **Identify your audience.** Because you will want others to read and enjoy your webpage, think about who will be reading it. Will your audience be primarily fellow classmates? Will students from the entire student body—both younger and older—be reading the page? What could you do to accommodate their interests? If your audience will include students outside your age or class group, avoid using inside jokes or jargon known only to your group. Remember your audience when you select graphics for your page. For example, avoid clowns and balloons if your page is intended for senior high students who want to learn more about preparing for college.

✔ **Choose a topic and a form.** Since this assignment will most likely involve several different types of writing (editorial, poetry, short story, and so on), you will need to work with your teacher to determine what type of article/writing you will add to the webpage. You should identify an issue, situation, topic, or problem that you would like to discuss or evaluate. Your piece could cover a recent sports event or review the school play, or you may want to critique a book you have read. You could also tell a brief story, analyze a cause-and-effect relationship you have noticed, or compose a poem appropriate to the webpage. In short, choose a type of writing that you have worked on already this year—one that fits into the structure you have predetermined.

✔ **Conduct research or collect information on your topic.** Use the writing assignments from previous chapters to remind yourself of the kind of information you will need to gather before writing the type of composition you have chosen. Review these chapters on your own before you begin writing.

✔ **Organize your webpage.** With your class, choose your major sections first and any subsections that are needed. Make sure that the section headings reflect the purpose that you decided upon earlier. The following headings are intended to inform senior high students about school happenings.

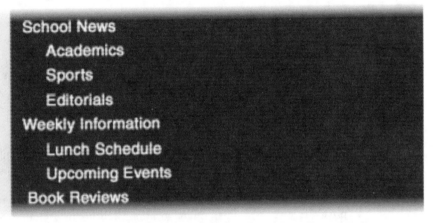

The sample headings below are intended to entertain the entire student body.

✔ **Plan the structure.** A visitor to your page should be able to find everything on your page without having to think too much. For example, in the first sample webpage above, all of the headings and subheadings are self-explanatory: a visitor would know immediately what he would find under "Sports" or "Lunch Schedule." In the second sample, visitors may be confused by "Funnies from the Hallway" (a section containing amusing school-related anecdotes) or "Weekly Interview" (a section devoted to interviewing a different student, parent, or teacher each week). If your cleverly worded heading is a must, consider adding a blurb to aid visitors in their navigation.

Funnies from the Hallway (Jokes, School-Related Anecdotes)

tip

Since new computer and Internet terms crop up nearly every day, dictionaries often do not contain definitions of technological terms.

Remember from first-hand experience that there are few things more frustrating than going to a site and not being able to find what you are looking for.

Because they are called to communicate the gospel, Christians have always been excited about advances in communication. In the second century AD, Christians developed the codex to replace the cumbersome scroll. During the Protestant Reformation, Martin Luther used the printing press so that his writings could be read by thousands of people all over Europe. Now the Internet gives the Christian a comparable opportunity. The following is what a missionary in Asia says about websites and the Internet: "I wanted a way to get helpful materials to people all over the world, but I found that not many resources were available in Chinese. It then occurred to me to make a website of helpful materials for Chinese-speaking people. They can download my articles and information and print them easily. Another example of technology's profitableness is the ability to put sermons on the Internet. One Sunday I preached in a church in the United States, and the church uploaded my sermon to their website. A week and a half later, I received an email from a lady in China who had listened to my sermon."

How could you use technology to help you do the work of a missionary? What things could you post that would be a witness? What kind of people would you target?

browser	A computer program that accesses webpages and files from the Internet or a network
button	A graphical link on which to click
download	To copy data to one's own computer from a host computer or server
filter	A program that blocks a computer's access to data or programs that meet certain criteria
hit	A user's accessing an item (such as a webpage) on a server
homepage	The first or main page of a website
hypertext	A retrieval system used to link specific information in a document/file to other related information
link	Media containing hypertext or a piece of text that, when clicked on, refers the user to another part of a document/file or to a new one
online	Connected to a computer network or to the Internet
post	To place text on an online location (website, newsgroup, etc.)
search engine	A program for searching the Internet or a database that allows users to input keywords or phrases and receive a list of applicable results
server	A computer with software that makes services, such as access to data files, data (also *file server*) storage, websites, or communications resources, available to users on a network or the Internet
usability	The accessibility and understandability of a program or document
webpage	A document on the Web
website	A set of interconnected webpages, usually including a homepage, created by a person or group as a means of relating information

Drafting

✔ **Employ effective Web writing.** Writing for the Web is very different from writing for other media. Most industry experts agree on several basic principles of Web writing, and you will do well to pay attention to them.

tip

In writing hypertext, make every word justify its existence. If it's expendable, cut it.

- Information needs to be in shortened form. It is widely held that most Web readers dislike scrolling from one screen to the next. If an article or story does not fit on a single screen, they tend not to read it at all. Sometimes a longer piece is called for, so the one-screen dictum must be broken. However, careful planning may help you to make your work brief in the first place or to shorten it after composing. Shortening your piece will involve cutting, hooking, and organizing.

CUTTING | Web content should be approximately fifty percent shorter than printed text. Write long if you must but then try to cut your piece in half. Cut transitional phrases and multiple examples. Use shortened words and phrases, e.g., *distinguish* instead of *make a distinction between*. In Web content, a paragraph of one hundred words can be deadly.

| **HOOKING** | Use your graphics and your words to catch your readers' attention. Readers are surfing into and out of sites, sometimes within seconds. Making your headings and subheadings attention grabbing as well as informative can cause your reader to stay at your page. Some common hooks are unusually worded statements, questions, and quotations, or addressing the reader directly. |

> **Word of Mouse**
> **Or, What I Learned on the Web**
> **Your Opinion Poll**

| **ORGANIZING** | Making hypertext readable usually involves giving information in readable chunks. A readable chunk is two or three brief paragraphs and lots of white space. If your piece is longer than that, consider adding headings, e.g., "Five Reasons to Read This Book," to break up the text. Use fragments for precision and emphasis. Bulleted lists are also great organizational tools. |

- Fonts need to be legible. This requirement includes avoiding using all caps unless absolutely needed. Capital letters tend to overemphasize what you are saying and make your content less credible. There are a number of standard fonts that are viewable across platforms, i.e., PCs and Macs. These include Arial, Helvetica, Times New Roman, Times, Courier, New Courier, Georgia, and Verdana. Using one of these fonts will insure that your text is being viewed for the most part exactly as you intended.

- Pages need to load quickly. On the Web, speed is essential. Users want to see content as quickly as possible; therefore, you should eliminate any images that do not add value to your content. Instead of adding images, use your layout and design to provide uniqueness to your page. The images you do use should be saved as low-resolution .GIF or .JPG to cut down on the file size.

✔ **Put the visitor first.** It will help to imagine yourself as a first-timer to your page. What do you want to see? Can you navigate through the page and access the information you need?

✔ **Start writing.** Jump right in and begin your first draft. Make sure that you follow the guidelines that your teacher has established for length, tone, and purpose of your piece.

✔ **Format your webpage.** Keep in mind the limitations of the webpage format. Most readers on the Web look for the following things when surfing.

- Keep your pages small. This refers to the size of the page file (not the screen size), including any images you scan. Most Web publishing tools allow you to see the size of the page and the approximate download time for someone accessing the page with a dial-up modem.

- Using the information you gleaned from your preview in the planning stage, try to make your webpage work the same way that other popular websites work. This will give new visitors an immediate advantage when they access your page.

- Be consistent with how the pages look. Once you establish the look for your webpage, be slow to change background colors or the navigational tools. Inconsistency and frequent changes become confusing to repeat visitors to your page. You can make slight changes as long as the overall look stays consistent.

- Have fun with your page. If your page is boring and useless to you, it probably will be for your visitors too!

Revising

tip

Look at your webpage as though you are viewing it through the eyes of a first-time visitor to the site.

✔ **Read your writing over and make corrections.** Does your work accurately reflect the point you were trying to make? Watch for words and phrases that are weak or that could be made stronger. Look for missing facts or information that might confuse your readers.

✔ **Think about the purpose of your webpage.** Does your webpage accomplish that purpose? Can a visitor easily access the information he wants? Is there any information that a potential visitor might be interested in that you could add to your page? Consider making changes that will improve usability and generate interest in your page.

✔ **Look at your color choices and graphics.** Make sure that they do not detract from your message. You could add your school's logo or use your school colors if they complement your overall design.

✔ **Get peer response to your piece and to your webpage.** Peers can offer feedback about the interest level accuracy of your writing. First-time visitors will provide you with valuable information about your page. Decide what information is useful for your purposes and incorporate that into your design.

Publishing

✔ **Post your webpage!**

✔ **Contact friends and relatives and tell them about your page.** Encourage them to respond to the page (if your page has that capability).

✔ **Print your article and send it to someone.** Or read it aloud to your family.

✔ **Let your local newspaper know about your webpage.**

THINK ABOUT IT

Inductive and Deductive Reasoning

Have you ever had a discussion with someone who was unreasonable? Let's say that you and your brother are discussing taking out the trash. You calmly explain that you have taken out the trash four times that week and now it is his turn. He says, "Well, you never let me borrow your bike anyway." What does a bicycle have to do with taking out the trash? This is obviously not a good argument. An argument is stating a set of statements or premises to support a conclusion. An argument is not a loud dispute or name calling similar to what might follow your brother's last comment. To give an argument, you must have adequate support for your conclusion.

The two basic kinds of arguments are inductive and deductive. Generally, an inductive argument moves from the specific to the general, while a deductive argument moves from the general to the specific. The premises of induction are usually based on observation and are intended to show that that conclusion is probable or most likely. The premises of deduction are usually laws and principles and are intended to prove that the conclusion must be true. Look at the following examples:

INDUCTION	I got an A on both the quizzes and the tests for this unit. I made an A on the quiz. Therefore, I will probably get an A on the test as well.
DEDUCTION	If I make A's on all my quizzes and A's on all my tests, then I will have an A in the class. I made A's on all my quizzes and tests. Therefore, I have an A in the class.

Identify the following arguments as _inductive_ or _deductive_.

_____ 1. All mammals are warm-blooded. Dogs are mammals. Therefore, dogs are warm-blooded.

_____ 2. Every time I go to the dentist, he finds a cavity. I am going to the dentist tomorrow. Therefore, he will find a cavity tomorrow.

_____ 3. I've noticed that many people in class who take notes usually make better grades on the test than those who do not take notes. I will start taking notes, and I will get better grades on the test.

_____ 4. In order to get an A for the project, every student must give an oral report. I did not give an oral report. Therefore, I will not get an A on the project.

_____ 5. My grammar book says that I must use an objective case pronoun after a preposition. I need to place either _who_ or _whom_ after the preposition _with_. Therefore, I will write, "With _whom_ are you going?"

_____ 6. I have noticed that in the sentence "With _whom_ are you going?" the objective case pronoun follows the preposition _with_. I have also noticed that objective case pronouns always follow prepositions in every sentence that I have studied today. It must be correct, then, to use objective case pronouns after prepositions.

_____ 7. Everyone who believes on the name of the Lord Jesus Christ will be saved. I have believed on the name of the Lord Jesus Christ. Therefore, I am saved.

_____ 8. Neither I nor anyone I have ever known has ever seen a UFO. Therefore, UFOs do not exist.

_____ 9. Everyone I know is going to a party tomorrow. Therefore, I should go to the party as well.

_____ 10. Mom says that I have to prepare the house for our guests tomorrow night. There is a lot of work to do. Therefore, I cannot go to the party.

Thinking It Through

Look at numbers 5 and 6 in the exercise. Write a set of similar arguments. One should be an inductive argument, and one should be a deductive argument. The conclusion of your inductive argument will probably be the first premise of your deductive argument.

Writers find the seeds of fictional stories in many places. Some start with a theme, an idea, that they want to present in an engaging way. Others are inspired by a real event, out of which they create a story and realize a theme. Still others start with a character, drawing on real people they know and the relationships they have with them. They create conflict between characters and reveal truth in the events that follow. Still others look back at moments of intense emotion and what caused that emotion. In doing so, they find a subject that is important to them and seek to evoke a response in the reader.

As you read Chekhov's story "Chameleon," consider what Chekhov might be trying to teach. The writing assignment in this chapter will help you write a short story that teaches a lesson or relates a truth in an interesting way.

Chameleon *by Anton Chekhov (translated by Ivy Litvinov)*

Police Inspector Ochumelov crossed the marketplace in a new greatcoat holding a bundle in his hand. After him strode a red-haired constable carrying a sieve filled to the brim with confiscated gooseberries. All around was silence. . . . There was not a soul in the marketplace. . . . The open doors of small shops and taverns gaped drearily out at God's world, like so many hungry jaws. There were not even any beggars standing near them.

All of a sudden the sound of a voice came to Ochumelov's ears. "So you'd bite, would you, you cur! Don't let it go, lads! Biting is not allowed nowadays. Hold it! Ow!"

A dog's whine was heard. Ochumelov glanced in the direction of the sound and this is what he saw: a dog came running out of the timberyard of the merchant Pichugin on three legs, pursued by a man in a starched print shirt and an unbuttoned waistcoat, his whole body bent forward; the man stumbled and caught hold of the dog by one of its hind legs. There was another whine, and again a shout of: "Don't let it go!" Drowsy faces were thrust out of shops, and in no time a crowd which seemed to have sprung out of the earth had gathered around the timberyard.

"Looks like a public disturbance, Your Honor!" said the constable.

Ochumelov turned, and marched up to the crowd. Right in front of the gate of the yard he saw the above-mentioned individual in the unbuttoned waistcoat, who stood there with his right hand raised, displaying a bleeding finger to the crowd. The words: "I'll give it to you, you devil!" seemed to be written on his tipsy countenance, and the finger itself looked like a banner of victory.

Ochumelov recognized in this individual Khryukin, the goldsmith. In the very middle of the crowd, its forelegs well apart, sat the culprit, its whole body a-tremble—a white borzoi pup, with a pointed nose and a yellow spot on its back. In its tearful eyes was an expression of misery and horror.

"What's all this about?" asked Ochumelov, shouldering his way through the crowd. "What are you doing here? Why are you holding up your finger? Who shouted?"

"I was walking along, Your Honor, as quiet as a lamb," began Khryukin, coughing into his fist. "I had business about some wood with Mitri Mitrich here, and suddenly, for no reason whatever, that nuisance bit my finger. Excuse me, but I'm a working man. . . . Mine is a very intricate trade. Make them pay me compensation—perhaps I won't be able to move this finger for a week. It doesn't say in the law, Your Honor, that we have to put up with ferocious animals. If everyone's to start biting, life won't be worth living. . . ."

"H'm . . . well, well," said Ochumelov severely, coughing and twitching his eyebrows. "Well, well . . . whose dog is it? I shan't leave it at this. I'll teach people to let dogs run about! It's time something was done about gentlemen who are not willing to obey the regulations! He'll get such a fine, the scoundrel—I'll teach him what it means to let dogs and cattle of all sorts rove about! I'll show him what's what! Eldirin," he continued, turning to the constable, "find out whose dog it is, and draw up a statement. And the dog must be exterminated without delay. It's probably mad . . . whose dog is it, I ask?"

"I think it belongs to General Zhigalov," said a voice from the crowd.

"General Zhigalov! H'm. Help me off with my coat, Eldirin. . . . Phew, how hot it is! It must be going to rain." He turned to Khryukin: "One thing I don't understand—how did it happen to bite you? How could it have got at your finger? Such a little dog, and you such a strapping fellow! You must have scratched your finger with a nail, and then taken it into your head to get paid for it. I know you fellows! A set of devils!"

"He burned the end of its nose with a lighted cigarette for a joke, Your Honor, and it snapped at him, it's nobody's fool! That Khryukin's always up to some mischief, Your Honor!"

"None of your lies, Squinty! You didn't see me do it, so why lie? His Honor is a wise gentleman, he knows who's lying and who's telling a God's truth. May the justice of the peace try me if I'm lying! It says in the law . . . all men are equal now. I have a brother in the police myself, if you want to know. . . ."

"Don't argue!"

"No, that isn't the General's dog," remarked the constable profoundly. "The General hasn't got a dog like that. All his dogs are pointers."

"Are you sure?"

"Quite sure, Your Honor."

"And you're right! The General's dogs are expensive, breed-dogs, and this one—just look at it! Ugly, mangy cur! Why should anyone keep a dog like that? Are you crazy? If a dog like that were to find itself in Moscow or Petersburg, d'you know what would happen to it? Nobody would worry about the law, it would be got rid of in a minute. You're a victim, Khryukin, and mind you don't leave it at that. He must be taught a lesson! It's high time. . . ."

"Perhaps it is the General's after all," said the constable, thinking aloud. "You can't tell by looking at it. I saw one just like it in his yard the other day."

"Of course it's the General's!" came the voice from the crowd.

"H'm! Help me on with my coat, Eldirin. . . . I felt a gust of wind. I'm shivery. Take it to the General's and ask them. Say I found it, and sent it. And tell them not to let it into the street. Perhaps it's an expensive dog, and it'll soon get spoiled if every brute thinks he can stick cigarettes into its nose. A dog's a delicate creature. And you put down your hand, blockhead! Stop showing everyone your silly finger. It's your own fault. . . ."

"Here comes the General's chef, we'll ask him. . . . Hi, there, Prokhor! Come here, old man! Have a look at this dog . . . is it yours?"

"What next! We've never had one like that in our lives!"

"No need to make any more inquiries," said Ochumelov. "It's a stray. What's the good of standing here talking. You've been told it's a stray, so a stray it is. Destroy it and have done with the matter."

"It isn't ours," continued Prokhor. "It belongs to the General's brother, who came a short time ago. Our General takes no interest in borzois. His brother now, he likes . . ."

"What, has the General's brother come? Vladimir Ivanich?" exclaimed Ochumelov, an ecstatic smile spreading over his features. "Fancy that! And I didn't know. Come to stay?"

"That's right."

"Just fancy! Wanted to see his brother! And I didn't know. So it's *his* dog? Very glad! Take it . . . it's a nice little doggie! Snap at his finger! Ha-ha-ha! Come now, don't tremble! Gr-gr . . . the little rascal's angry. . . . What a pup!"

Prokhor called the dog and walked out of the timberyard with it. The crowd laughed at Khryukin.

"I'll have you yet!" Ochumelov threatened him, and, wrapping his greatcoat around him, he continued his way across the marketplace.

USAGE

ADJECTIVE AND ADVERB USE

Showing Comparison with Modifiers

Adjectives and adverbs can show comparison. There are three levels, or degrees, of comparison. In the positive, no comparison is made. Two persons or things are compared in the comparative degree. The superlative degree indicates an extreme, especially when comparing three or more persons or things.

Adjectives
p. 13
Adverbs
p. 15

Positive	no comparison made	The meeting was long.
Comparative	comparison of two things or groups	The meeting was longer than previous meetings.
Superlative	comparison of three or more things or groups	The meeting was the longest meeting we had this month.

Regular Comparison of Adjectives

Nearly all one-syllable adjectives show the comparative form by the addition of *er* and the superlative form by the addition of *est*.

Positive	Comparative	Superlative
blue	bluer	bluest
damp	damper	dampest
warm	warmer	warmest

Also, some two-syllable adjectives take *er* and *est,* especially those that end in *y, ly,* and *le.*

Positive	Comparative	Superlative
clumsy	clumsier	clumsiest
sleepy	sleepier	sleepiest
funny	funnier	funniest
lovely	lovelier	loveliest
noble	nobler	noblest

Other two-syllable modifiers sound awkward with *er* and *est* and use *more* and *most* to make comparisons. Adjectives with three or more syllables make comparisons using *more* and *most*.

Positive	Comparative	Superlative
famous	more famous	most famous
complex	more complex	most complex
elegant	more elegant	most elegant
problematic	more problematic	most problematic

ESL Because the superlative degree indicates an extreme, the definite article *the* usually goes with it.

In this class, Bill is *the tallest*.
Mary is *the tallest girl*.

Absolute Comparative and Superlative of Adjectives

The comparative and the superlative are sometimes used in an "absolute" sense—that is, without any intention of specific comparison to other things. Usually this absolute sense is indicated by certain expressions that have become idioms in English.

ABSOLUTE COMPARATIVE | We lived in a *lower-income* housing development.
ABSOLUTE SUPERLATIVE | He told me the *saddest* story.

In the first example, the absolute comparative indicates "low income." It does not indicate a level lower than low income. In the second example, there is no comparison intended; the absolute superlative is used for emphasis to mean "a very sad story."

in SUMMARY

Adjectives and adverbs have three levels of comparison: **positive, comparative,** and **superlative.**

Nearly all one-syllable adjectives show the comparative form by the addition of *er* and the superlative form by the addition of *est.*

Some two-syllable adjectives take *er* and *est,* especially those that end in *y, ly,* and *le.*

Some two-syllable modifiers use *more* and *most* to make comparisons.

Adjectives with three or more syllables make comparisons using *more* and *most.*

The comparative and the superlative can be used as an **absolute modifier** without any intention of specific comparison to other things.

9.1 PRACTICE *the skill*

Underline the correct adjective from the choices in parentheses.

1. A kremlin is a *(secure, securer)* area in a Russian city.

2. The name *kremlin* is *(more recognizable, most recognizable)* than the Russian word *kreml* ("fortress"), from which the name comes.

3. The *(famousest, most famous)* kremlin is in Moscow.

4. Moscow's Kremlin has a *(long, longer)* history of government than one might think, dating back to the 1100s.

5. The czars ruled from the Kremlin from the mid-1500s to 1712, and the Communists established perhaps an even *(repressiver, more repressive)* government there in 1918.

6. When the Soviet Union collapsed in 1991, the Kremlin again became the *(official, more official)* center of Russian government activity.

7. The Kremlin is shaped like a triangle and is almost one and one-half miles around at its *(out, outer)* edges.

8. Enclosed within the *(massive, more massive)* walls of the Kremlin are towers, palaces, and cathedrals.

9. Today many Kremlin buildings are museums, housing some of the *(greatest, most great)* treasures of Russian history.

10. Without doubt, the inside of the Kremlin with its magnificent structures is *(inviting, more inviting)* than the walled outside.

REVIEW *the skill*

Write the correct form of the adjective in parentheses.

————————— 1. Russia is (*famous*) for its contributions to the arts.

————————— 2. Russians were involved in artistic endeavors from practically the beginning, the (*early*) days of their history.

————————— 3. But their efforts became (*noticeable*) to the outside world in the 1800s than they had been before.

————————— 4. Religion, Western thought, and local customs have all shaped the Russian arts so that it is difficult to tell which was (*influential*).

————————— 5. For example, Russian architecture shows the (*strong*) influence of the Byzantine church in the onion-shaped domes of its cathedrals.

————————— 6. However, buildings from the time of Peter I with their baroque style show (*great*) ties with the West than with the Eastern church.

————————— 7. In addition, early Russian music was (*simple*) than later developments, for it was mostly vocal, coming from folk tradition and the church.

————————— 8. The introduction of Italian opera and the combining of elements into a distinct Russian style, however, provided some of the (*beautiful*) music that the world has ever heard.

————————— 9. Furthermore, Russian painting began with (*holy*) purposes than it later showed.

————————— 10. While painting had its origins mainly in church decoration, the influence of the West led to a (*low*) level of art that rejected absolutes.

Regular Comparison of Adverbs

Many adverbs do not show comparison and therefore do not change form, but others have the same changes for comparison that adjectives have. Most dictionaries give you help as to whether to use *er* and *est* or *more* and *most*. One reliable rule is that adverbs made from adjectives by the addition of *ly* always take *more* and *most*, never *er* and *est*.

Positive	Comparative	Superlative
late	later	(the) latest
slowly	more slowly	(the) most slowly
cautiously	more cautiously	(the) most cautiously
brusquely	more brusquely	(the) most brusquely

Irregular Comparison of Adjectives and Adverbs

Some adjectives and adverbs have irregular comparative and superlative forms. The forms of these modifiers do not follow a regular pattern.

Positive	Comparative	Superlative
good (adjective)	better	best
well (adverb)	better	(the) best
bad (adjective)	worse	worst
badly (adverb)	worse	worst
much (adjective)	more	most
many (adjective)	more	most

in SUMMARY

Many adverbs have the same changes for comparison that adjectives have. Adverbs made from adjectives by the addition of *ly* always take *more* and *most*, never *er* and *est*.

Irregular adjectives and adverbs may have entirely different forms to show comparison.

9.3 PRACTICE *the skill*

Underline the correct adjective or adverb from the choices in parentheses.

1. Of all his classes this year, Slava likes geography (*better, best*).

2. Because he is from Russia, he studied the chapter on his home (*carefully, more carefully*) than the other chapters.

3. Russia is two and a half times (*larger, more large*) than the United States.

4. Russia covers (*more, most*) of the eastern half of Europe and stretches across the northern third of Asia.

5. Russia contains (*many, most*) mountain ranges, including the Tien Shan, Ural, Altai, and Caucasus Mountains.

6. The Caucasus Mountains contain the (*most high, highest*) peak in Europe, Mount Elbrus.

7. The Ural Mountains, which divide Europe from Asia, are (*famous, more famous*) for their gems and semiprecious stones.

8. At some places, the southern Ural Mountains spread (*more widely, most widely*) than in other places to cover widths of one hundred miles.

9. Europe's (*longest, most long*) river, the Volga, is in Russia.

10. Do you know the geography of Russia (*well, better*) than you did yesterday?

Write the correct form of the modifier in parentheses.

————————— 1. Russia is (*truly*) a land of superlatives.

————————— 2. It can claim to be the most unusual or the (*good*) in many aspects.

————————— 3. As the world's largest country, Russia can claim (*much*) land area than any other country can (over one-tenth of the land area in the entire world).

————————— 4. Russia must conduct its foreign affairs (*carefully*) than many other countries do, for it has the greatest number of neighbors—fourteen.

————————— 5. Possibly the (*bad*) part of having so many neighbors is that many of them are potentially dangerous.

————————— 6. The city of St. Petersburg can (*proudly*) claim the distinction of being the world's northernmost city of over one million people.

————————— 7. Its phenomenon of "white nights" from the middle of June to early July ensures that even those who stay awake (*late*) than usual—even all night!—will not see the sun set.

————————— 8. Russia should be able to accommodate fishermen (*well*) than many other countries can, for it contains some huge lakes.

————————— 9. For example, Lake Baikal, the deepest lake in the world, contains (*much*) water than all of the Great Lakes combined.

————————— 10. Finally, Russia, a land of great mineral wealth, produces (*much*) petroleum of all the countries in the world.

Problems with Modifiers

Avoiding Double Comparisons

Never use both *er* and *more* to form the comparative or both *est* and *most* to form the superlative. Using both is an error called a double comparison.

WRONG	This book is *more better* than that book.
RIGHT	This book is *better* than that book.

Avoiding Double Negatives

In standard English we use only one negative word to make a sentence convey negative meaning. The use of another negative word along with the adverb *not* is called a double negative. Double negatives should be avoided in both speaking and writing. To correct a double negative, eliminate or replace one of the negative words.

WRONG	We didn't have nothing to give.
RIGHT	We didn't have anything to give. We had nothing to give.

Distinguishing Between Adverbs and Predicate Adjectives

In the sentence pattern S-LV-PA, the linking verb is directly followed by a predicate adjective, not by an adverb. However, some verbs that can be linking verbs in one sentence can be transitive or intransitive in another sentence.

Sentence Patterns S-LV-PA, S-*be*-Advl
p. 41

LINKING VERB AND PREDICATE ADJECTIVE	The actor *looked* calm before his scene.
INTRANSITIVE VERB AND ADVERB	The actor *looked* directly at the audience.
LINKING VERB AND PREDICATE ADJECTIVE	The tree *grew* tall and strong.
ADVERB, TRANSITIVE VERB, AND DIRECT OBJECT	The gardener always *grew* several tomato plants.

In the first sentence, *looked* is a linking verb, and *calm* is a predicate adjective describing *actor*. In the second sentence, *looked* is an intransitive verb, and *directly* is an adverb describing *looked,* not *actor.* Be sure not to place an adverb directly after a linking verb. For example, it would be incorrect to write, "The actor looked calmly before his scene."

in SUMMARY

Do not use *more* or *most* with a modifier that already ends in *er* or *est.*

Use only one negative word to convey negative meaning.

Some verbs can be intransitive, transitive, or linking. Do not place an adverb directly after a linking verb or a transitive verb.

PRACTICE *the skill*

Underline the correct adjective or adverb from the choices in parentheses.

1. Over the years, the native Slavic music of Russia grew more (*complex, complexly*) as it gained Byzantine, Mongol, and western European elements.

2. Despite these foreign borrowings, Russian music was (*purer, more purer*) than that of many other countries for centuries.

3. Because Russia was isolated from foreign contact for much of its history, Russian music was not strongly influenced by (*any, no*) European ideas until the nineteenth century.

4. Of all the modern Russian composers, perhaps Peter Ilich Tchaikovsky is the (*most famous, most famousest*).

5. Of course, many people think that the music of Sergei Rachmaninoff and Igor Stravinsky is (*good, well*) too.

6. To nationalist composers such as Mussorgsky and Rimski-Korsakov, Tchaikovsky's European-style music affected Russian cultural life (*bad, badly*).

7. However, their compositions, which combined native Slavic melodies with the style of traditional Russian folk songs, sounded (*bad, badly*) to those who preferred Western music.

8. The music of Dmitri Shostakovich and Sergei Prokofiev grew (*popular, popularly*) during the Soviet era of the twentieth century.

9. Soviet government officials did not tolerate (*anything, nothing*) that they deemed unacceptable; therefore, they sometimes censured the music of Russian composers.

10. To the average listener, Prokofiev's *Peter and the Wolf* is probably (*better, more better*) known than his other works.

Tchaikovsky

REVIEW *the skill*

Rewrite each sentence, making the modifier clear or correct.

1. There isn't no denying that Russia is a huge, harsh country.

2. Russia's landscape and climate became importantly to the Russian people in times of war.

3. Twice Russia's geography fought almost more harder for the country than its soldiers did.

_____

_____

4. Napoleon and Hitler weren't expecting nothing like what their troops encountered in Russia.

_____

_____

5. In both cases the Russian army faced a more greater foe, but the Russians used their land to their advantage.

_____

_____

6. Rather than fighting near its western border, the Russian army drew the enemy more farther into the country.

_____

_____

7. As part of their scorched-earth policy, the Russians didn't leave nothing behind that would help the enemy survive.

_____

_____

_____

8. The weather grew coldly while the enemy was still in pursuit.

_____

_____

_____

9. The country that may have appeared pleasantly when the enemy entered became foreboding.

_____

_____

_____

10. Trying to conquer Russia may have been the most gravest mistake that Napoleon or Hitler made.

_____

_____

Placement of Modifiers

Misplaced Modifiers

Misplaced Prepositional Phrases p. 59

A modifier—whether it is a single word, a phrase, or a dependent clause—needs to be reasonably close to the word it modifies. If the position of the modifier makes it seem to modify the wrong word in the sentence, it is misplaced.

MISPLACED MODIFIER	Cole *almost* ate the entire pan of brownies
CORRECTION	Cole ate *almost* the entire pan of brownies.
MISPLACED MODIFIER	The students chased away the pigeons *in the second grade*.
CORRECTION	The students *in the second grade* chased away the pigeons.
MISPLACED MODIFIER	Last week we saw a submarine in the harbor *that had sunk.*
CORRECTION	Last week we saw a submarine *that had sunk* in the harbor.

Almost seems to modify *ate* in the first sentence. Cole may not have eaten any brownies, but he came close to eating them. In the second sentence, Cole clearly ate several brownies; he ate *almost* all of them. *Almost* clearly modifies *the entire pan of brownies*. In the third sentence, it would seem that it is the pigeons that are in the second grade; moving the prepositional phrase so that it clearly modifies *students* makes the sentence more logical.

One modifier that is frequently misused is the word *only.* Notice the difference in meaning this word can make:

Eric only waited one hour.

Eric waited only one hour.

Only Eric waited one hour.

The first sentence could mean that Eric only waited; he was not talking or reading a book. In the second sentence, *only* clearly modifies one hour. Eric could have been writing or exercising, but he had to wait only one hour, not two or three. In the third sentence, only Eric waited; no one else waited with him. Be sure that *only* and similar modifiers are as close as possible to the words they modify—usually just before the words or phrases they modify.

tip

Be more careful about modifier placement in writing than you are in speaking, where intonation and emphasis may make your meaning clear.

Two-Way Modifiers

A two-way modifier makes a sentence unclear because it stands between two sentence elements that it might modify. If the reader cannot tell which of the two it modifies, he cannot be sure what meaning the writer intended.

TWO-WAY MODIFIER	People who exercise frequently enjoy better health than those who do not exercise.

In the sentence above, the adverb is positioned between two verbs, and the reader cannot be sure whether *frequently* modifies *exercise* or *enjoy*. Correct a two-way modifier by moving the modifier to a clear position in the sentence.

CLEAR | People who frequently exercise enjoy better health than those who do not exercise.

People who exercise are likely to enjoy better health than those who do not exercise.

Depending on the meaning intended, more extensive revision may be necessary.

CLEAR | Frequent exercise improves a person's general health.

Dangling Modifiers

A dangling modifier is a modifier that does not actually modify anything. It is simply dangling there in the sentence. A dangling modifier cannot be corrected by moving it, for the word that it should modify is not in the sentence.

Participial Phrases p. 69

DANGLING MODIFIER | Rushing to the game, Kyle's bike toppled to the ground.

CORRECTION | Rushing to the game, Kyle lost control of his bike, and it toppled to the ground.

In the first sentence, who or what is rushing to the game? Kyle is rushing, not his bike. The modifier is "dangling" because the implied subject, *Kyle*, is not the same as the actual subject of the sentence. One way to correct a dangling modifier is to change the rest of the sentence so that the missing element is supplied right next to the modifier.

DANGLING MODIFIER | Although not on the official list, the security guard recognized me and allowed me to enter.

CORRECTION | Although I was not on the official list, the security guard recognized me and allowed me to enter.

Who is not on the official list? It is obviously not the security guard. A second way to correct a dangling modifier is to change the modifier into a complete clause that includes the missing element.

Modifiers That Split Infinitives

Sometimes a modifier comes between the *to* of an infinitive and the verb of the infinitive. The resulting construction is called a split infinitive. Split infinitives are not ungrammatical in English, but they may be awkward—especially if the modifier is several words long. You can usually improve a sentence by eliminating a split infinitive.

Infinitive Phrases p. 75

AWKWARD SPLIT INFINITIVE | She wanted to without hesitancy accept the position.

IMPROVED SENTENCE | She wanted to accept the position without hesitancy.

When the alternative would be awkward, some split infinitives are acceptable.

ACCEPTABLE | To really understand the play, you will need to see it.

AWKWARD | To understand the play really, you will need to see it.

in SUMMARY

To be clear, place a modifier close to the word it modifies.

Do not place a modifier between two sentence elements that it might modify.

Avoid dangling modifiers that do not modify anything in the sentence. Reword the modifier or the sentence.

In most cases, do not place a modifier between the *to* and the verb of an infinitive, creating a split infinitive.

PRACTICE *the skill*

Rewrite each sentence, making the modifiers clear or correct.

1. Anton Chekhov, one of Russia's famous writers, almost wrote a dozen plays.

   _____

   _____

2. Chekhov wrote just before his death *The Cherry Orchard,* his last play, which portrays the plight of an aristocratic family in danger of losing its home.

   _____

   _____

3. Lyubov, the family's matriarch, faces the imminent auction of her family's house and cherry orchard, returning from Paris.

   _____

   _____

4. Although their resources are few, Lyubov wastes money habitually giving parties.

   _____

   _____

5. Refusing to cut down the orchard, the neighbor Lopakhin's suggestion that part of the estate be leased out is rejected.

   _____

   _____

6. Lyubov and her brother, Gayev, ask an aunt to buy the estate that is estranged.

   _____

   _____

7. Musicians are hired by Lyubov for a party, wasting more money.

   _____

   _____

8. The two men return to reveal that Lopakhin, not Gayev, purchased the orchard estate during the party.

   _____

   _____

9. As they pack their belongings and leave, the audience hears the sound of axes chopping down the precious orchard.

   _____

   _____

10. Although the plot seems tragic, Chekhov intended it to actually be comic.

    _____

    _____

REVIEW *the skill*

Rewrite each sentence, making the modifiers clear or correct.

1. Siberia takes up alone a huge portion of Russia's geography.

_____

_____

2. In fact, Siberia is almost larger than any other country in the world.

_____

_____

3. Dramatically, temperatures during the winter months in Siberia can drop.

_____

_____

4. For example, in Verkhoyansk, in the far northeast, temperatures drop significantly only averaging -51° C (-60° F) during the month of January.

_____

_____

5. Nearly snowless at times, frost covers everything in sight.

_____

_____

6. Meaning "Sleeping Land," the Tatar language gives us the word *Siberia*.

_____

_____

7. During the Communist regime, political foes and criminals were sent to Siberia, where they were forced to without respite labor for their crimes.

_____

_____

8. Businesses that succeed primarily focus on mineral and industrial efforts.

_____

_____

9. Remaining permanently frozen, agriculture in the northern regions is difficult.

_____

_____

10. The top three to four feet only thaw, allowing mosses and shrubs to grow during the summer months.

_____

_____

CUMULATIVE *review*

Rewrite the paragraph, correcting the ten errors from these categories: subject-verb agreement, pronoun-antecedent agreement, pronoun reference, pronoun case, and adjective and adverb use.

During Soviet control of Russia, education was considered an important tool with which to correctly mold citizens. Public schooling was mandatory for all; therefore, almost everyone in Russia are literate. After the demise of communism, private schools appeared, and public schools began removing the influence of the Communist Party from textbooks. In Russia, daycare centers and preschools are popular, and they often begin attending preschool by age three. An eleven-year educational program (ages six to seventeen) are mandatory for all children. Russian students receive extensive training in reading and writing his language: it consumes ten to twelve class periods each week. After finishing grade nine, secondary schools offer two different programs. Either a general secondary school or a vocational-technical school are available. Secondary schools emphasizes science and mathematics. Schools that are in Russia currently struggle to maintain funds for teachers and materials.

SHORT STORY

But the wisdom that is from above is first pure, then peaceable, gentle, and easy to be intreated, full of mercy and good fruits, without partiality, and without hypocrisy.

James 3:17

For as long as there have been people, there have been stories. Many cultures have an oral tradition—that is, a treasury of tales that have been told aloud from generation to generation. These are similar to the oral anecdote you studied in Chapter 7. Families usually have such stories that they tell among themselves at gatherings to keep their history alive for their children.

A good story can always capture attention quickly. People who do public speaking often keep a collection of entertaining short narratives, sometimes factual and sometimes fictional, to support their ideas. Stories help us remember principles and motivate us to apply them. The Lord Jesus used parables and examples in just this way.

Many of the Lord's parables are not simple accounts of actual events but rather universal representations of life. They use common objects and familiar activities, not to show us one factual moment, as a history writer might, but to teach us through a crafted narrative some larger truth about humankind. When Christian writers compose fictional pieces, they should follow the example of the Author and Finisher of their faith. They should craft narratives of things *that are not* to illuminate things *that are.*

The Writing Process pp. 326-48

Your Turn

Write a short story based on a theme you feel strongly about. Your teacher will discuss the schedule for the rough draft, final draft, and publication of your story.

tip

Your journal is a great place to find writing ideas.

Planning

✔ **Look for an idea.** Where do you think Anton Chekhov found the seed for "Chameleon"? Perhaps he saw an argument in the street over a dog's biting someone. Perhaps he wanted to show how hypocritical people can be. Or perhaps he just wanted to show characters in a conflict. You may know someone like Ochumelov. Start by making lists of some of the following:

- Character traits that you admire or dislike
- Places you have lived or visited
- Moments of intense emotion
- Relationships you have with other people
- Jobs you have been responsible for
- Events that have changed you in some way
- Answers to prayer you have seen
- Your aspirations
- People who have influenced you

Clustering
p. 328

✔ **Make connections among the items on the lists.** A cluster diagram is a good way to show the relationships between the ideas you have listed. For example, do the people you admire have character traits that you listed? Write these ideas near your main idea and circle them. Draw lines connecting ideas to one another. An additional step will help you organize your cluster diagram: rank your ideas according to importance. You can do this by color or by number notation.

✔ **Select an idea to write about.** Which one of the ideas on your list particularly appeals to you? Perhaps you might want to model a story character after a person who has the character traits you listed. Has a moment of intense emotion changed you in some way? Maybe you could include a similar event in your story. Do you have some aspiration or ambition because of where you have lived? Perhaps this will suggest a theme to you. If at first you are unable to think of an idea that interests you, think about your favorite short story and what makes it your favorite. Writing about a similar event or emotion, as a form of modeling, might produce an interesting story.

✔ **Review the elements of a good short story.** Short story writers begin their stories with one of the key elements that make up a short story: plot, character, conflict, viewpoint, style, and theme.

Plot

Although it is almost impossible to think of only one element of a story in isolation from all others, it is helpful to consider plot first. Not many authors write detailed outlines for stories. Instead, they usually have a general order of events in mind. They know at least what will be the beginning (introduction of the conflict), middle (expansion of the conflict) and end (attempt at a resolution) of the piece. "Chameleon" begins by introducing the main character, Police Inspector Ochumelov, and quickly moves to the point of conflict: the biting dog and what to do about it. The story continues to reveal Ochumelov's wavering between disposing of the dog as a mangy cur and welcoming the dog as a beloved pet. "Chameleon" ends with the Inspector playfully teasing with the pup and striding across the market square and threatening—not the dog, but the man who was bitten.

Run your plot by a friend or family member to gauge its effectiveness. **tip**

Character

Many short stories depend heavily on character development. Character brings a story's action to life. The better acquainted the reader is with the characters, the more "alive" the story becomes. Character is revealed by what the characters say, what others say about them, and what they do. The author provides information about the characters either directly (description or dialogue) or indirectly (action). How many characters will you have? What are the main characters like? Why do they behave the way they do? What are their goals? At what points will they be at cross-purposes?

In "Chameleon" Chekhov reveals Ochumelov's character both directly and indirectly. In the author's exposition, Inspector Ochumelov is described as "coughing and twitching" as he decides what to do about the dog; however, he is chiefly revealed through his dialogue. Look again at how Ochumelov wavers with each new speculation about whose the dog is: "The dog must be exterminated without delay." "How could it have got at your finger? Such a little dog." "Ugly, mangy cur!" "A dog's a delicate creature." "Destroy it." "Nice little dog." What are the main characters like? What is the conflict between them? Why do you think each reacts as he does?

Conflict

Good stories, like life, include conflict, a point in the story about which there is tension and which demands a resolution. There are three basic types of conflict: man against a power or powers greater than himself (God, the sea, a tornado), man against himself (an insecurity, a moral issue), or man against another man. On the surface, Chekhov's main character wars with Khryukin, the goldsmith; but perhaps the real conflict is with himself about what to believe and what action to take about the dog. He struggles internally with how to present himself in the best light in front of the townspeople and the General.

Viewpoint

Each story could be told a different way depending on who did the telling. An East German guard would have written a different account of the fall of the Berlin Wall than did Andreas Ramos; John Vaughn had a different view of the fire than did his daughter Becky. How would Chekhov's story be different if Ochumelov told it? It would seem less objective, wouldn't it? What if Khryukin told it? Would any humor be lost? Would we gain a stronger sense of being part of the action?

First-person narrators make a reader feel close to the action because the author *becomes* one of the characters. He creates a trust with the reader. However, such a perspective is limiting—we can know only one person's thoughts and see and hear only what he sees and hears. The **omniscient viewpoint** enables the storyteller to know everything—including what all of the characters think and feel. A **limited-omniscient viewpoint,** as in "Chameleon," is like the first-person viewpoint in that we see and hear only what one character sees and hears; but limited-omniscient viewpoint allows the reader more space between himself and the story action since the story is told in the third person. Some beginning writers think that the easiest choice is omniscience—let the reader know what everyone is thinking. However, such freedom can make chaos. It is sometimes better to use the first-person or limited-omniscient viewpoint.

Writers choose carefully the point of view from which their stories are told. Who should tell your story? One of the characters? A narrator somewhat distanced from the story?

Style

The simplest indication of good writing style is that the reader never notices the style. It so perfectly suits the presentation that it draws no attention to itself. Style needs to be so much a part of the whole that the reader enters into the created world and becomes—for as long as he reads—a part of it.

Style is determined primarily by word choice (diction) and sentence structure (syntax). Choose the most precise words possible to convey your ideas without overloading the text with adjectives and adverbs. Vary your sentence structure rather than use all simple sentences or all compound-complex sentences. Above all, try to communicate such things as characters' emotions or motives indirectly, through details, rather than state them directly. We call this *showing* without *telling*. Let your reader discover for himself what is beneath the surface of your characters' words and actions.

Part of good style is good grammar and mechanics. Readers don't want to stop enjoying the world of the story to think, "Oh—there's a spelling error!" Nor do they want to have to reread a sentence to figure out what is being said. Everything the writer does should make it easier for the reader to enter into and stay in the story.

Theme

A theme is the recurring idea or central insight mirrored in the story's conflict and characters. Jesus' parables had a theme. What comment does your story make about human nature, about the way the people are, or about the way they should be? It should be something more specific than "friendship" or "honesty." See if you can state the idea in a single sentence (e.g., "People choose friends because of mutual trust and respect").

Christian writers have a responsibility to present themes from God's perspective. Many modern works promote a limited and humanistic worldview. Christian writers should ask themselves what their work is teaching. (Despite assertions that works can exist without really bearing any messages, in reality everything you write makes a statement about your way of looking at life.)

✔ **Remember your audience and purpose.** The purpose of most short story writers is to entertain their audience. Sometimes a writer wants to teach a lesson. Decide what you wish to accomplish with your story. Will your story be humorous or serious? Suspenseful or straightforward? Chekhov's purpose was probably to make us see the foolishness of hypocrisy, although he takes a humorous approach to this serious problem. Chekhov knew what kind of story his audience would respond to best. Analyze your audience to determine what kind of story they will benefit from or enjoy most.

✔ **Develop the story line.** Using the plot, character, conflict, viewpoint, style, and theme you have identified, add details to flesh out the basics of those key elements. In developing your story, write out at least the beginning of the chain of events that will get the story started. Include the beginning, middle, and ending ideas in this development.

Drafting

✔ **Write your first draft.** It does not matter where you begin writing—the beginning, the middle, or the end—just begin writing. Many writers write their conclusions first; that way they know exactly where they are headed. Don't allow yourself to get bogged down in crafting a masterful introduction or a perfect climax—you can come back to these parts in editing.

---

tip

Your opening sentence should be a hook that pulls readers in. Make it interesting!

Punctuating
Dialogue
pp. 280, 298

✔ **Use dialogue wisely.** Characters reveal much about themselves by the way they speak. Chekhov's Inspector is revealed mostly by his vacillating tirades. Remember that your characters may speak informally or formally, with or without dialect or slang.

✔ **Use figurative language.** Remember that similes, metaphors, and other figurative language can make your story more interesting. Be careful not to include overused similes and metaphors in your writing.

Figurative
Language
pp. 369-70

---

tip

Tape-record yourself reading the dialogue from your story. Play it back to see how natural or unnatural it sounds.

✔ **Remember to show, not tell.** Chekhov is careful to show us how Ochumelov is feeling by showing him taking his coat off and putting it back on as he becomes overheated and then cools down again. The author never says, "Now Ochumelov began to feel uncomfortable and embarrassed." Let your readers become involved in the story by allowing them to make decisions on their own. Just make sure that all of the details you include lead to the decision you intend.

✔ **Keep your theme in mind.** Include only those details, dialogue, and characters that will enhance your theme. Notice that Chekhov does not give excessive details about the dog or the constable. The only character we really get to know is Inspector Ochumelov because he is the vehicle for the theme.

✔ **As you write your story, consider several questions.**
- How does wrong appear? Undesirable or desirable?
- Does truth triumph ultimately?
- Do the characters who do wrong eventually appear in an unfavorable light?
- Do the characters who do right come across well in the end?
- How does the theme compare to the principles in God's Word?

The most important thing for a Christian writer is not what others think of him as a writer or what they think of his work. For him, the final goal is expressing well some theme that edifies his reader and glorifies his God.

Revising

✔ **Let your story rest.** Give yourself a day or two away from your story. Come back to the story fresh and reread it. You may find problems—of logic or plot—that you would otherwise miss.

✔ **Allow a peer reader to evaluate your story.** Letting someone else look at your story gives you valuable insight into how well your story is working. Ask your reviewer to tell you whether your characters and their dialogue seem convincing and realistic. Does the story develop and resolve a conflict? Is the viewpoint consistent and clear? Does the plot move steadily toward the climax? Is there anything about the style, including figurative language, that detracts from the story? Is the theme clear?

---
tip

Number the points in your plot and then check to see whether any numbers should be moved or eliminated.

✔ **Make changes in your draft.** Use the peer editing comments to make changes in your story. Evaluate the responses in light of your own decisions about the plot and theme. All changes should enhance the reader's understanding of the theme. Watch for problems in grammar and usage that your teacher has emphasized to you.

---
tip

Don't allow your word processor's spellcheck function to replace your own checks for grammar, usage, and spelling.

Publishing

✔ **Read your story aloud.** Family, friends, and classmates make a good audience for your story. Consider having a reading circle in which everyone gets a chance to read his own story.

Thinking Biblically

Many Christians believe fiction has little or no value. Such people might say, "Philippians 4:8 says we are to focus on 'whatsoever things are true.' Reading or writing fiction is at best a waste of time." The Bible itself, however, includes examples of biblical characters who use fictional stories to accomplish God's will. Nathan the prophet used a short story to confront King David with his sin (2 Sam. 12:1-4). David had refused to repent for months, but when Nathan skillfully told his story and applied it to David, the King of Israel broke: "I have sinned against the Lord" (v. 13). Why do you think Nathan's story was effective?

✔ **Make an anthology.** Collect several short stories of your own or gather your classmates' stories into a booklet complete with illustrations or photographs.

✔ **Adapt your story into a one-act play.** A short play based upon your short story could be presented for family or friends. Your play could be dramatic (with multiple characters, sets, and so on) or interpretive (a solo presentation with one person playing all of the parts and with minimal properties or costumes).

✔ **Submit your story to a magazine.** Check the guidelines for submission to an appropriate magazine. *The Writer's Market*, which presents such guidelines, is available in your local library or for purchase online.

Some Ideas to Consider

Bible

- Write about the dangers of jealousy or anger.
- Reveal the "deceitfulness of riches" as warned against in Matthew 13:22.

Political Science

- Describe the rise and fall of a politician who evidences selfish ambition. Or tell about a leader who is selfless.

Science

- Tell the story of a pioneer of the future and the lessons he or she learns.

LETTER FOR LETTER

Deadly Oath

Paul was severely punished for speaking the truth. On what falsehood were the hostile men basing their actions? Who tells the truth about Paul?

The torches on the walls only partially lit the back room of the dirty tavern. There, forty grimy men sloshed wine on the floor and down their throats, their voices growing louder and louder as they rehearsed the evils they had heard in the last three days.

One Jew turned to his comrade and hissed, "Jehovah will send me to the Gentiles. Look, my name is Paul, and I am Jehovah's messenger to the Gentile pigs. I'm going to teach the pigs about God."

His friend rejoined, "The Gentiles are good for nothing but slaves. You can't teach them the law. God doesn't want a Roman animal to worship Him."

Another man stands on a couch. "Brothers," he begins with a condescending smile, "my name is Paul, and Jesus, the Messiah—"

Shouts from the crowd interrupted him as he said the name of Jesus, but he held out his hands and continued.

"Jesus appeared to me and said, 'I am Jesus of Nazareth, whom you persecute; now go and witness for me to the Gentiles.'"

Raucous laughter erupted, and the man smiled as he stepped down from the couch and picked up his wine again. The bitter laughter from that room rang late into the night hours.

As the dawning light of morning peered through the windows of the tavern, it revealed a deserted room; sometime in the early morning hours the forty Jews had bound themselves together with a vow and had left to bring it to pass.

Nearby, Paul's nephew, Malachi, hurried through the streets to the Roman barracks where Paul was held. He asked to speak to Paul.

As he entered the room, Paul looked up in surprise, "Malachi, it is good to see you! What are you doing here?"

"Paul, listen to me. I have something very serious to tell you. While I was worshiping at the temple, a large group of men came and demanded to speak to Ananias. There were at least thirty men, maybe more, and since I knew it probably concerned you, I managed to get close enough to hear their discussion. Uncle Paul, I can't stand by and let you be killed. The entire band has sworn that they will not eat anything until they have killed you. They have talked Ananias into requesting that you return to the temple today, and the men plan to ambush you on the way. I heard all this from their own mouths."

Paul nodded gravely. "Thank you so much, Malachi, for bringing me this message." He then looked down the lengthy hall. "Centurion," he called. A stalwart soldier appeared. "Take this young man to the commander; he has something to tell him."

Minutes later, Claudius Lysias dismissed the young Jew and shook his head in amazement, muttering to himself, "Not today, my Jewish friends. You'll not take the life of a Roman today."

He sat down at his desk to write.

> Claudius Lysias unto the most excellent governor Felix sendeth greeting.
>
> This man was taken of the Jews, and should have been killed of them: then came I with an army, and rescued him, having understood that he was a Roman.
>
> And when I would have known the cause wherefore they accused him, I brought him forth into their council:
>
> Whom I perceived to be accused of questions of their law, but to have nothing laid to his charge worthy of death or of bonds.

Then he called two centurions and ordered them to prepare 470 soldiers to protect Paul on the trip.

That night, in a dark alley between the Roman barracks and Herod's temple, about twenty Jews waited impatiently as the sun descended lower and lower. Across the street, the other twenty felt their stomachs growl and tried to fight off sleep as they waited for Paul.

Meanwhile, 470 Roman soldiers accompanied Paul into the setting sun, toward Caesarea and Governor Felix and safety in the will of God.

For the full story, read Acts 22:24–23:35.
- *Why did the Roman guard refrain from flogging a Jew?*
- *How did the commander find out about the plot to kill Paul?*
- *What little detail did the commander leave out in his letter to the governor (Acts 22:24)?*
- *What do you think is the most important part of the letter?*
- *What are the consequences of this letter?*

Personal Response

Anyone who professes to be a follower of Christ should expect opposition. Write about a time when you suffered for doing right or write about how you should respond when someone persecutes you.

Have you ever wondered where a word like boulevard *came from? Or why we say* gesundheit *when someone sneezes? The authors of* The Story of English *describe how the English language became what it is today, including how foreign words became part of our vocabulary. In this selection McCrum, Cran, and MacNeil report on one of the significant contributions that American Indian culture has made to our present way of life—namely, the many native words that have become part of the Standard English lexicon. The research essay assignment later in this chapter will give you the opportunity to discover and explain the meanings and origins of other English words or phrases.*

The Story of English

by Robert McCrum, William Cran, and Robert MacNeil

The process whereby an Indian word became Standard English was often curious and tortuous. The animal we now know as a *racoon* was first recorded by Captain John Smith in 1608 as *raughroughouns.* By 1610, Virginians were talking about *aracouns,* and in due course the first syllable was dropped to give us the word we have today. The same process occurred to other Indian words, moving from the pidgin to the standard. *Scuppernong* meaning a yellow muscadine grape is first recorded as *askuponong. Opossum* became *possum. Skunk* began life as *segankn* or *segongw. Squash* (the fruit) was first recorded as *isquonter-squash* and *squantersquash* from the Narragansett word *askutasquash* meaning "vegetables eaten green".

Some borrowings from the American Indians had very interesting histories. *Pow-wow,* for instance, was adopted very early to mean a priest or medicine man. Within fifty years it was used to mean a ceremony in which magic was practised, together with feasting and dancing. A hundred years later, it had moved closer to its present English meaning and was used to describe an Indian council. After that it became generalized to refer, colloquially, to a conference or get-together of any kind.

The story of *mugwump* also shows how words can have lives of their own. It came from *mugquomp,* a Natick Indian word meaning "great chief" (the Massachusetts Bible used it to translate *duke* in Genesis xxxvi, 15). After that, the word gained a more jokey meaning and in 1884 it was used by Republican Party supporters of James G. Blaine to ridicule the breakaway Republicans who had thrown in their lot with Grover Cleveland, the Democratic nominee. In fact, the joke went against them because Cleveland won. Since then, *mugwump* has been used, often approvingly, in American politics to denote an Independent—but also derisively of a politician who straddles an issue or is ready to support either side.

CAPITALIZATION

Capital letters distinguish proper from common nouns and more important from less important words in titles. They also distinguish the beginnings of grammatical structures (for example, a sentence or a point in an outline). Using capital letters correctly not only will clarify your meaning for the reader but also will distinguish you as a capable writer.

People and Places

Family words used as proper nouns	Would you pick me up at 4:30 at the gym, **D**ad?
If the word is modified by an adjective, do not capitalize it.	I asked my **d**ad for a ride home.
Titles used with a name	**P**astor **K**irk **M**atthews **D**r. **L**ina **G**alli **S**enator **S**am **S**chuman **K**ing **G**eorge **I**
Do not capitalize a title used in place of a person's name.	The **p**astor will be gone next Sunday.
Terms used as descriptive substitutes for proper nouns	**O**ld **H**ickory (Andrew Jackson) the **L**iberator (Simón Bolívar)
Personifications	"The marvel of **N**ature shaking off sleep and going to work unfolded itself to the musing boy." ("Dawn in the Forest" by Mark Twain)
Countries and continents	**B**razil, **S**outh **A**merica
Cities and states	**D**es **M**oines, **I**owa
Streets and roads	101 **M**ain **S**treet
Bodies of water	**G**ulf of **S**uez **D**anube **R**iver
Geographic features	**C**arlsbad **C**averns **S**erengeti **P**lain
Do not capitalize a geographical noun unless it is part of a proper noun.	The **m**ountains rise majestically above the grassy **p**lains.
Sections of a country or the world	**N**ew **E**ngland **S**outheast **A**sia
Do not capitalize direction words when they refer to compass directions.	The farm is **s**outh of town.

Heavenly bodies	Neptune Cygnus
Capitalize the words earth, sun, *and* moon *only when they are used as proper names of specific heavenly bodies.*	The planets **V**enus and **M**ars are near **E**arth in our solar system.
Do not capitalize earth *when it is preceded by the.*	God prepared the earth for man to inhabit.

10.1 PRACTICE *the skill*

Underline each word that contains a capitalization error.

1. In the centuries after English settlers came to the new world, many words from American Indian languages became a part of English.

2. But the English did not have to leave england for their language to gain new words.

3. Huge forces from denmark and from France invaded at two different times early in English history, bringing with them foreign languages that would add many new words to English.

4. The "Great Army" of vikings from denmark was the first to come.

5. Between A.D. 865 and 870 they conquered almost all of england except a small section called wessex in the Southern part of england.

6. Things looked grim until 870 when a new King, Alfred the great, took the throne in wessex.

7. Alfred reorganized the English forces, and in 878, after a precarious winter on the isle of Athelney, he led them to a decisive victory over the danes and their Chieftain, Guthram.

8. As a result of his defeat, Guthram agreed to be baptized (with king Alfred as his Godfather) and promised never to invade wessex again.

9. But although wessex and (eventually) the City of London were saved, the vikings retained a large section of england that became known as the danelaw.

10. Many danes settled in the danelaw, and eventually much of their Old Norse vocabulary was incorporated into Old English.

Underline each word with a capitalization error and write the correction in the blank. If the sentence is correct, write C in the blank.

_____ 1. Alfred the Great, who is called the father of the English Navy, could perhaps best be described as Alfred the Educator, since his greatest legacy was in the intellectual realm.

_____ 2. After saving southwest England from the Vikings, Alfred began to support literacy and education in the land.

_____ 3. When Alfred was only four years old, his Father sent him to be educated by Pope Leo IV in Rome.

_____ 4. Once, Alfred's Stepmother offered a book as a prize for anyone who could memorize the book. With someone reading the book aloud to him, he memorized the entire book even before he knew how to read.

_____ 5. During this time, most people on the Earth were illiterate, but Alfred encouraged studies in both English and Latin.

_____ 6. His conviction concerning the importance of education was so strong that he believed the military attacks by Northern people were divine punishment for neglecting the study of ancient manuscripts, including the Scriptures.

_____ 7. In order to provide instruction for his people, Alfred brought Latin scholars all the way from the european continent to England.

_____ 8. He encouraged his people, the west Saxons, to translate Latin works into English; in fact, he translated several Latin works himself.

_____ 9. Because of the king's scholarly efforts, we still have a wealth of Anglo-Saxon literature.

_____ 10. The inscription on Alfred's statue in wantage, England, reads, "Alfred's name will live as long as mankind shall respect the past."

Constructions, Organizations, and Businesses

Buildings and structures	Pentagon Brooklyn Bridge
Monuments	Washington Monument
Aircraft and spacecraft	*Spirit of St. Louis* *Apollo 7*
Ships	*Monitor*
Trains	*Flying Scotsman*
Political parties	Republican Party Constitutional Union Party
Government departments	Internal Revenue Service (IRS)
Schools	Oxford University Paris Elementary School
Organizations	Future Farmers of America (FFA)
Members of most organizations	Tory Girl Scout
Do not capitalize members of an academic class.	The junior class will host a banquet for the seniors.
Businesses	Pizza Hut IBM
Do not capitalize the common noun for a business.	The department store downtown is having sidewalk sales.
Brand names of commercial products	Kleenex Jif Microsoft
Do not capitalize the common name of the product.	Kleenex facial tissue Jif peanut butter Microsoft software

PRACTICE *the skill*

Underline each capitalization error.

1. Changes in technology have caused an influx of new words like *software, hardware, ibm,* and *mac.*

2. The new york library contains hundreds of books about the history of our language.

3. Even the names of American political parties have changed: the democratic-republican party of the 1700s became simply the democratic party of today.

4. Astronauts named the *gemini* spacecraft after an astronomical constellation.

5. Arkansas's ouachita baptist university borrowed a Caddo Indian word for its name.

6. Some company names, like *microsoft,* come from a combination of words.

7. The name of organizations can be shortened: the veterans of foreign wars is well known simply as the VFW.

8. Sometimes the initials of an organization are pronounced as a single word; for example, *opec* stands for Organization of Petroleum Exporting Countries.

9. Businesses often take their titles from a family name: *J. C. penney, Wendy's,* and *wal-Mart* take their names from the founder or a member of his family.

10. Although *coke* is a brand name, some people use it to refer to all kinds of carbonated beverages.

REVIEW *the skill*

Underline each capitalization error and write the correction in the blank. If the sentence is correct, write C in the blank.

_____ 1. Like the Mississippi river and the state of Ohio, many American places are named with Native American words.

_____ 2. Greek or Roman words are often borrowed for heavenly bodies like orion and jupiter, but the word for earth comes from Old English.

_____ 3. She asked Papa, "Did you know that in Spanish your name can mean 'the pope'?"

_____ 4. The State department became the new name for the Department of Foreign Affairs.

_____ 5. NAACP, YMCA, FAA, and FDIC are all abbreviations for Organizations.

_____ 6. How did Americans get the nickname "the Yanks" during WWII?

_____ 7. The Federal Bureau of Investigation borrows the term *bureau* from French, meaning an "office."

_____ 8. The USS *constitution* obviously took its name from America's founding document, and the word *constitution* has been used in the legislative sense for at least eight hundred years.

_____ 9. Did you know that not every Facial Tissue is a Kleenex tissue?

_____ 10. "The green-eyed monster," a well-known idiom for jealousy, actually came from a famous Shakespearean play, *Othello*.

Religious, Cultural, and Historical Terms

Names of religions	Shintoism Hinduism
Nouns and personal pronouns referring to the one true God	The Holy Spirit performs His roles of comforting and convicting as He indwells the believer.
Do not capitalize common nouns or pronouns that refer to mythological gods.	Ares was the Greek god of war, but his fame was surpassed by that of the Roman god Mars.
The words *Holy Bible* or *Bible* and parts of the Bible as well as the sacred writings of other religions	Pentateuch Book of Mormon
Nationalities and languages	Spanish Russian
Ethnic groups	the Celts the Serbs

Months	January
Days	Monday
Holidays	Presidents' Day Hanukkah
Do not capitalize the names of the seasons unless personified.	We like to see the trees blossom in the spring. Wake up, O Spring, and shake off your wintry garb.
The abbreviations B.C. and A.D. *Notice that B.C. ("before Christ") is correctly placed after the year and that A.D. (anno Domini, "in the year of the Lord") is correctly placed before the year.*	Conservative scholars date the Exodus at 1446 B.C. William of Normandy conquered England in A.D. 1066.
Historical documents Historical events and periods	Declaration of the Rights of Man Treaty of Guadalupe Hidalgo Battle of the Bulge Roaring Twenties
Awards	Nobel Peace Prize Employee of the Month
The abbreviations A.M./P.M., a.m./p.m. *These abbreviations may be either capitalized or not but should be used consistently.*	I have appointments today at 10:00 A.M. and 2:00 P.M. We will need to leave for the reunion at either 11:30 a.m. or 12:00 p.m.

ESL

- A proper adjective referring to certain nationalities and languages can also be used as a noun (in singular form, always modified by *the*) to refer to persons from that country or area. Words of this type usually end in *ish* or *ese*, such as *Spanish, English, British, Portuguese, Japanese, Chinese, Alorese,* and *Vietnamese. French* also can be used this way.

  Historically, *the Japanese* have learned much from *the Chinese*.

- Many other proper adjectives referring to nationalities can be used as nouns in singular or plural form, according to the meaning of one or more than one person from that country or area. These are mostly words ending in *an*, such as *African(s), American(s), Cambodians(s), European(s), Italian(s),* and *Korean(s)*.

  Americans have many historical ties with *Europeans*.
  I met a *Cambodian* and two *Pakistanis* at the grocery store yesterday.

Underline each capitalization error. If the sentence is correct, write C in the blank.

_____ 1. Most people today use the Gregorian calendar, although some ethnic groups or religions, such as islam and judaism, follow different calendars.

_____ 2. The Gregorian calendar is named after Pope Gregory XIII, who reformed the Julian (or Roman) calendar in A.D. 1582.

_____ 3. In english, many months have names derived from Latin because they came from the Roman calendar.

_____ 4. Our twelfth month, december, comes from *decem*, the word for "ten" in Latin, because it was originally the tenth month of the Roman calendar.

_____ 5. Our month June (originally called junius) comes from the name Juno.

_____ 6. Juno was the Roman Goddess of marriage; Her Greek equivalent was Hera.

_____ 7. The romans, like the babylonians, named their days of the week after planetary bodies; for example, monday was originally Moon's day.

_____ 8. In English, some weekday names have roots in the languages of Old English and old norse; for example, wednesday (from Woden's day) is named after Odin, or Woden, the king of the gods in Norse mythology.

_____ 9. Month and weekday names of Latin or Anglo-Saxon origin are not found in the Bible because the Jewish calendar is used.

_____ 10. Since the Jewish and Gregorian calendars do not line up, Jewish holidays, such as yom kippur and Hanukkah, fall on different Gregorian dates every year.

Underline each capitalization error. If the sentence is correct, write C in the blank.

——— 1. In america, certain phrases and quotations from famous speeches and documents have become common in our speech.

——— 2. Most people associate "a house divided against itself cannot stand" with Abraham Lincoln's 1858 campaign speech, but Lincoln was actually referring to the words of christ from the scripture (Mark 3:25).

——— 3. The American civil war came just three years after Lincoln's warning.

——— 4. Lincoln described the government of the united states as being "government of the people, by the people, for the people" in his Gettysburg address.

——— 5. This Address was given at a ceremony consecrating a Civil War cemetery at the site of the battle of Gettysburg.

——— 6. The phrasing of the Declaration of Independence has been echoed in numerous political speeches and literally defines the way Americans view their rights.

Detail of *Lincoln and Douglas Debate*, Robert Root portrait, Abraham Lincoln Presidential Library & Museum (ALPLM)

——— 7. During the revolutionary war, Thomas Paine wrote the famous line "These are the times that try men's souls" in the first of his pamphlets entitled *the American crisis* series.

——— 8. Sometimes even a name becomes part of common speech. The pulitzer prize was created by and named for Joseph Pulitzer, a journalist who published a popular newspaper in new york during the 1880s.

——— 9. Alfred Nobel, the inventor of dynamite, founded the Nobel prize to honor significant achievements in physics, chemistry, medicine, literature, and peace.

——— 10. Even dictionaries and thesauruses bear names that come from individuals such as Noah Webster and Dr. Peter Mark Roget.

Titles and First Words

Capitalize the first and last words in a title as well as all other important words. Do not capitalize an article, a coordinating conjunction, the *to* of the infinitive, or a preposition of fewer than five letters unless it is the first or last word in a title.

Titles and First Words	
Newspapers and magazines	*Washington Post* *Newsweek*
Do not capitalize the word the *when referring to a newspaper.*	I advertised my car in the classified section of the *Detroit News.*
Literary works (including books, essays, poems, and plays)	*A Tale of Two Cities* *The Federalist Papers* "To a Mouse" *The Tragedy of Macbeth*
Sections of a book or play	Chapter 1
Some authorities do not capitalize the parts of a book or play unless they appear as a title.	Appendix Epilogue
Works of art	da Vinci's *Mona Lisa* Monet's *Water Lilies*
Musical compositions (including songs, operas, and instrumental music)	"Blessed Assurance" *Aïda* Brandenburg Concertos
Specific courses of study	Middle Eastern History Physics I
Do not capitalize the common noun for a course.	We are studying ancient Egypt in our history class today.
First word in a sentence	Put your books away.
First word in a line of dialogue	Before we left this morning, Dad said, "Be sure to feed your dog."
Do not capitalize the second part of a divided quotation unless the second part is the beginning of a new sentence.	"Yesterday you forgot," he continued, "and your mother had to do your job." "Yesterday you forgot," he commented. "Your mother had to do your job."
First word in a line of poetry	Water, water every where, And all the boards did shrink; Water, water every where, Nor any drop to drink. (from *The Rime of the Ancient Mariner* by Samuel Taylor Coleridge)

First word (and, of course, any proper nouns or proper adjectives) in each item of a formal outline	I. Official symbols of Minnesota
	  A. Bird
	  B. Flower
	  C. Slogan

First word and all nouns in the greeting of a letter	Dear Uncle John and Aunt Sue, Dear Friends,
First word in the closing of a letter	Cordially yours, Very truly yours,

Underlining for Italics
pp. 303-4

Quotation Marks
p. 299

Commas in Letters
p. 280

Write the letter of the choice that is capitalized correctly.

———— 1. A. In their book, *the story of English,* authors McCrum, Cran, and MacNeil strive to make a narrative of the changes in the English language.

B. In their book, *The Story of English,* authors McCrum, Cran, and MacNeil strive to make a narrative of the changes in the English language.

C. In their book, *The Story Of English,* authors McCrum, Cran, and MacNeil strive to make a narrative of the changes in the English language.

———— 2. A. Chapter 1, entitled "An English-Speaking World," discusses the amazing spread of English to all parts of the globe.

B. Chapter 1, entitled "An English-speaking world," discusses the amazing spread of English to all parts of the globe.

C. Chapter 1, entitled "An english-speaking world," discusses the amazing spread of English to all parts of the globe.

———— 3. A. Even students in a Linguistics 101 Class would recognize the Appalachian dialect as unusual.

B. Even students in a linguistics 101 class would recognize the Appalachian dialect as unusual.

C. Even students in a Linguistics 101 class would recognize the Appalachian dialect as unusual.

———— 4. A. The Appalachian folk song "Run To Fetch the Preacher" contains many examples of the regional dialect.

B. The Appalachian folk song "Run to fetch the Preacher" contains many examples of the regional dialect.

C. The Appalachian folk song "Run to Fetch the Preacher" contains many examples of the regional dialect.

———— 5. A. I. Influence on Scottish
II. Influence on Irish
III. Influence on other languages

B. I. Influence on Scottish
II. Influence on Irish
III. Influence on Other Languages

C. I. Influence On Scottish
II. Influence On Irish
III. Influence On Other Languages

_____ 6. A. O, my luve is like a red, red rose,
        that's newly sprung in June;
      o, my luve is like the melodie
        that's sweetly played in tune.

   B. O, my luve is like a red, red rose,
        that's newly sprung in June;
      O, my luve is like the melodie
        that's sweetly played in tune.

   C. O, my luve is like a red, red rose,
        That's newly sprung in June;
      O, my luve is like the melodie
        That's sweetly played in tune.

   (from "A Red, Red Rose" by Robert Burns)

_____ 7. A. "The best-laid schemes," my mother began, "of mice and men . . ."
   B. "The best-laid schemes," my mother began, "Of mice and men . . ."
   C. "The best-laid schemes," my mother began, "Of Mice and Men . . ."

_____ 8. A. Dear dr. Samuel Johnson,
   B. Dear Dr. Samuel Johnson,
   C. dear Dr. Samuel Johnson,

_____ 9. A. Your most humble servant,
   B. Your most Humble Servant,
   C. Your Most Humble Servant,

_____ 10. A. "Ode To a Nightingale" by John Keats
   B. "Ode To A Nightingale" by John Keats
   C. "Ode to a Nightingale" by John Keats

Write the letter of the choice that is capitalized correctly.

_____ 1. A. "Can you meet me at five?" asked Jared. "I am going to be a little late."

B. "That's fine." responded Josh, "Because I am going to be late as well."

C. "Let's meet at your house," Said Jared. "I'll be there as soon as possible."

_____ 2. A. Read Chapter 3 of your book.

B. Read Chapter 3 of your Book.

C. Read chapter 3 of your book.

_____ 3. A. Have you seen the Magazine called *Today's Christian Teen?*

B. Have you seen the magazine called *Today's Christian teen?*

C. Have you seen the magazine called *Today's Christian Teen?*

_____ 4. A. We have a beautiful painting called *The Signing of the Registry.*

B. We have a beautiful Painting called *the Signing of the Registry.*

C. We have a beautiful painting called *the signing of the registry.*

_____ 5. A. Would you like to purchase a subscription to The *Chicago Sun?*

B. Would you like to purchase a subscription to the *Chicago Sun?*

C. Would you like to purchase a subscription to the *Chicago sun?*

_____ 6. A. Dear Mr. Hensler and Family,

B. Dear Mr. Hensler And Family,

C. Dear Mr. Hensler and family,

_____ 7. A. Sincerely Yours,

B. Sincerely yours,

C. sincerely yours,

Proper
Adjectives
p. 15

_____ 8. A. *Fiddler on the roof* is a musical about a Jewish family living in Russia.

        B. *Fiddler on the Roof* is a musical about a Jewish family living in Russia.

        C. *Fiddler on the Roof* is a musical about a jewish family living in Russia.

_____ 9. A.   I. The history of France

        B. II. The Culture of France

        C. III. The people of france

_____ 10. A. I'm taking a Math Class called Linear Algebra.

        B. I'm taking a Math class called linear Algebra.

        C. I'm taking a math class called Linear Algebra.

Proper Adjectives and Other Words

Proper adjectives	**S**wiss cheese **C**hinese checkers
Do not capitalize a word modified by a proper adjective unless the two together form a proper name.	Bach was one of the great composers of the Baroque **e**ra. CiCi's **P**izza has a large buffet.
Personal pronoun *I*	How am **I** doing?
Archaic address-form *O*	Forgive, **O** Lord, and remember our sins no more.
Single letters used as words (including academic grades, vitamins, musical notes, and major musical keys)	Jesse hopes to get an **A** in her English class this semester. Orange juice is a good source of vitamin **C.** The highest **E** key on our piano always sticks. I prefer to play songs in the key of **C.**
Letters used to clarify a following word	It is illegal to make a **U**-turn at this intersection. The geese flew south in a **V**-shaped formation.

PRACTICE *the skill*

Underline each capitalization error and write the correction in the blank. If the sentence is correct, write C in the blank.

_____ 1. In A.D.1799, while on an egyptian expedition, one of Napoleon's officers made a startling discovery in the mud near the town of Rosetta.

_____ 2. His find was a 3'9"×2'4" black stone that came to be called the rosetta stone.

_____ 3. On the stone were hieroglyphics that had long stumped scholars. This stone, however, contained Egyptian and Greek Versions of the message written in hieroglyphics.

_____ 4. A frenchman named Jean François Champollion deciphered the meaning of the stone using the corresponding Greek text as a guide.

_____ 5. Champollion had to study from a copy of the stone because the English took the stone during the napoleonic wars.

_____ 6. The Greek and English Alphabets do not have exact correspondence with letters in hieroglyphics, making the message very difficult to decipher.

_____ 7. Champollion's knowledge of Coptic, a late stage of Egyptian that uses Greek letters, helped him to recognize some of the letters and words on the Stone.

_____ 8. Later, Champollion published a pamphlet that was the key to learning the ancient Egyptian language.

_____ 9. Today the Rosetta stone resides in a museum in London.

_____ 10. When we visited, the stone was under glass; i was slightly disappointed.

REVIEW *the skill*

Write the letter of the choice that is capitalized correctly.

_____ 1. A. In Food and Nutrition, we learned vitamin A is good for one's eyes.
B. In food and nutrition, we learned vitamin a is good for one's eyes.
C. In Food and Nutrition, we learned Vitamin A is good for one's eyes.

_____ 2. A. I made a C in a math class taught by Professor Knisley.
B. I made a c in a Math Class taught by Professor Knisley.
C. I made a C in a Math Class taught by Professor Knisley.

3. A. "Give ear to my prayer, O God; and hide not thyself from my supplication" (psalm 55:1).

   B. "Give ear to my prayer, o God; and hide not thyself from my supplication" (Psalm 55:1).

   C. "Give ear to my prayer, O God; and hide not thyself from my supplication" (Psalm 55:1).

4. A. I drove down Lakewood street in my brother's Ford mustang for the driving test.

   B. I drove down Lakewood Street in my brother's Ford Mustang for the driving test.

   C. I drove down Lakewood Street in my brother's Ford mustang for the driving test.

5. A. The anteroom in the Parkers' t-shaped home displays Victorian-style furniture and prints.

   B. The anteroom in the Parkers' T-shaped home displays Victorian-style furniture and prints.

   C. The anteroom in the Parkers' T-shaped Home displays Victorian-style furniture and prints.

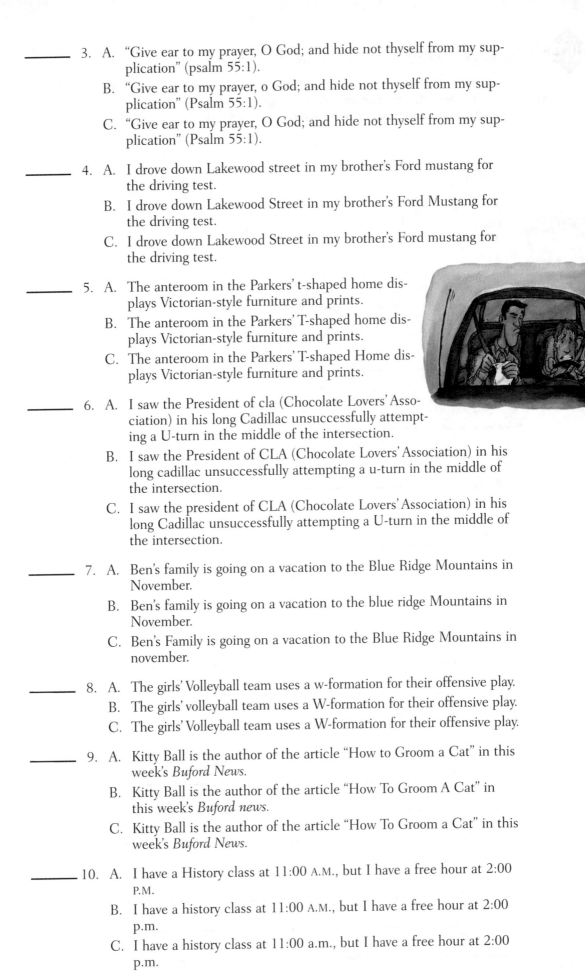

6. A. I saw the President of cla (Chocolate Lovers' Association) in his long Cadillac unsuccessfully attempting a U-turn in the middle of the intersection.

   B. I saw the President of CLA (Chocolate Lovers' Association) in his long cadillac unsuccessfully attempting a u-turn in the middle of the intersection.

   C. I saw the president of CLA (Chocolate Lovers' Association) in his long Cadillac unsuccessfully attempting a U-turn in the middle of the intersection.

7. A. Ben's family is going on a vacation to the Blue Ridge Mountains in November.

   B. Ben's family is going on a vacation to the blue ridge Mountains in November.

   C. Ben's Family is going on a vacation to the Blue Ridge Mountains in november.

8. A. The girls' Volleyball team uses a w-formation for their offensive play.

   B. The girls' volleyball team uses a W-formation for their offensive play.

   C. The girls' Volleyball team uses a W-formation for their offensive play.

9. A. Kitty Ball is the author of the article "How to Groom a Cat" in this week's *Buford News*.

   B. Kitty Ball is the author of the article "How To Groom A Cat" in this week's *Buford news*.

   C. Kitty Ball is the author of the article "How To Groom a Cat" in this week's *Buford News*.

10. A. I have a History class at 11:00 A.M., but I have a free hour at 2:00 P.M.

    B. I have a history class at 11:00 A.M., but I have a free hour at 2:00 p.m.

    C. I have a history class at 11:00 a.m., but I have a free hour at 2:00 p.m.

CUMULATIVE *review*

Rewrite the paragraph, correcting the ten errors from these categories: subject-verb agreement, pronoun-antecedent agreement, pronoun reference, pronoun case, pronoun courtesy order, adjective and adverb use, and capitalization.

The author of the first American dictionary, Noah Webster, was born in West hartford, Connecticut, in 1758. Webster wanted to write a dictionary to maintain a distinctly American language; he believed it was the best way to secure cultural independence for the United States. Appearing in 1828, Webster proudly published *An American Dictionary of the English Language*. In the dictionary, distinctly American words such as *skunk* and *hickory* was printed. When Webster died in 1843, George and Charles Merriam, whom owned a publishing business, secured the rights to the dictionary. The Merriam brothers instated Webster's own Son-In-Law, Chauncy A. Goodrich, as the editor in chief. Webster, who had studied lexicography thoroughly had trained Chauncy. The brothers' company, which became known as merriam-webster, was quite successful. Webster's work was acclaimed high by President James K. Polk and General Zachary Taylor. The Merriam-Webster dictionary continue to be one of America's leading authorities of the English language.

_____

_____

_____

_____

_____

_____

_____

_____

_____

_____

_____

_____

_____

_____

_____

_____

_____

RESEARCH ESSAY

In the beginning was the Word, and the Word was with God, and the Word was God.

John 1:1

What does the word *research* mean to you? Do you picture scientists in a laboratory? Or librarians looking through large reference books? Actually, almost everyone spends time researching almost every day. *Research* is simply another word for *investigation*—a method for discovering new information. Every time you search for an article on the Internet or look up a phone number in a directory, you are researching. The research essay assignment will allow you to investigate and then report the origins and meanings of English words or phrases that interest you.

McCrum, Cran, and MacNeil wrote about the American Indian origins of certain Standard English words. You will write about the origins of words that interest you. Choose a topic, research the topic, and write a research essay based on the information you find. Your essay should consist of an introductory paragraph, approximately three body paragraphs, and a conclusion paragraph, and it should be accompanied by a list of works cited.

Planning

✔ **Choose a topic.** Writing a research essay is a great opportunity to study something that you find interesting, especially if you don't know much about it yet. Use this project to research a topic that you have been curious about. Perhaps you've always wanted to know who named the lake near your house or why some suitcases are called valises. Use one of the techniques described in Chapter 13 to help you identify a topic. For example, asking questions is a useful strategy.

> **ESL**
>
> If your first language has in it a number of words that came from English, you might want to research and write about one or more of those words— that is, if research sources are available. In your research essay you might include information about how the word or words are used differently in the two languages.
>
> Another possibility is to write about one or more words that have come into English from your first language. You might be able to include information about how the words are used differently in the two languages.

✔ **Narrow your topic and determine your purpose.** Limit your topic to something that you can discuss thoroughly within the limits of your paper—approximately three paragraphs in addition to introduction and conclusion paragraphs. For example, you probably could not adequately explain the origin of every street name in your town, but you might be able to discuss the names of the streets in your neighborhood or the names of the large cities in your state or territory. The basic purpose of your essay will be to inform your reader about the meaning and origin of the words you choose to research. Always keep your topic and purpose in mind as you research and write.

Thinking Biblically

Many things worth knowing must be researched. This truth is sometimes difficult for Christians to accept since believers know that the most important ideas that humans can know are revealed by God in Scripture. We cannot research our way to knowing that there is only one God, that Jesus is the Son of God, or that Jesus died for the sins of mankind. Humans can know these truths only by faith in God and His Word. But does this mean that research is not important to the Christian? Read Luke 1:1–4. What do you think?

✔ **Find and evaluate sources.** Start by determining what you already know and what you need to find out. Identify specific questions that you want to answer. Now you're ready to find sources that provide the information you need. In addition to general reference works such as dictionaries and encyclopedias, explore the library's collection of other nonfiction books and articles about your subject. Don't forget to explore the online resources available to you. Perhaps you can even identify an expert to interview, such as a local historian. Just as important as finding sources is evaluating the usefulness of those sources. Ask yourself these questions about each source you use:

- Is this author an expert? Does he know what he's talking about? The biographical information included with the article or on the book jacket can tell you the author's background. Even the library catalog can help: if the author has written other books on this or related topics, he is probably considered an expert in the field.

- Does the author explain the information clearly? If you can't understand the book or article, you certainly won't be able to learn anything from it.

- Is the information current? Or does the author include outdated information that no longer applies or has since been proved untrue? For example, statistical information from a book published in 1970 may not be accurate any more, whereas facts from a current almanac are probably up to date.

- Do other experts value this source? Is it well respected? If you are researching current political slogans, the information in a newsmagazine is probably more reliable than information in a sports magazine.

✔ **Take notes and document sources.** As you research your topic, you will need to take two kinds of notes: source notes and content notes. Source notes record pertinent information about your sources themselves: the title of the book or article, the title of the periodical or electronic database (if your source is an article in a larger work), the author or editor, and the publication information (publisher, city of publication, and date of publication). If your source is an online reference, also note the date on which you accessed the website. The source notes will form the basis of the list of works cited to accompany your research essay. Content notes record the information you find in your sources. Keep your topic and purpose in mind as you research; record only the information that will be useful to you. Many of your content notes should be written in your own words—either summary or paraphrase—because your goal is to find information, not someone else's way of phrasing that information. Don't forget to include the name of the source and the number of the page on which the information was found.

✔ **Outline your essay.** Even if you choose not to make a formal sentence outline, using an informal outline helps you to organize your ideas in a clear, logical manner. First, list all the information that you plan to use in your essay, both research and your own ideas. Now is the time to delete any information that doesn't really fit your topic or purpose. Next, group related ideas together. Identify the main ideas in each group: these will become the main points of your outline. Then arrange the supporting details under the main points in some kind of logical order.

I. Word usage
 A. Compounds
 B. Singulars and plurals
 C. New words
 D. Old words with new uses

II. Loan words
 A. Hybrid phrases
 B. English prefixes and suffixes

III. Abbreviations
 A. Formal abbreviations (shortened words)
 B. Informal abbreviations (shortened words)
 C. Acronyms

Drafting

✔ **Prepare your thesis statement.** Remember your topic and purpose? If you haven't done so already, now is the time to turn those general statements into a formal thesis statement. Your thesis statement should include not only your topic but also the main idea that you want to communicate. It should be a statement, not a question, and it should be verifiable—something your essay demonstrates to be true.

[handwritten note:] English spoken in India has some different vocabulary from English spoken in North America.
I. Word usage
   A. Compounds

✔ **Draft your essay.** Using your outline as a guide, begin writing the body of your essay. You will probably want to turn each of your main outline points into a paragraph for your essay. First, rewrite an outline point as a topic sentence. Then turn the supporting points into supporting sentences. Work through each point of your outline this same way. You don't necessarily have to work through your outline in order. Some writers prefer to write the most important part first; others choose the section that interests them the most. Remember to incorporate your research as you write. If you found a compelling quotation, for example, use it to support one of the ideas you express in the paragraph.

✔ **Document your sources.** As you write, include the source information for every summary, paraphrase, or quotation. If you don't cite your source, your reader may assume that the ideas are completely original to you. Misrepresenting borrowed information as your own is plagiarism, a serious offense—morally and academically. Check with your teacher about the style you are to use. Parenthetical documentation is a common and useful style. A parenthetical citation identifies your source in the briefest way possible—usually just the author's last name— and specifies the page from which the information was taken. It appears in parentheses at the end of the sentence or at a natural pause in the sentence, before the punctuation. (If your readers want more information about your source, they can refer to the list of works cited at the end of your essay.) Here are some other tips for using parenthetical citations.

- If you mention the author's name in your sentence, do not repeat it in the parenthetical citation.
- If the authors of different sources share the same last name, include the author's first name too.
- If you use two or more sources by the same author, add a shortened form of the title after the author's name (separate the title and the author's name with a comma).
- If no author or editor is named, use a shortened form of the title instead.

✔ **Introduce your essay.** Your introductory paragraph sets the stage for everything to come. Catch your reader's attention with an interesting quotation, a startling fact, or an intriguing question. Then gradually lead your reader from that opening statement down to the specific point you plan to make in your essay: the thesis statement. Many writers prefer to write the introduction after they write the body of the essay because by then they know what it is they want to introduce. Of course, you may prefer to write your introduction first. Use whichever strategy works best for you.

✔ **Draw a conclusion.** One effective conclusion strategy is to begin with a restatement, not just a repetition, of your thesis. Then apply the information from your essay to your reader's life. What is the most important thing you want your reader to remember? Is there some action that your reader should take now that he has information you present in your essay? How will this information enrich his life?

> The vocabulary of English spoken in India is somewhat different from the vocabulary of English spoken in North America. English in India differs from North American English in other ways too, such as grammar and pronunciation. Although there are many differences, English-speakers from India and other countries are able to understand each other. This universality of English is one reason it has remained an important part of communication in India.

✔ **Compile a list of works cited.** Follow the directions your teacher provides for adapting the source information you compiled while you were researching. Most likely, you will list each source alphabetically by the author's last name, followed by his first name, the title of the work, and the publication information.

Revising

✔ *Re*-view the ideas of your essay. Read your draft again to examine its ideas. Does every paragraph serve the purpose of your essay? Do you present the information clearly? Does every sentence support the topic of that particular paragraph? Have you organized the information in a clear, logical manner? If not, then rework the essay to correct the problem.

✔ *Re*-view the style of your essay. Reread each individual sentence carefully, looking for problems within the sentence and for problems with the relationships between sentences. Then revise as necessary. Don't be afraid to mark up your text to indicate the changes you need to make.

- Do the important ideas in each sentence stand out? Or is the point obscured by vague language?
- Do the nouns and verbs convey accurate impressions? Or could you choose more precise words?
- Does every word serve an important function in the sentence? Or do you need to eliminate redundancies?
- Do the sentences follow one another smoothly and logically? Or do you need to add appropriate transitions?

First Draft

Indian words play a large part in the English of India.

a mixture of languages. *may* *mixed*
Many Indians speak kichiri. Kichiri ~~usually~~ includes English with

one or more
Indian languages. Kichiri is also the name of a food dish that com-

Indians who primarily speak
prises various food items mixed together. Even pure English ~~speakers~~

also
use Indian words in their speech. Indians combine English and

form hybrid words and phrases *For example,*
Indian words to ~~make new words.~~ Kaccha road means "dirt road,"

Indians *use*
and *ek minute* means "one minute." Often English prefixes and suf-

used
fixes ~~will be used~~ with Indian words, such as ~~adding~~ the suffix *fy* to

indicate an action is being done to a person. In Hindi, the word

muska means "to flatter," so *muskafy* means "to flatter someone."

Second Draft

Indian words play a large part in the English of India. Many Indians speak kichiri, a mixture of languages. Kichiri may include English mixed with one or more Indian languages. Even Indians who primarily speak English use Indian words in their speech. Indians also combine English and Indian words to form hybrid words or phrases. For example, *kaccha road* means "dirt road," and *ek minute* means "one minute." Indians often use English prefixes and suffixes with Indian words, such as the suffix *fy* used to indicate that an action is being done to a person. In Hindi, the word *muska* means "to flatter," so *muskafy* means "to flatter someone."

✔ **Proofread your essay.** After you revise your essay, prepare a clean copy of the final draft and examine it carefully. Check your essay for grammar, usage, capitalization, punctuation, and spelling errors. Recheck each of your summaries, paraphrases, and quotations too. Have you recorded the information accurately? Are all of the quotations enclosed in quotation marks? Are all of the source citations correct? If you find any mistakes or omissions, correct the errors and then prepare a new clean copy.

Publishing

✔ **Share your research with interested readers.** Is anyone you know studying the area you wrote about? Maybe you know someone who lives near one of the places whose name you discuss in your essay. If so, send a copy to him or her.

✔ **Submit your essay to a local publication.** If you researched the names of local places, your hometown newspaper might agree to publish your essay as a special contribution. Or perhaps the local historical society would include your essay in their newsletter or magazine.

✔ **Save your writing.** Add your research essay to your writing folder. Later, you'll enjoy rereading about the discoveries you made.

Some Ideas to Consider

Geography
- Write about the origins of specific place names: cities, countries, bodies of water, physical features such as mountains or plains, or man-made features such as streets or parks.

Literature
- Write about the origins of literary terms such as *metaphor, simile, novel,* or even *essay* itself.

Computer Science
- Write about the origins of technological terms used in the computer industry—*hardware, software,* or *programming.*

Biology
- Write about the etymology of medical terms or the Latin names and common English names for plants.

Foreign Language
- Write about the origins and meanings of common foreign words and phrases such as *à la mode, et cetera, kamikaze,* or *burrito.*

 THINK ABOUT IT

Inductive Arguments

You have already studied inductive and deductive reasoning, and you probably remember that an inductive argument intends to prove the likelihood of the conclusion. An inductive argument cannot be valid or invalid since it proves only the likelihood of an argument, but it can be **strong** or **weak.** If the reasoning provides sufficient support for the conclusion, then the argument is strong; if the reasoning provides little or no support, then the argument is **weak.** In this lesson you will learn three basic ways to make a strong inductive argument: appeal to authority, experience, or analogy.

An **appeal to authority** can be strong only if the authority is a qualified authority. If Tiger Woods praises a certain kind of golf club, then an argument for the golf club's superiority is a strong argument. However, if you use Tiger Woods as an authority on water polo, then that argument may be weak. Remember that the authority must be fully qualified; otherwise, the argument will be weak.

If your friend told you that he flew to Jupiter last night, would you believe him? Probably not. Claimed experience is not proof. However, an **appeal to experience** can be very strong. Let's say that you are planning to take your parents out for a nice meal at a certain restaurant. However, five friends tell you that they went there on separate occasions and the food and service were terrible. You would probably find another restaurant. An appeal to experience becomes more reliable as the number of witnesses increases.

An **appeal to analogy** is a commonly used argument. An analogy compares one situation to a similar situation. Analogy is used often to aid understanding and not just to convince. Perhaps your friend unwittingly laughs at your singing, and you have been taking voice lessons to correct your vocal problem. So you say, "You wouldn't like it if I made fun of your lack of basketball skills, would you?" Now your friend might understand how you feel and may apologize. A teacher may use an analogy to explain a difficult concept. Spiritual concepts that are especially difficult to explain can often be taught using analogy. When Jesus preached, He often used analogy in the form of a parable.

Identify the type of appeal used in the following inductive arguments as *authority*, *experience*, or *analogy*. Then identify the argument as *weak* or *strong*.

_____ 1. Eating chocolate is really good for you. I read that in *Chocolate Lovers* magazine.

_____ 2. My doctor, a nutrition specialist, says that eating dark chocolate in moderation is good for you.

_____ 3. Last year our July 4 party was rained out. We had better not plan one for this year.

_____ 4. Four of my friends have taken the driving test, and all of them have failed. The driving test must be difficult.

_____ 5. We put cats and dogs to sleep when they are old and sick. Isn't it all right to do the same with elderly people?

_____ 6. Just as a person would be foolish to look in the mirror and then ignore dirt on his face, it would also be foolish for him to look into the Word of God and not correct the problems he sees in his spiritual life.

_____ 7. It's legal, and so it can't be wrong.

_____ 8. I know someone from that school, and he is really smart. If you go to that school, you will be really smart too.

_____ 9. The Bible teaches that children are to obey their parents. Therefore, I should obey my parents.

_____ 10. Jeremy has a good family, and his parents let him stay up late; I should be allowed to stay up late as well.

Thinking It Through

Write an argument supported by at least one statement for each of the three types of appeals.

When you read a biography, it's as if you are taking part in that person's life. A biography is even more rewarding if you can identify with the experiences you are reading about. You can learn interesting things through sharing others' experiences.

This piece tells the story of the most important moment in a great man's life. The experience of coming to Christ forever changed Augustine. Notice how Bryan Smith coordinates and subordinates certain ideas in this excerpt. By creating dependent clauses and using coordinating conjunctions, he has tied the paragraph together in a precise fashion that is easy to follow.

Do you know someone whose life was dramatically changed when he or she surrendered to God? At the end of this chapter, you will have a chance to write a biographical essay about the salvation experience of someone you know or once knew.

The Way of the Word *by Bryan Smith*

The year A.D. 386 found Augustine a broken man, living in Milan. He had squandered his days in immorality, but the prayers of his mother followed him, as did the Holy Spirit's conviction. Previously, while living in Northern Africa, he had sought relief from a number of sources. One that had occupied many of his efforts was the false religion of Manichaeism. In time, however, this lie had lost its grip on him because it failed to answer adequately his perceptive questions. At last he moved to Milan, where he taught logic. There he became intrigued by the gospel preaching of a minister named Ambrose. Augustine longed to believe that gospel, but he could not give his whole heart to it because he was enslaved to his sin. One night, tormented by his seemingly helpless state, he wept alone in a garden. Suddenly, his sobs were interrupted by two commands pressing his soul: "Tolle, lege" (Take up, read). He grabbed a copy of the Scripture and providentially opened to Romans 13:13-14: "not in chambering and wantonness, not in strife and envying. But put ye on the Lord Jesus Christ, and make not provision for the flesh." He saw no vision; he simply wept and read God's Word. But the Lord was clearly at work, for there in the garden, Augustine submitted to the gospel. He left his life of sin and eventually became one of the most influential Christian leaders and theologians in history.

USAGE

PUNCTUATION

Imagine trying to drive in a crowded city with no traffic signals. Cars would be everywhere, and chaos would rule. Reaching your destination would be nearly impossible, not to mention incredibly dangerous. Traffic signals regulate and create order on the roads. Likewise, punctuation helps organize ideas on a page. Capital letters show a reader where to begin, commas indicate a yield, and periods bring the reader to a halt. Ideas must be organized if they are to be understood, and punctuation rules set a standard for that necessary order.

Four Types of
Sentences
p. 37

Exclamation Point

Expressions of strong emotion end with an exclamation point. These include exclamatory sentences, strongly stated imperative sentences, some interjections, and brief exclamations.

EXCLAMATORY SENTENCES	What a great shot!
STRONG IMPERATIVE SENTENCE	Pass the ball!
INTERJECTION	Hey! I'm open!
BRIEF EXCLAMATION	No way!

The exclamation point should be used sparingly.

Question Mark

Interrogative sentences end with a question mark.

> Have you ever read any of Gerard Manley Hopkins's poetry?

A question mark also follows a question tag at the end of a sentence.

> He's a great poet, isn't he?

Polite requests are not usually punctuated with a question mark. Remember that indirect questions will not end in a question mark either.

> Would you please read the poem aloud.

> The teacher asked me if I would read the poem aloud to the class.

Period

In Sentences

Most sentences end with a period.

> Hopkins wrote the sonnet "Thou Are Indeed Just, Lord, If I Contend."

Declarative sentences, which simply state facts, always end with a period.

> Hopkins lived only forty-five years.

Most imperative sentences (those not stated strongly) end with a period.

> Read "Pied Beauty" for tomorrow.

Indirect questions end with a period as well.

> Noel asked whether I had read "The Windhover."

For Initials and Abbreviations

Initials and some abbreviations end with periods.

Capitalization
pp. 240-41

For Initials and Abbreviations	
Personal names and titles	Mr. R. W. Hamilton Sr. Col. Jack Swayne
Periods are now usually omitted after acronyms and common abbreviations of the names of government agencies, most organizations, and well-known businesses.	YMCA (Young Men's Christian Association) MADD (Mothers Against Drunk Driving) IRS (Internal Revenue Service) NHL (National Hockey League)
Items in addresses	1406 Edgartown Dr. P.O. Box 50007
Periods do not follow state, province, or territory postal abbreviations, nor are periods used with ZIP codes or other postal codes.	Chesapeake, VA 23320
Time and dates	A.D. 1066 612 B.C. 7:30 A.M.
Measurements	120 lb. 5 ft. 2 in.
Metric measurements do not need periods.	10 km 20 cm

In Outlines and Lists

A period follows each number or letter that shows a division of an outline.

  I. Main idea
     A. Supporting idea
     B. Supporting idea

  II. Second main idea
     A. Supporting idea
        1. Supporting detail
        2. Supporting detail
     B. Supporting idea

A period follows each number or letter that precedes an item in a vertical list.

     A. Fill water bottles
     B. Peel oranges
     C. Get clean towels

A list within a sentence uses pairs of parentheses instead of periods.

> Before the game, make sure to (1) fill the water bottles, (2) peel the oranges, and (3) get clean towels.

For Decimals

Use a period as a decimal point.

6.3 million

$199.99

101.5°F

PRACTICE *the skill*

Insert any missing periods or decimal points, question marks, or exclamation points.

1. Do you know who is called the Father of Modern Missions

2. It is Mr William Carey, an Englishman

3. His life might be outlined as follows:

   I Life in England

      A Shoemaker

      B Baptist preacher

      C Missions promoter

   II Work in India

      A Bible translation and production

      B Evangelism and church planting

      C Education and medical services

4. Read Carey's sermon "Expect Great Things from God; Attempt Great Things for God" to understand his success as a missionary

5. Carey founded the first modern missionary society in AD 1792 and left as a missionary for India in 1793

6. The land of India, whose temperature can get up to 853°F even in January, must have been very different from cool, damp England

7. Carey accomplished an amazing amount of work in his forty-one years as a missionary

8. Would you notice that he participated in the translation of the Scriptures into thirty-six languages and in the production of a Bengali-English dictionary

9. Wow Carey also evangelized, started churches, provided education and medical services, pushed for social reforms, and participated in business

10. Do you think Carey was a model for modern missionaries

REVIEW *the skill*

Write the letter of the correctly punctuated sentence.

_____ 1. A. You might ask whether the work of William Carey is being continued today?

B. You might ask whether the work of William Carey is being continued today.

_____ 2. A. One of the modern mission agencies that follows in Carey's footsteps is Gospel Fellowship Association (GFA).

B. One of the modern mission agencies that follows in Carey's footsteps is Gospel Fellowship Association (G.F.A.).

_____ 3. A. The missionary portion of the association was established in AD 1961.

B. The missionary portion of the association was established in A.D. 1961.

_____ 4. A. The association's offices are located at 1809 Wade Hampton Blvd., Greenville, SC 29609.

B. The association's offices are located at 1809 Wade Hampton Blvd, Greenville, S.C. 29609.

_____ 5. A. You could visit the offices any weekday after 8:00 AM and before 5:00 PM.

B. You could visit the offices any weekday after 8:00 A.M. and before 5:00 P.M.

_____ 6. A. Dr Mark Batory is the executive director.

B. Dr. Mark Batory is the executive director.

_____ 7. A. It is amazing that Gospel Fellowship Association is sending missionaries to thirty-four different countries!

B. It is amazing that Gospel Fellowship Association is sending missionaries to thirty-four different countries?

_____ 8. A. It's somewhat surprising that one of its highest concentrations of missionaries is in North America, isn't it?

B. It's somewhat surprising that one of its highest concentrations of missionaries is in North America, isn't it.

_____ 9. A. Of course, North America includes Canada and Mexico as well as the approximately 301,1 million people of the United States.

B. Of course, North America includes Canada and Mexico as well as the approximately 301.1 million people of the United States.

_____ 10. A. Don't you think that William Carey would be pleased that people today still share his burden?

B. Don't you think that William Carey would be pleased that people today still share his burden.

Comma

Commas are the most frequently used—and misused—marks of punctuation.

In a Series

Commas often separate three or more items in a series.

Series of Three or More Items

Use a comma after each item (except the last item) in a series of three or more single words or groups of words of the same type that are joined by a conjunction.

> My neighbor hired us to *rake the leaves, clean the garage,* and *mow the lawn.*

> Do you like to watch *soccer, baseball, lacrosse,* or *basketball?*

In some situations (such as writing for a newspaper), the comma is omitted before the conjunction. However, since the comma before the conjunction is never wrong, it is safer to make a practice of always using a comma before the conjunction.

Coordinate Adjectives in a Series

Groups of adjectives can modify nouns in two different ways. **Cumulative adjectives** build on one another.

> *The mangled dog* dish belongs to Rex.

> *His new blue* collar fits well.

The and *mangled* tell which *dog* dish Rex has, and *his* and *new* specify which *blue* collar is being referred to. Both adjectives are necessary to identify the object. Adjectives building on each other in this manner do not need commas separating them.

However, sometimes two adjectives have a similar meaning so that both would not really be necessary to identify the object being described. These **coordinate adjectives** modify the noun separately and need to be separated by commas.

> He lives in that *old, weather-beaten* doghouse.

Participles can be coordinating in the same way.

> Rex is a *trusting, loving* dog.

A simple test can help you identify coordinate adjectives: coordinate adjectives can usually have *and* put between them and still sound correct.

> trusting and loving dog = trusting, loving dog

> (but not "his mangled and dog dish")

Independent
Clauses
p. 88

Two or More Independent Clauses

Use a comma before a conjunction that joins two independent clauses.

> Judson was born in Alaska, and his sister Jessica was born in Guam.

When two independent clauses are very short and closely related, the comma may be omitted.

> He is eighteen and she is fifteen.

If a compound sentence contains three or more independent clauses, use commas to separate them.

> The score is tied, the bases are loaded, and the crowd is silent.

Be careful to avoid using a comma before a conjunction that joins only the parts of a compound predicate.

> Emily *flew to Montreal on Tuesday* and *drove to Sept-Îles later that same day.*

Insert any missing commas. If the sentence is already correct, write C in the blank.

_____ 1. Constantine became emperor of the Roman Empire when persecution of Christianity was harsh, strong and cruel.

_____ 2. He looked at the Christians in a totally different way than his pagan barbaric predecessors had.

_____ 3. Christians had been recently persecuted under three emperors: Diocletian Galerius and Maximin.

_____ 4. In A.D. 311 the Edict of Toleration was issued and Christians were freed from their persecution.

_____ 5. He legalized the Christian faith and publicly embraced it.

_____ 6. People converted to Christianity and the church grew but many converts were insincere in their professions of faith.

_____ 7. Constantine was the first Roman leader to have a personal interest in Christianity and it was he who first used the term *Catholic*.

_____ 8. The Roman Catholic Church gradually began to be infiltrated with pagan rituals state politics and doctrinal errors.

_____ 9. Some called Constantine a pagan, some called him a Christian, and a few called him both but true Christians understood that his public religious policy did not necessarily reveal the inward state of his heart.

_____ 10. He was loved by some and disliked by others—he relieved the persecution of the church but he burdened it with unnecessary cares of the world.

Insert any missing commas. If the sentence is already correct, write C in the blank.

———— 1. Jesus Christ faced the ultimate persecution in His death on the cross and the Bible says that His followers will also face persecution.

———— 2. Enemies of Christ persecute Christians to stop the spread of the gospel but through persecution the church actually grows.

———— 3. It doesn't seem to make sense but it is true.

———— 4. Sometimes persecutors (or others witnessing persecution) will see in Christians such faith, determination and peace that they decide they want the same things in their lives.

———— 5. In this way, the testimony, or witness, of the persecuted church often leads others to Christ and the church grows under persecution.

———— 6. Persecution was not uncommon for the early church; in ancient Rome, Christians were often arrested and taken to coliseums where they were killed by gladiators, eaten by wild animals, or burned at the stake.

———— 7. People who willingly die for their Christian faith are called martyrs; Stephen, a brave faithful deacon in the early church, is considered the first martyr.

_____ 8. "The Martyr of the Catacombs" is a short story that depicts such persecution of Christians in Rome and it also shows how the testimony of those under persecution can help bring others to salvation.

_____ 9. In the United States, people have the freedom to worship as they choose, but persecution of Christians still takes place in many other countries around the world.

_____ 10. China, Saudi Arabia, Morocco and Cuba are just a few of the nations where present-day Christians face active persecution.

After Introductory Elements

Commas set off certain kinds of elements when they come first in a sentence.

Introductory Participial Phrases

Use a comma to set off an introductory participle or participial phrase.

> *Feeling the pressure,* Corey stepped up to bat.

Participial
Phrases
p. 65

Long Introductory Prepositional Phrases

Use a comma after a long prepositional phrase (usually five or more words) or multiple prepositional phrases at the beginning of a sentence.

> *At the top of the sixth inning of the championship game,* the score was tied.

Prepositional
Phrases
p. 57

Introductory Sequencing Words

Commas are often used after sequencing words like *first, second, next, finally,* and *last*.

> *First,* read your part through several times.

> *Next,* look up any unfamiliar words.

> *Finally,* read your part aloud in front of a mirror.

Introductory Adverb Clauses

A comma always follows an introductory adverb clause.

> *Before we read John Milton's poetry,* the teacher summarized his life for us.

Adverb Clauses
pp. 95-96

Other Introductory Elements

A comma should follow a sentence modifier.

> *To better understand his epic poetry,* familiarize yourself with epic conventions.

A comma is often used when the introductory phrase contains a verbal.

> *By reading a poem aloud,* you will hear how Milton's lines sing.

Insert any missing commas. If the sentence is already correct, write C in the blank.

_____ 1. In 1517 Martin Luther posted ninety-five theses on a church door and thus declared the hypocrisy and corruption of the Roman Catholic Church.

_____ 2. By making his grievances public Martin Luther ignited the fuse of the Protestant Reformation, a movement that would revolutionize religious practice in the sixteenth century.

_____ 3. With active determination Martin Luther obviously played an important part in the Reformation and the resulting spread of the gospel.

Martin Luther at 45 by Lucas Cranach, courtesy of German Information Center

_____ 4. After he had been banned by the Edict of Worms Luther spent much time at the castle of Wartburg working on a translation of the New Testament.

_____ 5. Because some church officials had prohibited the translation of the Bible into German Luther knew he would face much opposition in his work.

_____ 6. Accepting the principle of *sola scriptura* (belief in Scripture as the sole authority for man's faith), Luther thought the common people should not have to rely on the priest for God's Word.

_____ 7. Realizing that most people did indeed rely on the Catholic clergy Luther decided to translate the Bible into German.

_____ 8. Finally Germans would be able to read the Bible for themselves.

_____ 9. Although there was a German Bible already in existence it was flawed and difficult to read because it was written in a style similar to the Latin Vulgate, not a style similar to German speech.

_____ 10. To appreciate what Luther's translation meant to the German people imagine what it would be like if you had no readable Bible in your language.

11.6 REVIEW *the skill*

Insert any missing commas. If the sentence is already correct, write C in the blank.

_____ 1. When the fullness of time came God sent Jesus Christ into the world.

_____ 2. Obviously, God the Father prepared the first-century world for the coming of His Son.

_____ 3. First He used the Roman government.

_____ 4. With the strength of its armies Rome was able to enforce peace throughout its empire.

_____ 5. Besides peace throughout its empire Rome provided a well-constructed system of roads.

_____ 6. During the first spreading of the gospel both the peace of Rome and the roads of Rome allowed believers to travel freely with the good news.

_____ 7. Second God used the Greek language to prepare the world for Christ's coming.

_____ 8. With so many people speaking the same language it was easy to tell others about Christ.

_____ 9. Because they are God's chosen people the Jews played a special part in God's preparation.

_____ 10. By their presence the Jews kept before people the idea of one true God with a righteous character.

To Separate

Commas often set off a word or a group of words from the rest of the sentence. The number of commas needed depends on where the word or word group is—at the beginning, in the middle, or at the end of the sentence.

Nouns of Direct Address

Sometimes we address a person by his name or courtesy title when we speak to him. That name or title, called a **noun of direct address,** should be set off by commas.

> *Justin,* may I speak with you for a moment?

> Can you repeat that, *ma'am?*

> What I'm trying to say, *Donna,* is that you've done a great job.

Parenthetical Expressions

Use commas to set off phrases that could be left out of the sentence.

> *By the way,* that dinner was delicious.

> The dessert, *in my opinion,* was the best part of the meal.

> No one should eat too much dessert, *of course.*

Interjections
p. 21

Interjections

Most interjections are set off from the rest of the sentence by commas.

> *Yes,* you are correct.

> *Oh,* it was I who left that rose on your windowsill.

> Open the window, *please.*

Phrases That Show Contrast

Commas should set off a phrase that shows contrast, especially when the phrase begins with a negative word such as *not* or *never.*

> Deborah, *not Kindra,* will be running the 300-meter race.

> She always trains in the morning, *never the late afternoon.*

Appositive
Phrases
pp. 61-62

Appositives

Most appositives are set off by commas.

> Rob, *my next door neighbor,* owns a pharmacy.

> Robert A. Milikan, *an American physicist,* measured the electrical charge of an electron in his famous "oil drop" experiment conducted in 1911.

However, a "close appositive"—a short appositive that is more specific than the noun before it—should not have commas.

> In 1662 the Frenchman *Claude-François Menestrier* wrote the first history of ballet.

> My cousin Alyce ran a marathon last year.

Adjectives After a Noun

Adjectives or participles joined by a conjunction often come after the noun. The modifying phrase is then set off by commas.

> The rookie football player, *nervous and excited,* waited impatiently to enter the game.

Tag Questions

A declarative sentence can be turned into an interrogative sentence by adding a tag question to the end. The tag question is separated from the rest of the sentence by a comma.

> The weather is beautiful, *isn't it?*

> You did get my message, *didn't you?*

Conjunctive Adverb

Conjunctive adverbs like *however* and *though* are often said in such a way that there seem to be pauses before and after them. As long as the word does not come between two independent clauses, set if off with a pair of commas.

> The game may be canceled, *however,* because of the storm.

Conjunctive
Adverbs
p. 16

Restrictive and Nonrestrictive Elements

A **restrictive** modifier is one that is necessary to identify the particular thing being referred to. It restricts the possibilities and is not set off by commas.

A **nonrestrictive** modifier gives extra information that is not necessary for identification of the thing being modified. Nonrestrictive elements are set off by commas.

The modifiers, whether restrictive or nonrestrictive, may be of various types.

Dependent
Clauses
pp. 91-92, 95-96

NONRESTRICTIVE ADJECTIVE CLAUSE	Bowling, *which is one of the oldest and most popular indoor sports*, is their favorite weekend activity.
RESTRICTIVE ADJECTIVE CLAUSE	My friend *who is an avid bowler* owns his own bowling shoes.
NONRESTRICTIVE PHRASE	An avid bowler, *with his own shoes and a customized bowling ball*, may practice several hours a week.
RESTRICTIVE PHRASE	A player *with three strikes in a row* has bowled a turkey.
NONRESTRICTIVE APPOSITIVE	Bowling a perfect game, *earning a score of three hundred points*, is not easy to do.
RESTRICTIVE APPOSITIVE ("CLOSE APPOSITIVE")	My friend *Matt* bowled a 210.
NONRESTRICTIVE ADVERB CLAUSE	I always enjoy our youth group's bowling activities, *although I'm not much of a bowler.*
RESTRICTIVE ADVERB CLAUSE	My group had the highest score *because we had Matt on our team.*

PRACTICE *the skill*

Insert any missing commas. If the sentence is already correct, write C in the blank.

_____ 1. Do you know anything about the Septuagint Mr. Hernandez?

_____ 2. No please tell me about it.

_____ 3. The Septuagint a historic achievement was the first translation of the Hebrew Old Testament into another language.

_____ 4. The translators chose Greek, a common language of that day, for this endeavor.

_____ 5. Greek cultured and international was the ideal language for the spread of the ideas of both the Old Testament and the New Testament.

_____ 6. The language that brought the world the humanistic ideas of the Greek philosophers was used by God to convey knowledge of Himself.

_____ 7. Legend not fact surrounds the origins of the Septuagint.

_____ 8. The common abbreviation LXX may have been used because there were supposedly six translators from each of Israel's twelve tribes (close to 70).

_____ 9. Although not all Jewish scholars liked the Septuagint Jesus Himself sometimes quoted from the translation.

_____ 10. It appears that God used the Septuagint for the spread of Christianity doesn't it?

REVIEW *the skill*

Rewrite each sentence, correcting any errors in comma usage. (You may need to insert or remove a comma or commas.) If the sentence is already correct, write C in the blank.

1. Erasmus a scholar in the fifteenth and sixteenth centuries lived in northern Europe.

_____

_____

2. Although he entered a monastery as a young man, he spent most of his life traveling and studying Latin and Greek.

   _____

   _____

3. Erasmus was one of the ones, who criticized the corruption in the established church.

   _____

   _____

4. He did not however just offer criticism.

   _____

   _____

5. His solution, to the abuses, was the production of a Greek New Testament.

   _____

   _____

6. You see, Erasmus wanted to produce a Greek New Testament to demonstrate the imperfections of the Vulgate.

   _____

   _____

7. Erasmus used four Greek manuscripts ones available in his city for his New Testament.

   _____

   _____

8. He had to translate the last verses of Revelation from Latin into Greek because those verses were missing from all four of his manuscripts.

   _____

   _____

9. Erasmus by using the original language of the New Testament wanted to produce an accurate copy of the New Testament in Greek.

   _____

   _____

10. His activities, exposing corruption and providing the Scriptures, helped lead to the Reformation, even though Erasmus himself refused to leave the established church.

    _____

    _____

In Letters and with Quotations, Dates, and Addresses

Salutations and Closings

A comma is used after the salutation in a friendly letter.

> Dear Magda,

> Dear Mrs. Saunders,

In both business letters and friendly letters, a comma is used after the closing.

> Sincerely,

> Your friend,

Quotation
Marks
pp. 298-99

Direct Quotations

A "quotation tag" (Steve said, she said) is joined to the quoted sentence with one or two commas. One comma is used if the quotation tag comes at the beginning or at the end; a pair of commas is used if it comes in the middle of the quoted sentence. Notice that the comma always appears before the quotation marks.

AT THE BEGINNING	Jocelyn asked, "Who painted *Death on a Pale Horse*?"
IN THE MIDDLE	"Benjamin West," replied Dan, "painted that in 1802."
	"In that same year," added Jocelyn, "Beethoven composed his second symphony."

No comma is used at the end of a question or exclamation if a question mark or an exclamation point is used instead.

> "Do you like the painting?" asked Dan.

Dates

For dates that appear in month-day-year order, use a comma to separate the day from the year. If the date does not end the sentence, put another comma after the year.

> The twins were born on *December 24, 2000.*

> On *December 24, 2000,* the twins were born.

No comma is necessary for dates that appear in day-month-year order.

> The twins were born on 24 December 2000.

Addresses

Place commas between elements in an address. Also, use a comma after the last item in the address if the sentence is incomplete.

> Rachael was born in *San Diego, California,* and she moved when she was five to *Kingsville, Texas.*

Do not insert a comma between the state, province, or territory and the ZIP code or another postal code.

> Mail the invitation to 1131 Master's Row, Chesapeake, Virginia 23322.

In addresses on envelopes, use the standard two-letter abbreviation for the state, province, or territory with no punctuation before or after it.

> Mr. and Mrs. Thomas L. Gerald

> 57 Bridge St.

> Kingston NS B0P 1R0

> CANADA

PRACTICE *the skill*

Insert any missing commas in the following items.

1. Imagine a letter (slightly modernized) from a member of the early church to a friend, written on June 5 61.

2. It is addressed to Claudius, 1 Appian Way Rome Italy 00111.

3. Dear Claudius

4. I want to inform you of the arrival of a man named Paul on March 24, 61 to the city of Rome.

5. As my friend Tertius says "He is no ordinary man."

6. Paul has suffered much for his faith in Jesus Christ yet says, "I take pleasure in infirmities, in reproaches in necessities in persecutions, in distresses for Christ's sake."

7. "For to me to live is Christ, and to die is gain" says Paul of his life's philosophy.

8. "I am not ashamed of the gospel of Christ," Paul has asserted "for it is the power of God unto salvation to every one that believeth."

9. Your friend Jason of Athens Greece could tell you more about Paul because he has met him.

10. Sincerely Erastus

REVIEW *the skill*

Insert any missing commas in the following items.

1. Emily wrote her friend Trent to tell him about the decision she made for Christ on November 11 2000.

2. Dear Trent

3. "I want to tell you about the best decision that I ever made" she began.

4. "A friend told me that Jesus died on the cross to pay for my sins" she continued "and I asked Jesus to be my Savior."

5. From John 3:16 she quoted "For God so loved the world, that he gave his only begotten Son, that whosoever believeth in him should not perish, but have everlasting life."

6. Your friend Emily

7. "Thank you for your letter Emily," responded Trent.

8. "I have also accepted Jesus as my Savior" he wrote "and He gives me the strength I need each day."

9. He quoted "Be strong in the Lord, and in the power of his might" (Eph. 6:10).

10. This letter was sent to the attention of Emily Wahl, 134 Main Street Keeler, Wisconsin 54032.

Conjunctions
p. 20

Incorrect Commas

Commas in wrong places can be distracting and even confusing.

Before a Conjunction Joining Only Two Elements

Normally no comma should be used when only two words, phrases, or dependent clauses are joined by a conjunction.

INCORRECT	In 1894 Mark Twain published *Tom Sawyer Abroad,* and *The Tragedy of Pudd'nhead Wilson.*
CORRECT	In 1894 Mark Twain published *Tom Sawyer Abroad* and *The Tragedy of Pudd'nhead Wilson.*

After a Conjunction

A comma should not ordinarily follow a conjunction. Remember that a comma *precedes* a conjunction joining two independent clauses.

INCORRECT	The temperature dropped to below thirty, and, the wind began to howl in the chimney.
CORRECT	The temperature dropped to below thirty, and the wind began to howl in the chimney.

However, a pair of commas may set off an item following a conjunction as well as anywhere else.

> The weather had been fairly warm, but, surprisingly, it snowed this morning.

Between a Subject and a Verb

A comma should never separate a subject and a verb.

INCORRECT	In 1944 bacteriologist Oswald Avery, demonstrated that DNA is responsible for heredity.
CORRECT	In 1944 bacteriologist Oswald Avery demonstrated that DNA is responsible for heredity.

A pair of commas (not just one) may set off a nonrestrictive item between the subject and the verb.

> Theodore Von Kármán, *sometimes called the Father of the Supersonic Age,* was instrumental in the founding of the Jet Propulsion Laboratory in California.

Avoid using a comma to salvage a sentence that has an awkwardly long subject. Rewrite the sentence if necessary.

POOR	Reading a biography of Abraham Lincoln aloud to her grandfather, was Emily's solution to the silence of the long winter evenings.
BETTER	Emily filled the long winter evenings by reading a biography of Abraham Lincoln aloud to her grandfather.

Integrated Quotations

When a quotation functions as either the subject or predicate noun of a sentence, it should not be set off by commas.

SUBJECT	"These are the times that try men's souls" opens Thomas Paine's first *Crisis Paper.*
PREDICATE NOUN	The beginning of Milton's great epic *Paradise Lost* is "Of man's first disobedience and the fruit / Of that forbidden tree."

The rule for restrictive clauses applies to quoted matter: do not use commas to set off a quoted restrictive clause.

Dates

Do not use a comma between a month and a year or after a year (unless the comma is required for another reason).

INCORRECT	She visited London in August, 2008, and anticipates returning for a longer visit someday.
CORRECT	She visited London in August 2008 and anticipates returning for a longer visit someday.
	She visited London in August 2008, and she anticipates returning for a longer visit someday.

Circle any incorrect commas. If the sentence is correct, write C in the blank.

———— 1. Jeremy Taylor, theologian and writer, was born in Cambridge, England, in August 1613.

———— 2. Perhaps one of his best known works, is *The Rules and Exercises of Holy Living and Dying,* often referred to simply as *Holy Living and Dying.*

———— 3. Being from a poor family, Taylor, had to attend the University of Cambridge as a poor student; his lowly status meant that he actually had to serve the wealthier students.

———— 4. Taylor was not at first a distinguished person, but, after he gave a lecture in the absence of a colleague, he became a well-known preacher.

———— 5. Taylor eventually became quite popular, and people were especially attracted to his joyfulness, and to his godliness.

———— 6. He became the chaplain to the archbishop of Canterbury, and to Charles I.

———— 7. The 1600s were a time of political upheaval between the Puritans and the royalists in England, and Taylor suffered more than once for his loyalty to the king.

———— 8. Even in times of political suffering, however, Taylor devoted his time to writing.

———— 9. "God hath given to man a short time here upon earth, and yet upon this short time eternity depends", is a quotation of Taylor's from the opening chapter of *Holy Living and Dying.*

———— 10. Great men such as Charles Wesley and Oswald Chambers testify that their lives were richly blessed, and challenged by the reading of *Holy Living and Dying.*

REVIEW *the skill*

Circle any incorrect commas. If the sentence is correct, write C in the blank.

_____ 1. In *Holy Living and Dying* Taylor, proposes a set of "rules" that will help a believer fulfill his responsibilities as a Christian.

_____ 2. According to Taylor, an important rule regarding the use of time is, "In the morning, when you awake, accustom yourself to think first upon God."

_____ 3. "In every action reflect upon the end," is a rule regarding good intentions that means that before one begins an action, he should consider the results of that action.

_____ 4. In order to practice humility, Christians should never compare themselves favorably with others, and, every man should think himself the lowest of all men.

_____ 5. A humble man "is modest in his speech," writes Taylor, "and reserved in his laughter."

_____ 6. According to Taylor, a humble man "does not murmur against commands," and "patiently bears injuries."

_____ 7. "Let us not inquire into the affairs of others that concern us not," writes Taylor on the subject of propriety.

_____ 8. "Be reverent, modest, and reserved in the presence of thy betters," is a rule not often practiced in today's society.

_____ 9. Reading books is a good practice, but Taylor says, "Good sermons and good books are of excellent use, but they can serve no other end but that we practice the plain doctrines of Scripture."

_____ 10. Taylor died in Lisburn, Ireland, on 13 August, 1667.

Semicolon

A semicolon signals a stronger sentence break than a comma does. Remember that the semicolon always joins equal elements. A fairly strong mark of punctuation, the semicolon should not be overused.

Independent
Clauses
p. 88

Between Two Independent Clauses

A semicolon may connect two closely related independent clauses. Often the second independent clause reinforces the first, and there may or may not be a transitional word within the second independent clause.

> The race will be challenging; over half of the five miles are uphill.
>
> Many people will be racing; however, only a few will actually finish the race.

Comma with
Conjunctive
Adverb
p. 277

Notice that the conjunctive adverb *however* follows the semicolon as part of the second clause.

Before a Conjunction in a Long Compound Sentence

Usually a compound sentence has a comma before the coordinating conjunction; however, a semicolon is often substituted for that comma when the sentence, longer than usual, contains other commas.

Compound
Sentence
p. 103

> As the iron ore carrier passed beneath the aerial lift bridge in Duluth, Minnesota, the sailors waved to the tourists, who were standing along the canal; and the tourists waved back energetically.

Between Word Groups Containing Commas

Because it is a stronger mark of punctuation than the comma, the semicolon is used to separate word groups in a final series when any of the word groups contain internal commas. Note that the series must be at the end of the sentence.

> The new class officers are president, Kristen Markey; vice president, Joey Hayes; and chaplain, Ian Romig.

Even if a list does not have internal commas, it may still have semicolons if (1) the whole list is introduced by a colon and (2) the items in the list are somewhat long.

> The new class officers are as follows: President Kristen Markey; Vice President Joey Hayes; and Chaplain Ian Romig.

Semicolons also separate Bible references whenever a new chapter is mentioned.

> Hosea 6:3, 6; 10:12
>
> II Peter 1:4; Rev. 5:9-10

Colon

The colon is a strong mark of punctuation, separating elements almost as definitely as the period. The colon often points up what follows it, marking it as being important, explanatory, or more specific.

In Bible References and Expressions of Time

An unspaced colon separates the chapter and the verse in Bible references and in expressions of time.

> Proverbs 29:1
>
> II Corinthians 12:7-10
>
> 10:00 A.M.

After a Salutation of a Business Letter

Place a colon after the salutation in a business letter.

> Dear Sir or Madam:
>
> Dear Representative Adams:

Before a Series at the End of a Sentence

A colon can introduce a series that comes at the end of a sentence. Often *the following* or *as follows,* signaling a coming list, appears somewhere before the colon. A colon can set off a series only if the series is not part of the basic structure of the sentence. In other words, no colon should be used before a complement or the object of a preposition.

CORRECT	Please bring the following items to the meeting: theme ideas, something to take notes on, and a positive attitude.
INCORRECT	The boy who got the part was: energetic, talented, and well practiced.
CORRECT	The boy who got the part was energetic, talented, and well practiced.

The words *such as* or *including* should not be followed by a colon.

> Gretchen has many favorite books, including *Where the Red Fern Grows, Watership Down,* and *The Hobbit.*

The colon can also be used for emphasis to introduce a single appositive at the end of a sentence.

> The art collector slowly and dramatically pulled away the veil covering his new acquisition: a stunning portrait of his pet iguana.

Before a Long or Formal Direct Quotation

A colon is often used before a long or formal direct quotation, especially if the introduction to it is formal. The quotation must appear last in the sentence.

> After his conversion, John Donne composed moving poetic prayers, including the following from *A Hymn to God the Father:* "But swear by thyself, that at my death thy Son / Shall shine as he shines now, and heretofore; / And, having done that, thou has done; / I fear no more."

Between a Book Title and Subtitle

If a book has a subtitle, it will appear on the title page below the title; usually it is unpunctuated. However, when you refer to the book in your writing by both its title and its subtitle, you should insert a colon between the two parts.

> Kanchan found biographical information on T.S. Eliot in *Poetry in English: An Anthology.*

Insert any missing semicolons or colons.

1. An important way the kingdom of God grows is through the Bible God has preserved His Word so that man may know Him.

2. In Psalm 12 6-7 the Bible gives us the following important promise "The word of God . . . liveth and abideth for ever."

3. People can find out how to repent, believe, and receive Jesus just by reading the Bible but Christians should not stop witnessing, sharing, and preaching the good news of salvation.

4. Concerning the Bible, Christians should take the following steps memorize it to increase their Bible knowledge, practical wisdom, and spiritual insight apply it in making decisions, giving advice, and influencing others and meditate on it to understand God's will, abide in His presence, and walk in His way daily.

5. The Word of God is obviously powerful it is called a sword that can pierce the hearts of men (Heb. 4 12 Eph. 6 17).

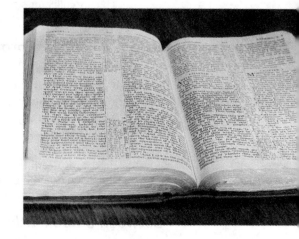

6. Dear Mr. Farley

7. I would like to order the commentary *Ecclesiastes A Study in Human Happiness* by G. L. Woodard at the list price of $24.95.

8. I will expect to receive the book no later than November 25, 2001, at 10 00 A.M., as stated in the shipping terms.

9. Thank you for the excellent service you provide in selling good Christian literature at reduced prices I am greatly indebted to you.

10. Sincerely, Herman Larkin

Insert any missing semicolons or colons. If the sentence is already correct, write C in the blank.

_____ 1. Heroes and heroines of the faith can be found in unusual places one heroine often lay in a sickbed.

_____ 2. This heroine was a well-known pastor's wife Susannah Spurgeon.

_____ 3. Mrs. Spurgeon could be described as dedicated, compassionate, and selfless.

_____ 4. Her life demonstrated biblical ideals for women (Prov. 31 26-30 I Pet. 3 1-4).

_____ 5. Mrs. Spurgeon, born Susannah Thompson on January 15, 1832, was saved as a young girl but she was not fully dedicated to serving the Lord until after she met her future husband.

_____ 6. The year 1856 brought the following changes to Susannah Thompson's life marriage to Charles Spurgeon, the birth of twin sons, and the beginning of a lifelong struggle with a weak body.

_____ 7. Despite her physical weakness, Mrs. Spurgeon made a lasting impression on church life in England for she developed an unusual burden, getting books to needy preachers.

_____ 8. She put much effort into establishing a Book Fund for these men she gave generously of her own funds and encouraged donations from others for many years.

_____ 9. In spite of her poor health, she lived a relatively long life she outlived her husband by eleven years and died in 1903 at the age of seventy-one.

_____ 10. Proverbs 31 31 well describes Mrs. Spurgeon "Give her of the fruit of her hands; and let her own works praise her in the gates."

Rewrite the following paragraph, correcting the ten mistakes from these categories: subject-verb agreement, pronoun-antecedent agreement, verb use, pronoun reference, adjective and adverb use, capitalization, and punctuation.

When the Romans captured Israel in the first and second centuries, most of the Jews left the region, and the area became known as palestine. Almost two thousand years later, the Jewish people began returning. In 1880 there were already twenty four thousand Jews living in Arab-occupied Palestine. At first the move seemed slowly, but by 1914 more than eighty-five thousand Jews had migrated to Palestine. In 1917 Britain issued the balfour Declaration, which supported the homeland for the Jews in Palestine, and after World War I Britain, receiving Palestine as a mandated territory, was supposed to aid the Jews in their building of a homeland. After six million Jews were killed in World War II by the Nazis, they demanded a state in Palestine. In 1947 the United Nations agreed to separate Palestine into a Jewish state, and an Arab state. On May 14, 1948, the state of Israel had officially began. Surrounding Arab nations attacked the new nation immediately, yet, it survived. Hostility in Israel and the surrounding regions continue, but the nation of Israel exists today.

_____

_____

_____

_____

_____

_____

_____

_____

_____

_____

_____

_____

_____

_____

_____

_____

_____

COORDINATION AND SUBORDINATION

> For the word of God is quick, and powerful, and sharper than any twoedged sword, piercing even to the dividing asunder of soul and spirit, and of the joints and marrow, and is a discerner of the thoughts and intents of the heart.
>
> *Hebrews 4:12*

Conjunctions pp. 20-21

When speaking, you may indicate the importance of certain ideas by the tone of your voice, animated facial expressions, or distinct gestures. In writing, however, different strategies—such as coordination and subordination—are necessary to show how ideas rank in importance. *Coordination* is making elements equal, and *subordination* is making certain elements less important (or less central) than others. Think of an outline—the main points are parallel and thus coordinate. The supporting points, subpoints, come under the main idea to support and strengthen it, and since they are less important, they are subordinate. The writing strategy of coordinating and subordinating ideas should become a part of your writing, whether you are writing a personal letter, a research paper, or a short story.

Write a brief biography similar to the excerpt at the beginning of this chapter. Your biography will tell the salvation story of someone you have known personally. As you craft your narrative, focus on the organization of your ideas—specifically, the way in which you coordinate and subordinate thoughts and details.

Planning

Thinking Biblically

Augustine left behind a spiritual autobiography written as a series of confessions to God. The following quotation taken from his book *Confessions* appears shortly after Augustine's account of his conversion.

"Thou, O Lord, art good and merciful, and Thy right hand had respect unto the depth of my death, and from the bottom of my heart emptied that abyss of corruption. And this Thy whole gift was, to nill what I willed, and to will what thou willedst. . . . [W]hat I feared to be parted from, was now a joy to part with. For Thou didst cast them forth from me, Thou true and highest sweetness. Thou castedst them forth, and for them enteredst in Thyself, sweeter than all pleasure" (*The Confessions of St. Augustine*. New York: Grosset & Dunlap, n.d., pp. 176-77).

✔ **Choose a topic.** You may choose any person that you know or have known well, such as a grandparent, a pastor, a teacher, or a friend.

✔ **Consider your audience.** Because your purpose for writing depends on your audience, you must carefully consider to whom you are speaking. For this assignment, imagine your biography will be appearing in your local newspaper's human-interest section. You will have unsaved readers, so be sure to present the gospel clearly.

✔ **Avoid jargon.** Using the specialized technical terms of a particular group can confuse and frustrate your reader. Consider the backgrounds of your readers. An unsaved person may not be familiar with terms such as *lost, justification,* or *propitiation.* Using unfamiliar words can also make the reader feel unintelligent or unaccepted since he is not on the "inside" with those sharing these foreign terms. You must give your readers easy access to your meaning. Sometimes technical terms are necessary; however, be sure to provide definitions for such terms.

tip

When defining specialized terminology, avoid using other equally unfamiliar terms in the definitions.

✔ **Clarify your goals.** Your basic purpose is to inform—to tell a story—and to offer clear presentation of the gospel. What other purpose could you accomplish in your biography? Could you present an example? An explanation? Can you encourage or inspire? Persuade?

✔ **Gather information.** Write out what you already know about the person you are writing about. Do you need more background information? Did this person publish an account of his or her conversion? Did he or she deliver it publicly where it would have been recorded? If possible, interview the person or others who were acquainted with your subject. Write out a list of well-thought-out questions before meeting with your interviewee. Keep an accurate record of the answers and be sure to ask permission if you plan to record the interview. Look for specific details. The more concrete your story is, the more effective your message will be.

Drafting

✔ **List the key idea or ideas you want to include in your narrative.**

> Went swimming at the quarry with Alex
>
> Almost drowned
>
> Saved by a man driving by in a car
>
> The man and Alex drowned
>
> Visited the church across from the quarry
>
> Heard how God gave His Son to die for us

✔ **Freewrite.** Read through all the information you have gathered. Then try to write it all out at one time. Include the ideas you listed in the previous step. Write down every detail that you might want to include. Remember that this is just a drafting exercise, one step in the process. Don't worry about revising and editing at this stage. Just write!

Coordination
p. 365

✔ **Organize your thoughts.** Since writing a biography is telling someone's story, you will most likely want to organize your ideas in a chronological order. However, you should feel free to be creative. You can begin *in medias res,* in the middle of the story, by setting the scene for the action or by describing the action itself. As you write, keep in mind the basic principles of coordination and subordination. **Coordination** of ideas is accomplished by using the conjunctions *and, but, or,* and *nor.* Linking thoughts together in this way implies they are of equal importance.

Coordinating
Conjunctions
p. 20

Elements needing equal emphasis within sentences may be coordinated. Remember that only parallel elements may be coordinated.

Neither *Tristen* **nor** *Alex* knew about the sinkhole.

On that hot summer day the boys *rode their bikes* **and** *played basketball.*

The water was *cold* **and** *refreshing.*

Alex and Tristen swam as hard as they could, **but** *they could not free themselves from the strong pull of the sinkhole.*

Subordination
p. 365-66

Information that qualifies and supports an idea should be **subordinated.** To subordinate, use a subordinating conjunction to make a dependent clause.

UNSUBORDINATED	The day was hot and humid. The boys wanted to go swimming.
SUBORDINATED	*Because the day was hot and humid,* the boys wanted to go swimming.

Making the first sentence a dependent clause stresses the causal relationship. If the day had not been hot and humid, then the boys would not have wanted to go swimming—because A, then B.

Try combining the following sentences using various coordinating and subordinating conjunctions. Notice how a shift in emphasis can completely change the meaning.

She plays basketball. She runs track. She is fast.

Frankie went to the class party. Amanda went shopping.

Greg likes dogs. Sonly likes cats.

Revising

✔ **Consider the responses from your peer "editors."** Did they suggest any changes in your organizational strategy? Carefully evaluate the responses to see whether they are accurate and necessary.

✔ **Check for jargon.** Do you define terms your audience may not be familiar with? Are the definitions clear and free of other jargon words?

✔ **Accomplish your purpose.** Does your narrative accomplish the goals you set at the beginning of the writing process?

✔ **Coordinate and subordinate.** Remember that coordination and subordination make your writing more precise. Are there any sentences that can be combined by making an equally important idea coordinate or a supporting idea into a dependent clause?

✔ **Proofread.** Check the spelling carefully; use a dictionary if you are not certain.

First Draft

~~Tristen~~ was born in South Carolina. ~~He~~ was an ordinary nine-year-old
boy. ~~Tristen~~ On hot summer days, he and his friend Alex ~~liked to ride their bikes to the basketball court. They also liked to ride their bikes~~ would play basketball, ride bikes, and go swimming. ~~They like to do these things in the hot summer.~~ One day Tristen and Alex rode their bikes.
~~They rode~~ by the quarry. ~~The water looked good. And~~ It was so cool, and the water . . . ~~it was so hot outside.~~
~~There was a sign that said~~ "No Swimming!" Ignoring the sign, the boys ~~Tristen and Alex didn't pay attention to the sign. They put their bikes down. They~~ climbed down to the water
and ~~They~~ jumped ~~into the cold water. Wow! It felt so good! It~~ in. The cold wetness was a welcome relief from
the heat. ~~The quarry~~ It ~~wasn't very big. The boys~~ Tristen and Alex decided to try to swim across the
quarry. They didn't get very far before. A strong current ~~started~~ began pulling them under
the water. The young boys kicked and struggled with all their might to free
themselves from the current. ~~The current~~ that seemed to be sucking them
straight down to the bottom. A man driving by saw the two boys struggling in
the water. He pulled his car over and ~~He~~ jumped into the water. ~~He fought~~ Fighting the
current, ~~He~~ h swam out to the boys. He hooked Tristen's neck in his arm and
managed to get him to safety. He went back for Alex. The two fought the
current, but t ~~The~~ force of the water was too strong. Alex and the man never made
it back. Tristen could not believe what had just happened. He had almost
died. ~~And~~ H his best friend was gone, along with a ~~this strange man~~ the stranger. That stranger ~~The man~~
had saved his life—and ~~he~~ died trying to save Alex.

Second Draft

Born in South Carolina, Tristen was an ordinary nine-year-old boy. On hot summer days he and his friend Alex would play basketball, ride their bikes, and go swimming. One day Tristen and Alex rode their bikes by the quarry. It was so hot outside, and the water looked so cool. Ignoring the "No Swimming!" sign, the boys climbed down to the water and jumped in. The cold wetness was a welcome relief from the dense heat. Tristen and Alex decided to try to swim across the quarry. It wasn't very big. They didn't get very far before a strong current began pulling them under the water. The young boys kicked and struggled with all their might to free themselves from the current that seemed to be sucking them straight down to the bottom. A man driving by saw the two boys struggling in the water. He pulled his car over and jumped into the water. Fighting the current, he swam out to the boys. He hooked Tristen's neck in his arm and managed to get him to safety. He went back for Alex. The two fought the current, but the force of the water was too strong. Alex and the man never made it back. Tristen could not believe what happened. He had almost died. His best friend was gone, along with the stranger. That stranger saved his life—and died trying to save Alex.

Tristen had to tell his story over and over to so many people. One Thursday night he went back to a church across from the quarry. Tristen had been at the church a few times before. He liked to go and play games there with his friends. They always had to sit through a Bible lesson. He had never really listened very carefully. But this time he listened. The teacher told the class about a man who had come to earth to die. He gave His life for us. "Greater love hath no man than this, that a man lay down his life for his friends." Then Tristen understood. That stranger had given his life to save him. And this man, Jesus, had come and had given His life for the world.

Publishing

✔ **Send a copy of your biography to the person you wrote about.** If that person is no longer living, send it to his or her family members.

✔ **Submit your biography to your church newsletter.**

✔ **Give an oral presentation of your paper.** Bring in photos of the person. If possible, have that person come and visit your class on the day you give your report.

✔ **Save your writing.** Put it in your portfolio along with a photo of whomever you wrote about.

Some Ideas to Consider

- If you are a Christian, think about the people who were influential in your coming to Christ. You may write about your pastor, your parents, a Sunday school teacher, or someone in your church that showed special interest in you.

- Do you know someone who is a faithful example, no matter what happens? You could write about a teacher or a parent or someone else that you spend a great deal of time with.

- Perhaps you have a close friend who has recently given his or her life to Christ. Or maybe a family member who had strayed from the Lord has recently surrendered his will to God's. The better you know the person, the easier the story will be for you to write.

LETTER FOR LETTER

A Love Letter

In Ephesians 4:15, Paul exhorted Christians to "[speak] the truth in love." Here Paul uses persuasion, but in a truthful and loving way. What truths did Paul use to persuade Philemon?

Philemon had the men sit down, as he always did. Every morning they met here, the master with the slaves, to go over the day's work on his estate outside Colosse. Being a Christian, he treated his slaves better than most because he wanted his men to see the love of Christ through him. But, he told himself, he was also a businessman who got things done.

"All right, does everybody know what's going on? Khamid, you have the southern fields again today. Balmada can help you. Keep trimming like you've been; I want those fields finished by sundown."

Khamid started. "Sundown? But that's impossible—"

"Sundown, Khamid. Don't come in till you're through."

"But without Onesimus, we can't do more than five or six acres. He knew those fields like the back of his hand and probably could do the whole thing by himself today, but I can't even find my way around down there. I'm not used to the southern fields."

"Khamid, we have a job to do, with or without Onesimus, and we will do it. You don't build a business by making excuses. Now get out there, all of you."

As the men sullenly left the room, Philemon wrestled with the same questions he'd had for weeks. Ever since Onesimus left, the men had seemed strange. Philemon wondered whether they were planning to run away too. Maybe he should have Onesimus flogged when they catch him to teach the others that running doesn't pay. That is, if they catch him; he could be as far as Rome by now.

Just then a messenger came in, with a letter in his hand. Opening it, Philemon smiled at the familiar signature of the Apostle Paul, his personal friend and mentor. As he read, his eyes grew wider and his mouth fell slightly open as he came across the words

> I beseech thee for my son Onesimus, whom I have begotten in my bonds.

For the full story, read the book of Philemon.

- *What are some of the reasons that Paul gives Philemon for Onesimus's release?*
- *Paul was Philemon's spiritual authority. Why do you think Paul did not write a firm letter to Philemon, insisting that he release Onesimus?*

Personal Response

Paul's request for Philemon to forgive Onesimus was based upon Christ's forgiving us. With Christ as our example, we should forgive others and completely restore fellowship with them. Is there someone who has wronged you that you have never forgiven? Write about a time when you forgave someone or when someone forgave you.

Examples of persuasive writing are all around you: newspaper editorials, advertisements, a note about why your brother needs to borrow your mountain bike. Each author uses various techniques to persuade you to espouse his point of view.

The following is an excerpt from a speech given by General Colin Powell on July 31, 2000, at the Republican National Convention in Philadelphia. He was trying to persuade his audience—those in the auditorium and those watching on television—to vote for then-Governor George W. Bush. Notice Powell's balance of argumentation, fact-giving, and emotional appeal.

Speech to the Republican National Convention

by Colin Powell

Ladies and gentlemen, we stand at an historic turning point in world history. For the first time in almost a century, America does not face an enemy fueled by an ideology claiming to be superior to our beloved system of democracy, free enterprise and the rights of men and women to pursue their individual destinies.

We defeated communism. We defeated fascism. We defeated them on the field of battle, and we defeated them on the field of ideas.

The sick nations that still pursue the fool's gold of tyranny and weapons of mass destruction will soon find themselves left behind in the dust bin of history.

They are investing in their own demise as surely as the Soviet Union did by investing in the Red Army. They are of the past, and we are of the future. Count on it.

Today, we are the most powerful nation on earth—militarily, economically, by any measure. We are that rarity in history, a trusted nation whose power is tempered by compassion, whose leadership is earned by example and whose foreign affairs will be guided by common interests and common sense.

The world is watching to see if all this power and wealth is just for the well-to-do, the comfortable, the privileged, or are we a nation that can make our dream real for all Americans so that all share in what we have been given by a generous God?

We must show to the rest of the world, the beauty and potential of democracy. Our greatest strength is the power of our example to be that shining city on the hill that Ronald Reagan spoke of and that the whole world looks up to.

To continue to be that place, we must all work together. We must reach down, back and across. All of us coming together to show the world what our American family can do. That is the challenge. This is the time. And in Governor George Bush, we have the leader.

MORE PUNCTUATION

You learned about six major marks of punctuation in the previous chapter. This chapter will continue the theme of punctuation with descriptions of seven additional marks. Though not as well known or frequently used as the period or the comma, these marks help to fine-tune and clarify your writing. Use them correctly, and both you and your writing will appear more polished.

Quotation Marks

Quotation marks have two main purposes. They show that a person's exact words are being quoted, and they indicate the titles of shorter works. Unlike the punctuation marks discussed in the previous chapter, quotation marks always appear in pairs.

Direct Quotations

Quotation marks indicate that the exact words of a writer or speaker are being reported.

> "I would like to present next year's student body president," announced the principal.

> The report stated, "Profits are expected to rise next quarter."

A quotation tag tells the reader who spoke or wrote the words. The quotation tags in the sentences above are *announced the principal* and *the report stated*. If a quotation tag appears at the end of a sentence, use a period after the tag.

> "Your test is scheduled for Tuesday," the teacher said. "Please be prepared."

Sometimes a quotation tag comes in the middle of a quoted sentence. When that happens, surround the quotation tag with commas and enclose both parts of the quoted sentence in quotation marks.

> "If you do not buy a ticket now," she warned, "it may be too late."

An exception to the rule regarding direct quotations is that certain well-known proverbs (including certain biblical sayings) are not enclosed in quotation marks.

> Kendra's dad taught her the concept that a penny saved is a penny earned.

Dialogue

When reporting dialogue, you should enclose each speaker's words in quotation marks and start a new paragraph whenever the speaker changes.

> "Where are we going for our picnic?" asked Tim.

> "We'll go to either the park or the lake," replied his mother.

> "Let's go to the lake," said Tim. "Then I can fish."

In the third line of dialogue, a period is used after the quotation tag because the preceding quotation is a complete sentence.

Do not use quotation marks for the speeches of dramatic characters within a play.

> **PRINCESS** | Here comes Boyet, and mirth is in his face.
>
> **BOYET** | O, I am stabb'd with laughter! Where's her grace?
> (William Shakespeare, *Love's Labour's Lost*)

Indirect Quotations

Sometimes only the idea of what a person said is recorded and not his actual words. Such a statement, called an indirect quotation, should not be enclosed in quotation marks.

DIRECT QUOTATION | Mom said, "You need to clean your room before you go out."

INDIRECT QUOTATION | Mom said **that I** need to clean my room before I go out.

Titles of Short Works

Titles of short works are normally enclosed in quotation marks. Works are typically considered short if they would not stand alone as published material. Examples are short stories, chapters of a book, short poems, essays, periodical articles, and songs. Individual episodes of a television or radio series are also put in quotation marks.

"The Gift of the Magi" is one of O. Henry's best-known short stories.

Everybody should read the article "Education in America" in this journal.

My favorite episode of that show was "Walking Distance."

There are two exceptions to the rule about titles of short works. First, major subdivisions of the Bible are capitalized but not put in quotation marks.

John is the last of the four Gospels.

The second exception is that quotation marks are not used with a title that stands as the heading of a work. An example of this exception is the title on a report that you write for class.

Capitalization of Titles
p. 249

Single Quotation Marks

Single quotation marks should be used when quotation marks are needed within quotation marks.

The song leader announced, "We will sing 'The Old Rugged Cross' next."

"Aunt Phylicia said, 'Come over tomorrow for lunch,'" Jackie told her sister.

Quotation Marks and Other Punctuation

In American usage, commas and periods always go before adjacent quotation marks.

"I have you scheduled to work Saturday," said Mr. Brown.

Tori eagerly replied, "I'll be there at 8:00."

Colons and semicolons always go after closing quotation marks. (Because the colon or semicolon is punctuation for the whole sentence, it stays outside the quoted item.)

I like the final words of "When I Survey the Wondrous Cross": "Love so amazing, so divine, / Demands my soul, my life, my all."

Question marks and exclamation points may go either before or after quotation marks, depending on the meaning of the sentence. If the words within the quotation marks are the question or exclamation, put the punctuation before the closing quotation marks. If, however, the entire sentence is a question or exclamation, put the punctuation after the closing quotation marks. The concluding period of a sentence is omitted if the sentence ends with an interrogative or exclamatory quotation.

The man behind me yelled, "Watch out for that car!"

Did you hear him say, "This is a dangerous place to walk"?

End Marks
p. 266

Comma
pp. 270-83

Semicolon and Colon
p. 286-87

Ellipses

Ellipses (or "ellipsis marks") are three spaced dots. Although the dots look like periods, each should have a space before and after it. Ellipses indicate the omission of something in quoted material or show halting or unfinished speech.

Omission of Words in a Quotation

Research Essay
pp. 258-59

Whenever one or more words are omitted within a sentence, ellipses should appear where the words would have been. Remember that omissions are acceptable only if they do not change the meaning of the original.

ORIGINAL	"Julius Caesar conquered Gaul in the century before Christ was born. The Gauls, a Celtic tribe, adopted Roman customs and became an integral part of the Roman Empire."
WITH OMISSIONS	"Julius Caesar conquered Gaul . . . before Christ was born. The Gauls . . . adopted Roman customs and became an integral part of the Roman Empire."

Sometimes you may quote multiple sentences, leaving out certain portions of the original. Place a period before the ellipses if both the words that precede and the words that follow the four dots are grammatically complete sentences (for example, if you delete only the end of the first sentence, leaving the main clause). The first letter of the sentence following the ellipsis may be capitalized, just as it would be at the beginning of any other sentence, regardless of whether it was capitalized in the original.

"Julius Caesar conquered Gaul. . . . The Gauls, a Celtic tribe, adopted Roman customs and became an integral part of the Roman Empire."

Ellipses are not needed at the beginning or end of a quoted passage.

According to my geography book, the Gauls "adopted Roman customs."

A full line of spaced dots may be used to indicate the omission of one or more lines of poetry.

ORIGINAL	"Come, we that love the Lord, And let our joys be known; Join in a song with sweet accord, And thus surround the throne." (from "Heavenly Joy on Earth" by Isaac Watts)
WITH OMISSIONS	"Come, we that love the Lord, ... Join in a song with sweet accord."

Halting or Unfinished Speech

Ellipses may also be used to show disruptions in the flow of speech. The disruption may be a hesitant pause in the middle of a sentence or a trailing off at the end of a sentence. If you are showing a pause in the middle, use just three spaced dots. If the disruption comes at the end of the sentence, place a period before the three dots.

Surprised by the commotion at the back of the hall, the speaker faltered as he said, "And in conclusion, let me say. . . ."

PRACTICE *the skill*

Insert any missing quotation marks. Circle any unnecessary quotation marks. If the sentence is already correct, write C in the blank.

_____ 1. Are you familiar with the book *"To the Best of My Ability: The American Presidents"*?

_____ 2. From the section "George Washington" to the section Bill Clinton to the information on campaigns and inaugurations, the book is full of details about the presidents' words and deeds.

_____ 3. Lincoln once confirmed that "he could not always control things during the Civil War by saying, 'I claim not to have controlled events, but confess plainly that events have controlled me.'"

_____ 4. But fewer have heard his predecessor's statement on leaving the White House: "If you are as happy, my dear sir, on entering this house as I am in leaving it and returning home, you are the happiest man in this country."

_____ 5. And so, my fellow Americans, ask not what your country can do for you; ask what you can do for your country: many people know that John F. Kennedy made that statement.

_____ 6. But who could guess who said "that the government had approached near to perfection"?

_____ 7. The same president featured a new song, The Star-Spangled Banner, as part of his first campaign.

_____ 8. James Monroe was not the only one to use music to attract voters; other campaign songs ranged from "That's the Ticket March" for William McKinley to Happy Days Are Here Again for Franklin Roosevelt.

_____ 9. Of course, a Republican would have said, "The song Happy Days Are Here Again is a little misleading. We are still in a depression."

_____ 10. "I was summoned," said George Washington, "by my country, whose voice I can never hear but with veneration."

Read the paragraph and determine whether the quotations following it are correct. Write the letter of the quotation that is punctuated correctly.

Though voting is one of the most important civil rights, it is also surely one of the most neglected. In 1988 only 50.1% of the electorate bothered to vote—the lowest turnout in sixty-four years. Christians who are able should make every effort not to be numbered with the apathetic. As a matter of stewardship they should use their ballot to make choices for the best government possible. As Edmund Burke observed, "The only thing necessary for the triumph of evil is for good men to do nothing."

(Passage from "Campaigns and Elections" in AMERICAN GOVERNMENT *for Christian Schools* by Timothy Keesee)

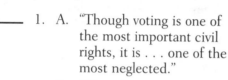

1. A. "Though voting is one of the most important civil rights, it is . . . one of the most neglected."

   B. "Though voting is . . . one of the most important civil rights, it is one of the most neglected."

2. A. "Christians . . . should make every effort not to be numbered with the apathetic."

   B. Christians...should make every effort not to be numbered with the apathetic."

3. A. "Christians who are able should make every effort not to be numbered with the apathetic. . . . They should use their ballot to make choices for the best government possible."

   B. Christians who are able. . . . should use their ballot to make choices for the best government possible."

4. A. "In 1988 only 50.1% of the electorate bothered to vote . . . Christians who are able should make every effort not to be numbered with the apathetic."

   B. "In 1988 only 50.1% of the electorate bothered to vote. . . . Christians who are able should make every effort not to be numbered with the apathetic."

5. A. "Christians who are able should . . . be numbered with the apathetic."

   B. "Christians . . . should make every effort not to be numbered with the apathetic."

6. A. "In 1988 only 50.1% of the electorate bothered to vote."

B. "In 1988 only 50.1% of the electorate bothered to vote. . . ."

7. A. "As Edmund Burke observed, "The only thing necessary for the triumph of evil is for good men to do nothing."

B. "As Edmund Burke observed, 'The only thing necessary for the triumph of evil is for good men to do nothing.'"

8. A. "Though voting is one of the most important civil rights, it is . . . one of the most neglected."

B. "Though voting is one of the most important civil rights, it is . . . one of the most neglected".

9. A. ". . . They should use their ballot to make choices for the best government possible."

B. "They should use their ballot to make choices for the best government possible."

10. A. "As a matter of stewardship they should use their ballot to make. . . . the best government possible."

B. "As a matter of stewardship they should use their ballot to make . . . the best government possible."

Underlining for Italics

Italic print is used primarily for identifying titles of books and other long works. A few other specialized uses are also discussed below. If you are writing out a paper by hand, you should underline words that would be italicized in print.

| HANDWRITTEN VERSION | Dumas constructed an elaborate tale of revenge in <u>The Count of Monte Cristo</u>. |
| WORD-PROCESSED OR PUBLISHED VERSION | Dumas constructed an elaborate tale of revenge in *The Count of Monte Cristo*. |

Capitalization
of Titles
p. 249

Long Works

Italicize or underline the titles of long literary and musical works.

BOOKS	*David Copperfield* (exception: the Bible)
PERIODICALS	*The Economist*
NEWSPAPERS	*Washington Post*
EPIC-LENGTH POEMS	*Beowulf*
PLAYS	*The Merchant of Venice*
TELEVISION OR RADIO SERIES	*The Lone Ranger*
MUSICAL COMPOSITIONS	Handel's *Messiah*

Works of Art

Italicize or underline the names of works of art.

PAINTINGS	*The Last Supper*
SCULPTURES	*Moses*

Capitalization
p. 243

Large Vehicles

Italicize or underline the names of large vehicles.

SHIPS	USS *Ronald Reagan*
TRAINS	*The Flying Scotsman*
AIRCRAFT	*Flyer*
SPACECRAFT	*Apollo 8*

Words, Letters, and Numerals Being Discussed

Italicize or underline words, letters, and numerals that are referred to as words.

The word *separate* is frequently misspelled.

The letter *l* and the number *1* can sometimes be confused with each other in writing.

The word *success* has two *c*'s and three *s*'s.

Notice that the plural suffix *s* is not italicized in the last sentence.

Foreign Words and Phrases

Italicize or underline unfamiliar foreign words and phrases used in a sentence.

For his birthday Paul would like *du gâteau au chocolat*—some chocolate cake.

12.3 **PRACTICE** *the skill*

Write the letter that corresponds to the sentence that is punctuated correctly.

———— 1. A. Shelly's article, "The Benefits of Debate," appeared in this week's issue of *Shelton High News*.

  B. Shelly's article, *The Benefits of Debate,* appeared in this week's issue of *Shelton High News*.

  C. Shelly's article, "The Benefits of Debate," appeared in this week's issue of "Shelton High News."

———— 2. A. He said, "I feel nauseous," but he should have used the word "nauseated."

  B. He said, "I feel nauseous", but he should have used the word *nauseated*.

  C. He said, "I feel nauseous," but he should have used the word *nauseated*.

———— 3. A. Even in awkward situations, my mother always exhibits "savoir-faire."

  B. Even in awkward situations, my mother always exhibits savoir-faire.

  C. Even in awkward situations, my mother always exhibits *savoir-faire*.

_____ 4. A. When you say the word *often,* you should not pronounce the letter "t."

B. When you say the word *often,* you should not pronounce the letter *t.*

C. When you say the word "often," you should not pronounce the letter "t."

_____ 5. A. The classic film "Ben Hur" features a thrilling chariot race.

B. The classic film *Ben Hur* features a thrilling chariot race.

C. The classic film Ben Hur features a thrilling chariot race.

_____ 6. A. *Death* is the third chapter of Tolstoy's famous novel *Anna Karenina.*

B. *Death* is the third chapter of Tolstoy's famous novel "Anna Karenina."

C. "Death" is the third chapter of Tolstoy's famous novel *Anna Karenina.*

_____ 7. A. "Andy on Trial" is a humorous episode of *The Andy Griffith Show.*

B. *Andy on Trial* is a humorous episode of "The Andy Griffith Show."

C. *Andy on Trial* is a humorous episode of *The Andy Griffith Show.*

_____ 8. A. Isaac Watts is the author of several hymns, including *When I Survey the Wondrous Cross.*

B. Isaac Watts is the author of several hymns, including "When I Survey the Wondrous Cross."

C. Isaac Watts is the author of several *hymns,* including *When I Survey the Wondrous Cross.*

_____ 9. A. The USS *Connecticut* is a Seawolf-class nuclear attack submarine.

B. The USS Connecticut is a Seawolf-class nuclear attack submarine.

C. The USS "Connecticut" is a Seawolf-class nuclear attack *submarine.*

_____ 10. A. In the Spanish language, there are no silent "e's."

B. In the Spanish language, there are no silent *e's.*

C. In the Spanish language, there are no silent *e's.*

Underline any words that should be italicized. If the sentence is already correct, write C in the blank.

———— 1. Alexander the Great, who had completely subdued the Greeks in the fourth century B.C., spread the Greek culture throughout much of the known world.

———— 2. He who richly distributed culture became himself a part of the culture of many nations. The famous story of the taming of his horse, Bucephalus, is told at the beginning of the movie The Black Stallion.

———— 3. Alexander studied with Aristotle as his private tutor; the young prince's favorite book was Homer's Iliad.

———— 4. Multitudes of books have been written about him. Alexander of Macedon: 356-323 B.C.: a Historical Biography by Peter Green is a classic work about the great conqueror.

———— 5. For those who enjoy watching rather than reading, Michael Wood's In the Footsteps of Alexander: A Journey from Greece to Asia is an exciting travel adventure film.

———— 6. Plays have been written about Alexander too, including Alexandre le Grande by the French playwright Jean Racine.

———— 7. Dryden's "Alexander's Feast" is a well-known short poem featuring the legendary hero.

———— 8. Even artists have used Alexander for inspiration. Alexander and Porus by Charles LeBrun in 1673 is only one of many paintings of the life of Alexander.

———— 9. Alessandro Magno, a bronze sculpture by Gemito Vincenzo, is found in Rome in the National Gallery of Modern Art.

———— 10. The words extraordinary and legendary certainly describe the man who may have believed he was a god. Yet he was a mortal man who died at the young age of 32.

Apostrophe

The apostrophe is used to indicate omissions, possessives, and certain plurals.

Omissions

Apostrophes can be used to show the omission of letters and numbers. Letters are commonly omitted within contractions, shortened forms of words or phrases. Apostrophes show where the omitted letters would have been.

Let us becomes *let's.*

Is not becomes *isn't.*

Cannot becomes *can't.*

Any noun or pronoun subject can form a contraction with an appropriate form of *be, have, will,* or *would.* Do not confuse the contraction *it's* (for *it is* or *it has*) with the possessive *its,* which should not contain an apostrophe.

POSSESSIVE	Someone's taken the torch from its case.
CONTRACTION	Who'd do such a thing? It's an important tradition to have the torch.

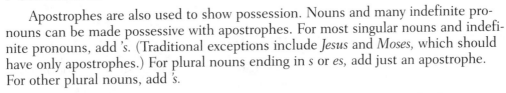

Some contractions with **not** change the spelling of the main word slightly.

> will + not = **won't**
>
> can + not = **can't**

Some words, such as *may* and *ought,* are rarely contracted with *not.* The contractions would be understood by a native English speaker, but they would sound very formal or old-fashioned. Avoid *mayn't* and perhaps *oughtn't.*

ESL

Apostrophes replace numbers in some instances. In informal writing, an apostrophe may take the place of the first two figures for a year.

> the blizzard of '97
>
> the '84 Olympics

Possessives

Apostrophes are also used to show possession. Nouns and many indefinite pronouns can be made possessive with apostrophes. For most singular nouns and indefinite pronouns, add *'s.* (Traditional exceptions include *Jesus* and *Moses,* which should have only apostrophes.) For plural nouns ending in *s* or *es,* add just an apostrophe. For other plural nouns, add *'s.*

Possessives
p. 14

SINGULAR	It is Charles**'s** turn to do the dishes and Anne**'s** turn to dry them.
PLURAL	Their parents**'** rule is that everyone takes a turn at the dishes.

Special rules govern sentences that show possession by more than one person. If the people own something together, only the last noun or pronoun is made possessive. But if they own items individually, each noun or pronoun should be made possessive.

> Frank and Neal**'s** restaurant is prospering.
>
> Frank**'s** and Neal**'s** savings had to be combined in order to start the business.

Special Plurals

Although the plural forms of regular common and proper nouns do not have apostrophes, there are a few plural forms that do. These forms include the plurals of letters or of words being discussed. They do not include the plurals of numbers, symbols, or dates.

> How many *s*'s are in the word *successful?*
>
> He tends to confuse his *two*'s and his *too*'s when writing.
>
> The same key on the keyboard makes *l*s and *!*s.
>
> The Cold War was a serious concern to Americans in the 1950s.

Hyphen

The hyphen, less than half as long as the dash, can be used either to join the parts of a single word or to join two or more words into one unit.

Word Divisions

Sometimes you may wish to divide a word between lines in order to achieve a symmetrical look on a paper. A hyphen can be used to show this division.

Word division can occur only between syllables, and it must meet the following guidelines: (1) A word should be divided only if it has at least two pronounced syllables. (2) At least two letters and the hyphen must remain on the first line. (3) At least three letters must appear on the second line.

Her work for the senior banquet was appreciated by the committee.

Numbers and Fractions

Multiword numbers from twenty-one through ninety-nine should be hyphenated when spelled out. This rule applies when these words stand alone as well as when they are part of larger numbers spelled out, as on a check. Fractions should also be hyphenated when spelled out, unless either the numerator or denominator already contains a hyphen.

twenty-one years old

five hundred ninety-six and no/100 dollars

one-eighth

eighty-eight hundredths

Omissions of Connecting Words

A hyphen can be used in place of a single connecting word such as *to* or *through*, especially when numbers are being connected.

Office hours are 8:00-5:00 every weekday.

You should complete problems 1-10 for your homework.

A hyphen should not be used to replace a pair of connecting words, such as *from* and *to* or *between* and *and*.

Please call me between 3:00 and 4:00.

Compounds

Compound
Nouns
p. 3

Hyphens are used to create some compound words. If you are unsure about whether a compound requires a hyphen, check a reliable recent dictionary.

sister-in-law   make-believe

Multiword Modifiers

When two or more words function as a single unit to modify a following noun, this "temporary compound" should be hyphenated.

dining-room table   weather-delayed flight

Prefixes

A hyphen is sometimes used when a prefix is added to a word. The prefixes *all*, *ex* (meaning "former"), *half*, and *self* are always hyphenated.

all-important, self-existent

The prefixes *non* and *anti* are used both with and without hyphens, but the trend is to go without.

non-fiction *or* nonfiction

Other prefixes are generally used without hyphens, with these exceptions.

1. Before a number, a proper adjective, or a proper noun

   pre-1900s, post-Depression

2. To distinguish a word with a prefix from one spelled similarly

   re-call vs. recall

3. If a prefix ends with the same vowel that begins a root word (Some words of this type are now regularly written without hyphens. If you are in doubt about whether to use a hyphen, check a recent dictionary.)

   re-elect, coordinate

12.5 PRACTICE *the skill*

Underline the words that contain mistakes in the use of apostrophes or hyphens.

1. The United States presidential election of 2000 remained undecided for weeks because the vote was tantalizingly close.

2. It wasnt the first election to be decided by only a few votes.

3. Rutherford B. Hayes defeated Samuel Tilden by only one electoral vote in '1876; the final vote was 185 to 184.

4. Although Tilden won the popular vote, Hayes won that all important extra electoral vote that gave him the presidency.

5. In 2000, history repeated itself in Bush's and Gore's presidential election race.

6. It came down to one state, Florida, where Bushs brother, Jeb Bush, was the governor.

7. At first, many member's of the media called the state for Gore; but by the time most of the votes had been counted, Bush was ahead only slightly, and it seemed too close to call.

8. A second tally also failed to resolve the controversy between Bush-Gore, although it confirmed that Bush received more votes.

9. Finally, the Supreme Court convened to rule on the non-sensical continued challenges to the election results.

10. In the end, George W. Bush became the forty third president of the United States of America.

Insert any missing apostrophes or hyphens. If the sentence is already correct, write C in the blank.

_____ 1. Unlike the government of the United States, a parliamentary system of government does not separate its legislative and executive branches.

_____ 2. The parliamentary systems executives, typically a prime minister and his ministers, are chosen out of the legislature.

_____ 3. The prime ministers leadership is over the largest party in a parliament, or sometimes he is the leader of a coalition.

_____ 4. The head of state, a monarch or a president, cooperates in the official appointment of the prime minister.

_____ 5. The other ministers are members of the prime ministers party, and the most important ones make up the Cabinet.

_____ 6. Another difference between the parliamentary system and the United States's system is the length of a term of office.

_____ 7. Terms in the United States are set for two to six years; only rarely is a term any shorter. Parliamentary terms, though established for a specific length of time, can be cut short for various reasons.

_____ 8. Probably the best known parliament is that of Great Britain, which was already developing in the 1000s.

_____ 9. Britains Parliament has a House of Commons and a House of Lords, but the House of Lords has lost power in the last 50 90 years.

_____ 10. Besides the peers and peeresses in the House of Lords, there are twenty judges and twenty six church officials.

Dash

The dash, a line about twice as long as a hyphen, is used to set off interrupting and summarizing elements. It is somewhat informal and should be used sparingly. Most word processing programs automatically convert two or three consecutive hyphens into a dash. Otherwise two unspaced hyphens are the standard typed substitute for a dash.

Interrupting Phrase or Clause

An interrupting phrase or clause is commonly set off by a pair of dashes.

> Carol Ann—usually the first to speak up—asked when it was time to eat.

> In the 1920s—they are sometimes called the Roaring Twenties—many Americans lived for the pursuit of pleasure and prosperity.

Do not overuse this kind of interruption in your writing.

Summarizing Statement After an Introductory List

The dash is also used in a sentence that starts with a list and then continues with a grammatically complete summary statement.

> Ham and cheese, egg salad, and peanut butter and jelly—these are my favorite kinds of sandwiches.

Commas with Nonrestrictive Elements
p. 277

Colon Before a Series at the End of a Sentence
p. 287

Parentheses

Parentheses (singular, *parenthesis*) are used to enclose extra information within a sentence. Often this information is relatively unimportant. Like quotation marks, parentheses always appear in pairs.

Supplementary Elements

The most common use of parentheses is to enclose additional, often explanatory information. That additional information may be a word, a phrase, a clause, or an entire sentence.

> My brother (the one in the blue shirt) will be running for class president.

> The sponsor for our senior class trip will be our principal (Mr. G, as we call him).

> We will visit relatives in Washington in June. (We'd like to see you when we come.)

Placement of Other Punctuation with Parentheses

End punctuation marks go outside of parentheses unless the material enclosed in the parentheses is a complete sentence. (Note the examples above.) The only exception to this rule is that a question mark or exclamation point would go inside the parentheses if the parenthetical material is a question or an exclamation.

> I think that Mrs. Serrano is the right person (do you agree?) for the position.

> Patrick is having his wisdom teeth removed (ouch!) this coming Monday.

If you are quoting a Bible verse and follow it with a reference in parentheses, place the end punctuation for the sentence after the final parenthesis, not before the quotation marks. If the quotation is itself a question or exclamation, punctuate it appropriately. However, you should still place end punctuation for the entire sentence after the final parenthesis.

> When asked the way to heaven, Jesus responded, "I am the way, the truth, and the life: no man cometh unto the Father, but by me" (John 14:6).

> Jesus described Nathanael by saying, "Behold an Israelite indeed, in whom is no guile!" (John 1:47).

Numbers or Letters That Identify Divisions Within a Sentence

Periods
p. 267

Numbers or letters that identify divisions within a sentence should be enclosed within parentheses.

> If you want to help your writing, you should purchase these reference works: (1) a dictionary, (2) a thesaurus, (3) a style manual.

> Craft entries can be made in the following categories: (a) woodworking, (b) leatherwork, and (c) needlecraft.

12.7 PRACTICE *the skill*

Insert any missing dashes or parentheses. If the sentence is already correct, write C in the blank.

_____ 1. It was not until the children of Israel left Egypt one could argue that they truly became a nation.

_____ 2. The Israelite political system consisted simply of God as their king and the maker of all their laws; this system is called a theocracy.

_____ 3. The theocratic government of Old Testament Israel existed under three different states: 1 Mosaic leadership, 2 judgeship, and 3 monarchy.

_____ 4. Guidance, protection, and the law all these came from God, while Moses served merely as mediator.

_____ 5. After Moses' death, Joshua who had served as Moses' aide took the role of human leadership over the Israelites.

_____ 6. During Joshua's leadership, the political system changed to a judgeship in which the people were led by judges (such as Deborah, Samson, and Gideon) who were chosen by God.

_____ 7. During Samuel's judgeship, the people demanded a king; God told Samuel, "Hearken unto the voice of the people . . . for they have not rejected thee, but they have rejected me, that I should not reign over them" I Sam. 8:7.

_____ 8. With the crowning of Saul, the political system passed from a theocratic judgeship to a theocratic monarchy. (Both were appointed by God.)

_____ 9. Saul an exceedingly tall man ruled Israel well at first, but later he rebelled against God.

_____ 10. Whenever the Israelites obeyed God's law, they were blessed; but when they rebelled against Him, they were brought under judgment. This pattern clearly shows don't you think? that every choice has consequences.

REVIEW *the skill*

Combine the following sets of sentences by using dashes or parentheses. (You may reword the sentences slightly and incorporate other punctuation if necessary.)

1. The Levites were a special tribe of Israelites chosen by God to do three things. They were chosen to teach the law, care for the sanctuary, and preserve God's covenant relationship with Israel.

   _____

   _____

   _____

   _____

2. Levites did not have land of their own. They lived in special cities located on land belonging to the other tribes of Israel.

   _____

   _____

   _____

3. The Levites were divided into three groups. The three groups were the high priest, the priests who offered sacrifices, and the Levites who cared for the sanctuary.

   _____

   _____

   _____

   _____

   _____

4. The majority of the Levites cared for the sanctuary. They were not allowed to offer sacrifices.

   _____

   _____

   _____

   _____

5. Priests who offered sacrifices were the only Levites allowed to fulfill this duty. They were all direct descendants of Aaron.

_____

_____

_____

_____

6. Representing the people before God, the high priest made atonement for their sins once each year. He was the only person ever allowed in the holy of holies.

_____

_____

_____

_____

7. Although they were born into the tribe of Levi, the priests had to meet certain qualifications. Not all Levites were priests.

_____

_____

_____

_____

8. Levites serving as priests had to be a certain age, and they could not have any physical defects. Priests had to be between thirty and fifty years old.

_____

_____

_____

_____

9. Priests underwent meticulous cleansing rituals. These rituals represented the purity required of the people by God. The rituals were for body and clothing.

_____

_____

_____

_____

10. The priesthood was a very significant part of the nation of Israel. It represented their election by God and their consecration to God.

_____

_____

_____

_____

Rewrite the following paragraph, correcting the ten errors in capitalization and punctuation. (Punctuation marks used as a pair are counted as a single error.)

Civil wars, revolutions, and political struggles have been common throughout all of history. A prime example of political intrigue in the Bible is the story of Athaliah, a wicked queen who reigned over Judah from 841 to 835 bc. Athaliah realized her chance to gain control of the government when her son, king Ahaziah, died. She killed all the legal heirs her own grandchildren and took the throne for herself. Unbeknownst to Athaliah, her daughter found Joash, one of the king's sons, still alive, and hid him in the temple for six years. In the seventh year the high priest of judah staged a coup d'état (a sudden overthrow of the existing government) on behalf of Joash. When Athaliah heard the noise from the temple she saw that Joash had been crowned king. "Then Athaliah rent her clothes" and accused the people of treason II Kings 11:14. She was executed the same day. Athaliah's wickedness should come as no surprise: she was the daughter of Ahab and Jezebel. Like her mother she turned the people of God away from him and toward the false god Baal.

_____

_____

_____

_____

_____

_____

_____

_____

_____

_____

_____

_____

_____

_____

_____

_____

> Blessed is the nation whose God is the Lord; and the people whom he
> hath chosen for his own inheritance.
>
> *Psalm 33:12*

A persuasive speech is similar in many ways to other types of persuasive writing. It takes a position on an issue. The speaker tries to persuade others to adopt his position. He presents arguments to support his position and reinforces them with specific facts and examples. A persuasive speech differs from other persuasive writing, however, in its presentation. A speech is presented orally. When writing a speech, keep in mind that you will have to reach your audience through their ears rather than their eyes, sometimes a more difficult task.

In the literature selection at the beginning of the chapter, Colin Powell attempts to persuade people to vote for George Bush. Think of a topic that concerns or interests you. Write a short speech to persuade an audience to adopt your viewpoint.

Planning

✔ **Choose a topic.** Because the purpose of this speech is to persuade, the topic should involve some degree of controversy. You may be trying to get your audience to accept something, to believe something, or to do something. Whichever is the case, choose a topic that you care about personally. Your speech will then carry the force of personal conviction. Reading the newspaper or brainstorming with family or friends may provide topic ideas.

tip

You can write about a recognized issue or encourage your audience to think again about something they take for granted.

✔ **Consider your audience.** Since they are the ones you are trying to persuade, it is helpful to know some things about them before you write your speech. How much do they know about your topic? Are they inclined either to agree or to disagree with your position? How does your topic affect them personally?

✔ **Clarify your goals.** Make sure you know what you want your audience to do with the information you give them. Do you want them to write a letter, an editorial, or an e-mail message? Do you want them to volunteer time or supplies or to give money? Do you want them to become active in a protest? When this is clear to you, find a way to include it in your speech.

✔ **Gather information.** You may be able to interview experts on the subject. If the issue has been around for some time, you should find information on it in books or reference works. If it is more recent, periodicals may be better sources. Consult *The Readers' Guide to Periodical Literature* for articles on your topic.

✔ **Consider the arguments for and against your position.** Perhaps list them in a chart. Use the strongest arguments for your position as the main points in your speech, but do not ignore the arguments of the other side. Opposing arguments may need to be addressed as subpoints. Once you have selected your arguments, you can organize your research to offer the best possible support.

Should Christians be involved in politics?

Yes—The Bible mentions a Christian's responsibilities in that area.

Yes—A Christian should be a good testimony to unbelievers.

Yes—Christians can influence political decisions.

No—Christians should be separate from the world.

No—The Bible never expressly calls for a Christian's involvement in politics.

No—Christians cannot win people if they are just like them.

✔ **Discuss your ideas with others.** Talk over your ideas and positions with other students, your parents, or teachers. Encourage them to share with you what they see as the pros and cons of your topic. Take notes on what you learn from other people.

Drafting

✔ **Prepare your introduction.** You may wish to start with a story, a statistic, a quotation, or some background information. The purposes of the introduction are to arouse interest and to show the response that you desire from your audience. Your introduction is your chance to make your issue compelling to them.

Here is one student's first draft of an introduction:

> When Matthew and Abigail Hill moved to a new state two years ago, they were prepared for a change in churches. They were prepared for a change in the sales tax and in the price of milk. They were even prepared for a change in the weather. But they were totally unprepared for the drastic change in the political climate. Matthew and Abigail talked to their new pastor and prayed about what they could do to change things. It was then that Matthew decided to run for public office. He was surprised to find that many of his friends opposed his decision and even told him that Christians should leave politics to others. But Matthew was convinced not only that he could be involved in politics but also that he had a mandate to do what he could to become active in the political arena. You too should seek involvement in the political process. Or maybe even run for office yourself.

✔ **State and support your position.** Make this statement clear and concise. One good tactic is to find common ground between you and your listener. This will put your audience on your side from the beginning and make them more willing to listen to your points.

✔ **Draft your speech.** Select an organizational method that will suit your topic. Some possibilities are cause and effect, comparison and contrast, problem and solution, and strength of argument.

Cause and Effect

Present the benefits of your point of view and the detrimental effects of the other side. Powell praises the democracy that defeated enemy ideologies on the "field of ideas"; he then asserts that the tyrannical nations that "pursue the fool's gold of tyranny" will end up "in the dust bin of history."

Comparison and Contrast

Examine the pros and cons of a position. These arguments for and against the position should convince your audience that you are right.

Problem and Solution

Present the problem fairly and then provide your solution. Powell presents the problem as a need to show the rest of the world "the beauty and potential of democracy." His solution is for Americans to work together—with Governor George W. Bush. Your speech should include facts that back up your solution. Since General Colin Powell is an accepted authority on his chosen topic, he was under less obligation to do so. He talks specifically of communism, fascism, and the Red Army.

Strength of Argument

Start with a better argument, move on to a good argument, and close with your best argument. The excerpt from Powell's speech gives only a part of one of his arguments. The text of the entire speech contains many more well-placed arguments.

Thinking Biblically

The Bible contains many examples of persuasive speeches. One of the best examples is Peter's sermon at Pentecost (Acts 2:14-40). What is Peter's thesis? How does he argue for his thesis? How does the audience respond?

---

tip

Take care not to overstate your position or use inflammatory language.

✔ **Use balance.** As you write, consider the need for a good balance of argumentation, presentation of facts, motivation, and appeal to emotions. Even in this excerpt it is obvious that Powell's speech is quite motivating. Look at the flow of the last paragraph: there is a mixture of long and short sentences building to a short, direct sentence that packs a punch.

✔ **Include a variety of evidence.** No one piece of evidence will sway your entire audience. Different types of evidence (anecdotes, quotations, statistics, and so on) appeal to different people.

---

tip

Consider using visual aids with your speech.

Fallacious
Argumentation
pp. 322-23

✔ **Avoid fallacies in reasoning.** As a speaker, you have a responsibility to use sound reasoning as you attempt to persuade your audience. Using tactics designed to manipulate or mislead your listeners is unethical, illogical, and un-Christian (see James 3:17). The following list includes a few of the reasoning fallacies that you should avoid in your speech.

Ad Hominem	attacking a person rather than the issue
Hasty Generalization	basing a conclusion on too little evidence
Bandwagon or Popular Opinion Technique	encouraging others to join an allegedly overwhelming majority on an issue
Card Stacking	intentionally presenting only one side of an issue
Testimonial	citing a well-known personality as an authority on something that he or she is not qualified to speak about

Concluding
Paragraphs
p. 341

✔ **Draw a conclusion.** This is a good time to restate the main idea of your speech. You might follow it up with an appeal to your audience to act on what they have heard. The more specific you make your appeal, the more likely you are to get a response. Another idea is to reinforce the message of your speech with a memorable story or quotation. Powell's "the challenge . . . the time . . . the leader" is quite an effective ending.

Oral Anecdote
pp. 187-91

✔ **Adjust for oral presentation.** Pay special attention to the sound of your speech. Repetition of sounds, words, or phrases will aid flow and memory. Notice the "We defeated . . . We defeated . . . We defeated" in the Powell speech. Also do what you can to include your audience in your speech. For example, address them directly when possible.

Revising

✔ **Get feedback.** Ask one or more persons to listen to your speech. Seek comments on content, style, and delivery.

✔ **Proofread your speech.** Look for any grammatical or stylistic errors. If you are writing the speech for class and your teacher will be grading the written copy, you will want to pay close attention to punctuation and spelling as well.

✔ **Record your speech.** Make a recording of your speech (both audio and visual if possible). Study your mannerisms and your arguments. Do you move around too much (or too little)? Are you buried in your notes, or do you make frequent and meaningful eye contact with your audience? If you were to take notes on your speech, would the notes make sense? Would they include any fallacies in reasoning?

tip

Use the recording experience to familiarize yourself with your script so that you will not be tied to your notes when you speak.

Publishing

✔ **Present your speech.** You could give your persuasive speech before your classmates or before a larger audience in your school or community. You might even consider entering a speech contest.

tip

The way you dress for your speech will either lend credibility to your message or detract from it.

✔ **Make a final recording.** This recording will serve as a historical record of your beliefs on an issue at a given time.

✔ **Print your speech.** Rework your speech and publish it as a pamphlet or brochure.

✔ **Save your speech.** Add this persuasive speech to your writing portfolio.

Some Ideas to Consider

Government

- Write about the opportunity to become involved in local, state, or national politics.
- Write about a law that you believe should be passed.
- Write about a foreign policy position that you would like to see adopted.

Church

- Write about a current issue that affects all believers.
- Write about a project that you would like to see your church or youth group undertake.

Education

- Write about the benefits of obtaining further education after high school.
- Write about the benefits of learning a trade.
- Write about the value of studying a particular subject (whichever one you choose).

Avoid Fallacies
in Reasoning
p. 320

Fallacious Argumentation

As you can see from our previous lesson, the task of thinking correctly and coming to logical conclusions all the time is not an easy one. One way to make the task easier is to recognize fallacies in arguments. Here are a few of the most common.

You know that analogy is a common argument. However, it can be one of the most misused. Suppose that your dad tells you to be in bed every night at 10:00 P.M. You would like to stay up later, so you say, "Dad, you respect your boss at work and you enjoy working for him. However, your boss does not tell you to be in bed at a certain time." Obviously, this is a weak analogy. A father and child have a very different relationship than a boss and employee have. In fact, if you use that **weak analogy,** you may find yourself going to bed even earlier!

Many arguments use **emotional appeals.** This means that the argument relies on feeling more than reasoning. Suppose a student comes to your door and offers to sell you a magazine. At first you refuse the offer because you never read magazines. Then the student says, "Please buy this. I've walked all day in the hot sun and not sold one single magazine, and if I don't sell all of these, I'll not get to go on the school trip." If you then buy the magazine, you did so due to an **appeal to pity.** You bought the magazine only because you felt sorry for the student. An ad against smoking may show several photos of people suffering from lung cancer. This ad uses an **appeal to fear.** The goal is for you to be afraid of getting sick and therefore not smoke. Appeals to pity and fear can be legitimate if other good reasons are also given. An **appeal to vanity** appeals to the pride and envy of the audience. Clothing ads often use this kind of argument. You may see an ad and want to look and dress like the models in the ad. These are only a few of the many different kinds of emotional appeals. Can you think of other arguments that appeal to our emotions?

If you simplify your opponent's argument into something that can easily be refuted, then you are guilty of setting up a **straw man.** For example, a politician might say, "All my opponent wants is for everyone to have a gun. She would love to see every crook and criminal on the streets with a loaded weapon." His opponent, who opposes gun control, probably has good reasons for her argument, and her position does not necessarily mean that she wants criminals to have unlimited access to weapons. The straw man that her opponent has set up, however, states her position in a way that is easily refutable.

An ***ad hominem*** argument attacks the person presenting the argument rather than the argument itself. Your friend warns you against eating too much junk food, and you respond, "I shouldn't listen to you; you drink sodas all the time." A former convict gives a speech about crime, and you say, "How could a lousy, no-good person like that have anything good to say?" Sometimes a person's character does have relevance to the integrity of his argument, but generally you should analyze what a person is saying and not the person himself.

These are just a few of the many types of fallacious argumentation. Remember, you might be arguing for a good cause, but you need to use reasonable arguments to support your position.

Identify each of the following arguments as *weak analogy, appeal to fear, appeal to pity, appeal to vanity, straw man,* or *ad hominem.*

_____ 1. "If you don't vote for me, you had better check the locks on your windows and doors, because this city is going to be an awfully scary place."

_____ 2. See how great this guy looks in this jacket. Don't you want to look like him?

_____ 3. Why would you listen to your aunt? She doesn't even remember what it's like to be your age!

_____ 4. Uncle Pete never finished school, and he's rich, so I don't have to finish school either.

_____ 5. They want to censor television programs for kids. This means that they want to take away the right of free speech and shelter kids from getting a realistic view of the world.

_____ 6. Please don't give me demerits. If I get any more, I'll be kicked off the team, and the last ones I got I didn't deserve anyway.

_____ 7. This judge supports the death penalty. All he wants to do is kill people instead of help them work through their problems.

_____ 8. If you aren't more careful, you are going to be hurt in a car accident.

_____ 9. You're an intelligent teenager. You know how to choose the best face wash for your skin.

_____ 10. It must be a bad idea because even the environmentalists are supporting it!

Thinking It Through

Find examples of weak arguments from television, magazines, newspapers, or blogs. Also find examples of strong or effective arguments.

In this excerpt, Peggy Noonan makes a strong case that American children watch too much television. Many writers like Noonan express their viewpoints in articles called editorials that appear in magazines and newspapers. What makes this editorial so effective? Can you identify the persuasive techniques Noonan uses? In this chapter, you will learn how to use persuasive writing to voice your opinions, and you will have the opportunity to write an editorial about a topic that is important to you.

The 12-Step Program Parents Need *by Peggy Noonan*

There is a commercial on television for a new minivan that I understand is selling well. It shows a happy family riding together through the plains and mountains of America. They're on vacation and it's going well—beautiful outside, peaceful inside. Then you notice the minivan is so quiet because the kids in the backseat are watching movies on individual monitors mounted above them.

When I saw this I finally realized: It's gone too far. TV-watching in America has gone too far. I'm not, of course, the only one who thinks so. A few months ago we all saw the report that said watching a lot of television is bad for children. The report, from the American Academy of Pediatrics, stated categorically, scientifically, and with authority that children under the age of 2 should never be allowed to watch TV, and older children should be limited to an hour a day.

The report wasn't exactly news to the nation's parents, not one of whom has ever been heard yelling, "Ben and Chloe, come in from that nice fresh air and watch television, and I mean now!" We all know that too much TV isn't good for children. So the report seems to be yet another illustration of Samuel Johnson's observation that men and women need not so much to be informed as to be reminded. It told us what we know.

THE WRITING PROCESS

This chapter is dedicated to the actual process that a writer goes through in order to turn thoughts into a finished product. Very few (if any!) writers sit at their computers and compose perfect text their first time through. All writing is a kind of process. The names given to the stages of the process may change, as will the particulars of style and organization, but each stage must be completed and is valuable and vital to the finished product. That is why this text includes the same four stages in every writing assignment: each stage is valuable and vital to the finished product.

As you further your study of the writing process, you will doubtless come across various names and divisions for the stages. The authors of this text have chosen the terms *planning, drafting, revising,* and *publishing* to describe four basic stages of the writing process. When you write, follow each of the steps of the writing process, no matter how abbreviated each may be for certain types of writing. Skipping one or more of the stages may not be obvious at first but will probably be painfully apparent later in the process. Lack of planning will lead to massive revision, no revision will lead to poor publication, and so on.

Whatever your talents or insecurities are as a writer, revel in the writing process. With it, you have a proven plan of attack for any writing task put to you. Using the process will make you grow as a communicator. Enjoy!

Planning

Good writing takes time and effort. And much of that time and effort goes into the planning stage. The energy you spend in choosing and narrowing your topic, analyzing your audience, determining your purpose, gathering information, and outlining your paper will pay off in a rewarding experience for both you and your readers. The planning stage is the time for creative thought and careful analysis. Many educators and writers call this stage the *prewriting* stage; this textbook chooses the term *planning* because the term seems to encompass the various aspects of the thoughtful design that occurs before beginning any important project.

Choosing Your Topic

For the writing assignments in this book, as well as for many others you will encounter, you will be given either a topic on which to write or a list of topics from which to choose. For your own personal writing—such as keeping a journal—you must come up with your own topic. In any case, at some point early in the writing process you must choose a topic. The best topic is one that you have some familiarity with and that you enjoy. Your enthusiasm for your topic will be evident in your writing and may even spread to your readers. Think of topics that pertain to your personal life experiences, or select an issue or subject that you would like to learn more about.

Every author has his own methods for selecting a topic. Some read over journal entries they have made and look for ideas that pertain to the assignment they have been given. Some are avid readers who take their topic ideas from the reading material they have been most recently exposed to. Still others keep track of current events and cull from those to find topics that interest them. The methods listed below will give you a good start when you feel uninspired on your own.

Making a List

On your computer or on a piece of paper, write down every event, experience, or person that you would be interested in writing about. Look at your own previous writings as well as the writings of others for ideas. Talk to parents and friends, inspect photograph albums, and read newspapers and magazines for topics. Become a reader—readers have almost limitless horizons because they have traveled and experienced and considered beyond what nonreaders have.

missions trip to Germany

failing my driver's license test

car wreck

best friend Jill

hurting my eye on a trailer hitch

Uncle Horace, the dentist

toothpaste

horses

ice skating

tip

Write down the first five nouns and verbs that occur to you. See if there's a topic in one of them.

Asking Questions

Ask yourself (or get others to ask) questions to get started. The journalist's questions (*who? what? where? when? why? how?*) are sometimes helpful in initiating ideas. Of course, one question often leads to another question and, in turn, to another idea. Below is an example of some possible questions.

Who is in the news recently? Why?

What unusual experience have I had?

What do I hope to achieve in the future?

Where would I visit if I could visit anywhere in the world?

When did the Lord first convict me of my need of a Savior?

Why do I believe _____?

How is _____ made?

Brainstorming

Brainstorming occurs when one or more persons list as many things as they can think of about a topic. A recorder writes every idea down for later review by the group or by each individual. As long as the ideas are morally pure and biblically appropriate, no idea should be considered irrelevant or wrong or too ridiculous to be included in a brainstorming list.

toothpaste	American Dental Association
flossing	dentists recommend?
brushing	paste or gel?
tubes	flavors
who invented?	new advances in?
bristles	cavities
electric toothbrushes	fresh breath

Brainstorming lists include topics that are both general and specific. Sometimes the topics generated by a brainstorming session are far afield from where you started; in these instances, further organization is needed.

tip

Successful brainstorming is flexible.

Clustering

When the topics from a brainstorming session are too broad or when further organization is needed, **clustering** can be a helpful tool. Clustering yields a diagram that shows relationships between ideas. At the center of your page write down the general topic idea and circle it. Then write down related ideas, circle them, and connect them with lines to the general topic idea. Next write down further ideas that relate to that second set. Group the ideas that go together and color-code or number them to show the hierarchy of importance.

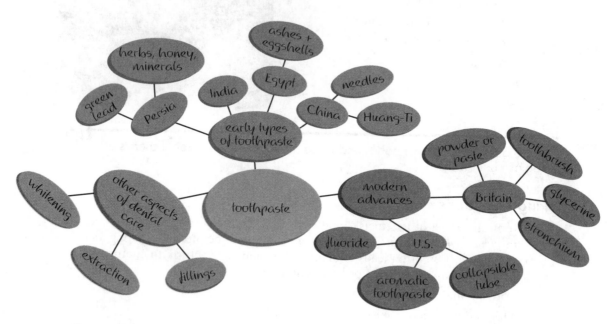

Freewriting

Like brainstorming, **freewriting** focuses on writing without worrying about ideas being inaccurate or irrelevant. As mentioned previously, no Christian writer ever writes without the restraint of biblical morality and conscience. However, you can relax in the knowledge that what you write is not for public consumption. Use one of the questions you generated under "Asking Questions" or ask yourself, "What am I thinking about right now?" or "What must I do today?" Set a time limit for yourself (five minutes, for example) and write for that amount of time. Write without stopping; aim to keep your fingers moving constantly. Refrain from changing spelling, grammar, or punctuation. Below is an example of freewriting from a student journal.

> After school I have to go right home and do my homework. I don't have that much—just science and history, and come up with one idea for a writing assignment. After that I need to help Mom with supper and hopefully have time to shoot some hoops against the garage. The garage door is stuck. Maybe it's a bike or the snowmobile up against it or a rake. It's almost fall and that means lots of raking. The tree out back is beautiful in the fall, but it has tons of leaves. Red, flaming orange, leftover limey green, shafts of sunlight. The smell of burning leaves in fall is delicious. But dangerous. The burning ordinances in our city leave something to be desired—someone needs to rethink them. Lots of property has been damaged because of leaf-burning fires.

Writers are sometimes faced with writer's block, the phenomenon that occurs when a writer can think of nothing to say. Often, writer's block happens when an author tries too hard to be perfect on his first try or when he limits his thoughts to that which is comfortable. Expanding your horizons (by reading or researching) or continuing to write when you think you are stuck will help you to get past writer's block.

Narrowing Your Topic

Once you choose your topic, you may need to narrow it. For example, the topic of *all city ordinances* is too broad. The topic *burning ordinances* is more likely to be a manageable topic for an editorial, letter to the editor, or brief article. Of course, some topics are too narrow. The topic of *burning leaves* would probably not yield enough information to write an entire paper.

If your topic is too broad, check your cluster diagram for one of the points coming off of the point you are considering. Perhaps this subpoint would make a better topic. In the toothpaste example above, you could write about the person who first developed toothpaste instead of trying to write about the history of toothpaste.

Another strategy might be to review your brainstorming to check for another idea. Sometimes an idea that you dismissed at first will, at second look, be a workable alternative. Remember to consider how long your paper will be and whether your topic can be covered adequately in the assigned pages.

Considering Your Audience

After you select your topic, ask yourself who your audience will be. **Audience** is the person or group to whom you are writing. This will determine both what you include in your paper and how you present the information. At times your teacher chooses your audience for you. Other times you are free to write to whomever you wish. Deciding who your audience is will help you better accomplish your purpose and meet your audience's needs. A student writing a letter to the editor about the city burning ordinance would write an informal piece (use of second person, occasional contractions); however, a student writing a petition to the mayor outlining the problems in the city burning ordinance would write a fairly formal piece (use of third person, no jargon or slang). Ask yourself *who is my audience? what information does my audience already know about my topic?*

Determining Your Purpose

Purpose is the reason for which you are writing. Your purpose may be to analyze, describe, inform, persuade, or entertain. Within a piece of writing you may have several purposes; however, the main point of the paper should have one driving purpose. For example, a story about the time you forgot all of your lines in the school play would be intended to entertain. A scientific research paper on the effects of glucosamine on joint health would have as its purpose to inform and perhaps secondarily to persuade. As you plan, ask yourself, *what is my purpose? what about my topic will interest my audience? what information about my topic will help me achieve my purpose?* Look again at the example under "Brainstorming." What information should the writer include if his purpose is to analyze the ingredients found in various brand-name toothpastes? How should the information included differ if the purpose is to entertain? The questions you ask yourself up front about audience and purpose will help you make decisions as you gather information and draft your paper.

Gathering Information

Now that you have chosen a topic, analyzed your audience, and determined your purpose, you are ready to gather information. You have already done some of this work in the initial stages of selecting a topic. The tactics you used there (*listing, asking questions, brainstorming, clustering*) can be helpful in information gathering as well. First, write down everything you already know about your topic that will be appropriate for your audience and will accomplish your purpose. Next, find sources that will expand upon the information you already have. Electronic resources are easily accessible, but remember that much of the content on the Internet is unsubstantiated or unreliable. Be sure that the e-sources you use are produced by recognized authorities or companies with good reputations. Books, magazines, and newspapers are valuable sources as well. Many college campuses have libraries that are open to the public and that contain material unavailable in conventional libraries. You might also consider interviewing someone in your area who is an authority on your topic.

When you have finished gathering information, ask yourself whether you have enough to interest your audience and achieve your purpose. If the answer is no, then you may need to re-think your topic. If the answer is yes—too much—then you will need to narrow the topic or change your idea. Using the questions generated in the brainstorming session above, one student came up with the following answers to his question about who invented toothpaste. Note how research on his initial question led to many other questions and answers.

> *Who invented?* a Chinese man; Huang-Ti's theories led to the development of a cream for teeth
>
> *When?* 500-300 B.C.
>
> *What were some of the other early advances in toothpaste?* 5000-3000 B.C. Egyptians used ashes of ox hooves, burned eggshells, pumice, and myrrh; Egyptians rubbed the paste onto their teeth with their fingers; Greeks and Romans improved toothpaste. Persians gave advice against hard toothpowders.
>
> *Check on other recipes for early toothpaste.*
>
> *When did toothpaste as we know it appear?* In Britain in the late 18th century, toothpaste was available in either paste or powder, and toothbrushes were used only by the rich; 1873 by the Colgate company—in a jar; 1896 in a tube
>
> *When did the first toothbrush appear?* check on this!
>
> *How has fluoride affected toothpastes?* check on this!

PRACTICE *the skill*

Read the following example and answer the questions at the end.

As you climb your family tree to its distant branches, one of the remarkable discoveries that awaits you is the number and diversity of lineages that flow together like streams in confluence to form your family. Consider, for example, that during a period of only ten generations, or roughly since the days of George Washington, every person has 1,022 direct ancestors drawn from over 500 different family lines. This accumulation of surnames represents keys to your past. So the answer to Shakespeare's well-worn question "What's in a name?" may be Danish and English, Russian and Prussian, Turkish and Yiddish. The rich diversity of names of families drawn to these shores from many lands is part of your heritage. As the building blocks of your genealogy, names warrant close study.
(from *Climbing Your Family Tree* by Timothy Keesee)

1. What is the purpose of this paragraph?

   _____

2. Who is the intended audience for this paragraph?

   _____

3. Who might the writer of this paragraph be?

   _____

Outlining the Paper

Outlining a paper before you begin drafting is always advisable. Some outlines are lengthy and detailed; others are sketchy and simply contain words or phrases arranged in order of presentation. Whatever outline type you choose (or that your teacher requires), taking the time to prepare one will help you remember to cover the important ideas in logical order. Use the ideas you wrote down during earlier stages in the planning process and rearrange them in the best order for your paper. You will probably end up omitting ideas that no longer seem relevant to your purpose.

Periods in Outlines p. 267

Tentative Outline

The tentative outline is used most often for extemporaneous writing or for in-class essays. However, it can be helpful for almost any form of writing. Simply arrange your written ideas showing the points and subpoints in the order of your plan of presentation. Tentative outlines very often do not contain numerals or letters. The following tentative outline was prepared after doing research on memorizing how to play a piece of music.

finding music piece you like

learning to play it as nearly perfectly as possible

memorizing short sections

seeing music in your mind

feeling where your hands and fingers will move next

reviewing

start memorizing

after memorizing, occasionally playing from written music for review

playing at least once a day to keep it fresh

breaking the piece into sections that flow well together, not into random sections

adding a section when confident of the previous section

playing with music in front of you but not looking at it

setting the music aside

playing with certain portion of it in front of you but not the whole piece

becoming familiar enough with the piece that memorization starts naturally

The next step is to group similar things together.

Finding music piece you like

learn to play it as nearly perfectly as possible

becoming familiar enough with the piece that memorization starts naturally

Start memorizing

memorizing short sections

breaking the piece into sections that flow well together, not into random sections

adding a section when confident of the previous section

playing with music in front of you but not looking at it

playing with certain portion of it in front of you but not the whole piece

setting the music aside

seeing the music in your mind

feeling where your hands and fingers will move next

Reviewing over and over

after memorizing, occasionally playing from written music for review

playing at least once a day to keep it fresh

Outline Forms

There are two types of outline forms that you can choose from if your outline will be seen by anyone else: topic outline and sentence outline. Choose one of these forms and follow it consistently; do not begin your outline with one form and then switch to the other form later in the same outline.

Parallelism
pp. 378-80

A **topic outline** uses phrases only—no sentences and no verbs except verbals. Each point within a numbered or lettered series should have the same grammatical form (participles or prepositional phrases or nouns or adjectives, and so on).

  I. Before memorizing
      A. Finding a piece of music
      B. Learning to play it
      C. Becoming thoroughly familiar with it

 II. Memorizing
      A. Planning ahead
      B. Breaking it up
      C. Getting away from the written music
      D. Seeing and feeling the music in your mind

III. After memorizing
      A. Reviewing without written music daily
      B. Reviewing with written music occasionally

In a **sentence outline** every point is a complete sentence; therefore, a sentence outline can include more information.

  I. A pianist must go through preliminary steps before he begins to memorize.
      A. He must find a piece of music that appeals to him.
      B. He must learn to play it accurately.
      C. He must become thoroughly familiar with it so that playing it becomes natural.

 II. A pianist must work hard to memorize the piece of music he has chosen.
      A. He must plan ahead; successful memorization takes weeks of time.
      B. He must break the piece up into meaningful sections based on phrases or the composer's divisions.
      C. He must gradually get away from the written music.
      D. He must get to the place where he sees and feels the music in his mind.

III. A pianist must follow through after memorizing the piece if he wants to fix it permanently in his mind.
      A. He must review the piece daily without looking at the written music.
      B. He must occasionally review the piece while looking at the written music.

Another advantage of the sentence outline is that your sentences can become the major points of your actual paper. Of course, most of the sentences will need at least some revision before they can be plugged into your paper.

tip

When taking an essay test, use an outline to keep your answer on track.

PRACTICE *the skill*

Arrange the following list of topics into an outline with three main points. Group the items logically. One item will be the topic heading for the outline.

Origins
Extended family
Nuclear family
Cousins
Forefathers
Children

Grandparents
Uncles and aunts
Ancestral family
The Structure of Kinship
Family tree
Parents

_____

_____

_____

_____

_____

_____

_____

_____

_____

_____

_____

Drafting

Aside from any freewriting you have done, the drafting stage is your first chance at getting your ideas down in the form of a cohesive whole. This first draft will be rough. In fact, your final composition may or may not resemble this first draft at all.

Some authors begin at the beginning (the introduction). Others jump into the middle of the paper; still others have an idea for the end and start there. Wherever you start, do not worry overmuch about grammar, usage, or punctuation. Neatness or form should not be a concern either. (Although you will need to be able to read your draft!) You will have a chance to correct these things in the revising stage.

Choosing a Mode

At this point in the writing process, you have already chosen your topic and determined your purpose. You probably also have a good idea of what mode you will use in writing since this is usually decided by that topic and/or purpose. **Mode** is a term for the form or method of writing. Each mode has some style and organizational patterns that are particular to it. (Note these in the writing assignments in Chapters 1-14.) Some writers select the mode that they will use at the beginning of their process; others wait to see where their information gathering leads them before they decide on a mode. In any case, when you draft, you must have a mode in mind. Different authorities have different names for the various modes of writing, but most agree on the following four modes.

Mode	Purpose	Example
Descriptive	describes an object, person, or place	"A Personal Account of the Fall of the Berlin Wall"
Expository	informs about a topic; explains or analyzes a process; defines or classifies a topic	"Growing Up Outdoors," "Baseball and the Great Depression"
Narrative	relates a story	"Proof Through the Night"
Persuasive	convinces readers about a topic	"The 12-Step Program Parents Need"

For the purposes of this book we add some other modes. Some of these are actually subcategories of the modes above, but because of the importance of the subcategory, we give it its own name.

Academic	focuses on learning a specific academic skill	*The Way of the Word*
Personal	tells an individual's own thoughts or feelings	Ann Judson's diary

Crafting a Thesis Statement, Topic Sentences, and a Concluding Sentence

Most expository and persuasive writing that you do will contain a thesis statement, topic sentence, and a concluding sentence. This includes in-class essays, reports and research papers, and speeches. Even many paragraphs in letters, anecdotes, and short stories will contain some sort of topic sentence. Writing a thesis statement, topic sentences, and a concluding sentence that are clear and logical is an important skill both for now and for later in your academic career.

Thesis Statement

The **thesis statement** expresses the main idea of the essay in a single sentence. A good thesis evidences that you understand the topic (or question) and tells what your approach will be. It may also communicate your point of view and organizational style.

POOR | A missile defense system is necessary for every country to be safe, so the United States should build one.

GOOD | The United States should set up a space-based missile defense system.

POOR | Robert Frost's poems use a lot of imagery.

GOOD | Robert Frost uses provincial imagery to discuss universal themes.

The first example is a poor thesis statement because it gives too much information. Rather than just stating his point, the writer has included the underlying reason for his position—something better left for the supporting sentences. The second example states the writer's main argument simply and clearly. The third example is poor because it gives too little information. It identifies the topic—imagery in Frost's poems—but it fails to indicate what the writer thinks about that topic. The fourth example makes both the writer's topic and his point of view clear.

The thesis statement is then worked into your introduction or, in the case of some essays, used as an introduction by itself. Your thesis will help to keep your writing on track. Referring to it often will focus your writing and force you to evaluate your facts, details, and anecdotes before you include them.

Topic Sentences

A topic sentence embodies the main idea of the paragraph. In this way it is similar to the thesis statement. Topic sentences may occur anywhere in the paragraph, but they are most often found at the beginning or end. When the topic sentence comes at the beginning, it establishes the groundwork for what will be said later. When it comes at the end, it summarizes or proves what has already been said.

If you used just a tentative outline or a topic outline to organize your paper, you will need to compose topic sentences as you write each individual paragraph. On the other hand, if you used a sentence outline, you may be able to use the main points of the outline as your topic sentences as you draft. (Of course, these sentences from your outline may need some changes as they are worked into your paper.)

For the paper on memorizing a piece of music outlined above, you might come up with these three topic sentences:

> Before beginning to memorize a piece, a musician must go through three preliminary steps.

> Because memorizing is hard, time-consuming work, the musician must plan ahead.

> Once a piece is memorized, the musician must follow through if he wishes to retain what he has learned.

13.3 ◢ ## USE *the skill*

Write a good topic sentence for the following paragraph. The sentence should both tell the topic of the paragraph and indicate what will be said about the topic. Make the topic of the paragraph the grammatical subject of the topic sentence.

In April 2001, the American Family Immigration History Center made online records available to the general public. Visitors to Ellis Island search the 22,000,000 records of immigrants, crewmen, and passengers who steamed into New York Harbor from 1892 to 1924. The database records information in ten categories including name, ethnicity, date of arrival, age, and gender. Statue of Liberty–Ellis Island Foundation members may add personal documents and photographs to the database for inclusion in this important national archive.

_____

_____

Concluding Sentence

Now that your paragraph has a topic sentence and supporting sentences, you need to write a concluding sentence. There are several ways to bring your discussion to an end. You could summarize your main idea or give a solution to a problem discussed in your paragraph. You could also ask your audience a question or make a prediction. The purpose of your paragraph will determine how you end your paragraph.

---

tip

Remember that your concluding sentence is your last chance to make an impression on your audience. Make it powerful.

REVIEW *the skill*

Choose the best concluding sentence for the following paragraph from the choices provided. Write the letter that corresponds to your answer.

God promises blessings for children who honor their parents, but most young people are not sure what the word *honor* means. Perhaps the best way to learn what honoring one's parents means is to look at godly young people in the Bible. Abraham's faithful servant traveled a long way to find a wife for his master's son Isaac. Did he go to the local market to find a bride? No, he went to the town well, and there he found Rebekah drawing water for her family. When Boaz, possibly the richest man in town, first sighted Ruth, she had just been gathering leftover grain for her mother-in-law. When the prophet Samuel came to the house of Jesse to anoint a king, David wasn't out with his friends; he was out in the field, watching his father's sheep. All of these young people were greatly blessed by God.

_____ A. Hard work and responsibility are necessary characteristics of every godly person.

B. Obeying your parents is another important way to honor your parents.

C. Honoring your parents will ensure that you will be successful in life.

D. Sharing the responsibility for the well-being of your family is honoring your parents.

Using the Components of Composition

Most pieces of writing that you do, whether for assignments in this book or otherwise, will be composed of a series of paragraphs. Most papers of any length contain an introductory paragraph, several body paragraphs, and a concluding paragraph. A **paragraph** consists of a group of sentences closely related to one another and to the main idea. Most well-constructed paragraphs reflect the structure of the entire paper: they contain a topic sentence, several supporting sentences, and a concluding sentence.

The secret to building good paragraphs is thorough planning. If you have done good research and organized your material well in the planning stage, your outline should become the basis from which you write each paragraph and, in turn, your entire paper. Each paragraph in the body (or main part) of your paper should consist of thoroughly developed sentences; each paragraph should cover a single division of your outline (I. or A., and so on). In fact, some writers mark the paragraph divisions of their papers directly on a copy of the outline.

Paragraph Development

Using the information gathered in the planning stage and armed with a topic sentence for each point in your outline, write individual paragraphs to further develop the idea of the topic sentence. To accomplish this, you need to write supporting sentences. **Supporting sentences** do what their name implies; that is, they support and develop the statement made in the topic sentence. These sentences may use details, examples, illustrations, or other methods to do so. There are several types of paragraph development. Many writers choose to back up the topic with facts, examples, details, or reasons. Still others define key terms or compare and contrast two things. Your writing will probably be a combination of two or more of these kinds of developmental strategies.

Kind	Definition
Fact	A statement that can be proved
Example	An instance or an event that illustrates a point
Statistic	A fact expressed in numbers
Incident/anecdote	A brief personal account that illustrates the topic
Sensory details	The use of sense words—sight, sound, smell, etc.
Reasons	The explanation of a truth
Comparison/contrast	Similarities and differences between two things

13.5 PRACTICE *the skill*

Identify the type of paragraph development the author used in the following paragraph.

The Medici family was very influential in Italy for several centuries. In the 1400s this obscure family gained influence and wealth in Florence, mostly through banking. Through strategic marriages they became affiliated with important families throughout Europe. This important family produced three popes (Leo X, Clement VII, and Leo XI) and two queens of France (Catherine de Médicis and Marie de Médicis). The family actively supported the arts and founded the Medici Library. With the exception of three short periods of exile, the family ruled Florence until 1737.

REVIEW *the skill*

Identify the type of paragraph development the author used in the following paragraph.

Many families go on summer vacations. One summer my family decided to spend the weekend at Clifty Falls, a small state park located near Madison, Indiana. Because the summer had been dry, there wasn't much water coming down the waterfalls, but there were many trails for hiking. We also visited some historical sites in Madison and had a picnic. The most memorable part of our vacation was when my little brother, Johnny, panicked on a hike behind a waterfall, and my dad had to carry him out.

Paragraph Organization

Organizing your ideas within a paragraph is much like organizing your entire paper. These sentences may use details, examples, illustrations, or other methods. You must consider both your audience and your purpose as you choose an organizational method that best suits the topic of your paragraph. The following chart shows the three major methods by which you can organize supporting sentences logically.

Paragraph Organization		
Method	**Definition**	**Used Most Often In**
Chronological order	A presentation of events in order of their occurrence	Stories, biographies, news reports, process or historical writing
Spatial order	A description according to how something is arranged in physical layout	Description of places or objects
Order of importance	A move from least important to most important or vice versa	Persuasive, informative, or descriptive writing

Choose an organizational method that fits your purpose.   **tip**

Each of the examples below uses a different organizational method to achieve a different purpose.

Chronological Order

Words and phrases such as *many years later, immediately, soon after,* and *early* indicate chronological order within a paragraph. What words in the following paragraph serve to indicate the order in which things happened?

Making a good cup of coffee is a fine art. First, grind the coffee beans—about one tablespoon of beans to every two cups of water. Then pour the ground beans into the filter. You may want to add some cinnamon and sugar to the grounds to sweeten the coffee. Next, pour water into the reserve. Make sure you don't add too much water, or you will have weak coffee. Now just wait patiently while the water percolates. Finally, when the water has finished dripping, pour your parents cups of the delicious, steaming treat.

Spatial Order

When describing a place or an object, the easiest method is to give the description from a single physical point of view; otherwise, the reader may become confused as he figuratively spins about the room trying to visualize the placement of objects. Prepositional phrases like *beside the table, under the rug,* and *in the well* help the reader visualize physical placement. What words and phrases indicate that the organization of the following paragraph is spatial?

> Last summer I went to a camp in Georgia. The campgrounds were beautiful, but the best part was the lake. From the road, before you turn into the camp, you can see the lake and the lodge. On the left side of the lake are two cabins and the chapel. A sidewalk coming down from the chapel goes to the lake and meets the bridge that goes over to the lodge. We caught many fish from the bridge. Next to the lodge, to the right of the bridge, is the dock. Beyond the bridge, on the left side of the lake, there is a gigantic water slide. This lake is the center of our fun at camp. I can't wait until next summer!

Order of Importance

In persuasive, informative, and some descriptive writing, the writer seeks to present pertinent information at the beginning of his piece. In that way he ensures that even if he loses his reader before the piece is concluded, he has gotten the most important part of his message across. Another technique is to build a case with increasingly important points to move the reader to action. Words such as *in the first place, most important, secondly,* and *last* clue your reader in to what is important to you.

> Reading widely will enrich your life. To begin, reading can help your writing. As you see the techniques used by good writers, you can incorporate them into your own writing. In addition, you will increase your vocabulary. Learning new words in context will help you remember the words and how to use them. Most important, reading a wide variety of books can help you become a better thinker. As you read, evaluate the situations created by the author. Do you agree with the philosophies the characters are promoting? What is the author's tone toward the subject? Learn now to cultivate an appetite for books.

13.7 PRACTICE *the skill*

Underline the words or phrases that indicate the type of order. In the blank write the type of paragraph organization used in the following paragraph.

The Tudor family reigned over England for almost 118 years. The first of the Tudor monarchs was Henry VII. He and his wife Elizabeth had eight children. The eldest, Arthur, died before his father, so Henry VIII ruled as the next king. Henry had a total of six wives. First, he married Arthur's widow, Catherine of Aragon. Their only surviving daughter was Mary I. After their marriage was annulled, he married Anne Boleyn, the mother of Elizabeth I. Next, Henry married Jane Seymour, who gave him the son, Edward VI, that he had so desperately wanted. None of Henry's other marriages yielded heirs to the throne. Edward, who had always been sickly, died at age fifteen. The next Tudor on the throne was Mary, who beheaded Lady Jane Grey, Edward's heir. She, in turn, was succeeded by Elizabeth, the last of the Tudor monarchs. Elizabeth reigned until her death in 1603.

Underline the words or phrases that indicate the type of order. In the blank write the type of paragraph organization used in the following paragraph.

Callie took the family portrait down from the mantle and looked at it. Dwight, her oldest brother, and his wife, Tessa, stood on the left in the back. Callie stood on a box next to them. To the right of her stood her other older brother, Bart, and his fiancée, Jade. In the middle, in front of Callie, sat her mother and father. Kneeling in front of them was her little sister, Trish. Callie placed the Hardy family portrait back on the mantle. They would need a new one now that Andrew had been born.

_____

Longer Compositions

Many longer compositions do not use the structured form of the topic sentence, supporting sentences, and concluding sentences. Instead, they follow a line of thought or a series of events from start to finish. For example, a personal letter will probably not contain an obvious topic sentence or thesis statement. Chekhov's short story "Chameleon" contains numerous one-sentence paragraphs of dialogue with no supporting sentences. However, both of these examples accomplish their purposes: a personal letter to entertain and inform and a short story to reveal a truth.

Introductory Paragraphs

In a longer work, the introductory paragraph is critical to encourage the reader to invest the time and effort to read your paper. A good introduction accomplishes several purposes:

- catches reader interest
- introduces the topic
- draws attention to the main idea, the thesis statement

Some writers use interesting stories, compelling questions, or problems to pull the reader into the work.

"What was that?" my little brother demanded. The ominous crash, followed by creaking and banging noises in the basement, worried me too. What if an intruder were in our house? Afraid to go downstairs, we ran to my room and hid inside. I didn't want to be caught in there, but the pounding fear kept me from venturing out. Finally, I forced myself to check the basement. A fallen tree branch had broken a window, and now the wind was moving the door back and forth on its creaky hinges. Although I certainly was not laughing at our unfounded fears, I was relieved to find that the threat was gone. This situation from my youth illustrates the power of sudden fear to keep a victim from thinking rationally or performing efficiently. Sudden fear can paralyze its victims. Scientific evidence reveals how this paralyzing effect occurs. First, fear-related hormones are released into the victim's bloodstream . . .

Concluding Paragraphs

Likewise, the concluding paragraph is crucial for the success of your work. A good concluding paragraph draws the essay's main ideas together and leaves the reader thinking about the essay's topic. Of course, the purpose of your paper will help determine how you conclude your essay. The concluding paragraph should do at least one of the following:

- summarize your main idea
- give a solution to a problem
- ask your audience a question

The conclusion is the final impression your reader will receive; therefore, your concluding paragraph should never introduce new or irrelevant material.

> Sudden fear is caused by surprise, reinforced by chemical reaction, and controlled only by practice. What, then, can be done to minimize the effects of sudden fear? Trust in God is the key. When our eyes are fixed on Him, we rest in the promises of His Word. Therefore, when precarious, fearful situations come, our faith carries us through the fear. Knowing how fear works is not enough, steeling oneself for calmness is impossible, and practice can only partly minimize fear. Only reliance upon God can bring calm to the worst situation.

Essays

You have studied the development and support of the paragraph and the writing of the thesis statement, the topic sentence, and the concluding sentence. All of these skills are necessary for a longer, multiparagraph work such as the essay.

An **essay** is a composition of several paragraphs all dealing with the same idea. Similar to the individual paragraph, the essay generally contains three parts: the introduction, the body, and the conclusion. The essay's main idea is stated in the thesis, which usually appears at the end of the introduction. Supporting paragraphs (just like supporting sentences in a paragraph) develop the thesis statement. The concluding paragraph unites all of the ideas in the essay, usually by restating the thesis.

In the three-paragraph essay, each part consists of one paragraph. In the five-paragraph essay, the body of the piece is expanded to be three paragraphs. In the in-class essay, with which you will become quite familiar, the entire piece may be only a single paragraph. In traditional in-class essay form, the thesis and the concluding statement become the first and last sentences of the essay.

> Life is hectic in the twenty-first century. Work, school, church, meetings, piano lessons, basketball practice, and study time—with all these activities it is difficult for an entire family to meet together for a meal, much less to find a time simply for being together. Since families are important, and most family members are quite busy, families should consider setting aside a time each day or each week for family devotions. Family devotions can consist of Bible study, songs, and prayer.

> There are several ways to study the Bible together as a family. First, a family can read through the Bible together. Members of the family can choose a book of the Bible to read, and each family member can take a turn reading verses aloud. A second idea is studying a biblical topic together. For example, if a family wants to learn about good and wholesome speech, each devotion time can cover a specific passage related to that topic. Lastly, a family can choose a passage to memorize, and they can recite and discuss the verses in the passage.

In addition to Bible reading, most family members enjoy singing their favorite songs of praise and encouragement. Even younger family members can participate by singing or requesting their favorite songs. A pleasant addition to music is sharing testimonies of praise and gratitude. Testimonies of gratitude inspire a spirit of gratitude in others, and a grateful spirit can strengthen and brighten any home. Testimonies of answered prayers and spiritual victories can also bring an awareness of the spiritual needs of other family members and create a greater sense of family unity.

Whether before or after Bible study and music, a time of prayer is an important part of family devotions. During this time, family members can share special prayer requests. Family members can take turns praying for the well-being of the family and the specific needs of each member. Prayer time is a good time to thank God for His blessings and to pray for missionaries, spiritual leaders, and government officials. God promises to be wherever two or more gather in His name—certainly He delights in a family who prays together.

Family devotions are an ideal way to promote spiritual growth as well as family unity in a home. The time of Bible study, songs, testimonies, and prayer can be held in the morning or the evening, and it can be for a short time or a more lengthy time. All family members should be included in this special time. For a family that is fast paced and always on the move, setting aside time for family devotions is always beneficial.

Revising

Writing Strategies pp. 356-85

After drafting your composition, you are ready to revise. Remember that revision of your draft should involve looking at your purpose for writing and at your audience to see whether you have accomplished what you set out to do. Sometimes, having a few days away from your piece will allow you to see problems or gaps in your writing more clearly.

Even experienced writers revise. Some revise as they write, continuously deleting phrases and moving chunks of text around. Others wait until they can read an entire hard copy of their piece before they edit. Careful revision will make you a better writer because it will make you aware of your recurring errors.

When you revise, consider three main areas: ideas, style, and correctness.

> Allow a peer or a family member to read your work during the revision stage.
>
> **tip**

Revising for Ideas

Revising for ideas requires that you rethink your purpose. Is the purpose clear and interesting to the audience for whom it was intended? Is the supporting information relevant and helpful? Or does it distract from the focus of the paper? A great temptation for beginning writers is to include tidbits of information that interest them but that at best do not advance the purpose of the paper. At worst they obscure or disprove the thesis. The following chart summarizes specific areas you need to consider as you revise.

Areas to Consider	Actions to Take
Clarity of Purpose Is your purpose clear from your topic sentence?	Focus on the main idea; eliminate irrelevant information
Interest Does the beginning grab the reader's attention? Do details throughout the piece make the reader want to continue reading?	Change the beginning. Use an interesting fact, question, or anecdote that will interest your audience.
Unity of Ideas Is everything included that needs to be included? Is there anything unnecessary in the piece?	Rewrite or eliminate sentences that do not relate to the topic of the paragraph.
Coherence Is the relationship among ideas, sentences, and paragraphs obvious and logical?	Include transitional expressions to link the various parts of the paper together.

The following paragraphs illustrate how careful revision corrects problems of clarity, interest, unity, and coherence.

First draft

In the Bible there are examples of different kinds of families. Joseph was taken away from his family. God used these circumstances to enable Joseph to rescue his entire family. Taken to the temple by his mother and father as a boy, Samuel grew up with the high priest; he later became an important person. Queen Esther, an orphan who had been reared by her uncle, saved the entire nation of Israel. Esther showed great courage in approaching the king before she was called for. Even though your family may be imperfect, your family was tailor-made for you by God, and He will use it to fulfill His purpose in your life.

Second draft

In the Bible God often uses nontraditional families to fulfill special purposes. For example, Joseph lost his mother and was later removed from his entire remaining family. God used these circumstances to enable Joseph to rescue his whole family. Taken to the temple by his mother and father as a boy, Samuel grew up with the high priest; he later became a great judge and prophet in Israel. Queen Esther, an orphan who had been reared by her uncle, saved the entire nation of Israel. You can see, therefore, that even though your family may be imperfect, God intended that family for you, and He will use it to fulfill His purpose in your life.

Rewrite the following paragraph, adding interest and correcting any problems in clarity, unity, and coherence.

Public education is available in the United States. Hundreds of thousands of American families teach their children at home. Some parents simply desire more time with their children. Parents feel they can have more personal time with their children. Different states have different laws regarding home schools. Many parents want to decide what values their children are being taught. More and more American families are combining home and school.

_____

_____

_____

_____

_____

_____

_____

_____

_____

_____

_____

Revising for Style

As you learned in the writing assignment in Chapter 11, writers can emphasize or downplay ideas by carefully choosing their placement or use in a sentence. Sentence length, type, and structure can affect what message stands out to the reader. Parallelism, coordination/subordination, and sentence rhythm also influence what the reader finds important in a sentence or paragraph. The following chart lists problems in style and possible solutions for those problems.

Read your papers aloud to "listen" for errors. **tip**

Areas to Consider	Actions to Take
Emphasis Do the important ideas stand out? Or are the wrong ideas being emphasized?	Put important ideas at the beginning or the end. (The end is the strongest position in the sentence or paragraph.)
Precise Words Are your nouns and verbs too general or imprecise? *(nice, relative)*	Use specific words. A thesaurus can help you find specific, precise words. *(friendly, uncle)*

Areas to Consider	Actions to Take
Conciseness Does your writing contain redundancy? Is your writing full of heavy dependent clauses?	Use fewer words. Reduce dependent clauses to shorter, simpler elements.
Smoothness Does any part of your writing sound awkward?	Rewrite using language and expressions that sound natural.
Fresh Words Is your writing replete with repeated words or phrases that have become clichéd?	Find a replacement word or phrase. Use new comparisons rather than overused ones.

13.10   REVIEW *the skill*

Rewrite the following paragraph, correcting any problems of emphasis, precise words, conciseness, smoothness, and fresh words.

    The Family Medical Leave Act (FMLA) became law on February 5, 1993. This law was passed to help people who need to leave their jobs temporarily from being discriminated against. The law affects almost all employers, with the exception of a few really small businesses that are privately owned. FMLA lets employees take a total of twelve weeks off work without pay in a twelve-month period for a bunch of different reasons. These reasons are giving birth or caring for a new baby, having an adopted (or foster) child placed in the home, caring for a relative who is ill, having a serious medical condition, and stuff like that. In most circumstances, the employee must be allowed to return to his job under the same conditions as when he left at the end of his medical leave.

_____

_____

_____

_____

_____

_____

_____

_____

_____

_____

_____

Revising for Correctness: Proofreading

The final step in revising is proofreading for correctness. Now is the time to make a clean copy of your paper to rid it of extraneous editing marks and changes that make the draft difficult to read. The clean copy will enable you to read smoothly and will increase your chances of detecting errors.

Use the following chart to help you look for specific problems in correctness.

Areas to Consider	Actions to Take
Sentence structure Does your paper contain sentence errors?	Correct fragments, comma splices, and fused sentences.
Usage Are there subject and verbs that disagree? How about pronouns and antecedents? Have you used correct pronoun case and reference? Have any incorrectly used words crept into your paper?	Correct agreement problems—both subject-verb and pronoun-antecedent agreement. Correct pronoun usage problems. Use troublesome verbs and other words correctly.
Spelling, Punctuation, Capitalization Do you have any spelling errors? Are your sentences punctuated and capitalized correctly?	Use the computer spellcheck as well as your own check to look for spelling errors. Correct punctuation errors. Correct capitalization errors.

tip

Do not depend upon a computer's spellcheck function to catch all of your errors.

Good proofreading is a skill that must be developed. You will not find every error in the first read-through. Professional proofreaders may read a piece three times or more. Another strategy professionals use is allowing others to read the manuscript. Fresh eyes can spot errors that someone who has been closely associated with the composition does not see. The following strategies will help you become a better proofreader.

- **Read slowly.** If necessary, use a blank sheet of paper to cover the part you have not read yet so that it does not distract you.
- **Read aloud.** You may hear an error that you would not otherwise have found.
- **Read backwards.** This will force you to look at each word individually.
- **Read specifically.** Look for a different type of error each time you read through the paper quickly. Look specifically for problems that you have had before. For example, if you have a tendency to make comma errors, read through once looking only for comma errors.

Remember that good proofreading can make an important difference in your paper, and the result can affect your grade and your audience's impression of your work.

Publishing

Now that you have drafted and revised your paper, you can make a copy worthy of publication. **Publishing** is the act of sharing your work with others. This can involve many possibilities—reading the work aloud, posting it in a school hallway, or sending it to a magazine or newspaper. Before you send your work anywhere, you need to prepare it for publication by choosing a title and making a final neat copy.

Choosing a Title

Some authors and many publishers consider the title to be one of the most important writing decisions you make. For an academic paper, a good title tells the reader something about what he will read. Generally speaking, the title should be no more than five or six words. The title should intrigue the reader and compel him to read more. Finally, a title for an academic paper should suggest the subject and perhaps the approach of that particular paper.

TOO GENERAL	Families in the Twenty-First Century
GOOD POSSIBILITIES	The Role of the Family in the Twenty-First Century
	Changes in the Family in the Twenty-First Century
	The Breakdown of the Family in the Twenty-First Century

tip

Select a title that would catch your attention if you saw it.

Titles for creative assignments will differ slightly from those for academic ones. Often a creative title leaves something to the reader's imagination and allows the reader to wonder what the connection will be. Creative titles are usually somewhat shorter than those for academic assignments. The creative writing title may name the subject directly (George Eliot's *Silas Marner*—a story about the title character), or it may suggest the subject in an indirect way (Agatha Christie's *The Mousetrap*—which is not about rodents at all but rather is a mystery set in a country house).

13.11 PRACTICE *the skill*

Choose the best title for the paragraph from the choices provided. Write the letter that corresponds to your answer.

Family reunions provide an opportunity for an entire extended family to get together—sometimes as many as four generations of the same family. In fact, a family reunion may be the only time that some relatives see each other. Some family members may not be able to visit often because they live several states away from the rest of the family. Others may live in the same state but still too far away for frequent visits. A well-attended reunion might include dozens of people.

_____ A. Family Get-togethers
      B. Fun, Food, and Fellowship
      C. Back Together: Family Reunions

Write a good title for the following paragraph. Make your title both informative and interesting.

Being a parent is not an easy job. Parents wear a variety of hats (such as chef's and chauffeur's). They also clean, manage, teach, nurse, comfort, discipline, mediate, and support the family. Sometimes parents have to do things they would rather not, such as correcting disobedient children. Sometimes parents must make difficult decisions that affect the entire family, such as taking a new job or moving to a different city or state. Besides all these tasks, a parent is a person who loves, nurtures, and helps a child become a mature adult. And that is not easy.

Making a Neat Copy

Your published paper should be as nearly perfect as you can make it—no handwritten corrections or crossouts allowed. Your audience expects and deserves a piece that is easy to read from a technical standpoint. In order to meet audience expectations, you will need to know the publication guidelines for your particular audience. If the paper is for a class, you must know what form the teacher expects and follow it carefully. Many teachers prefer that all papers, whether handwritten in class or word-processed, be double-spaced. Special attention must be given to margins as well. These areas allow the teacher's comments to be written directly on the paper.

If the paper is for outside publication, you must follow the guidelines from the chosen publisher. These are generally available online, at your local library, or in a recent copy of the publication itself. Follow publication guidelines exactly, since failure to do so can result in immediate rejection.

WRITING EDITORIAL

I will set no wicked thing before mine eyes: I hate the work of them that turn aside; it shall not cleave to me.
Psalm 101:3

Writing can be an effective tool for persuasion, and in many cases, "the pen is mightier than the sword." A well-written editorial can be a powerful way to promote your ideas, and a Christian can use an editorial to present truth compellingly. Peggy Noonan's editorial is an example of effective persuasion. After clearly stating her thesis (American children watch too much television), she supports her thesis with effective arguments. Her first argument is an appeal to authority. After she says that television watching has gone too far, she says, "I'm not, of course, the only one who thinks so." She goes on to cite specific statistics from the American Academy of Pediatrics. Her next argument is an appeal to human experience. No one can argue with her point that parents do not generally pull children away from productive activities and require them to watch television. An effective persuasive paper supports its claims with solid arguments.

Choose a topic that is important to you and write an editorial about that topic.

Planning

✔ **Begin by brainstorming for a topic.** What is something you feel strongly about? Is there something you would like to see changed? Your topic does not have to be a highly controversial topic, but it does need to be something important to you.

✔ **Write a thesis for your editorial.** What is the main point that you are trying to make? Your thesis is a concise statement of your opinion on a particular topic.

TOPIC	American teenagers and soft drinks
THESIS	American teenagers drink more soft drinks than they did twenty-five years ago.
REVISED THESIS	American teenagers drink a large amount of soft drinks, and the practice is significantly harming their health.
FINAL THESIS	American teenagers should reduce the amount of soft drinks they consume because the practice is significantly harming their health.

This is closer to the main point that you are trying to make, but it does not clearly state your opinion on the topic.

This may be good support for your paper, but this is not the main point you are trying to make.

Here you have clearly stated your opinion that American teenagers should reduce the amount of soft drinks they consume.

✔ **Generate support for your thesis.** Write out specific reasons for your argument. After you have written what you already know, do some research. For example, Noonan's article includes specific statistics from the American Academy of Pediatrics. If you were writing about teenagers drinking too many soft drinks, you would probably include statistics concerning how many soft drinks teenagers in the United States actually drink, and you would include documented medical research about related health problems.

✔ **If your main point identifies a problem, try to present a solution to the problem.** For example, if you were writing a paper concerning the amount of soft drinks that American teenagers drink, you might want to suggest that an alternative beverage be marketed. In the second half of Noonan's article, she proposes that a twelve-step program be offered to help parents and children break their television habit.

✔ **Determine your audience.** Knowing your audience is very important when writing a persuasive article. Who do you think is the target audience for Noonan's article? She is probably writing to parents, and most likely parents with school-age children. Do you think this article would be very popular in a publication for young teens? Why or why not? Who is your audience? What types of persuasion will be effective for your audience?

Paragraph
Organization
pp. 338-39

✔ **Organize your material to make it as effective as possible.** You may want to begin with your thesis, or you may want to begin with illustrations or statistics and then state your thesis later in the article. Determine the best organization for your editorial, and remember that strong arguments are generally needed at the beginning and ending of a persuasive work.

Drafting

✔ **Begin with a catchy opener.** Noonan's article begins with a narrative of a commercial that shows children watching television in a minivan. She uses the commercial as a vivid illustration of the problem that she is going to address. Presenting the problem effectively to the audience is a good way to begin a persuasive article.

✔ **Make the article interesting and relevant to your audience.** Your argument is not going to be effective if the reader does not care to finish the article. Include details that are relevant to your specific audience. For example, the high cost of dental bills caused by consuming soft drinks would not be a relevant detail to a teenage audience, but it would be a highly relevant detail for an article directed toward the teenagers' parents.

✔ **Note the tone of the argument.** Even if you are totally correct, your paper will lose its effectiveness if the tone is arrogant or malicious. If you must contradict someone, make sure your tone is kind and gracious.

INAPPROPRIATE STATEMENT	Sunshine Cola recently published an article stating that soft drinks are harmless refreshments that contain far less sugar and caffeine than is commonly assumed. This is a lie! This company only wants money and is totally unconcerned about anyone's health.
APPROPRIATE STATEMENT	Despite the article recently published by Sunshine Cola stating that soft drinks are harmless, nutritional experts have proved otherwise.

tip

An illustration can be an effective support for your argument.

✔ **Write a good conclusion.** In a persuasive work, the conclusion is especially important. Your conclusion, which can be one sentence or several sentences, should include a restatement of your thesis as well as provide a strong, confident ending for your argument. Do not include new or irrelevant information in your conclusion.

Revising

✔ **Read your article aloud.** Are there parts that sound dull or weak? Revise these parts to make them more interesting and convincing.

✔ **Be sure you have enough information.** Have you clearly explained the problem and offered a solution? Have you supported your statements with enough evidence?

✔ **Eliminate unnecessary words.** A persuasive article should be as clear and direct as possible. Unnecessary details can be distracting; therefore, every sentence in your article should support your thesis.

✔ **Check the tone.** Does your writing express confidence? Your audience is more likely to agree with you if you are confident about your opinion. Did you use exaggerated language? If you say that all teenage problems are caused by soft drink consumption, then your audience probably will not take you seriously.

✔ **Proofread for correct grammar and punctuation.** Misspelled words and incorrect grammar are distracting in any kind of writing, and they seriously reduce the effectiveness of persuasive writing.

Sentence Reduction pp. 374-76

Publishing

✔ **Submit your article to your school or local newspaper.** An editorial of this type, especially if you have chosen a topic of local interest, should be considered publishable by your local print sources. Make sure that you follow any publishing guidelines established by the paper.

✔ **Present your article to your class or family.** Read your work aloud and encourage feedback from your audience.

✔ **Post your editorial on your class or school webpage.** Depending on your topic, this article might be a perfect fit for your webpage. Encourage friends and family to read your views and respond in an editorial of their own.

Some Ideas to Consider

Government
- Should people with strong religious views be allowed to run for office?

Education
- Should vouchers be provided for home schools?

Health
- Are Americans being fueled primarily by fast food?
- Is being out in the sun good for you?

What's fueling you?

The Beginnings of Language

When God created the universe, He did not use His hands or any machinery. He simply spoke, using language to command the elements. On the sixth day He created Adam in His own image, giving him the gift of language. God and Adam communicated frequently, meeting together to talk and walk through Eden.

The English language you now speak descended from the language Adam spoke. This beginning of the history of language is recorded in Genesis. Genesis 10 explains that Noah's descendants would increase and divide into families, languages, and nations. Then Genesis 11:1-9 gives the specific history of the first division of language at the Tower of Babel. At that time, the people all spoke one language and lived together on the plain of Shinar. Becoming overly confident and endeavoring to be self-sufficient, the people began building a massive city with a tower to reach to heaven. Men wanted to make a name for themselves, independent of God.

When God saw the people banding together in rebellion, God, in a great act of mercy, took action to separate them. He confused their language, causing them not to understand one another. By creating the language divisions, God broke the strength of the people. No longer could they be independent and self-sufficient. Now they must live in dependence on Him—dependence for protection and for provision (see Acts 17:26-28).

Since the time that God created the first divisions, languages have been in constant gradual change. A people sharing a language would spread out over a wide geographic area and eventually lose contact with one another. Over time, the common language would change so much locally that people from one area could not understand people from another area. Once a language has changed this much, linguists say that the language has split into two or more new languages. These new languages are called "daughter languages," and the one from which they developed is the "parent language."

One of the languages that God made at the Tower of Babel seems to have been the one we call the parent Indo-European language. Over many centuries, this ancient language gradually changed, splitting into early Latin, early Greek, the early Germanic language, and many others. As the people kept spreading out, languages continued to change. For example, eventually Latin split into Portuguese, Spanish, French, and Italian. One of the early languages was the unwritten Germanic language, still spoken by northern tribes around the time of Christ. This language then also gradually split, eventually forming the Germanic languages such as Norwegian, German, and English.

On the chart below, the colored line traces the development of our English language. All of these languages are in the Indo-European language family. It is a large family of languages, but it is only one of the world's language families.

Simplified Chart of Indo-European Languages

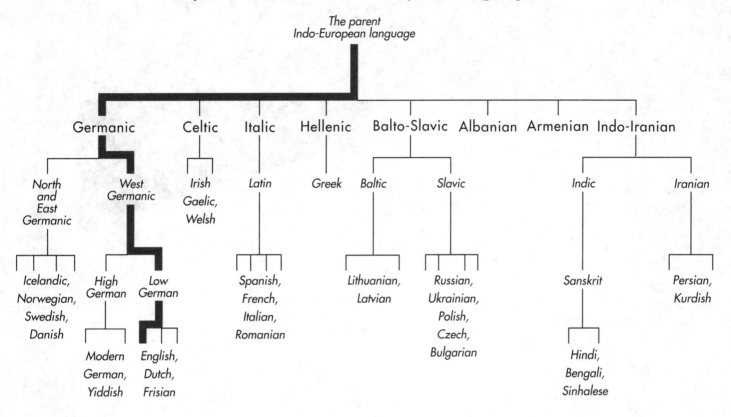

What about your first language? Is it part of the Indo-European language family? If so, you may be able to find it on the chart here (or you may not, since there are many more Indo-European languages than can be shown).

Otherwise, to find out what language family your language is in, start by looking up its name in a full-sized desk dictionary. (For example, the language definition for *Gujarat* is "the Indic language spoken in Gujarat," which is a region or a state in western India.) Then look at the classifying word (here *Indic*)—is it a branch of Indo-European, or a separate family? The chart here shows all the branches of Indo-European languages today, roughly from west to east: Germanic, Celtic, Italic (or Romance), Hellenic (or Greek), Baltic, Slavic, Albanian, Armenian, Indic, and Iranian. Thus the Gujarat language is in the Indic branch of Indo-European.

Now find your language, if you haven't already done so. If the dictionary gives the name of another language family, look it up too, and you should find out where the family is located and perhaps a few of the other languages in it. (If your language has more than one name, try more than one entry if you need to. Also, a few language families have alternate names, so different dictionaries could give different names for the family.)

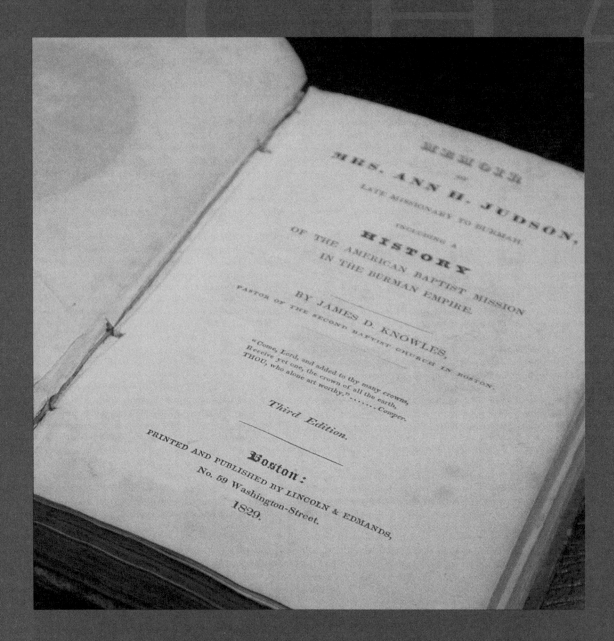

What is a journal? Most simply defined, a journal is a private place for a writer to record his thoughts. A journal could take the form of a diary, where the writer records daily experiences and his personal responses to them. A journal could also provide a place to "try out" creative ideas for stories, poems, or other works of art. Many Christians keep devotional journals, where they record their meditations on Scripture reading or keep track of answers to their prayers. For your journal entry try to keep your writing personal and expressive—an insight into your thoughts.

The excerpts from Ann Judson's journal below give us some insight into her thoughts. Does reading this journal make her seem more "real" to you? What do you think was her purpose in recording her thoughts as she began her voyage to a foreign mission field with her husband in 1812?

Memoir of Mrs. Ann H. Judson *by Ann Hasseltine Judson*

Feb. 18. Took leave of my friends and native land, and embarked on board the brig Caravan, for India. Had so long anticipated the trying scene of parting, that I found it more tolerable than I had feared. Still my heart bleeds. O America, my native land, must I leave thee? Must I leave my parents, my sisters and brother, my friends beloved, and all the scenes of my early youth? Must I leave thee, Bradford, my dear native town, where I spent the pleasant years of childhood; where I learnt to lisp the name of my mother; where my infant mind first began to expand; where I entered the field of science; where I learnt the endearments of friendship, and tasted of all the happiness this world can afford; where I learnt also to value a Saviour's blood, and to count all things but loss, in comparison with the knowledge of him? Yes, I must leave you all, for a heathen land, an uncongenial clime. Farewell, happy, happy scenes,— but never, no, never to be forgotten.

19. Sea-sick all day, and unable to do any thing. My thoughts, more than usual, fixed on divine things. Longed for the enjoyment of God's presence on our passage, that we may be preparing for usefulness in future life. In the night had many distressing apprehensions of death. Felt unwilling to die on the sea, not so much on account of my state after death, as the dreadfulness of perishing amid the waves.

21. Somewhat relieved from sickness, and able to read a few chapters in the Bible. Never had a greater sense of our obligations to live devoted to God, resulting from his distinguished mercies. Even on the ocean, confined as I am, I find many sources of enjoyment, and feel as happy as when on land, in the midst of my friends.

Feb. 22. O for a heart to live near to God, and serve him faithfully. I need nothing so much as ardent piety. I should feel happy in the consideration of having left my native land, and my father's house, if by making this sacrifice, the kingdom of Christ should be promoted. May it be my great object to live a useful, holy life, and prepare to die a peaceful death.

27. This day has been regarded by our friends on land as a day of fasting and prayer for the prosperity of the Mission, and I hope the same object has not been forgotten by us on the sea. I spent some time this evening on deck. The weather was pleasant; the motion of the vessel gentle, though rapid; the full moon shone clearly on the water; and all things around conspired to excite pleasing though melancholy sensations. My native land, my home, my friends, and all my forsaken enjoyments, rushed into my mind; my tears flowed profusely, and I could not be comforted. Soon, however, the consideration of having left all these for the dear cause of Christ and the hope of being, one day, instrumental of leading some poor degraded females to embrace him as their Saviour, soothed my griefs, dried up my tears, and restored peace and tranquility to my mind.

29. The weather continues pleasant, so that we are able to spend much time on deck. I see that there is no situation in life in which trials and enjoyments, pains and pleasures, are not intermingled. I calculated on nothing but difficulties and distresses, during the voyage, and am disappointed in finding many pleasures. God frequently deprives his children of the good things of this world, that they may be sensible they have no portion here. Have I not, then, reason to fear that I am receiving my *only* portion? And yet my heart tells me, that I do not wish to take these things as my portion. I would rather be deprived of them than that they should deprive me of the enjoyment of the light of God's countenance. I desire a heavenly inheritance that will never fail me. I desire that the great, the infinite God, may be my portion, my friend, my all.

WRITING STRATEGIES

Once you master the basics of the four-part writing process, you have a plan that can help you complete almost any writing project. The additional writing strategies you will encounter in this chapter are tools that you can use to improve the actual words and phrases and sentences that make up your writing. They will help you to achieve sentence variety, emphasis, and energy and to show clear relationships between sentence ideas. Some of the strategies will help you state ideas more logically and with less chance of misunderstanding based on faulty comparisons or a use of biased language. Mastery of these strategies can help ensure that the words of your mouth are correct and pleasing to Him who made all language (Ps. 19:14).

Sentence Emphasis and Variety

In order to be successful, your writing must capture and maintain your audience's interest. Variety and emphasis are the two elements that sustain reader engagement throughout a piece. A speaker whose vocal patterns undulate in the same monotonous pattern, never slowing, never speeding, delivering everything at a sort of nursery-rhyme gait, will soon lose his audience. Or at least find their eyes glazing over.

The principle holds true for writers as well. An effective writer uses variety—of sentence types, length, beginnings, and so on—to keep his readers interested. He also manipulates his words and phrases and sentences to provide proper emphasis to his important ideas.

Achieving Emphasis

Proper emphasis is essential for good sentence construction. As a writer, you want your readers to get the message and the emphasis you intend. If a reader finishes a piece and comes away thinking, "What was that paragraph about?" the author has not been successful. The following general guidelines for achieving emphasis are ordered from the least important to the most important.

Certain kinds of words are stronger, and therefore more emphatic, than others. Generally speaking, nouns and verbs are the strongest of the parts of speech. Determine to select strong verbs and well-chosen nouns rather than rely on their adverb and adjective sidekicks.

Parts of Speech
pp. 2-22

WEAK	At the gun, Williams *quickly ran* out of the starting blocks.
STRONGER	At the gun, Williams *exploded* out of the starting blocks.
WEAK	Where the river had been, there was nothing but a *little bit of water*.
STRONGER	Where the river had been, there was nothing but a *trickle*.

A short sentence before or after a series of longer ones can be emphatic. The contrast of varying sentence lengths gives the reader a break—or a much-needed jolt. The same is true of varying sentence types.

> There was a formidable obstacle. Every Prussian man must serve three years in the army; and classical students who had passed the university examination were forced to serve only one year. Muller had not yet received his army training, and without an exemption he could not obtain a passport to leave the country. His application for exemption was denied, and Muller felt much depressed because of the denial. But God had plans for this exemption. (from *George Muller: Man of Faith and Miracles* by Basil Miller)

Putting the important word or phrase at the end of the sentence achieves natural emphasis. Since these words are the last the reader will see, they naturally become the most important. You can manipulate your sentence by moving modifiers and phrases and by using differing verb types to create this kind of emphasis. The same emphasis is obtained by putting the important item before an interrupting word or at the end of a dependent clause. Look at the following sentences that have been carefully manipulated to place emphasis on differing ideas.

EMPHASIS ON CONCERN WITH THE PRESENT	Some historians readily admit that before they interpret the past, they concern themselves with the present.
EMPHASIS ON INTERPRETING THE PAST	Some historians readily admit that they concern themselves with the present before they interpret the past.

Moving an idea other than the subject to the beginning of the sentence or clause gives a certain amount of emphasis also, albeit to a lesser degree.

> Lying he could not forgive.

> Crouched and motionless, the panther waited for its prey.

Of course, these three guidelines should not be overused. Too much emphasis is as tiring as reading a computer screen full of capital letters.

Certain types of sentences break the normal routine of your writing. These unusual sentences should be used only occasionally for effect. Since they are unusual, they provide sentence variety, but they should be used primarily for emphasis.

Each of you has heard someone ask, "What do you think you are doing?" The question is not always meant to get an answer; it can be used simply for effect, such as to express surprise. We call this type of question a **rhetorical question.** The rhetorical question can be used for emphasis.

NORMAL SENTENCES	We don't need coats. It's ninety-three degrees outside.
RHETORICAL QUESTION	Why would we need coats? It's ninety-three degrees outside.

As with other sentence manipulation devices, rhetorical questions should be used sparingly. Their overuse can be tiresome or distracting.

Special emphasis can also be achieved by using an **inverted sentence** from time to time. Inverted sentences can have the complement at the beginning of the sentence, or they can bring the main verb to the front of the sentence or clause, thus emphasizing both what is at the beginning and what is at the end.

COMPLEMENT AT THE BEGINNING	Shy she definitely is not!
MAIN VERB AT BEGINNING OF CLAUSE	Crying? The three-year-old was talking and laughing, but crying she definitely was not.

Inverted sentences should also be used with care, and when the main verb becomes too distant from the subject or from the rest of the verb, they should be avoided altogether. As always, the goal is clarity and ease of understanding.

Do not overuse unusual sentence types. **tip**

14.1 PRACTICE *the skill*

Using the guidelines in parentheses, rewrite the sentence to improve emphasis.

1. Ninety percent of Egyptians are Muslims, and helping them become Christians can be difficult. *(Use a stronger subject for the second independent clause.)*

   _____

   _____

2. William Borden was a dedicated Christian who committed his life to being a missionary to Muslims. *(Shorten the sentence. Use inverted order for emphasis.)*

   _____

   _____

3. His ministry seemed to be a waste in the eyes of many. *(Make this a rhetorical question and put the important word at the end.)*

   _____

   _____

4. When he died at age twenty-five soon after arriving in Egypt, a failure is what many considered him to be. *(Put important words at the end.)*

   _____

   _____

5. However, William Borden's life caused others to give their lives completely to Christ and His service. *(Use a stronger verb.)*

   _____

   _____

USE *the skill*

Using the above guidelines for proper emphasis, write a paragraph that answers this question: How can Christian teens participate in missions?

_____

_____

_____

_____

_____

_____

_____

_____

_____

_____

_____

_____

_____

_____

Varying Sentence Length and Complexity

Ideally, the length of sentences in a piece of writing varies among short, medium, and long sentences. Too many short sentences make a piece seem simplistic; too many long ones make for difficult reading. Of course, varying length probably means varying complexity: some sentences will be simple, some compound, and some complex or compound-complex.

The following paragraph contains sentences of similar length and complexity. Its style is choppy and disjointed, and all ideas seem equally important.

> William Borden was a successful person. He had money. He was talented. He was good looking. He was athletic. Also, he was popular. Borden could have chosen anything. He chose, however, to be a missionary.

Revised, the paragraph flows better and achieves proper emphasis through the variety of sentence types.

> Anyone would have considered William Borden successful. He had money, good looks, and prestige; and he was a champion wrestler in college. He could have chosen to do anything he wanted with his life, but in giving his life to Christ, William Borden became truly successful. Many thought he was throwing his life away, but Borden had set his eyes on higher goals. He became a missionary.

Sentence
Patterns
pp. 40-44

Varying Sentence Patterns

As you write, you probably do not even think about the sentence patterns you are using. Indeed, good writing seems naturally to include a variety of basic sentence patterns. During the revising stage, however, many writers realize that they have overused one particular sentence pattern. Recognizing and changing a pattern that has been repeated too often can vastly improve a piece of writing that seems lacking in interest value.

Young William Borden grew up happy, full of love and enthusiasm for life. He played often with his friends. He eagerly labored with the men. One day, his mother entered into a close walk with God. Her whole life changed. William noticed as she revealed a new love for God and life itself. They began attending regularly at the Moody Church where Dr. R. A. Torrey was the pastor. Soon Borden himself was ready to become a Christian.

By introducing some new sentence patterns into the same paragraph, the writer was able to improve variety and therefore interest.

William Borden was a happy child, full of love and enthusiasm for life. He filled his time with playing with his friends or working with the men. When Borden was seven, his mother met Christ and began a close walk with God. The change in her life became clearly and immediately evident, and William noticed her new love for God and for life itself. They began attending regularly at the Moody Church where Dr. R. A. Torrey was pastor, and Borden himself soon desired to become a Christian like his mother.

Varying Sentence Beginnings

Phrases
pp. 56-77

Clauses
pp. 88-103

If every sentence you write begins with the word *the* or with the subject of the sentence, your writing will be tiresome. To achieve variety, try moving a phrase (verbal or prepositional) or a dependent clause to the beginning of your sentence. Modifiers, especially compound ones, can also make your sentence starters interesting. Of course, as with any strategy, overuse of a certain type of beginning, no matter how striking, can make the writing boring. Below are some examples of varied sentence beginnings.

REGULAR SUBJECT AND VERB	Kristy sang a solo for a vocal competition.
ADJECTIVES	Confident and happy, she faced the audience expectantly.
PARTICIPIAL PHRASE	Opening her mouth, she began to sing a piece by Puccini.
DEPENDENT CLAUSE	After she had finished, the audience applauded.

Check your writing for new ways to begin your sentences. **tip**

PRACTICE *the skill*

Rewrite the paragraph, following the suggestions below.

¹Before William Borden entered college, his parents sent him on a year's tour of the world. ²Accompanying him was a fine Christian tutor recently graduated from Yale. ³His name was Walter Erdman. ⁴He was an interesting and competent guardian for William. ⁵He was, more importantly, a man of strong Christian convictions. ⁶Borden began to see the needs of people all over the world. ⁷Seeds of missionary work were being sown in Borden's life.

1. Change the sentence pattern of sentence 1 to S-InV.

   _____

   _____

2. Combine sentences 2 and 3 to add complexity.

   _____

   _____

3. Change the sentence pattern of sentence 4 to S-LV-PA.

   _____

   _____

4. Vary the beginning of sentence 5.

   _____

   _____

5. Combine sentences 6 and 7 to add complexity.

   _____

   _____

USE *the skill*

Write an original paragraph, varying sentence beginnings, the length and complexity of the sentences, and the sentence patterns. When you finish writing, answer the questions about your paragraph.

_____

_____

_____

_____

_____

_____

_____

_____

_____

_____

_____

_____

_____

1. How many sentences did you write?

   _____

2. Write down the number of times you used the following sentence patterns: *S-InV, S-TrV-DO, S-TrV-IO-DO, S-TrV-DO-OC, S-LV-PA, S-LV-PN,* and *S-be-Advl.*

   _____

3. Write down the number of times you used the following sentence types: *simple, compound, complex, compound-complex.*

   _____

4. List the types of structures that begin your sentences.

   _____

5. How many different beginning structures did you use?

   _____

Choosing Between Constructions

Most of the choices we make as we write—the verbs we use or the phrases we routinely employ—are automatic. As we look closely at a piece of writing, however, we may wish to edit our choices to improve variety or to change emphasis.

Active or Passive

Most interesting text is written in active voice. In general, active verbs make a sentence more direct and vivid. However, there are times when a passive verb is the better choice. For example, using the passive to move important information from the subject position to the end of the sentence can change the emphasis.

Active and Passive Voice p. 160

| NORMAL SENTENCE | You can use different methods to achieve sentence variety. |
| PASSIVE USED TO MOVE A PHRASE TO THE END | Sentence variety can be achieved by different methods. |

Moving *methods* to the end of the sentence prepares the reader for a listing of the various methods.

Passive voice can also be used to keep the same subject for several verbs in a row. This may help you emphasize different objects with the same subject.

| INCONSISTENT SUBJECTS | When the neighbor asked Heather for a rake, Heather gladly gave one. If the neighbor needs Heather to help with the raking too, Heather will need to change clothes first. |
| BETTER (CONSISTENT SUBJECTS) | When Heather was asked for a rake, she gladly gave one. If she is needed to help with the raking too, she will have to change clothes first. |

---

tip

The active voice is usually the better choice.

Remember as you choose between active and passive voice that it is best not to overuse passive voice verbs. An occasional passive is permissible, and in some cases desirable. But when in doubt, use active voice.

Sentence Patterns p. 41

Indirect Object or Prepositional Phrase

Sometimes a sentence that contains an indirect object could also be worded to include a prepositional phrase. Depending on which construction you use, a different idea can be emphasized.

Prepositional Phrases pp. 57-59

| WITH INDIRECT OBJECT | Curtis e-mailed his friend the article. |
| WITH PREPOSITIONAL PHRASE | Curtis e-mailed the article to his friend. |

Notice the difference in the information located at the end of the sentence, the location of strength. In the first sentence, the emphasis is on the article. The suggestion is that perhaps he e-mails him other things regularly. In the second sentence, the emphasis is on the friend, suggesting that Curtis had already e-mailed it to someone else. Choose carefully which construction you use, depending on what information is more important.

PRACTICE *the skill*

Rewrite the following sentences to give the emphasis indicated in parentheses.

1. William Borden often gave the unsaved the gospel. (*Use a prepositional phrase instead of an indirect object.*)

   _____

   _____

2. Missions conference speakers told the need for the gospel all over the world to Borden. (*Use an indirect object instead of a prepositional phrase.*)

   _____

   _____

3. While the needs of all peoples were important, the conference especially emphasized the needs of Muslim people. (*Use passive to have consistent subjects.*)

   _____

   _____

4. He heard that in China alone more Muslims could be found than in all of Persia, Egypt, or Arabia. (*Use active for variety.*)

   _____

   _____

5. He became burdened for those people, and God was asked by him whether he should go to the Chinese Muslims. (*Use active instead of passive.*)

   _____

   _____

REVIEW *the skill*

Write an original paragraph, using active and passive correctly and indirect objects and prepositional phrases correctly. Answer this question: What thoughts would a new missionary have as he travels to the field in which he will serve?

   _____

   _____

   _____

   _____

   _____

   _____

   _____

   _____

Coordination and Subordination

Another way to achieve variety in your sentences is to use coordination and subordination in your paragraphs. The main purpose of coordination and subordination is to show how ideas and thoughts are related to one another. Thoughts can be related on an equal basis or on an unequal basis. Joining thoughts equally is known as coordination; joining thoughts unequally is called subordination.

Coordination &
Subordination
pp. 291-94

Coordination

Coordination joins ideas of equal importance. Coordinate ideas can be left in separate sentences or joined on an equal basis. We usually join coordinate ideas with coordinating conjunctions (*and, or, nor, for, but, yet*). Use of conjunctions to show coordination reduces the number of sentences and varies the structures of sentences.

Coordinating
Conjunctions
p. 20

ORIGINAL SENTENCES	William Penn obtained the rights to Pennsylvania in 1681. He soon became friendly with the Indians settled there.
COORDINATED SENTENCE	William Penn obtained the rights to Pennsylvania in 1681, and he soon became friendly with the Indians settled there.
COORDINATED PREDICATE	William Penn obtained the rights to Pennsylvania in 1681 and soon became friendly with the Indians settled there.

Successful coordination requires that ideas be equal in importance or nature. You can think of coordination as tines on a fork: each part spreads equally.

FAULTY COORDINATION	In Shakespeare's *Love's Labour's Lost,* Don Armado is a clown, and he tries to woo Jaquenetta.
CORRECT COORDINATION	In Shakespeare's *Love's Labour's Lost,* Don Armado is a clown and a friend of the king.

In the first sentence the ideas of being a clown and attempting to woo are dissimilar, whereas in the second sentence *clown* and *friend* are equal in nature. Another aspect of coordination requires that two parts be similar grammatically.

FAULTY COORDINATION (TWO NOUNS AND A VERB)	Robyn is a singer, a songwriter, and plays piano.
CORRECT COORDINATION	Robyn is a singer and a songwriter, and she is a pianist as well.
	Robyn is a singer, a songwriter, and a pianist.

Subordination

Subordination joins ideas of unequal importance. These ideas are joined on an unequal basis, with one idea subordinate to, or less important than, the other. Subordinate ideas are usually contained in dependent clauses or in phrases.

Subordinating
Conjunctions
pp. 21, 95

ORIGINAL SENTENCES	Penn's intent was to found a colony. That colony would be based partly on religious freedom.
SUBORDINATED (DEPENDENT CLAUSE)	Penn's intent was to found a colony *that was based partly on religious freedom.*
SUBORDINATED (PARTICIPIAL PHRASE)	Penn's intent was to found a colony *based partly on religious freedom.*

Because subordination shows ideas to be unequal, the ideas must be joined in such a way that the reader can tell which is the more important part and how it is related to the subordinate part.

| FAULTY COORDINATION | We studied the hymn writer Adelaide Pollard, and her best-known hymn is "Have Thine Own Way, Lord." |
| APPROPRIATE SUBORDINATION | We studied the hymn writer Adelaide Pollard, whose best-known hymn is "Have Thine Own Way, Lord." |

Notice that the information contained in the adjective clause of the second sentence seems to branch off the information of the main clause. This sentence better represents the relationship of the more important idea to the less important idea.

Complex Sentences p. 103

Most errors in subordination occur when unequal ideas are joined as though they are equal or when the less important idea is emphasized over the more important one. Make sure that the more important idea is located in the main clause and the background idea is in the dependent (subordinate) clause.

NO SUBORDINATION	The hymn "Spirit of God, Descend upon My Heart" was written by George Croly, and it is very powerful.
POOR SUBORDINATION	The hymn "Spirit of God, Descend upon My Heart," which is very powerful, was written by George Croly.
BETTER SUBORDINATION	The hymn "Spirit of God, Descend upon My Heart," which was written by George Croly, is very powerful.

If the main thrust of the sentence is the power of the hymn, then only sentence three puts the proper perspective on the relative importance of the two ideas. Sentence one makes the two ideas equal; sentence two makes the idea of the power of the hymn subordinate.

14.7 **PRACTICE** *the skill*

Rewrite the following sentences, correcting any illogical coordination or subordination. If the sentence is already correct, write C in the blank.

1. Many short-term missionaries go to the field and teach in a Bible college and learn about the country.

   _____

   _____

2. Short-term missionaries go to the field, and their terms are usually for just a few months or a year or two.

   _____

   _____

3. Short-term missionaries can find it difficult to adjust to the foreign countries; the language is unknown to them.

   _____

   _____

4. Short-term missionaries can go to certain countries; the missionary's native language is spoken by some of the people there, and the language is not as great a barrier.

   _____

   _____

5. Short-term missionaries must do a hard task, which is adjusting to a new culture.

   _____

   _____

6. The food that the missionary must eat can be very different from what he usually eats.

   _____

   _____

7. In Mexico, a missionary might be invited to eat grasshoppers that have been deep fried or partake of fish-head soup or goat-milk cheese.

   _____

   _____

8. A short-term missionary can help full-time missionaries by singing special music in church and being the teacher of a Sunday school class, or a short-term missionary could lead Bible studies.

   _____

   _____

9. Some short-term missionaries do maintenance work, or they can be carpenters.

   _____

   _____

10. There is another ministry that is short term and important; when missionaries need to go home on furlough for a year, they may need a replacement.

   _____

   _____

Sentence Energy

Variety and emphasis are not the only elements that make a sentence come alive for a reader. Vivid verbs, details, accuracy, and figurative language also make sentences and paragraphs that infuse your writing with vitality. More important, these elements help *show* the reader what you are trying to say rather than merely *tell* him.

Action Verbs

As you have read and heard many times before, action verbs are preferred to state-of-being verbs in almost every case. (Remember that not all state-of-being verbs are linking verbs.) When you write or edit, look for state-of-being verbs (especially forms of the verb *be*) that can be replaced with an action verb.

STATE-OF-BEING VERB	After the eruption of Mount St. Helens in 1980, many of the nearby forests *were* no longer intact.
ACTION VERB	The eruption of Mount St. Helens in 1980 *flattened* many of the nearby forests.

Action verbs energize your writing.   tip

Paragraph
Development
p. 337

Details

Energetic writing includes details that provide the reader with enough information to visualize what he is reading. Details should focus primarily on strong nouns and verbs and should engage the five senses: sight, sound, smell, taste, and touch.

FEW DETAILS	Christian radio can reach many places with the gospel.
MORE DETAILS ADDED	Christian radio can reach countries closed to missionaries, remote peoples hard to reach, and nearby islands that have been isolated from the gospel.

Before you begin writing, be sure that you yourself can visualize the situation or scene. You will then be in a position to help the reader do so.

Accuracy

Using the right words in the right way is important for good writing. Sloppy, inaccurate work reflects poorly on you as the writer and makes it difficult for the reader to understand what is being said. There are four categories of accuracy that you should be aware of as you write.

- Accurate Words—Choose words carefully to be sure that you convey the meaning you intend. A dictionary will help you determine shades of meaning, and a thesaurus will help you choose among words with similar meanings.

WRONG WORD	Roshni believed her umbrella to be *imperceptible* to rain.
CORRECTION	Roshni believed her umbrella to be *impervious* to rain.

- Accurate Phrasing—Sometimes whole phrases can be used incorrectly.

INACCURATE PHRASING	Barry was sure his brother would drive him *up the edge* with his impressions.
CORRECTION	Barry was sure his brother would drive him *over the edge* (or *up the wall*) with his impressions.

- Appropriate Connotation—**Connotation** is the suggested or implied meaning of a word, the general usage implications of the word. At times the connotation of a word is as important as what the word refers to, the denotative meaning. Note the following examples:

| INAPPROPRIATE CONNOTATION | The tightrope walker wobbled on the bouncing wire like a *top.* |
| APPROPRIATE CONNOTATION | The tightrope walker wobbled on the bouncing wire like a *toddler learning to walk.* |

- Specific, Concrete Words—Use a specific word instead of a general word if at all possible. Specific words allow the reader to "see" what you are writing.

| GENERAL | From an early age, Wilson wanted to go to college. |
| SPECIFIC | From his sixth birthday onward, Wilson wanted to attend Harvard University. |

Figurative Language

Poetry and Metaphor pp. 141-46

Often the best way to describe something is in terms of something else. **Metaphor** is the general term for these types of comparisons. Metaphors are stated or implied comparisons like the following:

| STATED COMPARISON | Johann is the sophomore class clown. |
| IMPLIED COMPARISON | Pretending to trip on his way into a room is part of Johann's act. |

In the second sentence, the implied comparison is that Johann has a routine that he goes through—much as a clown would.

A **simile** is a comparison that uses *like* or *as* as part of the statement:

> When Johann acts *like a clown,* he gets lots of laughs.

Figurative language like the metaphor and simile can be useful to the writer. However, do not overuse these devices. Metaphor after metaphor in a piece can be distracting or annoying.

Aside from overuse, the most frequent problem with using metaphors is the mixing of metaphors. The mixed metaphor uses two (or more) metaphors when comparing the same object. The resulting confusion—or comedy—distracts from your message.

| MIXED METAPHORS | Sparkling like diamonds, a blanket of snow covered the little town. |

A blanket made of diamonds? Diamonds covering a town? Using the two metaphors to describe the snow is both confusing and ludicrous.

MIXED METAPHORS	Marla *ran out of gas* before gym class, so she *wolfed down* a granola bar between English and history.
POSSIBLE IMPROVEMENTS	Marla *ran out of gas* before gym class, so she *refueled* with a granola bar between English and history.
	Marla *ran out of gas* before gym class, so she *ate* a granola bar between English and history.
	Marla *was hungry* before gym class, so she *wolfed down* a granola bar between English and history.

The improvements either continue the metaphor begun with the phrase *ran out of gas* or use neutral words and phrases in one or both positions. Be aware of metaphorical language that has become so much a part of our normal speech that we no longer think of it as metaphor. The verb *wolfed* is a comparison to a wolf's voracious eating.

PRACTICE *the skill*

Revise the following sentences according to the instructions in parentheses. Restructure the sentence if needed.

1. Missionary work has changed somewhat since the days of the early church. (*Give more details.*)

   _____

   _____

2. For example, some missionaries embark upon the launching of Bible schools to coach national pastors in the work of the Lord. (*Correct the mixed metaphors.*)

   _____

   _____

3. Christian radio stations can be lighthouses in foreign fields. (*Use an action verb.*)

   _____

   _____

   _____

   _____

4. Many also begin printing ministries that make the gospel acceptable in printed form. (*Use a more accurate word.*)

   _____

   _____

   _____

   _____

5. All these are attempts to fulfill the mandate in Matthew 28:19: "Go ye . . . and teach all nations." (*Use an action verb instead of* are.)

   _____

   _____

Revise the following paragraph to add action verbs, details, accuracy, and figurative language.

There is much training involved in becoming a missionary. He usually is a student at a Christian college and is in a degree program such as Christian missions or biblical studies. For most, the training continues in even higher education. Additionally, among peoples where foreign languages are spoken, linguistics training and language school are often needed. Some missionaries also need further study in ancient languages for lands where the translation of the Bible has been limited. Some study medicine, or radio broadcasting, or aviation to complement their ministries. A missionary, then, evolves into a smart person who is indeed "fit for the Master's use."

_____

_____

_____

_____

_____

_____

_____

_____

_____

_____

_____

_____

_____

_____

_____

_____

_____

_____

_____

_____

Sentence Expansion and Reduction

Sometimes in your drafting or editing stage you find that all of your sentences are the same: simple sentence after simple sentence. Sentence expansion and reduction techniques can help you to develop or combine your thoughts. **Sentence expansion** makes a sentence more interesting and shows connections between certain ideas. **Sentence reduction** helps you express information in fewer words. Skilled expansion and reduction will create better flow in your writing.

Expansion of Sentences

Sentence expansion usually involves adding thoughts and ideas to your sentences to make them more interesting and meaningful. Expansion techniques enable the writer to add information and to change the rhythm of a piece of writing. Descriptive phrases and clauses also add interest to sentences that might otherwise be dull and uninspiring.

Using Clauses

Clauses
pp. 91-100

By carefully combining independent and dependent clauses, the writer increases variety, clarity, and sophistication.

An **adjective clause** modifies a noun or pronoun.

> Maximilian was the emperor of Mexico. He was also an archduke of Austria.

> Maximilian was the emperor of Mexico *who was also an archduke of Austria.*

An **adverb clause** usually modifies a verb, but it can also modify an adjective or another adverb.

> He was unpopular with his Mexican subjects. He received the support of Napoleon III.

> *Although he was unpopular with his Mexican subjects,* he received the support of Napoleon III.

A **noun clause** functions as a noun: subject, direct object, and so on.

> Many people realize something about Maximilian. Maximilian was betrayed by one of his own officers.

> Many people realize *that Maximilian was betrayed by one of his own officers.*

Using Phrases

Phrases
pp. 57-77

Descriptive phrases (such as prepositional phrases and verbal phrases) add complexity of meaning and richness of detail.

ORIGINAL SENTENCE	Father pulled the pup from the burning building.
REVISED	With his bare hands Father pulled the pup from the burning building.
ORIGINAL SENTENCE	Tyra sat still.
REVISED	Tyra sat still, bravely facing the swinging door.

The revised sentences are better than the originals; however, you should beware of adding too many descriptive phrases to a sentence. The result may be a convoluted sentence rather than an interesting one.

> Running quickly through the tall grass and remembering the times he had been in trouble with his teacher at school before this, Jordan came upon the lake near the park, and, breathing heavily with some amount of trouble, he fell into the water at the edge.

Sentences like this one are in desperate need of reduction rather than expansion.

PRACTICE *the skill*

Using the words in parentheses, combine the following pairs of sentences by making one of them a dependent clause.

1. All missionaries receive training before they go to the mission field. Sometimes they specialize in learning to translate the Bible into the language of the people to whom they will minister. (*although*)

   _____

   _____

2. Some missionaries decide to become translators. They must have a thorough grasp of how languages work. (*who*)

   _____

   _____

3. As translators, these missionaries will be going to a foreign country. The foreign country will have a language different from the one the missionaries know. (*that*)

   _____

   _____

4. Missionaries need to translate the Bible into one of the languages of the foreign country. They will have to learn that language. (*because*)

   _____

   _____

5. Future translators often must learn the Bible's original languages. The original languages of the Bible are Hebrew, Aramaic, and Greek. (*which*)

   _____

   _____

   _____

6. Most future translators study Hebrew. They discover that Hebrew reads from right to left. (*when*)

   _____

   _____

   _____

7. Hebrew is a difficult language to learn. Most translators find it most helpful to use Hebrew to translate the Old Testament. (*even though*)

_____

_____

_____

8. Aramaic comprises only about one percent of the Old Testament. Many translators do not learn Aramaic. (*since*)

_____

_____

_____

9. Hebrew letters do not recognizably match up with English letters. Many Greek letters correspond to the letters of the English alphabet. (*although*)

_____

_____

_____

10. Missionaries want to be translators. They may take a language aptitude test. (*if*)

_____

_____

_____

Reduction of Sentences

The result of sentence expansion is usually added interest and a clear connection between ideas; however, sometimes the result is too complicated or too lengthy. In those instances, the writer must use sentence reduction techniques to make the writing more clear. Sentence reduction can make a paragraph tighter and more effective—the reader gets to the point more quickly. There are several ways to reduce sentences. The most obvious way is to make a compound sentence a simple sentence with a compound part. Look at the sentence reduction examples below:

> Many waste management sites *process tons of solid waste,* and (they) *employ innovative measures to do so.*
>
> Some of the facilities use compressed natural gas for *waste collection trucks,* and others (will use compressed natural gas) for *electricity.*
>
> Thirteen nationwide glass recycling facilities handle *over 800,000 tons of container glass,* and (they handle) *other kinds of glass as well.*

Most writers complete the kind of reduction process shown above automatically. We delete the repeated word or words and eliminate redundancy. What remains in the first and third examples is a simple sentence with a compound part. The second example ends up with an elliptical second clause (since the subject is still present).

Some dependent clauses can be expressed more briefly by reducing them to phrases. Often a clause can be shortened to a single word—usually an adjective. This reduction technique can greatly reduce wordiness.

Never expand or reduce sentences at the expense of clarity.

Reducing Adjective Clauses

If the subject of an adjective clause is a relative pronoun, you can usually reduce the clause to just a phrase or even a word. Usually, you can drop both the relative-pronoun subject and either the auxiliary *be* or the verb *be,* leaving the rest of the former adjective clause.

Adjective
Clauses
pp. 91-92

Adjective Clause to Prepositional Phrase

An adjective clause that includes a prepositional phrase after a relative pronoun subject and a form of *be* can be reduced to just the prepositional phrase.

Please bring me the sweater ~~that is~~ beside the bed.

Please bring me the sweater beside the bed.

Sometimes an adjective clause with no prepositional phrase can still be reworked into a prepositional phrase.

Anyone who has a cold should bring cough drops.

Anyone with a cold should bring cough drops.

Prepositional
Phrases
pp. 57-59

Adjective Clause to Participle or Participial Phrase

Many adjective clauses can be reduced to simple participles.

The actor bowed to the audience members, ~~who were~~ clapping.

The actor bowed to the clapping audience members.

Adjective clauses can sometimes be reduced to participial phrases.

Those ~~who are~~ making piñatas should bring a bag of candy.

Those making piñatas should bring a bag of candy.

Verbal Phrases
pp. 63-77

Adjective Clause to Single Adjective or Appositive

Any adjective clause that contains a predicate adjective after a relative-pronoun subject and a form of the linking verb *be* can be reduced to the adjective alone.

The audience enjoyed the performance ~~that was~~ lively.

The audience enjoyed the lively performance.

When an adjective clause contains a predicate noun after a relative-pronoun subject and a form of the linking verb *be,* the clause can be reduced to an appositive.

My cousin, ~~who is~~ a costume designer, shops for interesting fabrics.

My cousin, a costume designer, shops for interesting fabrics.

Appositives
pp. 61-62

Punctuation of
Appositives
pp. 276-77

Reducing Adverb Clauses

Although certain clauses should be expressed fully, some adverb clauses can be reduced to simpler structures.

Adverb Clause to Prepositional Phrase

Some adverb clauses can be reduced to prepositional phrases.

of
Because ~~there were~~ special visitors, I chose a back row seat.

Because of special visitors, I chose a back row seat.

Adverb Clauses
pp. 95-96

Adverb Clause to Verbal Phrase

An adverb clause that has the same subject as the main clause and expresses time, cause, or condition may be reducible to a participial phrase.

Being
~~Since we were~~ well prepared, we finished the race easily.

Being well prepared, we finished the race easily.

An adverb clause that expresses the same purpose and has the same subject as the main clause can often be reduced to an infinitive phrase.

to
Danielle and I trained four times a week ~~so that we would~~ be ready for the upcoming race.

Danielle and I trained four times a week to be ready for the upcoming race.

Remember that modifiers should appear as close as possible to the words they modify.

tip

Noun Clauses
pp.99-100

Reducing Noun Clauses

Sometimes a noun clause is reducible to a gerund phrase or an infinitive phrase.

Our decision was [that we would go to Williamsburg].

GERUND | Our decision was *going to Williamsburg.*
INFINITIVE | Our decision was *to go to Williamsburg.*

14.11 PRACTICE *the skill*

Rewrite the following sentences by reducing the italicized clauses to the shorter constructions suggested in parentheses.

1. Isaac Watts, *who was a hymn writer,* wrote the well-known hymn called "Jesus Shall Reign." (*appositive*)

   _____

   _____

2. As the basis for his hymn, Isaac Watts used Scripture *that was relevant.* (*single-word modifier*)

   _____

   _____

3. Watts decided *that he would use* Psalm 72 for his hymn "Jesus Shall Reign." (*infinitive*)

   _____

   _____

4. Psalm 72:15, *which tells about the praise Christ receives every day,* shows up in stanza three: "Endless praises crown His head." (*participial phrase*)

   _____

   _____

5. *Since it focuses on people of all nations worshiping God, "Jesus Shall Reign" reminds us of the importance of missions.* (*participial phrase*)

_____

_____

REVIEW *the skill*

Reduce the following sentences using the techniques discussed in this section.

1. The missions hymn "From Greenland's Icy Mountains" by Reginald Heber focuses on the privilege all believers have that they must take the gospel to the whole world.

_____

_____

2. The places mentioned in the first stanza are Greenland, India, and Africa, which represent the many regions that need the gospel.

_____

_____

3. The second stanza presents the island of Ceylon, which is now called Sri Lanka, as an example of how God uses nature to show Himself to the unsaved.

_____

_____

4. In spite of all the natural beauty of Ceylon, most of the people that are religious are Buddhists and do not believe in Christ.

_____

_____

_____

5. The third stanza of the hymn exhorts believers to carry the message that saves men's souls to the whole world until every nation has heard the gospel.

_____

_____

_____

Parallelism

Parallelism refers to the joining of sentence elements of the same form. Parallel structures should have the same grammatical form and be joined by a coordinating conjunction. Effective use of parallelism helps your writing to flow smoothly and, like subordination, shows the relationship between ideas. The following sentence is acceptable but can be improved by using parallelism.

ACCEPTABLE	Marcelline took French II this year as an elective. Creative writing was another of her electives, and she also took an extra physical education class.
IMPROVED WITH PARALLELISM	Marcelline took French II, creative writing, and an extra physical education class as electives.

Notice that the second version groups three similar things together, making the sentence both shorter and more intelligible.

Parallelism can be overdone—especially if every sentence contains groups of two or three related structures. However, the use of parallel structures can greatly improve your writing.

Three cautions concerning parallelism are in order.

Use Parallelism Only for Parallel Ideas

Many beginning writers make the mistake of using parallelism for ideas that are not truly of the same type.

ILLOGICAL PARALLELISM	Marcelline wants to study French so that she can be a teacher, missionary, or visit France some day.
CORRECTION	Marcelline wants to study French so that she can be a teacher, a missionary, or just a visitor to France some day.

All three parts are now nouns, and each one has its own article.

Sometimes one part of the structure is either more or less general than the other parts.

ILLOGICAL PARALLELISM	The Franklin family checked out travel books about England, France, and European countries.
CORRECTION	The Franklin family checked out travel books about England, France, and other European countries.

Adding the word *other* in the second sentence eliminates the logic problem of having the last item in the series include the other two.

Use the Same Part of Speech

Parts of Speech
pp. 2-22

Parallel structures joined by coordinating conjunctions must be of the same grammatical type. They must also be of the same part of speech.

	S TrV
NOT PARALLEL	The Franklins have read that Germany has an excellent

DO | **DO** | **PA?**
highway system, good public transportation, and enjoyable to visit.

	S TrV
PARALLEL	The Franklins have read that Germany has an excellent high-

DO | **DO**
way system, good public transportation, and enjoyable sightsee-
DO
ing opportunities.

Use the Same Type of Structure

Not only should parallel structures be of the same part of speech, but they should also represent the same type of structure: the same kinds of words or phrases, the same kinds of verbals, or the same kinds of clauses.

Verbal Phrases
pp. 63-77

Kinds of Words or Phrases

Although verbals function as different parts of speech (gerunds act like nouns, participles act like adjectives, and so on), they should not ordinarily be used in parallel structures with those parts of speech.

| NOT PARALLEL | The family will travel extensively for education, pleasure, and witnessing. |
| PARALLEL | The family will travel extensively for education, pleasure, and evangelism. |

---

tip

Use sentence pattern labels to help you determine whether you have used the same type of structure in your sentence.

Note that the first sentence above shows the use of a gerund in a parallel structure with other nouns. The result is a sentence that is not parallel. Sentence two corrects the problem in parallelism by changing the gerund to a regular noun. Another example shows the use of a prepositional phrase with adjectives in a sentence.

| NOT PARALLEL | The Franklins present a program that is earnest and under thirty minutes. |
| PARALLEL | The Franklins present a program that is earnest and brief. |

The second sentence reworks the prepositional phrase into an adjective.

Kinds of Verbals

Just as the writer should not mix parts of speech or kinds of words, he should never mix gerunds, participles, and infinitives in the same construction.

NOT PARALLEL	Nomar grew up in the Caribbean, where he learned snorkeling, to surf, and playing tennis.
PARALLEL	Nomar grew up in the Caribbean, where he learned to snorkel, surf, and play tennis.
	Nomar grew up in the Caribbean, where he learned snorkeling, surfing, and playing tennis.

Phrases and Clauses

Ordinarily, you should not join a phrase and a clause with a coordinating conjunction. Try making the phrase into a clause or the clause into a phrase.

NOT PARALLEL	Nomar learned early the pleasure of serving others and that he could be a real help in his father's church.
PARALLEL	Nomar learned early *that it is rewarding to serve others* and *that he could be a real help in his father's church.*
ALSO ACCEPTABLE	At an early age Nomar learned the joy of *serving others* and of *helping in his father's church.*

Remember that correlative conjunctions such as *both—and* should be used with care. The same kind of structure should follow each of the two words.

| NOT PARALLEL | Nomar both attends the church his father pastors and the school. |
| PARALLEL | Nomar attends both the church his father pastors and the school his father oversees. |

Kinds of Clauses

A dependent clause and an independent clause should not be joined by a coordinating conjunction. Check yourself if you write a sentence with a pair of words like *and which* or *and where*. *And which* requires two *which* clauses, and *and where* requires two *where* clauses.

NOT PARALLEL	They are located at a strategic spot on the island, and where they can walk to nearly everything.
PARALLEL	They are located at a strategic spot on the island, and they can walk to nearly everything.
ALSO ACCEPTABLE	They are located at a strategic spot on the island, where they can walk to nearly everything.

14.13   PRACTICE *the skill*

Rewrite the following sentences, correcting any illogical or incorrect parallelism. If the sentence is already correct, write *C* in the blank.

1. The Apostle Paul endeavored to win souls to Christ and starting churches in each city to which he came.

   _____

   _____

   _____

2. Many missionaries have followed that pattern, and which it is very effective.

   _____

   _____

   _____

3. Another pattern is to head to the field, start one church there, and pastor it for life.

   _____

   _____

   _____

4. Many Christians give the name "church planter" to a missionary who first in one place and then going another place begins churches.

   _____

   _____

   _____

5. This type of missionary wants to start as many churches as possible and to nurture those churches as they grow in Christ.

   _____

   _____

   _____

6. If there is a particular problem in a certain church, and he will probably return there to teach the church what the Bible says about the problem.

_____

_____

_____

7. Bible translators, church planters, and missionaries are needed in the work of Christ.

_____

_____

_____

8. In an area with many languages, a church planter may have a native convert interpret for him, to assist him in various tasks, and acting as his guide.

_____

_____

_____

9. This convert is very valuable in practical matters, in cultural adaptation, in teaching the Word to other converts, and in the ministry.

_____

_____

_____

10. The main differences between the more stationary missionary and the pioneering church planter are the number of miles of travel and the number of churches over which the missionary has oversight.

_____

_____

_____

Sentence Logic

If you have ever read a sentence and asked yourself, "Huh? What is this author talking about?" you have probably been the victim of someone's faulty logic. When the grammatical constructions or the meanings do not fit together quite right, sentences seem illogical. This section of the chapter will help you find ways to correct and improve the logic of your sentences.

Logical Comparisons

When comparing two or more similar things, state the comparison in a clear and logical way. Using the correct forms of the comparative and superlative degrees of adjectives and adverbs is the first way to ensure a logical sentence. The comparative, of course, is used to compare two things whereas the superlative is used when considering three or more things at once.

Things being compared must be separate. That is, one cannot be part of another.

FAULTY COMPARISON	*A Tale of Two Cities* is better than any book I have read.
CORRECTION	*A Tale of Two Cities* is better than any *other* book I have read.

The comparison is illogically stated because *A Tale of Two Cities* is one of the books the speaker has read and as such cannot be compared with itself.

The indefinite pronoun *anyone* is often found in illogical comparisons.

FAULTY COMPARISON	She spoke more clearly than anyone in the debate.
CORRECTION	She spoke more clearly than anyone *else* in the debate.

In the first version of the sentence she was speaking more clearly than herself. The word *else* solves the problem.

Clear Comparisons

Often the second part of a comparison can be understood from the context of the sentence. Look at the following examples.

Miranda writes poetry more than prose. (*more than* she writes *prose*)

Ron has traveled more than Drew. (*more than Drew* has traveled)

It is not only acceptable but also often advisable to leave out the second part of a comparison when it is not needed. However, do not leave out anything that is needed for clarity.

UNCLEAR	Colin e-mails Nancy as much as Barb.

In the sentence above *Barb* could be meant to be either the subject or the direct object of the understood verb *e-mails*. The sentence needs clarification. This can be accomplished by adding the second part of the comparison.

POSSIBLE CORRECTIONS	Colin e-mails Nancy as much as Barb does. Colin e-mails Nancy as much as he e-mails Barb.

Subject Placement

Subjects
pp. 33-34

In order to create a natural flow from one sentence to another, you should make sure that the subjects fit together well. Do not jump around needlessly from one topic to the next within a single paragraph.

POOR PARAGRAPH WITH SUBJECT SHIFTS	Of the many fields that need missionaries, perhaps one of the most neglected fields is the city. The cities of the world contain much of the world's population. People in the cities generally come from a variety of ethnic backgrounds. The languages that these various ethnic groups speak are all different. The differences also extend to the people's cultures. Missionaries have many opportunities to minister to many different kinds of people who need the Lord in the city.
IMPROVED	The cities of the world desperately need missionaries. Besides containing much of the world's population, the cities often have people from a variety of ethnic backgrounds. Each ethnic group speaks its own language and has its own culture practices. Through their large population and various ethnic groups, the cities provide the missionaries with abundant opportunities to minister to people who need the Lord.

Notice that the improved paragraph has only two subjects, *the cities* and *each ethnic group,* as compared with the first paragraph that has six different subjects. The second paragraph has greater coherence and unity because of the greater consistency of subjects.

14.14 PRACTICE *the skill*

Rewrite the following sentences, correcting any sentence logic problems. If the sentence is already correct, write C in the blank.

1. Tokyo has more people than any city in the world.

    _____

    _____

2. The city of Tokyo contains more than twenty-five percent of Japan's population.

    _____

    _____

3. Are you assuming that people in the urban areas need missionaries more than anyone?

    _____

    _____

4. Cities have more people groups than rural areas.

    _____

    _____

5. Maybe you more than anyone should consider being a missionary to a city in North America or abroad.

    _____

    _____

Rewrite the following paragraph to reduce the number of subject shifts.

Both the urban areas of a country as well as its rural areas are mission fields, even though there are many differences between them. Usually the living conditions in the urban areas are more crowded than in the rural areas. The people are easier for the missionary to get to in the urban areas because they all live in a relatively small space as opposed to being spread out in the rural areas. The urban areas might not have as much space as the rural areas to build a church building. Missionaries can obtain supplies more readily if they live in the urban areas. A lot of criminals usually live in the urban areas, so the urban areas have a higher crime rate than the rural areas. In the end, the superficial differences between the urban and the rural areas do not matter because both places need missionaries to tell people of Christ, the Savior of the world.

_____

_____

_____

_____

_____

_____

_____

_____

_____

_____

Biased Language

A Christian communicator must painstakingly avoid giving unnecessary offense to his listeners or readers. The stereotype is the most common type of offense. **Stereotypes** are oversimplified generalizations of persons or events usually based on either ignorance or animosity. These stereotypes mirror and perpetuate unfair and inaccurate prejudices against groups of people. Generalizations that are based solely on age, cultural background, gender, race, or physical characteristics have no place in the Christian's spoken or written communication.

Use caution when making generalizations. **tip**

| STEREOTYPE | He lost his keys—that's just like a man! (Many people lose keys; gender had nothing to do with the loss.) |
| CORRECTION | He lost his keys. |

STEREOTYPE	The teenaged driver slid on the icy overpass. (The problem is inexperience or icy conditions, not the age of the driver.)
CORRECTION	The inexperienced driver slid on the icy overpass.
	The driver slid on the icy overpass.
STEREOTYPE	Like most rich Republicans, she voted for the tax cut. (The sentence implies that Republicans are rich and always vote the same way.)
CORRECTION	Like many other Americans, she voted for the tax cut.
	She voted for the tax cut.

Notice that most of the corrections can be made simply by deleting the biased word or phrase. Being sensitive to others' preferences or limitations will make you a better communicator. The Bible tells us, "The words of a wise man's mouth are gracious" (Eccles. 10:12). Avoiding biased language will help to make your communication more gracious to your audience.

14.16 PRACTICE *the skill*

Underline biased language in the following paragraph. Then rewrite the paragraph, correcting the bias in language and overall tone.

Although Emanuel, the new short-term missionary teacher at the *Escuela de la Ciudad,* had several mistakes typical of youth to overcome, his first year was more or less successful. He did not watch the students in his class closely enough. If he had, certainly many of the problems of the year would have been avoided. But Emanuel grew up in a wealthy North American family, so he could not be expected to understand problems in poorer people's lives. He had trouble relating to the uncouth, rowdy guys of South America and to the quiet students, mostly girls, of course. His support from home remained steady. Especially wonderful were some of the low-class congregations that supported him. They gave very sacrificially. While everything was not, as they say in Spanish, *color de rosa,* Emanuel was able to finish his first year with success and satisfaction.

_____

_____

_____

_____

_____

_____

_____

_____

USE *the skill*

Revise the following paragraph, using all the skills discussed in this chapter.

A hymn that is probably familiar to most Christians, but perhaps not often considered a missions hymn, is A. Katherine Hankey's hymn "I Love to Tell the Story." This hymn says what must be at the heart of every believer if that believer desires to be a missionary. In this hymn, the writer tells her reasons for loving the story. The story has given her joy in life more than anything she has. It is curious what makes her say that the story gives her joy. It is because the story is about Christ. The story could be about another person. The joy would not be the same. The story brings her joy. The story tells what Christ did for her. Christ came to earth. His death on the cross was for her eternal salvation. Then He rose from the grave. She loves the story. She tells the story. She tells the story simply because not everyone knows the story. She tells it because Christians need to be reminded of the riches that they have in Christ. She tells the story because she wants to practice now so that she will be ready to sing it for all of eternity. Hankey loves the story. She tells the story. She values the story. This hymn is a missions hymn.

My flesh and my heart faileth: but God is the strength of my heart, and my portion for ever.

Psalm 73:26

Imagine how it would feel to be the first American female to take the gospel of Christ to a country where most of the people had never even heard the name of Jesus! Ann Judson wanted to remember the details of her experience herself in later years, and she wanted to leave a record of it for others. How do you think she felt? Nervous? Excited? Sad? Brave? Fearful? Lonely? Her emotions were probably a mixture of all of these. She was leaving the only life she had ever known—family, friends, homeland—for a complete unknown, a life she correctly believed would bring hardship, danger, and perhaps an early death. As we read her journal, we see the tension between what she was feeling and what she knew to be true from God's Word. Only through a disciplined turning of her thoughts to Christ and His sacrifice—the reason for her own sacrifice—was she able to find peace. Only through thinking of the people she must reach rather than of herself was her anxious mind quieted.

A journal can be a private place to record your thoughts. It can also be a starting place for a more formal or public piece of writing. As you record your impressions in a loose, unstructured format, you will begin to see serious themes emerging. Which of your ideas would you like to explore and develop further?

Keep a journal over a period of two weeks. You decide what the content will be and in what format you will record your thoughts. Notice that journal entries don't have to be long; Ann Judson's entries varied in length, and some were quite short. Try to write fluidly, without a lot of long pauses for thought. Make sure to spend at least ten to fifteen minutes writing in the journal each day. At the end of the two weeks, select five entries to be rewritten and turned in.

Planning

✔ **Choose a place in which to record your journal entries.** The book or notebook in which you record your thoughts should be one that you like and that you will want to take along with you to school, on a bus, in the car, on vacation, to the park, and so on. Select a size that you are comfortable carrying and a cover that interests you. You could even make your own cover. Choose lined or unlined paper according to what you prefer.

✔ **Decide whether you will include sections.** Some journalists enjoy dividing their journals into sections that might include a reading response area, a writing idea area, and a place to record daily events. Other journalists prefer to write strictly chronologically. Decide beforehand which method you prefer.

✔ **Seek writing inspiration.** For the journal, you should draw directly from your own personal experience. You may choose to write in your journal in the evening, reflecting on various events of the day. What one thing from your day stands out to you the most? Did you find out some good news? Did you meet anyone new? Is there something on your mind that you don't want to tell anyone? The journal is a good place to explore your thoughts and to think through and respond to issues. What areas were you successful in? Was there anything you could have done better? Did you learn any important lessons? How did the Lord reveal Himself to you throughout the day? Did you see any answers to prayer?

Thinking Biblically

Psalm 119, an autobiographical poem consisting of twenty-two stanzas, is a kind of journal. Each stanza functions in a way similar to a journal entry as the author unfolds his life's story. He begins by recording his decision to live in obedience to God's Word (vv. 1-8). In a later stanza he expresses sorrow for failing to live up to that decision (vv. 25-32). In time he matures and thanks God for enabling him to grow spiritually through the Scriptures (vv. 65-72). This psalm, however, is different from most journals because it is written as a prayer to God. Psalm 119 is an encouragement to Christians to consider writing their own journals as prayers. Instead of heading an entry "Dear Diary," a Christian may wish to use the greeting, "Dear God." If a Christian writes his entries to God, his journaling will strengthen not only his writing skill but also his prayer life. As the years pass, he will have much more than a record of his life. He will have an intimate account of God's faithfulness in guiding his life and answering his prayers.

tip

Perhaps begin your journal with a brief history of yourself. Tell where you were born, what your family is like, what you like to do, and so on.

✔ **Remember that you are your own audience.** You are writing to yourself now and to your future self. Someday you may want to remember what it was like to be in high school. Be specific and include lots of details so that later—even ten years from now—you will vividly remember what you were writing about.

tip

Include newspaper clippings, photographs, postcards, and drawings that are a part of your memories.

✔ **Think about your goals for journaling.** A journal can be a record of events. It can be the place you express your thoughts and feelings. It can be a record of your spiritual growth and struggles. In reality, it will most likely be all these. Think about what you will want to remember in years to come.

Drafting

✔ **Date your entries.** Dated entries will help you remember the chronology of events when you look back on your journal in a few years. If you make more than one entry in a day, include the time of day too.

✔ **Consider including the circumstances of your writing.** You can tell where you are physically and what has prompted you to write. Did something just happen that you don't want to forget? Did you just have a great idea? The more specific and detailed your entries are, the easier it will be for you to remember the significance of the moments you are recording.

✔ **Begin writing.** Find an environment that does not distract you. Spend a few minutes thinking about what you would like to record. Record your responses to a current political situation or a community event. Tell your feelings about what is going on and what you think should be done differently. Years from now someone may read your account as history.

Tell a story from your point of view. Talk about something that interests you—a hobby, a book, a lesson. Describe something unusual you saw. Write about your friends—how you met, what you do together, some of your favorite memories with them. Describe your family members and family traditions. Tell what you are learning in your devotions. Write about something you heard in a sermon.

✔ **Be relaxed but never unrestrained.** There is always the possibility that someone will read your journal. Write honestly, but use discretion. God is always a part of your audience, so be sure what you write is pleasing to Him.

✔ **Allow for peer response.** After you select entries to turn in, copy them and ask a few classmates to read them. What did they like? What could you work on?

Revising

✔ **Reread your entries.** Read your entry while the details of the events are still fresh. Be sure you have been accurate and have not left out anything important.

✔ **Structure your entry if you plan to publish.** Of course, most of your journal entries will remain private—for your eyes alone. However, if you decide to develop an entry further, you will need to organize your ideas more strictly than you may have in your journal. Journal writing should be more fluid, but more formal writing needs structure to aid in clear communication of your thoughts.

✔ **Look at your entry through someone else's eyes.** Are the essential facts clear from your entry? Will someone who doesn't know you or the situation be able to understand what is going on? If there are weak areas, take time to go back and fill them in so you have a concrete, vivid entry.

✔ **Proofread your piece.** Read your entries aloud. Then check the mechanics—punctuation, grammar, and spelling.

Publishing

✔ **Develop an entry.** Select an entry (or part of an entry) that you would like to explore more fully. Develop that idea in several paragraphs. Make a copy of the journal entry you drew from and staple it to a copy of what you wrote.

✔ **Make a collection of one entry from each student in your class.** Select your most interesting entry. Or every student could submit an entry from the same day. The collection could be titled "A Day in the Lives of Sophomores."

Some Ideas to Consider

Politics
- What are the current issues? What do you think about them?
- What bills are being discussed? How will they affect your future?

Education
- What do you think is the purpose for education?

HISTORY OF THE ENGLISH LANGUAGE

Language Families

We have seen that the first language differences were caused directly by God at the Tower of Babel. As people multiplied and scattered and as language changed over a period of time, these first languages were used in different ways. The local varieties, known as dialects, eventually became different enough to be called separate languages. Today, the languages that have come from any one of the first languages make up what linguists call a language family. The Indo-European family, for example, came from one of the first languages. It includes many "descendants," as you can see from the chart on page 353.

The Indo-European family is only one of the many language families of the world. For instance, Tagalog is a Philippine language in the Malayo-Polynesian family. Hebrew and Arabic are in the Semitic family, which is part of the large Afro-Asiatic family of North Africa and the Middle East. Although the Indo-European family is just one of many language families, its languages are now spoken by nearly half the people in the world.

The Indo-European language chart shows how close English and German are. They both developed from the Western variety of the unwritten Germanic language. Barbarian tribes—sometimes raiders and plunderers—who lived mostly in northwestern Europe, spoke this language. Because of their common heritage, English and German have clear similarities in many of their basic words.

The Organization of the Library

Resources in a library are usually organized into several sections. The largest is usually the main section of bookshelves, which is called the **stacks.** Another major division of the library is the **periodicals.** Many libraries have separate periodical rooms for both research and leisurely reading. The **reference** section contains encyclopedias and other materials that cannot be checked out of the library. Many libraries offer various **audio-visual** materials, and some libraries offer other **special sections** such as a collection of rare books. A common one is a local-interests section that contains historical documents from your city or state. Many of these materials carry a special label that indicates the library section to which they belong.

Kinds of Material	Examples	Label
Books	fiction and nonfiction books, both hardcover and paperback	
Periodicals	newspapers, magazines, microfiche, microfilm, and journals	PER
Audio-Visual Materials	audiocassettes, CDs, videocassettes, filmstrips, works of art, puppets, and games	AV
Reference	encyclopedias and other noncirculating materials that can be used only in the library	R or REF
Children / Young Adult	books, periodicals, and audio-visual materials designed especially for children or teens	J or JUV (juvenile) or YA
Special Sections	local interests, genealogy rooms, rare books	

The Arrangement of Books

Parts of a Book
pp. 412-15

Fiction

Fiction books are shelved alphabetically according to the author's last name. If two or more authors have the same last name, their books are arranged alphabetically by the authors' first names. If a library has more than one book by the same author, that author's books are arranged alphabetically according to the first words of the titles (not including *A, An,* or *The*). The list below shows the order in which these books would appear on a library shelf.

> Cather, Willa. *O Pioneers!*
> Chute, B. J. *The Fields Are White*
> Chute, B. J. *Greenwillow*
> Chute, Marchette. *The Innocent Wayfaring*
> Collins, Wilkie. *The Moonstone*

Some libraries separate certain kinds of fiction books from the rest of the fiction collection. For example, a library may have separate shelves for mystery fiction, science fiction, or westerns. The book spines are usually marked with letters that indicate that special section, such as *MYS* for mystery fiction. Also, paperback fiction books may be separated from the hardcover books. Paperback books are usually marked with the letters *PB*.

Nonfiction

Nonfiction books are arranged by topic. Almost all libraries organize nonfiction books according to one of two classification systems: the **Dewey decimal system** and the **Library of Congress system.**

Dewey Decimal System

The **Dewey decimal system** is named for its creator, American librarian Melvil Dewey (1851-1931). This system gives every nonfiction book a number according to its subject matter. This number appears on the spine of the book and in the library catalog. Here are the ten major classifications in the Dewey decimal system.

Number	Category	Examples
000-099	Generalities	encyclopedias, general reference works, computing, journalism
100-199	Philosophy and psychology	logic, ethics
200-299	Religion	theology, denominations
300-399	Social sciences	economics, education, etiquette
400-499	Language	linguistics
500-599	Natural sciences and mathematics	astronomy, chemistry, botany
600-699	Technology (applied sciences)	medicine, engineering, home economics
700-799	The arts	architecture, photography, music, sports
800-899	Literature and rhetoric	novels, short stories, plays
900-999	Geography and history	travel, biography

Thinking Biblically

"The earth is the Lord's, and the fulness thereof; the world, and they that dwell therein" (Psalm 24:1). This world belongs to God, and Christians are to show others that this is so. Libraries contain a wealth of information about God's world. Most of this information is not directly connected to God and what He is doing in the world, but believers can—and should—learn to see this information in a Christian way. Of course, a believer cannot begin to do this unless he knows the Bible well. That's one reason that Bible is an important subject in Christian education. But a Christian also needs to know his way around the library. That's the reason this chapter is very important. Suppose a friend said, "The Bible can't be trusted because it talks about people who didn't exist. I've heard that Belshazzar—the king of Babylon in Daniel 5—never lived." Could you use the library and what you've learned in Bible class to respond to this claim?

The Dewey system is called a decimal system because it is based on divisions of ten. Each division can be divided by ten as many times as necessary. For instance, here are the ten divisions within the 600 division.

600-609	General technology	650-659	Management
610-619	Medical sciences and medicine	660-669	Chemical engineering
620-629	Engineering	670-679	Manufacturing
630-639	Agriculture and related technologies	680-689	Manufacture for specific use
640-649	Home economics and family living	690-699	Buildings

Each subdivision can be further divided. The number 636, animal husbandry, is a subdivision of 630, agriculture and related technologies. Further levels of subdivision use a decimal point: 636.7 indicates dogs, and 636.73 indicates dogs for the blind.

The 900s division includes **biography,** but some libraries separate the biographies and autobiographies from the other nonfiction books and shelve them in a separate area. A capital letter *B* or the Dewey decimal number *920* on the spine of a book indicates that the book is a biography or autobiography. These books are arranged alphabetically by the last name of the subject, not the author. For example, Courtney Anderson's biography of Adoniram Judson would be shelved under *J,* not *A.* Other libraries shelve biographies with the appropriate subject area. A biography of a philosopher would be shelved in the 100s with the other books about philosophy.

Under a book's Dewey decimal number is a number that identifies the book by its author or perhaps by one or more letters of its title. This number is called the Cutter number. The **Dewey decimal number** and the **Cutter number** together make up the **call number** of the book.

Library of Congress System

Some large libraries use the **Library of Congress system** instead of the Dewey decimal system. The Library of Congress system uses a combination of letters and numbers to classify books. There are twenty-one basic categories in the Library of Congress system.

A	General works	M	Music and books on music
B	Philosophy, psychology, religion	N	Fine Arts
C	Auxiliary sciences of history (such as archaeology, genealogy, biography)	P	Language and literature
D	History: general and old world	Q	Science
E	History: America	R	Medicine
F	History: America (local)	S	Agriculture
G	Geography, anthropology, recreation	T	Technology
H	Social sciences	U	Military science
J	Political science	V	Naval science
K	Law	Z	Library science
L	Education		

PRACTICE *the skill*

Answer the following questions about the library.

1. Which section of the library contains the books?

   _____

2. Which section of the library contains the materials that may not be checked out of the library?

   _____

3. How are fiction books shelved when two or more authors have the same last name?

   _____

4. How many major divisions does the Dewey decimal system have?

   _____

5. Why is the Dewey decimal system called a decimal system?

   _____

6. In the Dewey decimal system, what two main ways can biographies and autobiographies be classified?

   _____

7. How are biographies alphabetized?

   _____

8. In the Dewey decimal system, what two numbers make up the call number of a book?

   _____

9. Which system for organizing nonfiction books uses a combination of letters and numbers?

   _____

10. How many categories does the Library of Congress system have?

    _____

REVIEW *the skill*

Using the Dewey decimal chart on page 398, write the number range of the correct category for each of the following books.

_____ 1. *Church Councils and Their Dates*

_____ 2. *Fossils in Focus*

_____ 3. *Inside Africa*

_____ 4. *Aesthetics and Technology in Building*

_____ 5. *The Income of Nations and Persons*

_____ 6. *World Book Encyclopedia*

_____ 7. *Wild Animals of the World*

_____ 8. *Spanish Thought and Letters in the Twentieth Century*

_____ 9. *Two Models of Grammatical Description*

_____ 10. *Ergonomics at Work*

_____ 11. *Critical Thinking*

_____ 12. *Latin America: the Development of Its Civilization*

_____ 13. *Megachurches and America's Cities*

_____ 14. *Negotiating the Maze of School Reform*

_____ 15. *The Molecules Within Us: Our Body in Health and Disease*

Where Do I Start?

Now that you are familiar with the different sections of the library and you understand the organization of the library, you need to know how to use the resources available to you. Whether you are working on a school project or a personal project, following these steps will help you get the most from your library.

The Library Website

Many libraries maintain a website that gives information about the library's hours, policies, and resources. Using the website, you may be able to renew books, request books for interlibrary loan, or e-mail reference questions to the library staff. The website will probably tell you about specific resources that a particular library offers and give you a schedule of special events and classes taking place at the library.

Webpage Design pp. 207-12

The Catalog

Online catalog

Usually the best place to start your research is the library catalog. Most libraries today have an **online catalog,** sometimes called **OPAC** (online public access catalog). Many public libraries allow patrons to access their computer catalogs from home through the Internet. An online catalog contains electronic records for each book. Each record includes the title, the author, the place of publication, the date of publication, the publisher, the number of pages, and the call number (for a nonfiction book). Many electronic records include a summary of the book, and almost all computer catalogs include each book's status. The status information will tell you whether the book is currently available, reserved for another patron, or already checked out. It may even tell you when the book is due to be returned to the library.

You can search the online catalog by typing in the author, the title, or the subject of the book you want. The computer will begin to search for the book by comparing the words you typed to the information in its database. When it finds a match, the screen will display the record. If you search by subject, the screen may display several lines of more specific subjects. For example, if your search word is *dogs*, more specific lines may include the following: dogs—breeds, dogs—diseases, dogs—grooming. To view books in a given subject area, type the number displayed next to that entry. To see the record for an individual book, type the number displayed next to that entry or click on it. If you want more information about the book, you may need to type or click on an additional command, such as *F* for *full title record*.

MATERIAL: Book

CALL NUMBER: 636.7 Am 35c

date of publication

AUTHOR: American Kennel Club

publisher

TITLE: The complete dog book: the photograph, history, and official standard of every breed admitted to AKC registration, and the selection, training, breeding, care, and feeding of pure-bred dogs.

city of publication

EDITION: 15th ed.

number of pages

PUBLICATION: New York: Howell Book House, 1975.

contains illustrations

DESCRIPTION: 672 p., ill.; 24 cm

NOTES: "Breed standards corrected to May 1, 1975."

height of book's spine

SUBJECT: dogs

Card catalog

A **card catalog** is a cabinet with small drawers filled with cards containing information on each book in the library. Like the online catalog, the card catalog can be searched by author, title, or subject. The cards for all of these categories are usually alphabetized together. Each kind of card has a different top line: the author card starts with the author, the title card starts with the title, and the subject card starts with the subject. Each card includes the title, the author, the place of publication, the date of publication, the publisher, the number of pages, and the call number (for a nonfiction book).

PRACTICE *the skill*

Using the catalog entry below, answer the following questions.

MATERIAL: Book
CALL NUMBER: 917.4 R248
AUTHOR: Redington, Robert J.
TITLE: Survey of the Appalachians
EDITION: 1st ed.
PUBLICATION: South Egremont, Mass.: Taconic Publishers, c1978.
DESCRIPTION: 132 p., ill., maps (2 fold. in pocket); 22 cm
NOTES: Bibliography: p. 130-32
SUBJECT: Appalachian Mountains

1. What is the complete title of the book?

   _____

2. What company published the book?

   _____

3. What is the book's call number?

   _____

4. Where was the book published?

   _____

5. What year was the book published?

   _____

6. Does the book include illustrations? How do you know?

   _____

7. How would you find other books by the same author using the computer catalog?

   _____

8. What is the author's name?

   _____

9. Under what subject would you find other books on the same topic?

   _____

10. Does the book contain a list of sources that the author used? How do you know?

    _____

REVIEW *the skill*

Using a library's catalog, find at least one book for each of the following topics. List the title, the author, and the call number for each book.

1. Jury system

_____

_____

2. Creationism

_____

_____

3. Bilingual education

_____

_____

4. Crown jewels

_____

_____

5. Economic geography

_____

_____

6. Radio advertising

_____

_____

7. Birth order

_____

_____

8. Papermaking

_____

_____

9. Jewish history

_____

_____

10. Malaria diagnosis

_____

_____

Finding Reference Materials

There are several methods you can use to find reference materials—in the library or even from home.

Gathering Information pp. 258, 329-30

- Use the online catalog or card catalog to locate reference materials related to a topic. Reference resources will appear with the label *R* or *REF*. These materials will be located in the reference section of the library.

- Browse the reference section for resources related to a topic. For example, if you were doing a research project on Mark Twain, you might notice that many of the sources have call numbers with Dewey decimal numbers beginning with 817 and 818. Instead of writing down all of the entries you find, you may want simply to browse this section for related materials.

- Look for bibliographies in the reference materials. Many good reference books will give you a listing of excellent resources for further study.

- Use online reference materials. Several important reference materials are now online, and using them can save you time. Find out what online reference materials your library offers.

- See "Special Reference Tools" on pages 405-7 for a list of important reference materials that may be helpful in your research.

Finding Books

These methods will help you find books on particular topics.

- Use the online catalog or card catalog to locate books related to a topic. Write down the call numbers of books that can possibly be helpful in your research. The location of a book may be designated as *stacks* (the main section of bookshelves in a library). After you have located a particular book, browse the shelf where it is located for similar books that might be helpful.

- Find the section of the stacks that covers a topic of interest to you (check the classification table that your library uses and then find the shelves labeled with the relevant number or letter). Then simply browse the stacks for books that look helpful.

- Use online resources. Many works are now available online as electronic texts. Locating poems and other short works online may be faster than searching for a particular work in a book. For example, the Project Gutenberg website contains texts of over 20,000 ebooks in the public domain.

Finding Periodicals

Finding an article in a periodical usually requires using one of several special reference tools.

- Use **periodical indexes.** The library catalogs will help you find books and audio-visual materials, but they will probably not help you find specific articles in magazines or newspapers. To find relevant articles, you need to consult periodical indexes. Remember to read the introduction to the index for the list of magazines indexed and the directions for understanding entries.

- Use the *Readers' Guide to Periodical Literature*. This is the most generally useful periodical index. It lists articles from over two hundred magazines by subject and by author. An online version of the *Readers' Guide* is also available. The index is updated regularly throughout the year. Soon after publication, articles are listed in one of the paperback volumes issued during the year. At the end of each year, these volumes are combined and reissued in a single large volume.

  To find an article about a particular subject, look up the keyword. Under the subject heading, you may find "See also" entries that suggest related subject headings. Each individual entry includes the article's subject, its title, its author, the magazine in which it appears, the volume number or date of the magazine, and the page numbers of the article. If the article has illustrations, the entry will include that information too. The listings use several abbreviations explained in the front of each volume.

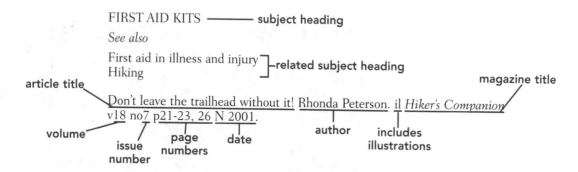

- Use the *New York Times Index*. Most public libraries subscribe to several newspapers. In addition to local newspapers, many libraries also carry the *New York Times* and its index, both of which are available in print and electronic versions. The *New York Times Index* lists articles that have appeared in that newspaper only. However, it can assist your search for information in back issues of other newspapers as well as the *New York Times* since it will help you discover the dates of newsworthy events.

- Use **subject indexes.** If you need detailed information about a particular subject, you may want to check other periodical indexes. Examples of other indexes include the *Social Sciences Index* and the *Humanities Index,* both of which cover scholarly journals in certain fields of study.

- Use **online databases**. Some libraries have online databases indexing the entire archives of certain periodicals. These databases are easily searched electonically and yield summaries or full texts of articles. Articles only summarized can be obtained from the library's collection or through interlibrary loan.

Finding Information on the World Wide Web

The Internet, especially the World Wide Web, is a rich source of information. Use these techniques to find the specific information that you need.

Webpage
Design
pp. 207-12

- Use a good Web search tool. When you are connected to the World Wide Web, you can access several search engines and search directories. A search directory contains a large base of websites categorized by subject. When you type in a subject, the search directory looks for sites related to your subject. A search engine uses the keyword that you typed and actually searches the Web for sites that contains those words. For example, if you type the word *schools,* a search directory will give you sites that are about schools or related to schools. A search engine will give you sites that actually contain the word *schools.* Some search tools employ a combination of the search directory and the search engine.

- Limit your search query. When conducting a keyword search, most search tools recognize certain terms and symbols. There are some terms and symbols that are common among many search tools.

Boolean

Use AND when you want both terms to be in the site. (Use all capital letters for these terms.)

Use NEAR when you want the first term to appear within a few words of the second term.

Use OR when you want at least one term to appear in the site.

Use NOT when you want sites that do not contain that term.

> **EXAMPLE** | dogs AND breeds NOT grooming

Plus/Minus

Use a plus sign [+] before a term if you want sites that contain that term.

Use a minus sign [-] before a term if you want sites that do not include that term.

> **EXAMPLE** | +dogs+breeds-grooming

Phrases

Use quotation marks around a phrase to search for an exact phrase or similar phrase.

> **EXAMPLE** | "breeds of dogs"

- Evaluate information you find on the Web. The Web contains a great deal of useful information, but it also contains a large amount of unreliable information. Before you use information on the Web, evaluate the sites based on these standards.

AUTHORSHIP	Is it signed? Any site with no author listed is unreliable.
AUTHORITY	Is the author an authority on the subject? Was the site created by a trustworthy organization?
CURRENCY	When was the site created and has it been updated recently? An old site or a site without a date posted is likely to be unreliable.
BIAS	Many Internet sites contain strong bias. For example, a political site with strong partisan views may not be able to provide you with unbiased information about political history.

PRACTICE *the skill*

Answer the following questions about finding information.

1. List the three ways to search for reference materials and books.

2. Which periodical index is the most generally useful periodical index?

3. What periodical index would help you discover the dates of newsworthy events?

4. What are two examples of other helpful periodical indexes?

5. Assuming that you want at least one of the following terms to appear in a site on the World Wide Web, write out a Boolean search query for the terms *cat, leopard, panther.*

6. Assuming that you want your first term, *eagle,* to appear within a few words of the second term, *endangered species,* in a site on the World Wide Web, write out a Boolean search query using these two terms.

7. Assuming that you want all three of your terms, *black bear, polar bear, brown bear,* to appear in a site on the World Wide Web, write out a Boolean search query using these three terms.

8. Assuming that you do not want the word *experimentation* to appear in a site on the World Wide Web, write out a plus/minus search query for the terms *rat, mouse, experimentation.*

9. Write out the phrase *save the animals* as you would type it to do a phrase search query on the World Wide Web.

10. What are the four criteria you should use to evaluate sites on the World Wide Web?

Use the following entry from the *Readers' Guide to Periodical Literature* to answer each question.

SALT WATER FISHING

Fishing off the Great Barrier Reef. Tim McManus *Outdoor Leisure* v105 no4 p56-63 My 2008.

1. What is the title of the article?

   _____

2. When was the article published?

   _____

3. What is the subject heading under which the article is listed?

   _____

4. On what page of the magazine does the article end?

   _____

5. What is the title of the magazine in which the article appears?

   _____

6. What is the number of the issue in which the article appears?

   _____

7. Who is the author of the article?

   _____

8. An article can be located in what two ways?

   _____

9. How could you find other articles by the same author?

   _____

10. What is another subject heading that could be searched for related topics?

   _____

USE *the skill*

Use the resources you have been learning about to answer the following questions.

1. Use the online catalog or card catalog to look up the keyword *buffalo* and write down two general reference books and one bibliography reference book relating to this topic.

   _____

   _____

2. Use the online catalog or card catalog to look up the keywords *wildlife preservation* and write down call numbers for three books relating to this topic.

   _____

   _____

3. Use the online catalog or card catalog to look up the keyword *bird* and write down three periodicals related to this topic.

   _____

   _____

4. Using the *Readers' Guide to Periodical Literature,* look up the keyword *bison* and write down the first entry.

   _____

   _____

5. Using the *New York Times Index,* look up the keyword *environment* and write down one article relating to this topic.

   _____

   _____

6. On the World Wide Web, do a Boolean search using the terms *mountain lion, jaguar, extinction* with the word NOT and write down the top three hits.

   _____

   _____

   _____

7. On the World Wide Web, do a Boolean search using the terms *deer, gazelle, elk* and the word OR and write down the top three hits.

   _____

   _____

   _____

8. On the World Wide Web, do a Boolean search using the terms *wolf, dog, coyote* with the word AND and write down the top three hits and their authors (or indicate the lack of authors).

_____

_____

9. On the World Wide Web, do a plus/minus search using the terms *fish, license, season,* write down the top three hits, and indicate whether the author of the site is an authority on the subject.

_____

_____

10. On the World Wide Web, do a phrase search for *Yellowstone National Park;* then write down the top three hits and indicate the date each site was posted on the Web.

_____

_____

Special Reference Tools

Almanacs and Yearbooks

Both almanacs and yearbooks supplement encyclopedias by giving current information about statistics and recent events. Most almanacs, and all yearbooks, are published every year.

Almanacs include tables of weights and measures, lists of sports statistics, names of award winners, information about government agencies and programs, summaries of recent events, and other facts. You can find the information you need by looking in the almanac's index, which may appear at the front of the book like a table of contents.

Yearbooks tend to concentrate on special subjects. For instance, the *Year Book of Sports Medicine* includes information on topics such as treating athletic injuries, and the *Supreme Court Yearbook* has summaries of every decision made by the Supreme Court that year.

Atlases and Gazetteers

Atlases are books of collected maps. Most atlases also contain information about weather, geography, population, and other statistics. The index lists the page number for each map in the collection. **Gazetteers** are indexes of place names. Some gazetteers include additional information, such as elevation or population, for each place listed.

Bible Commentaries and Concordances

Bible commentaries are verse-by-verse or section-by-section explanations of Scripture. Some commentaries cover individual books of the Bible; longer works cover the entire Bible.

Bible concordances are alphabetical indexes to the words of the Bible. They are helpful for locating a passage and sometimes for studying a subject through the Bible. Some concordances include the Hebrew or Greek word from which the English word was translated. When you can remember only part of a verse, look up an important word from the verse in the alphabetical list. If the particular passage you want is not listed, try another keyword. Not all keywords or passages will appear in every concordance.

Some commentaries and concordances are available in electronic versions, which make searching the Scriptures even easier. Finding all the occurrences of a particular word or phrase in a printed concordance would be time consuming. But with an electronic version, your search would take only a few seconds.

Biographical Sources

In addition to book-length biographies of particular people, the library contains a number of sources for more concise biographical information. Prominent people living today appear in **biographical dictionaries,** such as *Current Biography, Contemporary Authors,* and the various *Who's Who* publications. Persons no longer living may be described in older editions of these works and in sources such as the *Dictionary of American Biography* and the British *Dictionary of National Biography.* Most of these sources are arranged alphabetically by the subject's last name; some of the multivolume works may be arranged alphabetically within chronologically arranged sections. Check the index to find the pages that discuss the person you are researching.

Dictionaries

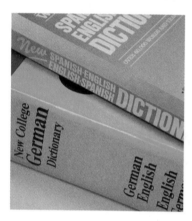

Dictionaries contain a wealth of helpful information about words and languages. Large **unabridged dictionaries** contain several hundred thousand words. Abridged dictionaries, or **desk dictionaries,** are much shorter, but even they contain thousands of words, usually all the words we use on a regular basis. **Special-purpose dictionaries** include Bible dictionaries, dictionaries of synonyms, foreign language dictionaries, and dictionaries of subjects like sports or the sciences. Some dictionaries are available in both printed and electronic versions.

Finding the Word

The **entry words** are arranged alphabetically according to each letter in the entry, whether it is one or more words. **Guide words** at the top of each page indicate the first and last words included on that page.

Understanding the Entry

The **pronunciation,** a respelling that indicates how to pronounce the word, usually appears right after the entry word itself. Some words have two or more different acceptable pronunciations. The introduction to the dictionary will explain which pronunciation is the preferred one.

One entry word may be able to function as several different parts of speech. Each **part of speech label** is listed with the definition to which it applies. For example, the word *read* can function as a noun or as a verb. Dictionaries usually classify verb meanings into two groups. Transitive verb meanings are labeled *tr.* (or *v.tr.* or *vt*). Intransitive verb and linking verb meanings are both labeled *intr.* (or *v.intr.* or *vi*). Every verb has at least one of these labels along with its meaning or meanings.

The entry may also include **inflected forms,** words that differ from the main entry because of the addition of suffixes or because of other changes. Inflected forms include irregular plural forms of nouns, certain verb forms, and comparative and superlative forms of modifiers. Some dictionaries also include **related words** at the end of the entry, such as the adjective *botanical* at the end of the entry for the noun *botany.*

If a word can be spelled correctly more than one way, the entry will include the **variant spellings**, including hyphenation. The correct **capitalization** will also be indicated.

If a word has more than one **definition**, each definition will be listed and numbered. The entry may also list **synonyms** (words with the same or similar meaning).

Most entries will include an **etymology.** An etymology is the history of the word, including the language from which it came originally. The abbreviations for the languages are explained in the front of the dictionary.

Certain entry words will also have **usage labels.** Usage labels point out special areas of meaning. A **field label** points out a definition that applies to a particular field, such as music or biology. A **stylistic label** limits a word or a definition to a particular usage level, such as *informal* or *obsolete.*

Spelling
pp. 430-33

Hyphens
p. 308-9

Capitalization
pp. 240-53

History of
the English
Language
pp. 352-53

Encyclopedias

Encyclopedias contain articles that give brief introductions to many subjects. Most major encyclopedias are available in both print and electronic formats. Some are available on the Internet. Electronic versions usually offer keyword-searching options.

Printed encyclopedias usually consist of several volumes, each labeled with one or more letters and a numeral. The articles are arranged alphabetically. Guide words at the top of the page tell you the topic of the first article on that page. Information on some subjects may be included in several different articles. The index lists all the pages that contain information on a particular subject. Some encyclopedias have an index in each volume; others have a separate volume (usually the last volume) that is the index for the entire set. Many encyclopedia articles list cross-references to other related articles under a heading such as "See also."

Indexes

Indexes are listings that make it easy to find information. Most useful are the periodical indexes. In addition to the *Readers' Guide,* useful indexes include *Book Review Index, Essays and General Literature Index,* and **books of quotations** such as *Bartlett's Familiar Quotations.* A book of quotations allows you to find a famous quotation by looking up its author, a keyword, or the topic. Most books of quotations also list each quotation's original source and date.

Thesauruses

A **thesaurus** is a treasury of synonyms and antonyms. Some thesauruses list the main words alphabetically, while others group all words by meaning, directing you to the meaning groups from a detailed index in the back. In either case, you choose a synonym included in the words you find listed. A dictionary and a thesaurus are often well used together—the thesaurus to help you think of a word and the dictionary to confirm that the word is in fact the one you need.

PRACTICE *the skill*

Write the letter of the reference tool you would use to find the answer to each question.

A. almanac or yearbook
B. atlas or gazetteer
C. Bible commentary
D. book of quotations
E. biographical dictionary
F. desk dictionary
G. special-purpose dictionary
H. encyclopedia
I. index
J. thesaurus

_____ 1. What is a synonym for the word *deliver*?

_____ 2. What is the Latin word from which we get the English word *creed*?

_____ 3. What is the name of the bay between India and Burma?

_____ 4. What Major League Baseball team won the American League pennant in 1987?

_____ 5. To what event in Jesus Christ's life would some people say Psalm 2:7 applies?

_____ 6. What is Emily Dickinson's birth date?

_____ 7. What does the word *approbation* mean?

_____ 8. What magazine includes an article about butterflies?

_____ 9. What are some quotations from Alexis de Tocqueville's *Democracy in America*?

_____ 10. What is the population density of Panama?

USE *the skill*

Using the sources you identified in Practice 15.8, answer the following questions.

1. What is a synonym for the word *deliver*?

_____

2. What is the Latin word from which we get the English word *creed*?

_____

3. What is the name of the bay between India and Burma?

_____

4. What Major League Baseball team won the American League pennant in 1987?

_____

5. To what event in Jesus Christ's life would some people say Psalm 2:7 applies?

_____

6. What is Emily Dickinson's birth date?

_____

7. What does the word *approbation* mean?

_____

8. What magazine contains an article about butterflies?

_____

9. What are some quotations from Alexis de Tocqueville's *Democracy in America?*

_____

10. What is the population density of Panama?

_____

HISTORY OF THE ENGLISH LANGUAGE

A Developing Language

The three main aspects of any language are sounds, vocabulary, and grammar. Over time, a language changes in all three of these areas. Many factors can influence a particular language, even another language. Languages influence each other the most in the area of vocabulary. Many of the English words we use today were borrowed from other languages centuries ago.

English developed from the ancient Indo-European language. Linguists believe the people of central Europe spoke this language around 3000 B.C. Much later, some of the people who spoke this language moved north and west, forming the Germanic tribes. Sometimes in war and sometimes in trade, the Germanic tribes came into contact with the Latin- and Greek-speaking people of the Roman world. The Germanic people borrowed words from the Romans—words having to do with cooking, trade, and travel. Words such as *dish, kettle, cook, kitchen, plum, cheap, monger* ("dealer"), and *mile* tell us something about what the early Germanic people learned from the Romans.

The Germanic tribes also borrowed words having to do with religion. After the Roman emperor Constantine legalized Christianity in A.D. 313, churches became well known to the invaders because their gold and silver cups and their ornaments made them profitable places to raid. At that time, the West Germanic tribes knew about churches, not from attending them, but by breaking into them. Since the idea of a church was new to them, they did not have a word in their own language. So they borrowed the Greek word for church—*kurika* or *kirika*. It came down into Scottish English as *kirk* and into German as *Kirche*. The central and southern Old English language used *circe*, with the *c*'s having a *ch* sound instead of the old *k* sound. And today the word is *church*.

Improving Your Study Time

Learning and using good study skills will help you improve your mind and your character. More important than the facts you learn is that you learn *how* to learn. If you train yourself to be alert and to think logically, you will be better able to assimilate and evaluate the new information that you encounter throughout your life. Students who diligently prepare develop good work habits regardless of what grade they earn. Don't be satisfied with just making a good grade. Be satisfied when you have done your best. Use these tips to develop great study habits.

Keep a good attitude. Having a negative attitude about school will make studying harder. If you have the right goals and avoid last-minute panic studying, you will succeed more easily. In fact, reaching your goals through diligent work gives a sense of satisfaction. No matter what your I.Q., you can achieve a high level of success with a positive attitude.

Get plenty of sleep, exercise, and nutrition. It is very hard to concentrate when you are tired, out of shape, or malnourished. Medical professionals recommend that teenagers get eight to ten hours of sleep each night, exercise regularly, and eat a well-balanced diet.

Be organized. It is almost impossible to do well in school if you can't find your homework or if you forget to study for tests. First, write down all your assignments and their due dates in a notebook, calendar, or computerized program designated just for that purpose. Then transfer that information to a monthly calendar that includes other activities such as sports events and trips. This strategy allows you to know when you will have busy weeks and when you will have time to work on projects. Don't forget to take home every book you need for that day's assignments. When you finish your homework and studying, store your completed homework papers in a specific place in your notebook. Having your materials ready and organized will make both study time and class time more profitable.

Be prepared for class. Try to preview your assignments the night before class so that you know what you need to learn during class time. Be on time and make sure that you have your textbook, the assignments that are due, and the appropriate supplies for taking notes.

Make good use of class time. If you read the assignment the night before class, you will be ready to listen carefully and participate in class. Ask questions about material that you don't understand and share other information that you know about the topic when appropriate. Sit attentively in your chair; do not slouch. Good posture will help you to stay alert and to write legibly. Of course, you should also avoid daydreaming.

Take clear, well-organized notes. Listen carefully to your teacher's lesson. Most speakers use expressions such as *first, in addition,* and *finally* to signal new information. Anything that the teacher writes on the board or on an overhead projector is probably something that you should add to your notes. Try to write down the main ideas in your own words, but record specific facts such as names and dates accurately. If the teacher gives you a definition of a key term, record it in exactly the same words that the teacher uses. Follow the main idea with a brief explanation of the concept or a listing of details about the topic.

Have a specific study time. Set aside a certain time each day to study. This will keep you from waiting until the last minute and enable you to get projects done ahead of time. Study in a comfortable (but not too comfortable!) and well-lighted place that is free from distractions.

Read over your notes regularly. If you review your notes each night or at least each week, your study time before the test will be considerably easier. Begin with your hardest subject first. When you have finished with your other subjects, go back and review that first subject again. You may want to study with a friend occasionally; each of you will be able to share things that the other might have missed during class.

Master each concept. During your study time, try to master each concept presented that day. Don't just finish the exercise. Study until you fully understand the concept.

Get help from a teacher or a tutor. If you follow these steps yet continue to struggle in any subject, you need to ask your teacher or a tutor for help. Every student is different; you may need more explanation than what is presented in class.

Don't give up. Review this chapter several times during the year. We often forget good advice and need to be reminded occasionally. If your grades don't improve immediately, don't stop trying. Just start over again and keep going.

Using the Parts of a Book

Organization is very important to most writers, especially writers of nonfiction works such as textbooks. Most nonfiction books include features to help you, the reader, follow the organization of the book easily and find information quickly. The features may not be the same in all books, but most books contain many of the parts described in the following paragraphs.

Every book begins with a **title page,** which gives the title of the book, the name of the author or editor, the name of the publisher, and the place of publication. On the back of this page is the **copyright page,** which states the year that the book was copyrighted and the name of the copyright holder. *Copyright* means that the author or publisher has the legal right to that book; no one else can reprint any part of it without permission.

A **table of contents** tells you two important things: the major topics in the book and the logical organization the author uses to discuss those topics. He may start with the simplest and proceed to the most difficult concept, or he may discuss the information in chronological order. The table of contents lists the chapter or unit divisions with page numbers in numerical order. A **list of illustrations** is similar to a table of contents; it lists the location and sequence of pictures in the text.

Some books also include **acknowledgments,** the names of people the author or editor wants to thank. Some books also have an **introduction** or **preface,** which states the purpose of the book or provides important background information.

The largest part of a book is the **text.** In both fiction and nonfiction books, the text is usually divided into units, sections, or chapters. Chapters in textbooks usually display clear organization. The chapter may have bold headings that introduce main topics and smaller bold headings to introduce smaller parts of the main subject. The rest of the information is usually in lists or paragraphs. Try to find the topic sentence in each paragraph. Then look for details that support that topic sentence. Also read the information in captions under illustrations and study the pictures and illustrations themselves.

Many nonfiction books also contain additional sections of information that are placed after the text. One of these is the **bibliography;** it lists either the books that the author used in writing the text or the titles of some additional books about the same subject.

Extra helps, such as charts, diagrams, long lists, and notes of explanation, are included in the **appendix.** One kind of appendix is a **glossary,** which gives the definitions of special vocabulary words used in the text. Many textbooks have glossaries and other appendixes.

An **index** is an alphabetical listing of key words and phrases with all the page numbers where they appear in the text. Sometimes the index also lists the page numbers of the illustrations.

You may notice that many fiction books have only a title page, a copyright page, a table of contents, and a text. This is true because the main purpose of fictional writing is usually to entertain, not to inform.

16.1 PRACTICE *the skill*

Write the letter of the correct book section that would give you the information requested. Letters may be used more than once.

A. Title Page
B. Copyright Page
C. Table of Contents
D. List of Illustrations
E. Acknowledgments
F. Introduction or Preface
G. Bibliography
H. Appendix
I. Glossary
J. Index

_____ 1. a list of sources the author used

_____ 2. the name of the copyright holder

_____ 3. the names of people the author wants to thank

_____ 4. the pages on which a certain key word appears

_____ 5. the titles of individual chapters

_____ 6. important background information

_____ 7. the definitions of special vocabulary words

_____ 8. additional charts and diagrams

_____ 9. a list of pictures in the text

_____ 10. the place of publication

Use the sample table of contents below and the index (page 415) from *UNITED STATES HISTORY*, **Third Edition** (© 1991, 2001 BJU Press) to answer each question.

_____ 1. Which unit includes information about the philosophy of Manifest Destiny?

_____ 2. Which page would tell you about the Albany Congress?

_____ 3. Which chapter discusses the Acadians?

_____ 4. Which two chapters include information about the Alien and Sedition Acts?

_____ 5. Which chapter includes the illustration *All Creation Going to the White House?*

_____ 6. Which pages have information about the Algonquin Indians?

_____ 7. On what page does an illustration of the Alamo appear?

_____ 8. Which unit contains a special section about the Eastern Indians?

_____ 9. On what page does the list of maps begin?

_____ 10. Which chapter should cover the Tea Act of 1773?

Contents

Index

Italic type indicates that an illustration of the entry appears on that page.

Improving Your Reading Comprehension

Learning in school usually requires reading. Becoming an avid reader and improving your reading comprehension skills will increase your knowledge and your ability to learn. But if you don't understand what you read, you're not going to benefit much. You probably do not always have time to look up the meaning of every unfamiliar word. Using the following strategies will help you discover the meanings of words quickly while you continue to read your assignments.

Context Clues

The context of an unfamiliar word, those other words and structures that immediately surround the unknown word, can often help you understand it better. If you discover enough clues from the context of an unfamiliar word, you will probably have a good idea of its meaning.

Verbal Context

The most useful context clues may be other words in the sentence. Sometimes a writer may define an unfamiliar word by including explanatory words or a synonym.

> Often the director of a company has *carte blanche,* complete authority to make decisions over every matter.

If you know French, you know that *carte blanche* means "blank ticket." When we use this expression in English, however, it has an additional connotation. The sentence itself defines *carte blanche* for the reader as "complete authority."

If the text does not include a definition of the word, look for examples that may explain the word.

> Jesse James was *infamous*. History, as well as legend, states that he robbed numerous banks and trains across at least five states and territories.

The additional information in this passage makes it clear that an *infamous* person has a very bad reputation.

Sometimes an unknown word may be compared or contrasted with another word. If you know the meaning of the second word, it can help you discover the meaning of the unknown word.

COMPARISON	Like Wayne, who seems to talk all the time, my little sister loves to *prattle*.
CONTRAST	Instead of asking permission to plant her garden partly on Mr. Grantley's property, Salfia *encroached* upon his land.

By comparing the sister's behavior to Wayne's, you can guess that *prattle* means to chatter or talk aimlessly. Because you know that Salfia did not have permission to use Mr. Grantley's property, you should realize that *encroached upon* means *intruded on*.

You may be able to determine the meaning of the unfamiliar word if the context expresses a cause-and-effect relationship.

> After Mr. Mikelsohn lost the family's savings when his business failed, he was unable to find another job. Consequently, the family was reduced to *penury* until Mrs. Mikelsohn began working at the police department.

What happens when a person loses his money and his job? Were you able to determine that *penury* means *poverty*?

Grammatical Context

The grammatical structure of the sentence can also be a clue to help you discover the meaning of an unfamiliar word. Notice any parallel structures, look for associations between the words that you know, and then try to find the associations between those words and the unfamiliar word. For example, if the unfamiliar word appears in a list, try to determine what the listed words have in common.

> Are those antlers from a caribou, a *wapiti,* or a moose?

Because it is listed with *caribou* and *moose,* you probably guessed that a *wapiti* is a kind of large deer or elk.

PRACTICE *the skill*

Write the letter of the word or phrase that most closely matches the meaning of the italicized word. Be prepared to explain what context clues you used.

_____ 1. Collin possessed a *magnanimous* spirit toward the man who had robbed him, even embracing the man when he asked Collin to forgive him.
A. gracious in pardoning
B. helpful in trouble

_____ 2. The Wheelers placed *luminaries* at the end of their driveway so that we could find it in the dark.
A. rocks
B. lights

_____ 3. Although Denae was a *lithe* gymnast when she was younger, after her back injury she couldn't even bend to touch her toes.
A. lightweight
B. flexible

_____ 4. The *erudite* professor always seems to have a correct answer for every question his students ask him.
A. learned
B. aged

_____ 5. The *enigma* of who had robbed the bank remained a mystery for ten years until new evidence helped police identify the robber.
A. case
B. riddle

_____ 6. In his *taciturn* manner, Curtis ordered his ice cream cone by merely pointing to his choice of ice cream in the case.
A. untalkative
B. direct

_____ 7. Although her answer to the question was prompt, it was neither *lucid* nor rational. No one understood her answer.
A. clear
B. correct

_____ 8. His teacher insisted that Gavin *desist from* his rowdy behavior because he was disrupting the class with all the animal noises he was making.
A. retreat from
B. stop

_____ 9. The woman sitting by the pond looked like Nevan's deceased great-great-grandmother. Nevan wondered whether what he saw was an *apparition*, but he didn't believe in visions or ghosts.
A. specter
B. look-alike

_____ 10. Zayna knew that she should be able to figure out the algebra problem, but this one just seemed to be like a confusing *labyrinth* that she would never find her way through.
A. maze
B. difficulty

Write a definition of the italicized word. Be prepared to explain what context clues you used.

1. No one ever knew how to respond to Martin's *capricious* decisions. Martin wasn't like his brother Melvin, who always made reasonable choices.

   _____

2. Lillian was in a state of *euphoria* after she found out that she passed her chemistry final. Now she could graduate from high school!

   _____

3. Derek's eating habits, including drinking ten cans of pop a day, were an *impediment* to his having good health.

   _____

4. Monica recounted the story of her plane ride through a rainstorm in her typically *histrionic*, emotional way, acting the story out as if she were in a play.

   _____

5. Astoria's parents gave her permission to visit her aunt in Switzerland for a *fortnight* in October. They decided that two weeks was long enough for Astoria to be out of school.

   _____

6. The feeling seemed to be *prevalent* that the school should be closed for two weeks because of an epidemic of lice among the students.

   _____

7. When I broke my leg in a snowmobile accident, my mother took care of me like a *solicitous* nurse.

   _____

8. The mob that was rioting in the streets sounded like a pack of *vociferous* dogs that keeps neighborhoods awake at night.

   _____

9. The other day in the post office, Lloyd gave his friends a *diatribe* about the grocery store's always being out of the vegetables that he needs and about stores like that being allowed to stay open.

   _____

10. Because Lex *prevaricated* about the amount of money he had spent on the advertising aspect of the budget, his boss fired him. His boss wanted to have a truthful person in charge of the company's finances.

    _____

Word Parts

Another way to discover the meaning of a word is to analyze its parts. If you understand the meaning of the prefix or the suffix, you might be able to determine the meaning of the whole word. Look at the charts below to note the spellings and definitions of several roots, prefixes, and suffixes that came into English from Latin.

Dictionaries pp. 406-7

Roots

A root is the main part of the word.

Root	Meaning	Example
dic/dict	speak, say	dictate
fer	bring, bear	transfer
ject	throw, cast, or hurl	projection
pel/pulse	drive	dispel
port	carry	disport
tract	draw, pull	protract
vene/vent	come	contravention

Prefixes

A prefix is added to the beginning of a word.

Prefix	Meaning	Example
a/ab/abs	away from	abstraction
contra	against, opposite, contrasting; lower in pitch	contradict
dis/di	apart, away	distract
in	in, on, within	indict
pro	for, favoring; in place of; forth, forward	project
trans/tra	across	transfer

Suffixes

A suffix is added to the end of a word.

Adding Suffixes p. 433

Suffix	Meaning	Example
ance/ence	one that does or causes a particular action	inference
ant/ent	*adj.*, performing or causing a particular action; being in a particular condition	propellant
	noun, one that does or causes a particular action	
ate	to act upon in a particular manner	dictate
ion	action, process; result of an action or process	transportation

PRACTICE *the skill*

Using the definitions of the roots, prefixes, and suffixes given on page 419, guess the definitions for the words given below.

1. abstract _____

2. contradict _____

3. contravene _____

4. dictation _____

5. disport _____

6. infer _____

7. propellant _____

8. propulsion _____

9. transference _____

10. transport _____

REVIEW *the skill*

Compare the definitions you wrote in Practice the Skill 16.5 to the dictionary definitions. Write a sentence using the word correctly.

1. abstract _____

   _____

2. contradict _____

   _____

3. contravene _____

   _____

4. dictation _____

   _____

5. disport _____

   _____

6. infer _____

   _____

7. propellant _____

   _____

8. propulsion _____

_____

9. transference _____

_____

10. transport _____

_____

Using Profitable Memory Techniques

After you complete your daily reading and written homework assignments, you will need to study for your tests and quizzes. Here are some techniques to improve your memory.

Read through the class notes for each class on a daily basis. Frequent review of the material will help you to remember it more easily.

Pay attention as you study. Determine to remember, and remind yourself not to be mentally lazy.

Ask yourself questions about your notes and answer them aloud. Write down questions about material that is unclear to you. Try to find the answer in a reference source or ask the teacher for more information when you return to class.

Make flash cards from your study notes. Write a question on one side and the answer on the other side. Use the flash cards to quiz yourself or ask a friend or family member to help you.

Create your own written quizzes as you study. Put the quiz away for a day or two and then try to answer the questions. Those that you cannot answer correctly are the ones that you need to study again. You can also ask a friend or family member to quiz you occasionally.

Cluster information that you are learning. When you need to study a large amount of information at one time (such as for a final exam), try to organize the material into related groups or clusters. Learn the information by category groups: the structure of leaves, the structure of roots, the structure of stems, and so forth.

Use mnemonic [nĭ·mŏn´ ĭk] devices to help you remember. Create rhymes, acronyms, acrostics, or other word games during your study times to help you remember detailed information. An acronym is a word in which each letter stands for another word. An acrostic most often takes the form of a phrase in which the initial letter of each word stands for another word or phrase.

RHYME	To remember the fates of the six wives of England's King Henry VIII, use this rhyme: Divorced, beheaded, died, Divorced, beheaded, survived.
ACRONYM	*Laser* is an acronym for a specific physical process taking place: **L**ight **a**mplification by **s**timulated **e**mission of **r**adiation.
ACROSTIC	To remember the order of the planets, use this acrostic: **M**y **V**ery **E**ducated **M**other **J**ust **S**howed **U**s **N**igeria (Mercury, Venus, Earth, Mars, Jupiter, Saturn, Uranus, Neptune).

Taking Tests

Studying and doing homework are part of learning, but they are also part of an organized plan to help you do well on tests and quizzes. You have no doubt learned that waiting to study until the night before a test is not a good way to earn a good grade. The more often you review material and the longer the period of time over which you review, the more information your memory will retain. In addition, the following test-taking strategies can help you succeed.

1. Before you begin, look over the test to determine the number and type of questions there are.

2. Read all directions carefully.

3. Work through the entire test in one of three ways:

    * Start at the beginning of the test and keep going. Answer those questions about which you are confident and those about which you are 50 to 75 percent certain of the answers. In some way mark those questions that you do not know or that you need to spend more time thinking about. Come back to them later.

    * Scan the test for the easiest section or the easiest questions and answer them first. Then spend the rest of the time on the more difficult questions.

    * Start at the most difficult section of the test and do it first. Again, mark questions with which you are having problems and come back to them later. This strategy can be helpful if the difficult questions are worth more credit because it ensures that you have time to answer those questions before you answer those that will earn you less credit. (Be careful, however, not to spend too much time on the difficult questions! Save some time to answer those questions whose answers you know.)

    All three of the strategies can be helpful, but most students prefer one to the others. Find the strategy that works best for you. You may even want to use different strategies for different kinds of tests.

4. Try to answer all questions, even if you have to guess at some.

5. Think carefully and be selective about what you write. It is better to write a little about what you do know than to write a lot about what you do not know.

6. Write neatly. Correct answers will not count if the teacher cannot read what you have written.

Most classroom tests, and some standardized tests, are a mixture of objective questions, which ask for a specific, factual answer, and subjective questions, which allow you to give your own thinking, using your own words. Unfortunately, a student may sometimes miss a question whose answer he knows because he is unfamiliar with the format of the question. Knowing how to answer different kinds of questions will help you avoid that problem.

How to Answer Essay Questions

Essays
pp. 341-42

Most subjective questions are essay questions. An essay allows you to show connections among the facts that you present. Of course, you must first know the facts. Then you can demonstrate your mastery of the material. Learning to write a well-organized essay within the allotted time limit is a useful skill.

1. Carefully read the directions and the question or questions. If you are to answer only one question from several options, read them all to find the one you are best prepared to answer.

    * Pay special attention to the verb in the question and do only what it asks you to do. Some verbs frequently used in essay questions include *compare, contrast, explain, describe, discuss,* and *evaluate.*

- Notice the nouns in the question. If you are told to compare two poems by Shakespeare, you will not write about Shakespeare himself or about his plays. If the question asks you to compare the figures of speech in the poems, don't write about the rhyme scheme or the sound devices.

- Understand what format you are to use. Do the directions indicate that you should write one well-developed paragraph? Or should you write a multiparagraph essay with separate introduction and conclusion paragraphs? Be sure to allow yourself enough time to produce the right kind of essay.

2. Create a scattergram. Jot down your ideas on a separate piece of paper. Include any dates, names, or places that you don't want to leave out.

Making a List pp. 326-27

3. Organize your ideas. What is most important? What is least important? Which ideas belong together logically? Use arrows and other markings to indicate the order you will use in your essay. Now you have a rough outline.

4. Write a thesis statement. One of the best strategies is to turn the question into a sentence. If possible, indicate the basic organization of your essay as well.

Tentative Outline p. 331

| QUESTION | Contrast the governments of ancient Greece and ancient Rome. |
| THESIS | The governments of ancient Greece and ancient Rome differed in three major respects. |

5. Write a topic sentence for each main point on your rough outline. Be sure that each topic sentence relates directly to your thesis statement.

Crafting Thesis and Topic Sentences pp. 334-35

6. Support each topic sentence with specific detail. Make your answer as thorough as possible within the time limit. Do not assume that the reader will accept a statement without sufficient proof.

7. Conclude the essay with a restatement of the thesis. Do not merely copy the thesis from the beginning of your essay; instead, state it another way.

Paragraph Development p. 337

| RESTATEMENT | These three differences clearly contrast the government of ancient Greece with that of ancient Rome. |

8. Quickly proofread your essay, if you have time. Correct any obvious errors—factual or grammatical—and add any necessary clarification.

Proofreading p. 346

How to Answer Objective Questions

The most common types of objective questions are multiple choice, matching, and true or false. Short answer questions are objective if they ask you to state a fact rather than to give an opinion or draw a conclusion.

Multiple Choice

1. Read each question carefully. Formulate an answer before you look at the choices.

2. Read all of the choices carefully. Eliminate those that you know are wrong.

3. Choose the best answer from the choices that are left.

Matching

1. Read each question carefully. Formulate an answer before you look at the choices.

2. Match the questions and answers that you know are correct. If you are allowed to mark on the test paper, check off the answers as you use them.

3. From the remaining choices, choose the best answer for each question.

True/False

1. Read each item carefully. If any word in the item is false, the entire item is false.

2. Look for words like *always* or *never;* these words often (but not always) signal a false item.

Short Answer

1. Accurately and completely answer the questions that you know.

2. If you do not know the answer, make the best guess you can. You may receive partial credit for your answer.

How to Take Standardized Tests

Periodically you will be required to take standardized tests. Standardized tests often contain types of questions different from those on classroom tests. You will have a better chance of doing well if you are familiar with the types of questions usually included on standardized tests.

Reading Comprehension

The reading comprehension section tests your ability to analyze a written passage. The questions may ask about the main ideas, details, or meaning of the passage. You may have to evaluate information or draw conclusions. The following strategies will help you on this part of the test:

1. Look at the questions briefly.

2. Read the paragraph thoroughly and then answer the questions you definitely know.

3. Read the other questions carefully as time allows, eliminating answers you know are incorrect.

4. Choose the most logical answer from those remaining.

With a height of 3,212 feet, Angel Falls is easily the highest waterfall in the world. The upper part plummets over half a mile straight down, and then it cascades down rocks for the remaining 564 feet. (from GEOGRAPHY)

Example: ___**B**___ In this passage the word *plummets* means
A. to decline at an angle
B. to plunge
C. to progress gradually downward
D. to rise suddenly

The passage has no information leading the reader to think that *plummets* means *to rise suddenly.* The other three options all express falling motion, but "to decline at an angle" does not describe an action that goes "straight down," and "to progress downward gradually" cannot describe the fast action of a waterfall. The correct answer is *B,* "to plunge."

Vocabulary

Standardized tests usually also contain a vocabulary section that tests your knowledge of common English words. This section may include two types of questions. One type gives a sentence (or part of a sentence) with a word in bold print. You must then choose the word that best matches the meaning of the word in bold print. Context clues will help you choose your answer.

Example: _____**A**_____ Moira and Alistair often **perambulate** through the park after dinner.
A. to roam or stroll
B. to run
C. to swim

"To swim" is clearly wrong because the sentence indicates that *perambulate* is something one can do in a park, not a body of water. Although the context does not clearly state the speed at which the subjects *perambulate,* the timing—after dinner—implies that it is probably not a strenuous activity. The best answer is A, "to roam or stroll."

Another type of question may list several sentences, each including the same underlined word. You must choose the sentence in which the word has the same meaning as in the original sentence.

Example: _____**C**_____ Please <u>raise</u> your hand if you have a question.
A. The silent auction <u>raised</u> eleven thousand dollars for the relief fund.
B. Those rowdy spectators <u>raised</u> quite a commotion after the game.
C. The engineer instructed the workers to <u>raise</u> the foundation of the building by one foot.
D. Georgette earned another <u>raise</u> through hard work and dedication to her employer.

In the original sentence, *raise* means "to elevate." *Raise* in the first choice means "to collect money." In the second choice, *raise* means "to instigate or incite." In the fourth choice, *raise* means "an increase in salary." The correct answer is the third choice, in which *raise* means "to elevate," as in the example.

Analogy

Many standardized tests also contain an analogy section. An analogy is a comparison of one thing to another. Analogy questions on standardized tests ask you to compare the relationship of one pair of words to the relationship of another pair of words. Analogies are similar to vocabulary questions because they test your understanding of the meanings of words. But they are different from vocabulary questions because they ask you to think about the relationship between the words.

In an analogy question, you must choose the pair of words whose relationship most closely matches that of the original pair of words. The two words in a set are usually separated by a colon that stands for the phrase "is to"; and the two sets of words are separated by a double colon that means "as."

Example: _____**C**_____ raisin : grape ::
A. date : pear
B. orange : grapefruit
C. prune : plum
D. pea : pod

First, read the question as an interrogative sentence. This question would be read as "*Raisin* is to *grape* as *what* is to *what?*" Then change that question into a statement that expresses the relationship between the two words: *A raisin is a dried grape.* Now you are ready to compare the other sets of words to the original set. The original set expresses a relationship between two forms of the same fruit; the first three choices also name kinds of fruit, and both the first and third choices name dried fruit. But only choice C expresses a relationship between the original fruit and its dried form, just like the original pair of words. The question and answer together would be read as "*Raisin* is to *grape* as *prune* is to *plum.*"

Grammar, Usage, and Mechanics

Standardized tests often combine questions about grammar, usage, and mechanics in one section. Other tests include several separate sections of questions. Depending on the test, the questions may appear in different formats. For example, the test may show a sentence with several words underlined and labeled, requiring you to choose the word that contains the error. If the sentence is correct, you choose the "no error" option.

Example: ___**B**___ Jamie was <u>surprised</u> by the size of the
A

<u>turkies</u> at the nature <u>preserve</u>. <u>No error</u>
B **C** **D**

The correct choice is *B* because the correct spelling should be *turkeys*.

Another type of question may show you a sentence with part of the sentence underlined. You must choose one of the possible replacements for the underlined part. If the underlined part is correct, choose the answer that indicates no change is necessary.

Example: ___**D**___ Someone made meatballs for dinner; <u>they smell</u>
delicious.
A. they smells
B. it smells
C. it smell
D. correct as is

Choice *D* is correct because the pronoun *they* agrees with its antecedent, *meatballs*. The verb *smell* is also plural.

Other standardized tests have separate sections for mechanics (capitalization and punctuation). The question may divide one sentence into several parts with each part on a separate line. You choose the part that contains an error. If the sentence is correct, choose the answer that indicates no change is necessary.

Example: ___**A**___ A. After he learned to drive
B. Jackson began saving money
C. for a car of his own.
D. no mistakes

Choice *A* contains an error. A comma should follow an introductory adverb clause.

16.7 PRACTICE *the skill*

Reading Comprehension: Read the paragraph and answer the following questions. Write the letter of the correct answer.

Since before the time of Christ, the Jews have classified their scriptural books into three main divisions: the Law, the Prophets, and the Writings. The last of these divisions was sometimes called "the Psalms" because Psalms dominates that section. These divisions include the same thirty-nine books that we have in our Old Testament. The Jews, though, arranged them in a different order, beginning with Genesis and ending with II Chronicles. To us it seems odd to put II Chronicles last, because it does not cover the last period of Old Testament history. However, the Jews focused on the date of *writing,* and they believe that Ezra wrote II Chronicles as the last scriptural book around 424 B.C. (from *How Firm a Foundation* by Kent Ramler and Randy Leedy)

_____ 1. The topic of the above paragraph is
A. the Jewish view of the Old Testament.
B. the modern Christian view of the Old Testament.
C. the date of the book of II Chronicles.

_____ 2. In this paragraph the word *divisions* means
   A. an arithmetic function.
   B. a disagreement of opinion.
   C. the parts or sections of a whole.

_____ 3. According to this paragraph, the Jewish Old Testament ends with II Chronicles because
   A. II Chronicles covers the last period of Old Testament history.
   B. Jews believe that II Chronicles was the last Old Testament book written.
   C. II Chronicles dominates the last section of the Jewish Old Testament.

Read the paragraph and answer the following questions. Write the letter of the correct answer.

Countless cities and rural areas across the world do not have a Bible-believing church. Billions of people do not know about Jesus and His power to save them from sin. A church-planting missionary seeks to evangelize an area and begin a local church for the believers. He may begin by passing out tracts, talking to people, and trying to win them to Christ. Services often start with just the missionary's family and grow as people are saved or hear about the meetings. The church planter will teach the new converts how to win others to Christ and how to live as a Christian. Those with leadership potential may be trained to guide the work when the missionary leaves. (from *Publish Great Things* by H. Douglas Garland)

_____ 4. A good title for this paragraph would be
   A. Local Churches.
   B. Church Planting.
   C. How to Evangelize.

_____ 5. In this paragraph the word *tracts* means
   A. large sections of land or water.
   B. athletic race courses.
   C. pamphlets that contain Bible verses and the plan of salvation.

_____ 6. This paragraph does **not** discuss
   A. the need for Bible-believing churches.
   B. writing a church constitution.
   C. the work of a church planter.

Vocabulary: Write the letter of the definition that most closely matches the word in bold print.

_____ 7. Unable to reach a **consensus,** the council decided to vote again.
   A. agreement
   B. dissension
   C. victory

_____ 8. The gardener needed more **loam** for his plants.
   A. twilight
   B. a machine for weaving
   C. soil with a mixture of ingredients

Write the letter of the sentence in which the definition of the underlined word most closely matches that of the first sentence.

_____ 9. Did your grandmother make the lace <u>mat</u> under this lamp?
    A. The gymnast never practices without a <u>mat</u> under the apparatus.
    B. After you clear the table, please shake the <u>mats</u> too.
    C. Wipe your feet on the <u>mat</u> before entering the house.

_____ 10. Angelo enjoyed the audience's <u>positive</u> reaction to his performance.
    A. The critics' <u>positive</u> response to the book gratified the first-time author.
    B. After checking the dictionary, Xue was <u>positive</u> that she had used the word _perambulate_ correctly.
    C. The test came back from the laboratory with a <u>positive</u> result.

16.8 REVIEW _the skill_

Analogy: Write the letter of the pair of words whose relationship most closely matches the relationship of the original pair of words.

_____ 1. bird : nest ::
    A. bear : den
    B. bird : bee
    C. hive : bee

_____ 2. ink : pen ::
    A. ink : paper
    B. pen : pencil
    C. graphite : pencil

_____ 3. card : envelope ::
    A. stamp : letter
    B. film : camera
    C. heel : shoe

_____ 4. book : page ::
    A. leaf : stem
    B. second : minute
    C. sentence : word

_____ 5. dog : cat ::
    A. wolf : lion
    B. fish : bird
    C. kitten : puppy

Grammar, Usage, and Mechanics: Write the letter that corresponds to the error in the sentence.

_____ 6. My <u>friend</u> Grace will be <u>visiting</u> her cousins in <u>wyoming</u> next week.
    A   **B**   **C**
    <u>No error</u>
    D

_____ 7. <u>Grace's</u> <u>neice</u>, Janelle, will be driving to <u>Cheyenne</u> with her. <u>No error</u>
    A   **B**   **C**   **D**

Write the letter of the correct replacement for the underlined section of the sentence. If the sentence is correct, choose D.

_____ 8. The guides didn't know that no one <u>had brought their</u> lunch on the hike.
   A. had brought his
   B. have brought their
   C. have brought his
   D. correct as is

Write the letter of the section that contains an error. If the sentence is correct, choose D.

_____ 9. A. The Tobels hired a contractor
   B. to oversee the renovations
   C. to their house.
   D. no mistakes

_____ 10. A. Although the Tobels will paint the house,
   B. the contractor had to hire
   C. carpenters, electricians and plumbers.
   D. no mistakes

HISTORY OF THE ENGLISH LANGUAGE

A Nation Settled

The history of the English language itself begins with the settlement of England by Germanic peoples. The first known inhabitants of Britain were the Celts. In A.D. 43 the Romans began to conquer the Celts. The Romans ruled Britain until A.D. 410, when Roman troops withdrew from the island. Then, around A.D. 450, some of the Germanic tribes sailed across the North Sea and invaded Britain. These Germanic invaders belonged to three tribes: the Angles, the Saxons, and the Jutes. Each tribe spoke a different Germanic dialect, but they most likely could understand each other. The Angles settled the whole central and northern section, and the Saxons settled all of the southern part except for the rather small southeastern section settled by the Jutes.

In conquering and settling Britain, the Germanic tribes partly pushed back and partly absorbed the Celtic-speaking Britons they found there. However, even today two of the Celtic languages survive in Great Britain: Welsh to the west of England (in Wales) and Gaelic in Ireland and Scotland.

Old English, the language as it was after A.D. 450 and before A.D. 1100, is sometimes called Anglo-Saxon after the two larger tribes. The largest tribe gave its name to the country ("Angle-land") and to the language ("Angle-ish").

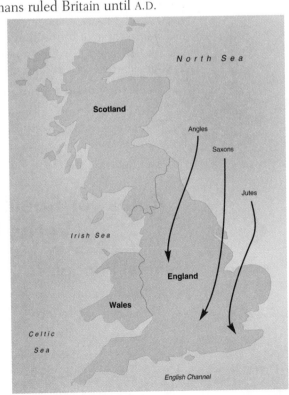

Good spelling is an essential writing skill. Whether you are writing a research paper or a personal letter, your message is communicated most clearly by your using the right words and spelling them correctly. Use these spelling hints and master these rules so that you will be a competent writer.

Spelling Hints

Pay attention to the spelling of new words.

Make a point of focusing on the spelling of new or unfamiliar words. When you read, you certainly read for meaning; but an occasional focus on spelling can help you become a good speller. (Spell the word softly to yourself and try to learn it.)

Spell by syllables.

Dividing a word into its individual syllables will help you to spell it correctly. Think about prefixes, suffixes, and other word parts as you spell words by syllables.

op + en	open
prai + rie	prairie
pen + cil	pencil

Dictionaries
pp. 406-7

Use a dictionary.

Look up the spelling of words when you are unsure of the correct spelling. Keep a good dictionary available when you are writing. Although you might be unsure of a word's exact spelling, you probably know enough of the word to find it in a dictionary.

Keep a list of words that are problems for you.

Whenever you misspell a word and then locate the correct spelling of that word, put it on your list of problem words. Study your list systematically. Begin by writing a word several times, concentrating on its appearance and pronunciation. Repeat this procedure three or four different days of the next week. Then have someone quiz you on that word. If you can write the word correctly without hesitation, transfer it to your "learned" list. If a problem remains, keep working on the word.

Look for possible groupings among your problem words.

If you find a group of similar words, try to formulate or find a rule for that group. For example, several of your problem words may contain *ie* and *ei*. Learning the rules for *ie* and *ei* will allow you to spell an entire group of words correctly.

An important step to good spelling is mastering the basic spelling rules.

Rules for Spelling Singular Present-Tense Verbs and Plural Nouns

Plural nouns
p. 2

General Principles

If the word ends in *ch, sh, s, x,* or *z,* add *es.*

crutch	crutches
bush	bushes
cutlass	cutlasses
box	boxes
waltz	waltzes

Present Tense
p. 154

If the word ends in *y* preceded by a consonant, change the final *y* to *i* and add *es*.

victory	vict**i**e**s**
directory	direct**ori**es
pantry	pant**ri**es

If the word ends in *y* preceded by a vowel, add *s*.

holiday	holidays
key	keys
buoy	buoys

If the word ends in *f* or *fe*, consult your dictionary. For most, add *s*; for others, change the *f* to *v* and add *es*.

plaintiff	plaintiffs
safe	safes
reef	reefs
knife	kni**ve**s
shelf	shel**ve**s

Add *s* to most other words.

power	powers
microchip	microchips

If the word ends in *o*, consult your dictionary. For most, add *es*; for others, add *s*.

potato	potatoes
go	goes
portfolio	portfolios

Musical terms are more likely to require *s* than *es*.

piano	pianos
arpeggio	arpeggios
concerto	concertos

Some nouns have irregular plural forms. Consult your dictionary for nouns with irregular plurals.

goose	geese
ox	oxen
woman	women

Plurals of Proper Nouns

The plurals of proper nouns are made by adding *s* or *es* according to the preceding rules, but without any other spelling changes. Never use an apostrophe in making the plural of a proper name.

the Thompsons	the Hugheses	the Pettys	the Kuchikis

Plurals of Compounds

Attach the suffix to the end of most compounds.

whitewash	whitewashes
watchdog	watchdogs
overdo	overdoes

Pluralize the first element of certain compound nouns—those in which the first element is felt to be the most important part of the compound. When in doubt, consult your dictionary.

sister-in-law	sisters-in-law
bachelor of arts	bachelors of arts
lady in waiting	ladies in waiting

Plurals of Numbers

Use *s* alone for the plural of a number that is expressed in figures.

The **1500s** marked the beginning of the Modern English period.

Among the scores on the tests were two **100s.**

(ESL)

Pronunciation of Possessives, Plurals, and Singular Present-Tense Verbs

The same pronunciation rules apply to three English suffixes—the possessive suffix for nouns (spelled *'s*), the regular plural suffix for nouns (spelled *s* or *es*), and the third-person singular suffix for present-tense verbs (spelled *s* or *es*). The pronunciation of all of these suffixes depends on what kind of sound precedes the suffix.

- These suffixes are pronounced /əz/ after **s, z, sh, zh, ch,** and **j** sounds (sounds similar to the /s/ and /z/ sounds of the suffixes). These sounds include the **x** and **ge** spellings.

  Examples: *buses, axes, oozes, pushes, garages, watches, George's.*

- The suffixes are pronounced /s/ after other voiceless consonant sounds (sounds that you form with your mouth but do not say with your vocal cords): **f,** voiceless **th, p, t,** and **k.**

  Examples: *Jeff's, Ruth's, cups, bats, kicks.*

- The suffixes are pronounced /z/ after other voiced sounds (sounds that you both form with your mouth and say with your vocal cords): **v,** voiced **th, b, d, g, m, n, ng, l, r, w, y,** and all vowels.

  Examples: *leaves, soothes, rubs, leads, drags, Tom's, Dan's, songs, pills, cars, arrows, boys, sofas, dictionaries, pianos.*

Rules for Spelling with *ie* and *ei*

When the sound is "long *e*," put *i* before *e* except after *c*.

i before *e*	except after *c*
believe	receipt
fierce	conceive
piece	deceive

Exceptions: *caffeine, leisure, protein, seize, sheik, weird; either* and *neither,* in their more common American pronunciation, are also exceptions to this rule.

When the sound is "long *a*," put *e* before *i*.

weigh	neigh
eight	vein

When the two vowels are pronounced separately, spell according to the pronunciation of the first vowel.

piety	brier
sobriety	deist

Rules for Adding Suffixes

Doubling a Final Consonant

If a one-syllable word ends with a single consonant preceded by a single vowel, double the final consonant before adding a suffix that begins with a vowel.

pan	pan**ning**
pop	pop**ped**
skip	skip**per**

If a multisyllable word with its main accent on the final syllable ends with a single consonant preceded by a single vowel, double the final consonant before adding a suffix that begins with a vowel.

offset	offset**ting**
begin	begin**ning**
deter	deter**rence**

Exceptions: The consonant does not double when the suffix causes the main accent to shift away from the final syllable: ***conference*** vs. *conferring*.

If a word ends with a single consonant preceded by two vowels, do not double the final consonant before adding a suffix.

keep	keep**ing**
float	float**ing**
boor	boor**ish**

Changing the Final *y* to *i*

If a word ends with a consonant and *y*, change the final *y* to *i* before adding a suffix.

vary	var**ied**
many	man**ifold**
glossy	gloss**iness**

Exceptions: Some words keep the *y*: *babyhood, shyness*.

However, if the suffix itself begins with *i*, do not change final *y* to *i*.

deny	deny**ing**
pay	pay**ing**
carry	carry**ing**

Dropping the Final Silent *e*

Drop the final silent *e* that is preceded by a consonant before adding a suffix beginning with a vowel.

rewrite	rewrit**ing**
shove	shov**ing**
debate	debat**able**

Exceptions: The *e* is kept to signal the "soft" pronunciation of *c* or *g* before a suffix beginning with *a* or *o*: *noticeable, courageous*.

Keep the final silent *e* before adding a suffix beginning with a consonant.

erudite	erudite**ly**
base	base**ment**
fate	fate**ful**

Exceptions: *truly, argument, judgment*

Chapter 1 Review: Parts of Speech

Nouns
Identify each italicized noun as *proper*, *compound*, or *collective*.

_____ 1. Bethlehem is perhaps best known as the *birthplace* of the Messiah.

_____ 2. *Bethlehem* is located six miles southwest of Jerusalem.

_____ 3. Bethlehem is not on the *seacoast* of the land of Israel.

_____ 4. As a *class,* you can learn more about Bethlehem by reading a Bible encyclopedia.

_____ 5. Actually, two towns mentioned in the *Old Testament* have the name Bethlehem.

Pronouns
Identify each italicized pronoun as *personal*, *demonstrative*, *interrogative*, or *indefinite*.

_____ 6. Between *you* and me, Bethlehem is one city that I would like to visit.

_____ 7. The Messiah was born in Bethlehem. For *whom* was He born?

_____ 8. *Both* of the locations of the Old Testament towns of Bethlehem are known to scholars today.

_____ 9. *This* is what I learned: the other town of Bethlehem is mentioned in Joshua 19:15.

_____ 10. Like *many* of the towns in the Bible, Bethlehem has its share of visitors today.

Identify each italicized pronoun as *reflexive*, *intensive*, *relative*, or *reciprocal*.

_____ 11. According to Matthew 2:5-6, the priests and scribes *themselves* knew the prophecy that the Messiah would be born in Bethlehem.

_____ 12. Bethlehem is a city *that* is approximately 2,300 feet above sea level.

_____ 13. People who called *themselves* sons of David went to Bethlehem for the census.

_____ 14. Ruth, *who* was the great-grandmother of David, lived in Bethlehem.

_____ 15. The two Bethlehems do not rival *each other* in importance.

Verbs
Identify each italicized verb as *action*, *state-of-being*, or *auxiliary*.

_____ 16. David *was* the shepherd in charge of his father's sheep in Bethlehem.

_____ 17. David *wrote* many psalms to God when he was a shepherd.

_____ 18. The psalms that David wrote have profoundly *affected* believers of all ages.

_____ 19. As evidenced by his writings, David *walked* with God.

_____ 20. *Do* you have a favorite psalm?

Adjectives and Adverbs
Underline each adjective once and each adverb twice.

21. Some important people are buried either in or near Bethlehem.

22. Whose tomb do you think is near Bethlehem?

23. Rachel, the wife of Jacob, has her tomb there.

24. Rachel was very beautiful; however, she was also a deceitful woman occasionally.

25. Genesis 31 tells us that she stole her father's idols and then hid them.

Prepositions, Conjunctions, Interjections
Identify each italicized word as *preposition*, *conjunction*, or *interjection*.

_____ 26. *Not only* did Rachel deceive her father, *but* she *also* deceived her husband.

_____ 27. Jacob did not know that Rachel had the idols in her possession when Laban went *into* the tent to look for them.

_____ 28. In a sense, Jacob was reaping the fruit *of* his own sin of lying.

_____ 29. Jacob had lied to his father about who he was, *and* as the leader of his home, he set the example for Rachel to follow.

_____ 30. *Oh*, may we not be deceitful like Rachel and Jacob!

Chapter 2 Review: Sentences

Finding the Subjects and Predicates
Underline each simple subject once and each simple predicate twice.

1. Why do many people think of pyramids as Egypt's only burial ground for the pharaohs?

2. The Egyptians buried and preserved their deceased monarchs in more than one place.

3. There are some burial sites in the Valley of the Kings.

4. The valley and its graves are located near the Nile River.

5. What was the reason for the different burial grounds?

Underline each complete subject once and each complete predicate twice.

6. Archeologists and scientists guess at the reason for this new burial ground.

7. What do you think about the site's appearance and location?

8. The site, named el-Qurn, forms a shape similar to a pyramid, and it is not easily accessible.

9. The Egyptians mummified their pharaohs, transported them to the Valley of the Kings, and then buried them there.

10. For homework, please study more about the Valley of the Kings.

Identifying Four Types of Sentences
Identify each sentence as *declarative, exclamatory, imperative,* or *interrogative.* Place the appropriate punctuation mark at the end of the sentence.

_____ 11. One of the most famous tombs of the valley is Seti I's tomb

_____ 12. What made his tomb so famous

_____ 13. His tomb had elaborate wall paintings and inscriptions

_____ 14. Please do not touch the inscriptions

_____ 15. Look at those incredible paintings

Analyzing Sentence Patterns

Label the sentence patterns *S-InV, S-TrV-DO, S-TrV-IO-DO, S-TrV-DO-OC, S-LV-PN, S-LV-PA,* or *S-be-Advl.*

16. Over a period of many years, the Egyptians built their pharaohs these tombs.

17. First, workers would dig a cave into the mountain.

18. Then workers made rooms in the cave.

19. Next, other workers would make the walls of the rooms smooth.

20. Others painted pictures and messages on the walls.

21. Many of the pictures are still clear today.

22. The workers were in the caves a lot.

23. The workers were probably men.

24. The air in the caves was probably stale.

25. The workers worked by lamplight.

Chapter 3 Review: Phrases

Prepositional Phrases

Place parentheses around each prepositional phrase and underline the complete object of each preposition. Write the word or words that each phrase modifies.

_____ 1. Computers have drastically altered life in the workplace.

_____ 2. Scarcely any industry exists that has not been affected by this invention.

_____ 3. Seemingly everything has been automated with computers.

_____ 4. A machine operator in a factory programs small computers to run the machines.

_____ 5. He saves time when he uses his skills with the computer to make adjustments that used to be made manually.

Misplaced Prepositional Phrases

Underline each misplaced prepositional phrase and insert a caret (∧) at its correct location. If a sentence is already correct, write C in the blank.

_____ 6. Actually, the modern computer combines several inventions with its many features.

_____ 7. Benjamin Franklin's research on electricity obviously was an important step towards the computer in the 1750s.

_____ 8. A monumental step for technology, however, was taken when the transistor was invented.

_____ 9. The invention about two hundred years after Franklin's studies in electricity of the transistor chip shrank the amount of room needed by the computer.

_____ 10. Previously, computers could occupy huge areas of space.

Appositive Phrases

Underline each appositive phrase. Write the word that the appositive renames.

_____ 11. Often these machines, the computers before transistors, stretched from the floor to the ceiling.

_____ 12. Owning such a computer was made both impractical and undesirable by the devices used before transistor chips or microprocessors, vacuum tubes.

_____ 13. After the invention of the transistor, the basic component of the microprocessor, the race to make a user-friendly personal computer began.

_____ 14. The general public began looking upon computers, desktop machines now, with more familiarity and less fear than before.

_____ 15. Both large, established companies like IBM and small, upstart companies like Microsoft pushed to develop the software and the hardware, the actual components of the computer, that were needed to market a practical personal computer.

Participial Phrases

Underline each participle and place parentheses around each participial phrase. Write the word that the participle modifies.

_____ 16. Actually, the real race was between the Apple Macintosh computer and the IBM personal computer using Microsoft Windows.

_____ 17. Both platforms, competing to become the standard, developed visual screen formats people could understand and use.

_____ 18. At first, the system now named Microsoft Windows was called "Smoke and Mirrors" pejoratively.

_____ 19. Rushed into development, it became the standard on all IBM-compatible machines.

_____ 20. Complemented by Windows, IBM-compatible computers eventually won most of the personal computer market over Macintosh.

Misplaced and Dangling Participial Phrases

Underline each participle or participial phrase. Rewrite any sentence that contains a misplaced or dangling participle or participial phrase, correcting the error. If a sentence is already correct, write C in the blank.

21. Finding a different niche, dominance has been obtained by Macintosh in the area of computer graphics.

_____

_____

22. For this reason, aspiring computer graphics professionals learn to use the Macintosh.

_____

_____

23. The art is often truly astonishing created by computers.

_____

_____

24. Motion media, along with still media, are also produced on supercharged computers.

_____

_____

25. Changing all the time, the motion pictures of years gone by are exceeded in quality by

the video of today.

_____

_____

Gerund Phrases

Underline each gerund or gerund phrase. Identify its function as subject (S), direct object (DO), predicate noun (PN), indirect object (IO), or object of the preposition (OP).

_____ 26. The modern computer was developed by the combining of many different inventions.

_____ 27. Having been repeatedly enhanced makes the computer more complicated than ever.

_____ 28. The computer industry continues making faster and better computers.

_____ 29. The challenge is incorporating all the new technology as quickly as it is developed.

_____ 30. In fact, some analysts, by having predicted the replacement of mankind by machines, have made computer technology seem dangerous.

Infinitive Phrases

Underline each infinitive and place parentheses around each infinitive phrase. Identify the function of each infinitive phrase as noun (Noun), adjective (Adj), or adverb (Adv).

_____ 31. To tell about a computerized house running itself without any humans is one of Ray Bradbury's objectives in "August 2026: There Will Come Soft Rains."

_____ 32. All the humans have perished in a nuclear blast, and the computerized house needs to be repaired so that it can function correctly.

_____ 33. After a terrible fire to complete the destruction, only one wall of the computerized house still stands.

_____ 34. A voice from the wall tries to give the date: "Today is August 5, 2026, today is August 5, 2026, today is . . ."

_____ 35. Some people fear that computers will soon make people unnecessary; however, computers are used to make our work more productive.

Chapter 4 Review: Clauses

Distinguishing Dependent and Independent Clauses

Identify each italicized clause as dependent (DC) or independent (IC).

_____ 1. Does anyone know *where the country of Albania is located?*

_____ 2. Albania is part of the area of southern Europe and is on *what is sometimes called the Balkan Peninsula.*

_____ 3. The Mediterranean Sea is to the south of Albania, and *across the sea lies the country of Libya.*

_____ 4. *Albania is in the Balkans surrounded by Macedonia to the east, Greece to the southeast, the Adriatic Sea to the west, and both Montenegro and the territory of Kosovo to the north.*

_____ 5. *Although Italy is Albania's neighbor to the west,* Albania is separated from Italy by the Adriatic Sea.

Adjective Clauses

Place parentheses around each adjective clause. Write the word it modifies. Underline each relative pronoun once; underline each relative adverb twice.

_____ 6. In the early 1990s, the people of Albania overthrew Communist rule and replaced it with a multiparty democracy, which they replaced with a socialist system in the late 1990s.

_____ 7. During this time, many Albanians immigrated to Greece where they hoped to be able to start life over.

_____ 8. Some Albanians had already been living in other countries whose nearby locations made them easy to emigrate to.

_____ 9. Not only did internal struggles plague Albania during the 1990s, but an external conflict, which would eventually involve NATO peacekeeping forces, also affected the country.

_____ 10. The Albanians living in the province of Serbia known as Kosovo were told by Serbia either to leave the country that they had lived in all their lives or die.

Adverb Clauses

Place parentheses around each adverb clause. Write the word or words it modifies. Underline each subordinating conjunction.

_____ 11. The Albanians did not want to leave the land whereas the Serbs wanted them to go.

_____ 12. Although most of the people living in Kosovo were Albanians, the province was part of Serbia.

_____ 13. If an Albanian decided to stay, he risked his life.

_____ 14. The NATO forces entered the conflict because they wanted to stop the mass murders.

_____ 15. Until the territory declared independence from Serbia in 2008, NATO kept a tenuous peace in Kosovo.

Identifying Noun Clauses

Place parentheses around each noun clause. Identify the function of each noun clause as subject (S), predicate noun (PN), direct object (DO), indirect object (IO), object of the preposition (OP), or appositive (App). Underline each subordinating conjunction once; underline each indefinite relative pronoun twice.

_____ 16. The varied and complex history of the Albanian people requires that one understand something of it to understand the present-day enmity between the Albanians and the Serbs.

_____ 17. The question of what began the enmity between the Albanians and the Serbs is answered by examining the invasion of Albania by the Ottoman Turks in the fifteenth century.

_____ 18. A very important fact, that the Albanians had converted to the Turks' religion of Islam, angered the Serbs.

_____ 19. That most Serbs did not convert to Islam put a religious difference between them and the Albanians.

_____ 20. This difference in religion was what caused, at least in part, the enmity between the Serbs and the Albanians.

Identifying Types of Sentences

Identify each sentence as simple (S), compound (Cd), complex (Cx), or compound-complex (Cd-Cx).

_____ 21. In addition to religious differences, the national differences between the Serbs and the Albanians also divide them.

_____ 22. The Ottoman Empire ruled over almost all the Balkan area, but the empire never quite conquered the whole country of what today is Austria.

_____ 23. The Ottoman Empire lasted for approximately six centuries, but the 1800s brought with them the end of the Ottoman Empire.

_____ 24. After the Ottoman Empire collapsed early in the 1900s, wars broke out between the Balkan states.

_____ 25. One result of these Balkan wars was that Serbia gained possession of Kosovo, which had been part of Albania.

Identifying Errors

Identify each group of words as a sentence (S), a fragment (F), a comma splice (CS), or a fused sentence (FS).

_____ 26. Communist leader Hoxha gained control of Albania after the First World War.

_____ 27. Hoxha ruled Albania for about forty years he kept the country isolated from the rest of the world.

_____ 28. His reign considered by many to be a reign of terror because during his rule about 50,000 Albanians were exiled, killed, or imprisoned for committing crimes against the state.

_____ 29. Working with their new freedom, Albania decided to try a democracy, making Sali Berisha the president, the country was officially a democracy.

_____ 30. However, the economy of the democracy collapsed, the Albanians reverted to a socialist form of government.

Chapter 5 Review: Agreement

Subject-Verb Agreement

Subjects and Predicates

Underline the simple subject(s) of the verb in question. Then underline the correct verb from the choices in parentheses.

1. Many Christians today (*is, are*) using hymns as part of their devotional time.

2. A hymn (*is, are*) actually just a poem set to music.

3. A story (*exists, exist*) about how most hymns were written.

4. Both the hymn writer and the composer of a hymn (*writes, write*) to honor the Lord.

5. Neither the hymn writer nor the composer (*wants, want*) fame for himself when he writes.

Problems with Subject Identification

Underline the simple subject(s) of the verb in question. Then underline the correct verb from the choices in parentheses.

6. Hymns (*is, are*) a great source of comfort and inspiration for many believers.

7. There (*has been, have been*) many hymns written in the past two hundred years.

8. People (*has sung, have sung*) hymns in church for many years.

9. The text of the hymn, not the musical notes, (*was, were*) the part of the hymn that Daniel Whittle typically wrote.

10. One of the hymns that he wrote (*was, were*) called "I'll Stand By Until the Morning."

Problem Nouns and Problem Pronouns

Underline the simple subject(s) of the verb in question. Then underline the correct verb from the choices in parentheses.

11. Everybody who sings this hymn (*agrees, agree*) that the theme of the hymn is Christ standing by believers in their times of distress.

12. Imagine that you (*is, are*) living in the nineteenth century, learning facts about Daniel Whittle.

13. Daniel Whittle, in one of his hymns, (*employs, employ*) a sailing theme.

14. The United States (*is, are*) where Daniel Whittle lives and works.

15. The evangelistic team of Whittle and McGranahan often (*travels, travel*) across the sea to Britain.

16. Ten years (*represents, represent*) the approximate amount of time that James McGranahan has been helping Daniel Whittle with his evangelistic meetings.

17. Most of the tunes to Whittle's hymns (*is, are*) written by McGranahan, who leads the singing at the evangelistic meetings.

18. Some of the people at the evangelistic meetings (*realizes, realize*) that McGranahan replaced Philip Bliss as Whittle's song leader.

19. Many (*knows, know*) the story of Philip Bliss's death in a train accident.

20. Bliss's death is the event that (*has, have*) the status of inspiring James McGranahan to use his musical talents for the ministry.

Pronoun-Antecedent Agreement

Nouns as Antecedents and Compound Antecedents
Underline the correct pronoun from the choices in parentheses.

21. When Philip Bliss wrote the hymn "Hold the Fort," (*he, it*) found the idea in one of Daniel Whittle's sermons.

22. Philip Bliss heard Daniel Whittle, an evangelist, preach on Revelation 2:25; (*it, they*) speaks of Christ's command to believers to "hold fast" until Christ's return.

23. Whittle used an illustration from the Civil War; (*he, they*) talked about not quitting when the battle seems hopeless.

24. Both the verse and the illustration gave (*its, their*) inspiration to Philip Bliss for his hymn.

25. Neither the Christian nor the soldier in war should give up (*his, their*) fight.

Indefinite Pronouns as Antecedents
Write an appropriate personal pronoun to complete each sentence.

_____ 26. Either of the men, Whittle or Bliss, could be called a great hymn writer of _?_ time.

_____ 27. Some of the other hymns that Bliss wrote had _?_ inspiration in life experiences.

_____ 28. Nobody who wrote hymns wrote them so that _?_ would be famous.

_____ 29. Everybody seems to be able to find out more about Philip Bliss than _?_ can about Daniel Whittle.

_____ 30. Anyone who has music composition skills could use _?_ talents to write hymns today.

Chapter 6 Review: Verb Use

Principal Parts

Underline each main verb once. Underline each auxiliary twice. Then identify the principal part of the main verb as *present*, *past*, or *past participle*.

_____ 1. Every closet stores shoes.

_____ 2. Shoes have become essential for any lifestyle.

_____ 3. Barry, like most people, considered shoes necessary, but certainly not interesting.

_____ 4. Some people, however, have practically collected shoes.

_____ 5. Others design them.

Perfect Tenses

Underline each complete verb. Then identify its tense as *present*, *present perfect*, *past*, *past perfect*, *future*, or *future perfect*.

_____ 6. The United States imports shoes from all over the world.

_____ 7. Many people have found the designs from Europe interesting.

_____ 8. Others will buy shoes manufactured in Asia only.

_____ 9. On his trip to Israel, my uncle bought sandals like those worn during Bible times.

_____ 10. He had always thought more highly of imported shoes than domestic ones.

Progressive Tenses

Write the progressive form of each italicized verb. Do not change the tense of the verb.

_____ 11. People *find* many different uses for shoes.

_____ 12. To meet these needs they *purchase* many different types of shoes.

_____ 13. A hiker *had wanted* the soles of his shoes to be thick, durable, and tractive.

_____ 14. The hiker *examined* the soles' ability to grip a surface.

_____ 15. As a result of his examination of the soles, the hiker *will purchase* the shoes shortly.

Voice

Underline the verb in each independent clause. Then identify its voice as *active* or *passive*.

——————————— 16. The weight of the shoe would be considered by a runner to be an important criterion.

——————————— 17. Jose will not buy a heavy shoe.

——————————— 18. For basketball players, traction and ankle support are deemed important.

——————————— 19. Since they stand all day long, many salespeople like stylish yet comfortable shoes.

——————————— 20. They look for good arch support and plenty of softness to avoid foot pain at the end of the day.

Mood

Identify the mood of the italicized verb as *indicative*, *imperative*, or *subjunctive*.

——————————— 21. In the past, shoes *were made* for other reasons.

——————————— 22. If you see my favorite sandals, please *buy* me some in a size nine.

——————————— 23. If I *had been* a knight, I would have needed strong boots built for protection.

——————————— 24. For comfort, *wear* sandals like the ones they wore in Bible times.

——————————— 25. Sandals *allow* your feet to breathe in a warmer climate.

Chapter 7 Review: Pronoun Reference

Ambiguous Reference and Remote Reference
Identify each sentence or group of sentences as having clear pronoun reference (C) or unclear pronoun reference (U).

_____ 1. Sometimes culture, religion, or climate influences the hat that a person wears. It distinguishes one person from another.

_____ 2. In the Middle East, some women wear hats on their heads and veils over their faces. It helps women meet the standard of modesty in their culture.

_____ 3. Turbans are made of certain fabrics, and they have a variety of colors. In some cultures, this indicates what religion the people belong to.

_____ 4. In colder climates, a person wears fur caps and coats, hoping that these will protect him from the winter.

_____ 5. In countries like Indonesia, where the sun blazes down most of the year, the men wear wide-brimmed hats because they help keep the sun out of their faces.

_____ 6. Hats have varied over the centuries because people like to be innovative. Different cultures have developed different styles for numerous other reasons as well, depending on the use of them.

_____ 7. Assyrian men wore turbans or cone-shaped hats while the women wore shawls over their hair and veils over their faces. The women also sometimes decorated them with gold.

_____ 8. The Greeks invented their own unique style. Most of them usually didn't wear hats. They were different from others.

_____ 9. The Egyptians substituted a hairpiece for a hat. These wigs were decorated with headbands, and they were usually black.

_____ 10. People who traveled around and lived in the desert often wore hats that looked like hoods because they needed to protect their heads from the climate.

Reference to an Implied Noun and to a Noun That Is a Modifier
Rewrite each sentence to correct any unclear pronoun reference. If the antecedent is already clear, write C in the blank.

11. In the fifteenth century, to match the long, flowing trains of their dresses, they wore tall hats with cloths draped from them.

_____

12. In contrast to the women, they wore small caps to suit their obligations of work.

_____

© 2009 BJU Press. Reproduction prohibited.

13. The women's hats, who cared more about style than the men did, were more elaborate.

_____

_____

14. The Italians began to make straw hats, probably because Italy had so much of it.

_____

_____

15. To make one straw hat, he would work for many hours.

_____

_____

Indefinite Reference of Personal Pronouns and Reference to a Broad Idea

Identify each sentence as correct (C) or incorrect/informal (I).

_____ 16. In Spain, they wear mantillas sometimes.

_____ 17. When you read an entry about hats in a typical encyclopedia, it says that in some countries today people wear certain hats for important occasions.

_____ 18. If a person wants a hat, he can go to a department store and buy one.

_____ 19. Some women wear hats in church.

_____ 20. The tag inside the hat may say which way to wear the hat.

_____ 21. In Italy, some men wear large flat hats, and some men wear small round hats; they tell what their profession is.

_____ 22. The weatherman says that it is going to be extremely windy today. Hang on to your hat!

_____ 23. American women sometimes wear bandanas or scarves to cover their heads, and this came from Greece.

_____ 24. Sometimes hairpins beautify Japanese women's hair instead of hats because they are their custom.

_____ 25. It is a long way from China, where some people wear coolie hats, to South America, where some people wear *chullos*.

Chapter 8 Review: Pronoun Use

Pronoun Case
Provide an appropriate personal pronoun. Then identify it as subjective (S), objective (O), possessive (P), or independent possessive (IP).

_____ 1. The women's suffrage movement officially started in the 1800s; ? began in Seneca Falls, New York.

_____ 2. At the convention in Seneca Falls, some women and men wrote a document outlining ? goal of gaining rights for women.

_____ 3. ? was a difficult battle because people were not used to the idea of women's rights.

_____ 4. Women had voiced a desire to vote before the 1800s, but not much attention had been given to ? .

_____ 5. However, one state, New Jersey, had allowed ? women to vote from 1790 to 1807.

_____ 6. From 1691 to 1780, though, Massachusetts allowed a woman to vote if ? possessed land.

_____ 7. However, by the time the women's suffrage movement started, ? were not allowed to vote.

_____ 8. Two of the main leaders in the movement were Susan B. Anthony and Elizabeth Cady Stanton; some people respected ? at that time, but not many.

_____ 9. Both of these women used ? skills not only for the suffrage movement but also for the abolition and temperance movements.

_____ 10. Susan B. Anthony and Elizabeth Stanton worked together for women's suffrage; ? had a goal to accomplish.

Compound Constructions, Appositives, and Comparisons Using _Than_ or _As_
Underline the correct pronoun from the choices in parentheses.

11. Susan B. Anthony and (_she, her_) led the women who wanted to amend the Constitution in order to gain the right to vote.

12. Other women disagreed with Susan B. Anthony and Elizabeth Stanton. (_They, them_), with their leaders, Lucy Ward and Julia Stone, sought to gain this right through the state governments.

13. Even though these groups disagreed on method, they both would have wanted (_we, us_) women to have the right to vote.

14. When Elizabeth married Henry Stanton, she was as much an abolitionist as (_he, him_).

15. Elizabeth Stanton lived in the same time period as Susan B. Anthony, but Elizabeth Stanton was five years older than *(she, her)*.

Using *Who* and *Whom*
Write the correct pronoun *(who* or *whom)* for each sentence.

_____ 16. _?_ can tell me what state allowed women to vote in the 1800s?

_____ 17. Senator Aaron A. Sargent was from California. He is the man _?_ first proposed a constitutional amendment for women's suffrage to the Senate.

_____ 18. For _?_ was the amendment made?

_____ 19. After _?_ was the amendment named?

_____ 20. _?_ knows when the amendment was passed?

Courtesy Order and Use of Reflexive and Intensive
Underline the correct pronoun or pronouns from the choices in parentheses.

21. These women took upon *(them, themselves)* the responsibility of securing the right to vote for all the women of America.

22. These women shaped the history that affects *(me and you, you and me)* today.

23. The right to vote should be exercised by *(you and your fellow citizens, your fellow citizens and you)*.

24. I'm glad these women won the right for *(me, myself)* to vote.

25. *(You and your classmates, your classmates and you)* have learned something about the history of voting.

Chapter 9 Review: Adjective and Adverb Use

Comparison of Adjectives
Underline the correct adjective from the choices in parentheses.

1. The toy store was the (*largest, most largest*) one I had ever seen.

2. The model castle with all its detailed instructions looks like the (*more interesting, most interesting*) toy in the store.

3. The clerk climbed the ladder and got the ball that was the (*close, closest*) to him.

4. The battery-operated car that I wanted to buy was the (*fastest, most fastest*) car in the store.

5. My sister wanted the (*shorter, more shorter*) jump rope so that she would be able to use it more easily.

Comparison of Adverbs
Write the correct form of the adverb in parentheses.

_____ 6. The glowing stars shone (*bright*) than the glowing planets.

_____ 7. Of all the toys in the store, Sam decided that he liked the marbles (*well*).

_____ 8. The puppet from San Reno was made (*well*) than the puppet from Tulsa.

_____ 9. The model ant farm must be used (*carefully*) than the building blocks.

_____ 10. That is the (*bad*) looking kite I have ever seen!

Problems with Modifiers
Underline the correct adjective or adverb from the choices in parentheses.

11. The blue yo-yo is (*better, more better*) than the yellow one.

12. The store didn't have (*nothing, anything*) besides toys.

13. The toy xylophone sounded (*good, well*).

14. The little boy looked (*wondering, wonderingly*) at the bike.

15. The bike looked (*exciting, excitingly*).

Placement of Modifiers
Rewrite each sentence, making the modifiers clear and correct.

16. From the highest shelf, the boy wanted the big beach ball.

17. His mother said he would only get it if he behaved.

18. The store's clown who juggled skillfully impressed the children with his tricks.

19. Running down the aisle, the boy's untied shoelace tripped him.

20. The store's goal is to successfully sell toys to children.

21. Although not on the sale flyer, the manager gave me the sale price on the bike.

22. My manager told me to without delay load the toys on the truck.

23. Shoppers who buy often find their children have more toys than they can use.

24. They only have three infant rattles left.

25. They needed to accurately assemble the toy stove.

Chapter 10 Review: Capitalization

People and Places
Underline each word that contains a capitalization error.

1. My Italian Mama is a wonderful cook.

2. Once a month, she cooks a special lasagna dinner for dad, Uncle Luigi, and me.

3. The Fork and knife dance in my uncle's hands and utter strange clicking sounds.

4. My mother and uncle are originally from Venice, Italy, near the northern Mountains.

5. Uncle Luigi usually stays and eats until the Moon shines.

Constructions, Organizations, and Businesses
Underline each word that contains a capitalization error.

6. The Grand canal meanders through Venice in an S-shaped pattern.

7. The *mayflower* would not be able to fit through most of the canals of Venice.

8. The nazis took over Venice during World War II.

9. My uncle attended the University institute of Architecture in Venice, which he reached by trenitalia Railroad.

10. Venetian streets contain small Designer Clothing stores but not large Department stores.

Religious, Cultural, and Historical Terms
Underline each word that contains a capitalization error. If the sentence is correct, write C in the blank.

_____ 11. Catholicism is the major religion of Italy.

_____ 12. Roman Catholics believe that the apocrypha is part of God's inspired scripture.

_____ 13. Many jews lived in Venice around the time of World War II, and their neighborhoods were called ghettos.

_____ 14. Venice was first inhabited about a.d. 400.

_____ 15. My favorite event in Venice occurred at 8:00 p.m. on May 24, 2000, when my uncle received the Distinguished Citizen Award at the Bridge of Sighs.

Titles and First Words
Underline each word that contains a capitalization error. If the sentence or phrase is correct, write C in the blank.

_____ 16. The Venice *times* announced two new courses at the University of Venice: Rwandan history and The Glory of Modern Art.

_____ 17. Some famous artistic works about Venice are *The Merchant of Venice*, a Shakespearean play; *Portrait of Georgio Cornaro*, a painting by Titian; and *Farnace*, an opera by Vivaldi.

_____ 18. "If to Do Were as Easy as to Know" was the title of the review of the newly opened *Merchant of Venice* performance in The *New York Times*.

_____ 19. i asked Uncle Luigi, "have you ever seen *The Merchant of Venice*?"

_____ 20. "I have," he replied. "Let none presume / To wear an undeserved dignity. / O! that estates, degrees, and offices / were not deriv'd corruptly, and that clear honor / were purchas'd by the merit of the wearer."

_____ 21. *The Sights of Venice,* by Caryn Langley

_____ 22. In the book, chapter 1 focuses on the canals in Venice.

_____ 23. Dear mom and dad,

_____ 24. With Love from Venice,

_____ 25. Roses are red, / Violets are blue.

Proper Adjectives and Other Words
Underline each word that contains a capitalization error.

26. Do venetian blinds come from Venice?

27. My mother knows that i do not like to clean the blinds each week.

28. "For me, o mother, it is sheer torture," I said.

29. She told me that if I had at least a b average on my next report card, she would let me skip a month of cleaning the blinds.

30. I will do a complete u-turn in my study habits to pursue this reward!

Chapter 11 Review: Punctuation

End Marks and Other Uses of the Period

Insert the correct end mark for each sentence. Insert any missing periods or decimal points in the following sentences.

1. I have one sister and one brother

2. My brother is almost seven feet tall

3. We used to live at 12 Crest Rd in Monson, Massachusetts

4. School did not start until 9:00 am when I was in kindergarten, did it

5. You should visit Massachusetts sometime

Commas: In a Series, After Introductory Elements

Insert any missing commas. If the sentence is already correct, write *C* in the blank.

_____ 6. Massachusetts has beautiful leaves in autumn, lots of snow in winter and little humidity in summer.

_____ 7. A small white picket fence sat in front of our blue two-story house.

_____ 8. My sister and brother liked to play outside but I liked to read.

_____ 9. Before turning the lights out at night, I would often read a book.

_____ 10. First I had to make sure that the book was all right with my mother.

Commas: To Separate, In Letters, and with Quotations, Dates, and Addresses

Insert any missing commas. If the sentence is already correct, write *C* in the blank.

_____ 11. Volleyball my favorite sport took place during September and October.

_____ 12. "You didn't forget your uniform did you?"

_____ 13. My friend Heather received the MVP award.

_____ 14. "Congratulations, Heather" I said.

_____ 15. We graduated from Faith Baptist Christian Academy in Palmer Massachusetts, on May 29 2008.

Incorrect Commas

Circle any incorrect commas. If the sentence is already correct, write C in the blank.

———— 16. My brother played basketball, and soccer.

———— 17. My sister played volleyball, but, she enjoyed basketball more.

———— 18. My mother, taught my brother at home for a year.

———— 19. My sister, who also attended Faith Baptist Academy, worked at Mountainview Bible Camp for many summers.

———— 20. She graduated in June, 2007.

Semicolons

Insert any missing semicolons or colons. If the sentence is already correct, write C in the blank.

———— 21. It is faster to fly than to drive from Massachusetts to South Carolina the distance is over five hundred miles.

———— 22. If you drive to South Carolina from Massachusetts, you will probably go through Connecticut, New York, Pennsylvania, Maryland, Virginia, and North Carolina and you might not want to drive all those miles.

———— 23. New England has a very different culture from the South therefore, it may take Americans from other areas a while to get used to either one.

———— 24. School starts earlier in the South than in the North, usually around 800 a.m.

———— 25. If you move from the South to the North in the winter, you would want to have the following items to go to school boots, a thick jacket, and ear muffs.

Chapter 12 Review: More Punctuation

Quotation Marks and Ellipses

Read the following paragraph and determine whether the quotations following it are correct. Identify each item as correct (C) or incorrect (I).

Then they took away the stone from the place where the dead was laid. And Jesus lifted up his eyes, and said, "Father, I thank thee that thou hast heard me. And I knew that thou hearest me always: but because of the people which stand by I said it, that they may believe that thou hast sent me." And when he thus had spoken, he cried with a loud voice, "Lazarus, come forth." And he that was dead came forth, bound hand and foot with graveclothes: and his face was bound about with a napkin. Jesus saith unto them, "Loose him, and let him go" (John 11:41-44).

_____ 1. "Then they took away the stone. . . And when he thus had spoken, he cried with a loud voice, 'Lazarus, come forth.'"

_____ 2. "And Jesus . . . said, 'Father, I thank thee that thou hast heard me.'"

_____ 3. Jesus knew that "his prayer was heard by the Lord."

_____ 4. "And he that was dead came forth, . . . and his face was bound about with a napkin."

_____ 5. "Jesus saith unto them, 'Loose him, and let him go'."

Quotation Marks and Underlining for Italics

Insert any missing quotation marks. Underline any words that should be italicized.

6. Handel's Messiah recounts the life of Christ as described in the Bible.

7. George Herbert's poem Prayer describes the meaning of prayer for believers.

8. Pastor Hardwick sailed on the ship the Mediterranean when he visited the Holy Land. He especially enjoyed seeing the Mount of Olives where Jesus prayed.

9. The song Teach Me to Pray, Lord encourages believers to learn to pray as Christ prayed during His earthly ministry.

10. If you want to learn more about Christ's prayers, you can read With Christ in the School of Prayer by Andrew Murray.

Apostrophes and Hyphens
Insert any missing apostrophes and hyphens.

11. Jesus prayers included The Lords Prayer, in which He taught His disciples to pray.

12. The disciples prayer lesson taught them how to petition God for the needs of His kingdom and for their personal needs.

13. Jesus prayed aloud at Lazaruss tomb to increase peoples faith in Him.

14. How many *a*s are in the name *Lazarus?*

15. Lazarus had two sisters but no brother in law, because neither of his sisters was married.

16. When Jesus prayed at the feeding of the five thousand, the number five thousand represents only one third to one half of the people who were there, since the number did not include women and children.

17. Some believers dont pray much, not because they cant, but because they wont.

18. The God blessed prayer is one that is prayed from a humble heart.

19. My great aunt prays 5:00 7:00 every morning.

20. Surely its self evident that Jesus is the all important model of a person who truly prays.

Dashes and Parentheses
Insert any missing dashes or parentheses.

21. In the Upper Room, at the feeding of the five thousand, and at the Mount of Olives all these were instances when Jesus prayed.

22. The Lord's Prayer actually only sixty-six words long is given by Jesus as an example for us.

23. One could easily follow the steps Jesus used in the Lord's Prayer: 1 acknowledge God's person, 2 ask for God's provision, 3 appeal for God's pardon, 4 apply for God's protection, and 5 aim for God's glory.

24. Jesus exemplified a life of prayer, and He taught us much about it for example, in the Sermon on the Mount.

25. He especially denounced hypocrites often the religious leaders! who prayed simply to be seen of men.

INDEX